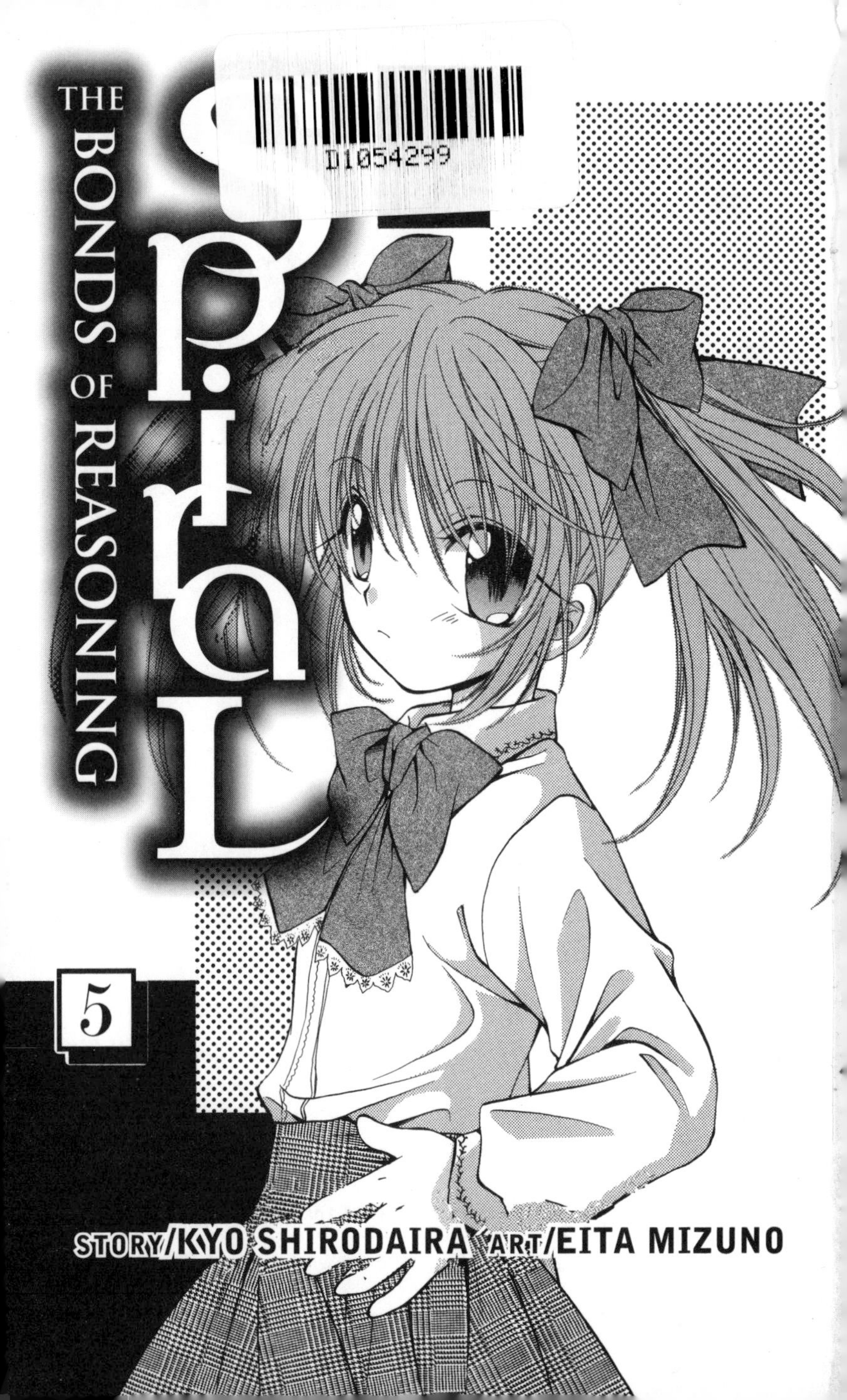
THE BONDS OF REASONING
5
STORY/KYO SHIRODAIRA ART/EITA MIZUNO

CONTENTS

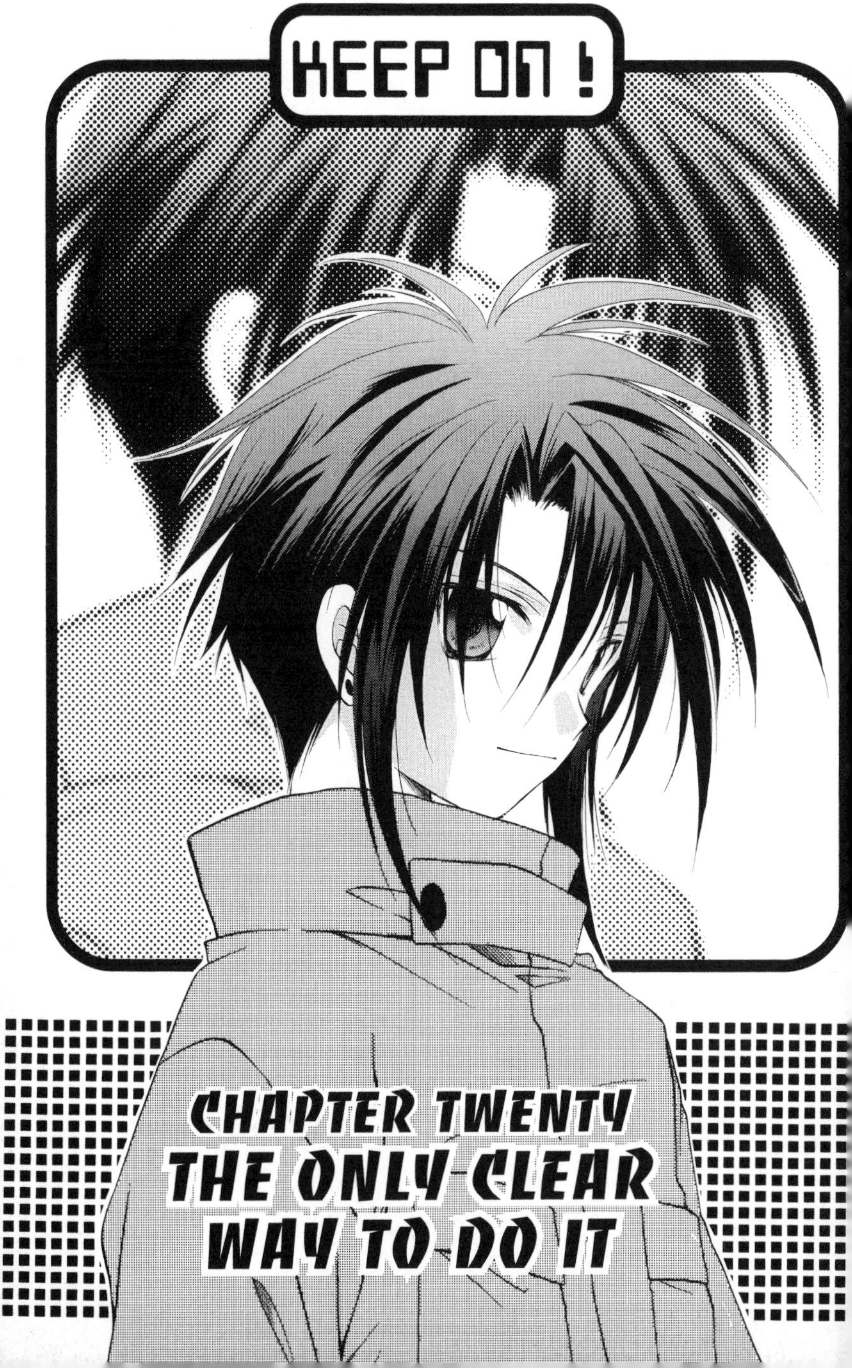
KEEP ON!
CHAPTER TWENTY
THE ONLY CLEAR WAY TO DO IT

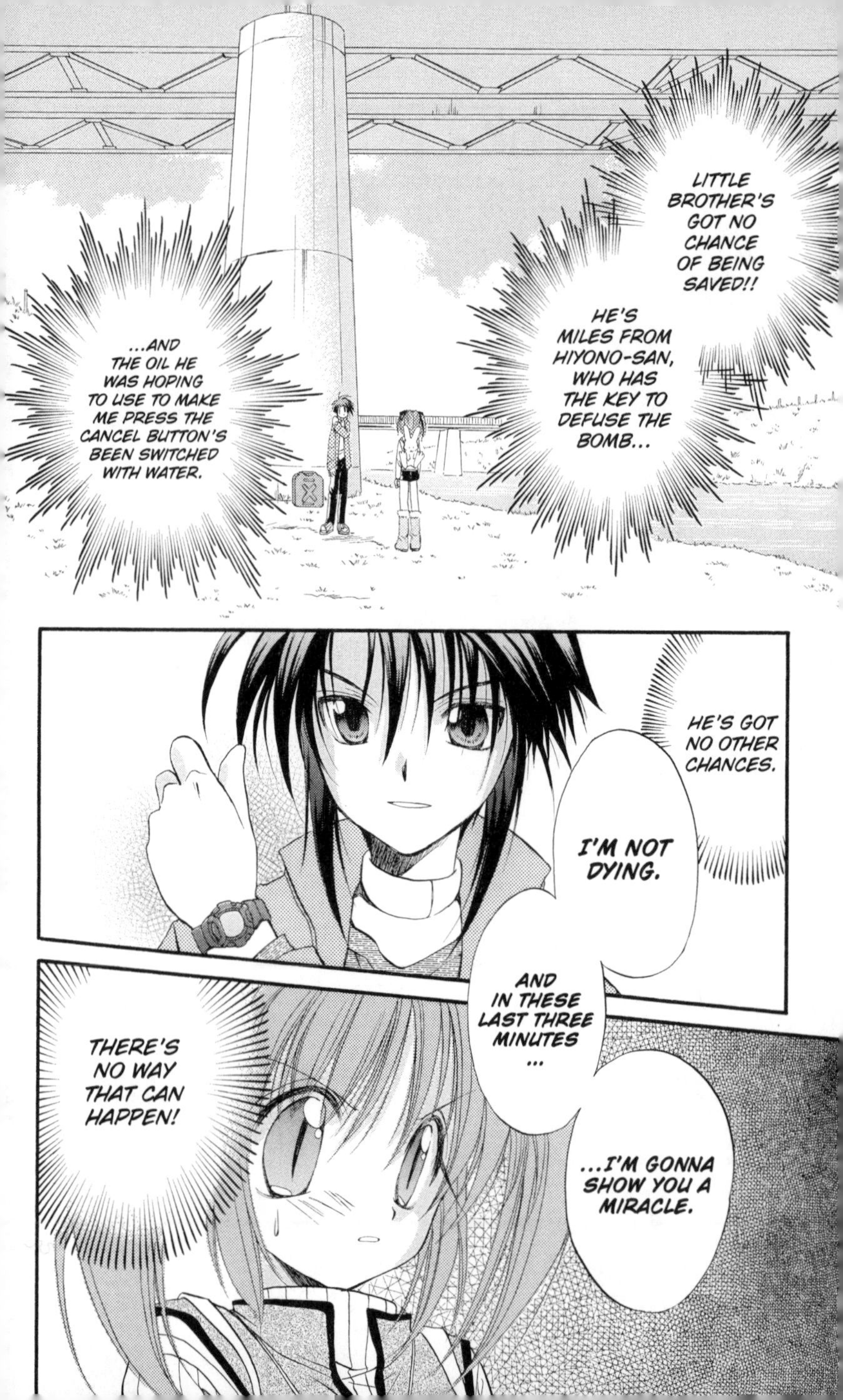
HE'S MILES FROM HIYONO-SAN, WHO HAS THE KEY TO DEFUSE THE BOMB...
...AND THE OIL HE WAS HOPING TO USE TO MAKE ME PRESS THE CANCEL BUTTON'S BEEN SWITCHED WITH WATER.
LITTLE BROTHER'S GOT NO CHANCE OF BEING SAVED!!
HE'S GOT NO OTHER CHANCES.
I'M NOT DYING.
AND IN THESE LAST THREE MINUTES ...
...I'M GONNA SHOW YOU A MIRACLE.
THERE'S NO WAY THAT CAN HAPPEN!

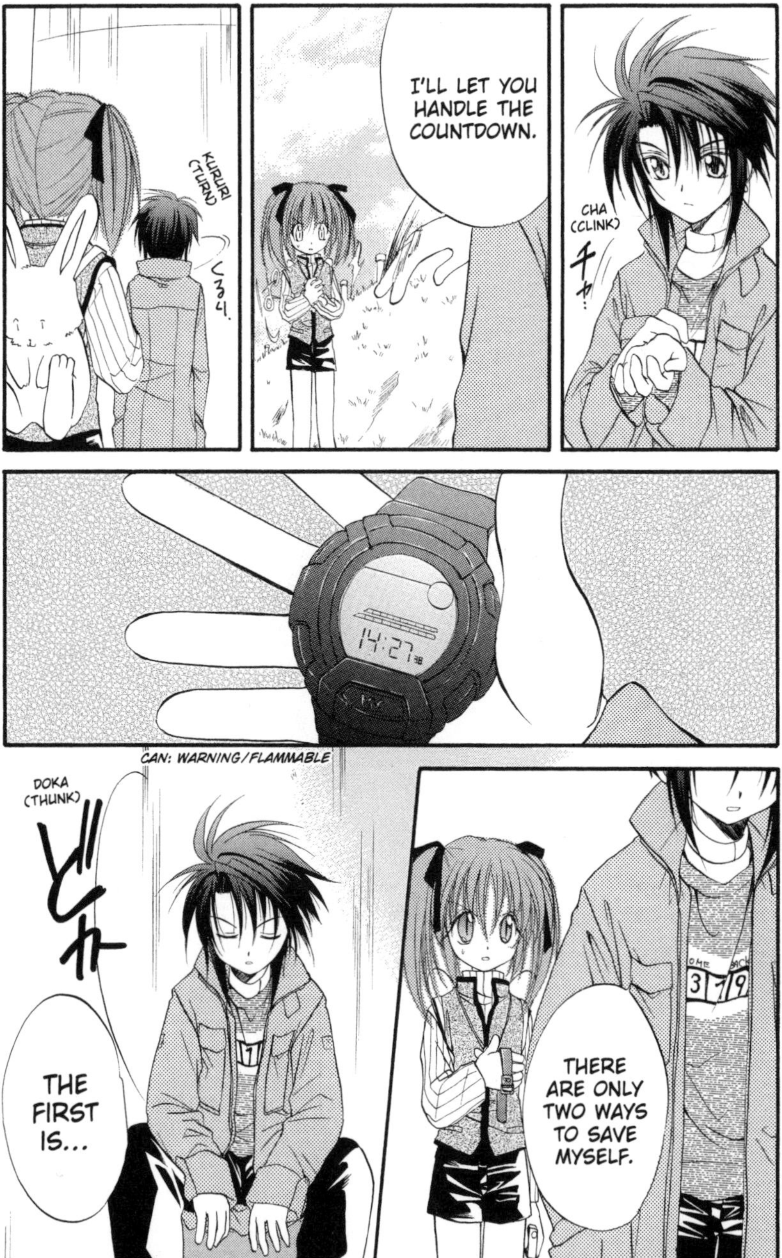
CHA (CLINK)
チャ…
I'LL LET YOU HANDLE THE COUNTDOWN.
KURURI (TURN)
くるん
14:27
THERE ARE ONLY TWO WAYS TO SAVE MYSELF.
CAN: WARNING/FLAMMABLE
DOKA (THUNK)
THE FIRST IS…
火気厳禁

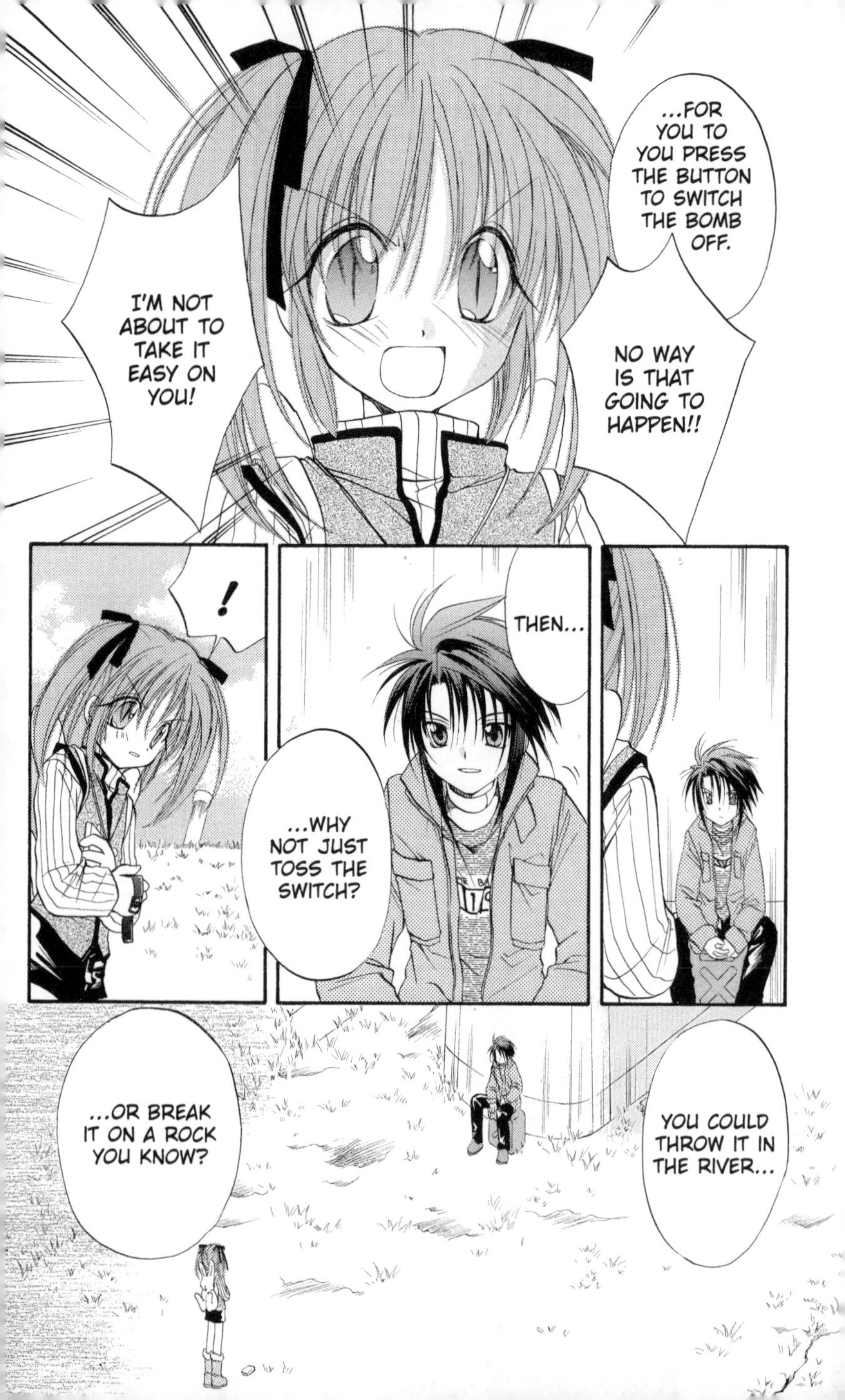
...FOR YOU TO YOU PRESS THE BUTTON TO SWITCH THE BOMB OFF.
NO WAY IS THAT GOING TO HAPPEN!!
I'M NOT ABOUT TO TAKE IT EASY ON YOU!
THEN...
...WHY NOT JUST TOSS THE SWITCH?
!
YOU COULD THROW IT IN THE RIVER...
...OR BREAK IT ON A ROCK YOU KNOW?

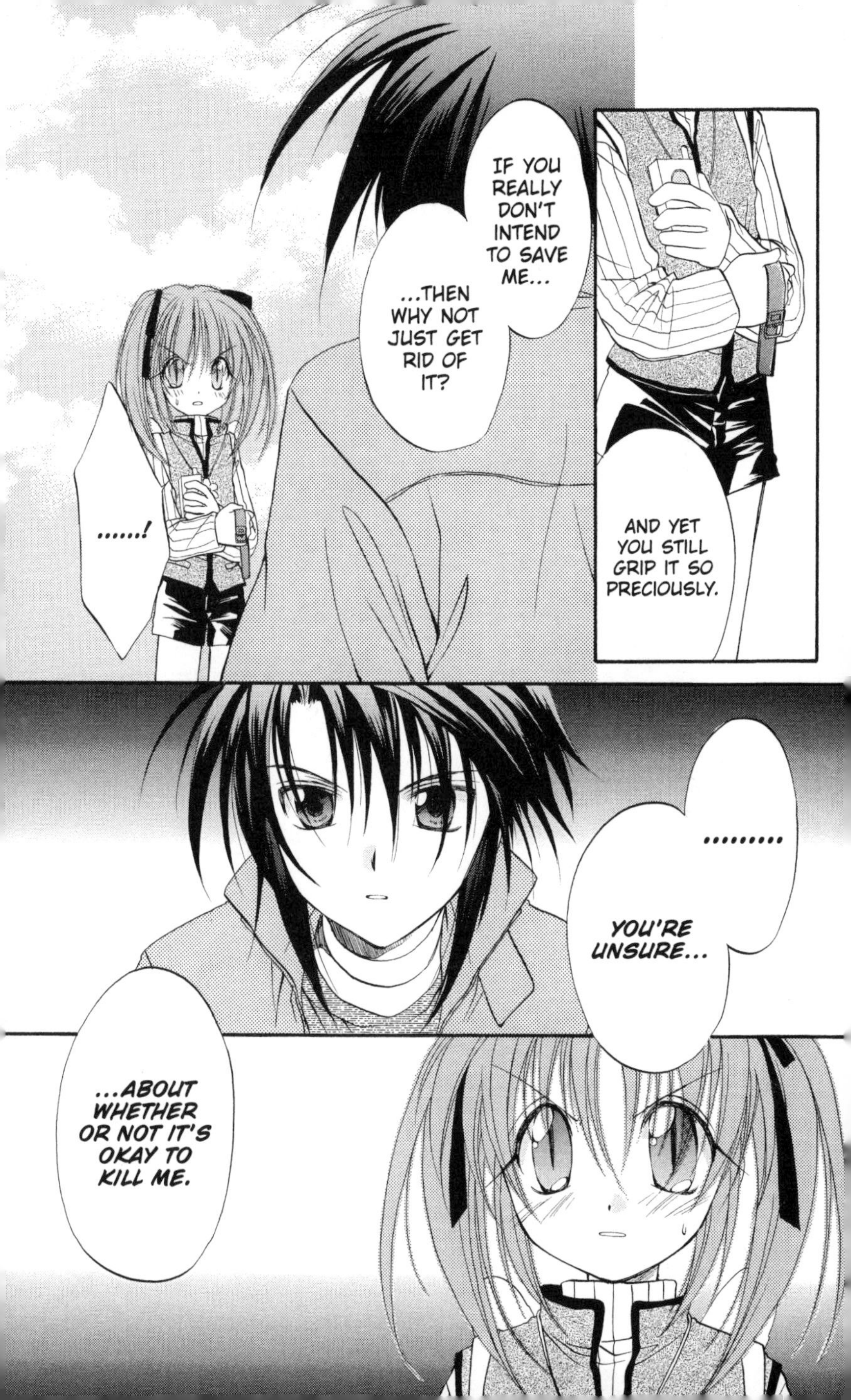
IF YOU REALLY DON'T INTEND TO SAVE ME...
...THEN WHY NOT JUST GET RID OF IT?
AND YET YOU STILL GRIP IT SO PRECIOUSLY.
......!
....
YOU'RE UNSURE...
...ABOUT WHETHER OR NOT IT'S OKAY TO KILL ME.

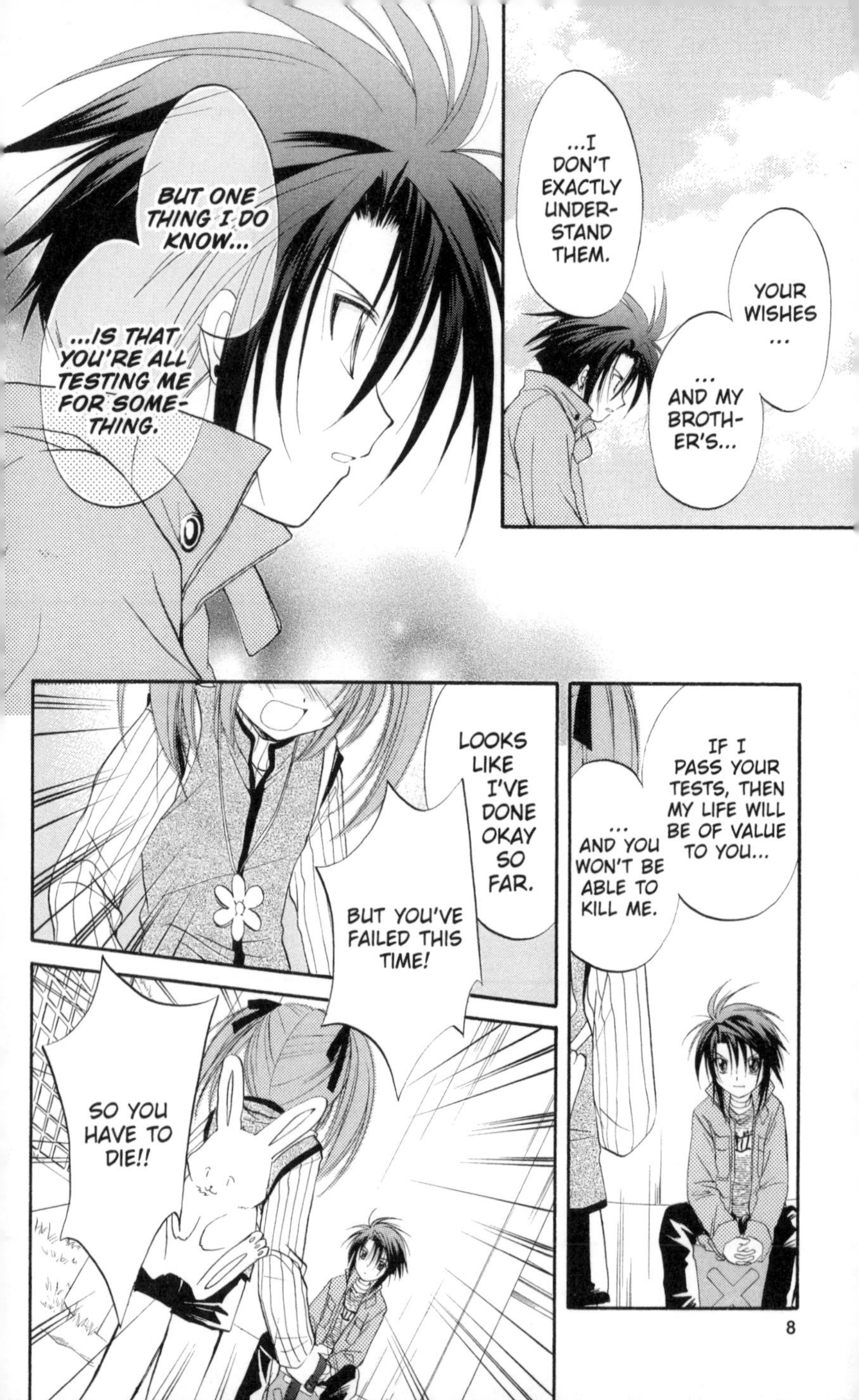
YOUR WISHES...
...AND MY BROTHER'S...
...I DON'T EXACTLY UNDERSTAND THEM.
BUT ONE THING I DO KNOW...
...IS THAT YOU'RE ALL TESTING ME FOR SOMETHING.
IF I PASS YOUR TESTS, THEN MY LIFE WILL BE OF VALUE TO YOU...
...AND YOU WON'T BE ABLE TO KILL ME.
LOOKS LIKE I'VE DONE OKAY SO FAR.
BUT YOU'VE FAILED THIS TIME!
SO YOU HAVE TO DIE!!

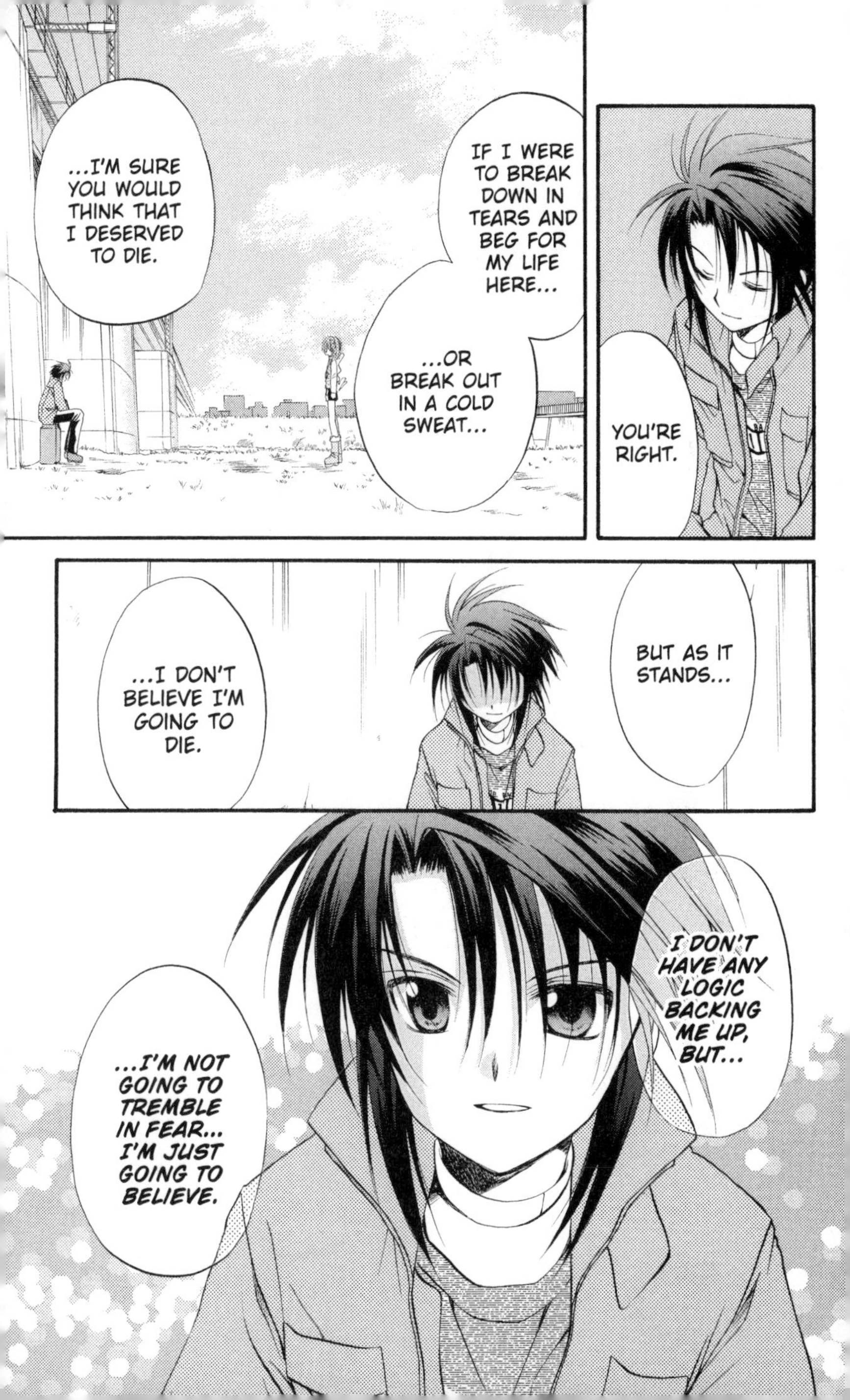
YOU'RE RIGHT.
IF I WERE TO BREAK DOWN IN TEARS AND BEG FOR MY LIFE HERE...
...OR BREAK OUT IN A COLD SWEAT...
...I'M SURE YOU WOULD THINK THAT I DESERVED TO DIE.
BUT AS IT STANDS...
...I DON'T BELIEVE I'M GOING TO DIE.
I DON'T HAVE ANY LOGIC BACKING ME UP, BUT...
...I'M NOT GOING TO TREMBLE IN FEAR... I'M JUST GOING TO BELIEVE.

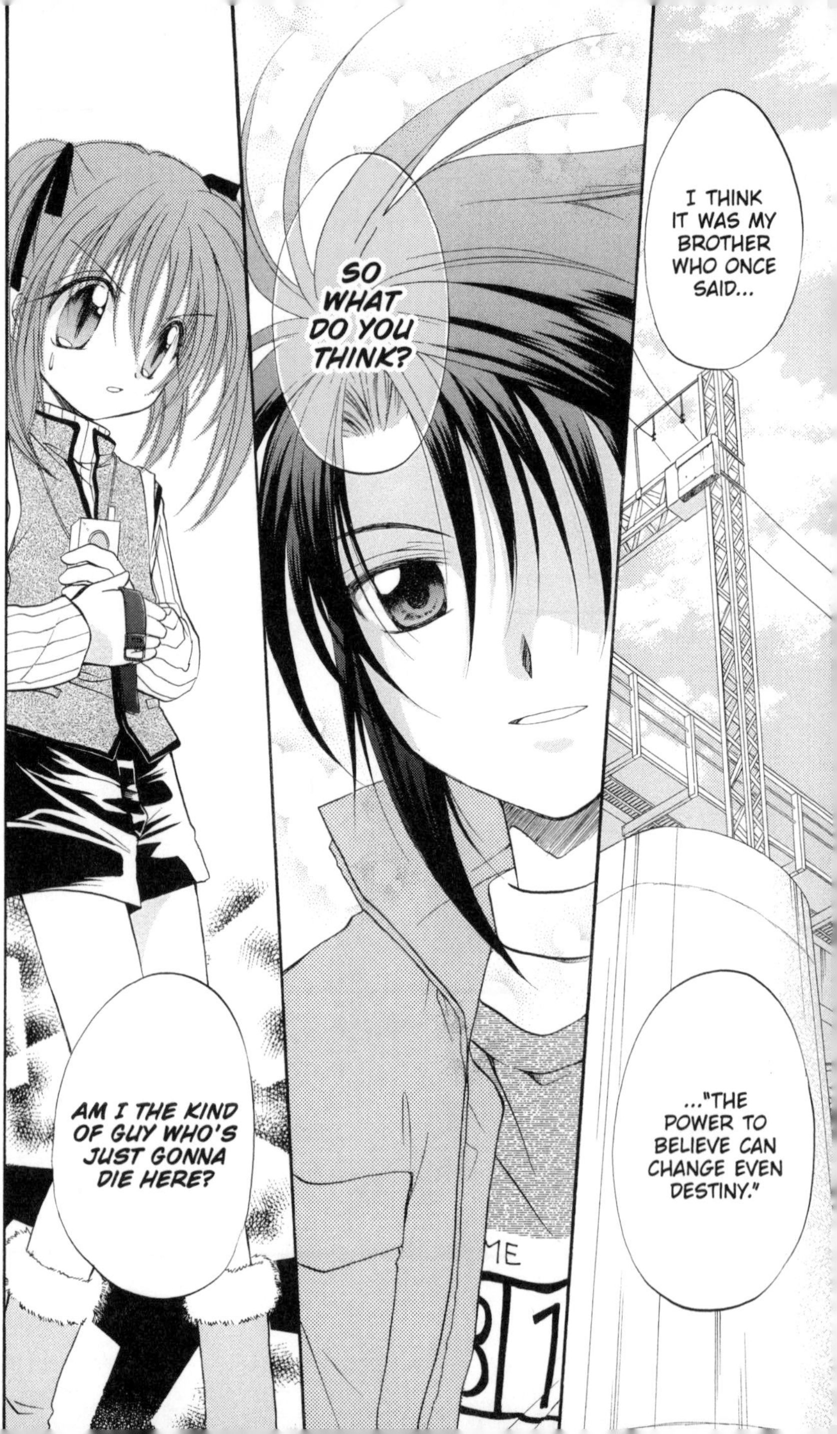
I THINK IT WAS MY BROTHER WHO ONCE SAID...
..."THE POWER TO BELIEVE CAN CHANGE EVEN DESTINY."
SO WHAT DO YOU THINK?
AM I THE KIND OF GUY WHO'S JUST GONNA DIE HERE?

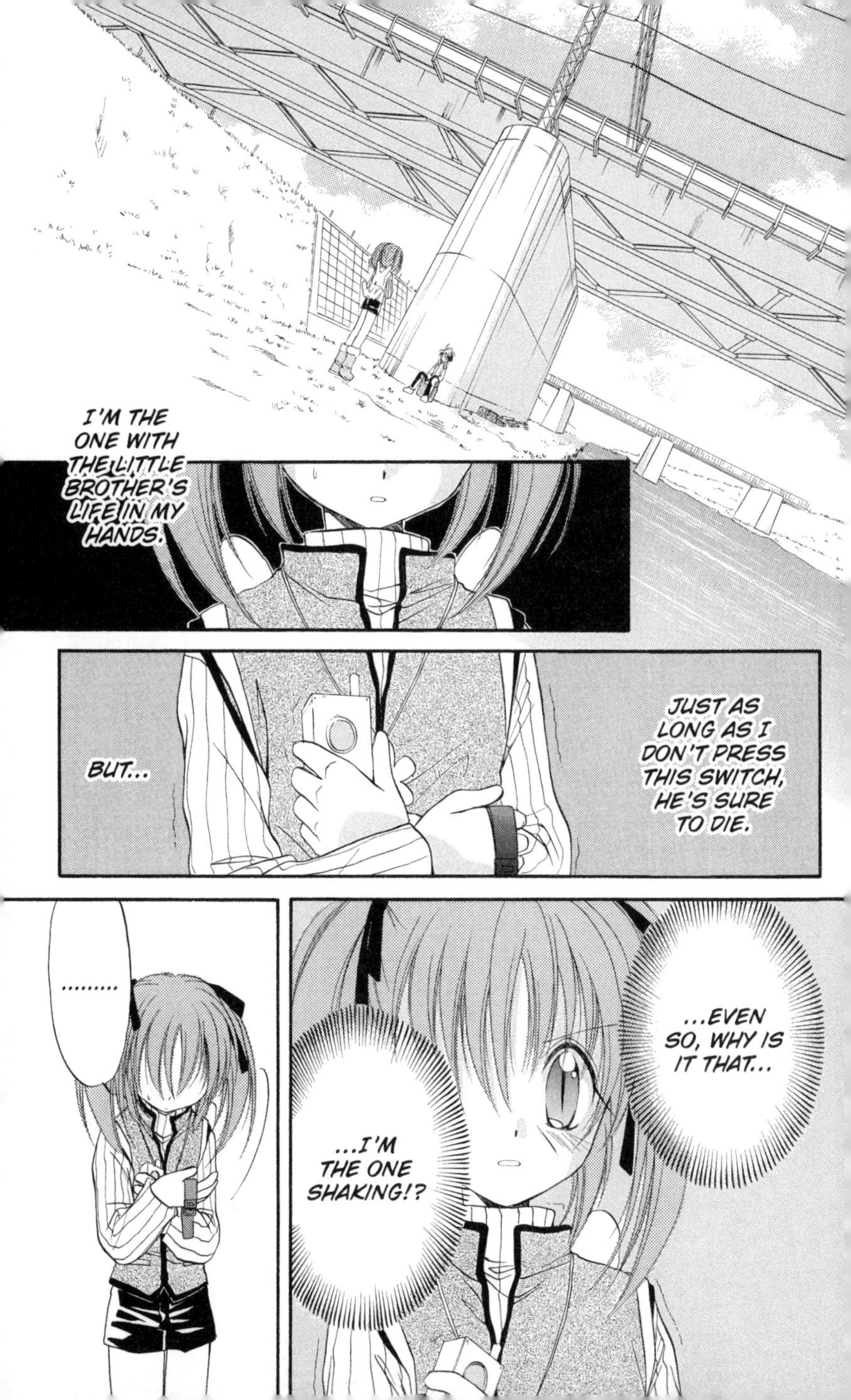
I'M THE ONE WITH THE LITTLE BROTHER'S LIFE IN MY HANDS.
JUST AS LONG AS I DON'T PRESS THIS SWITCH, HE'S SURE TO DIE.
BUT...
...EVEN SO, WHY IS IT THAT...
...I'M THE ONE SHAKING!?
....

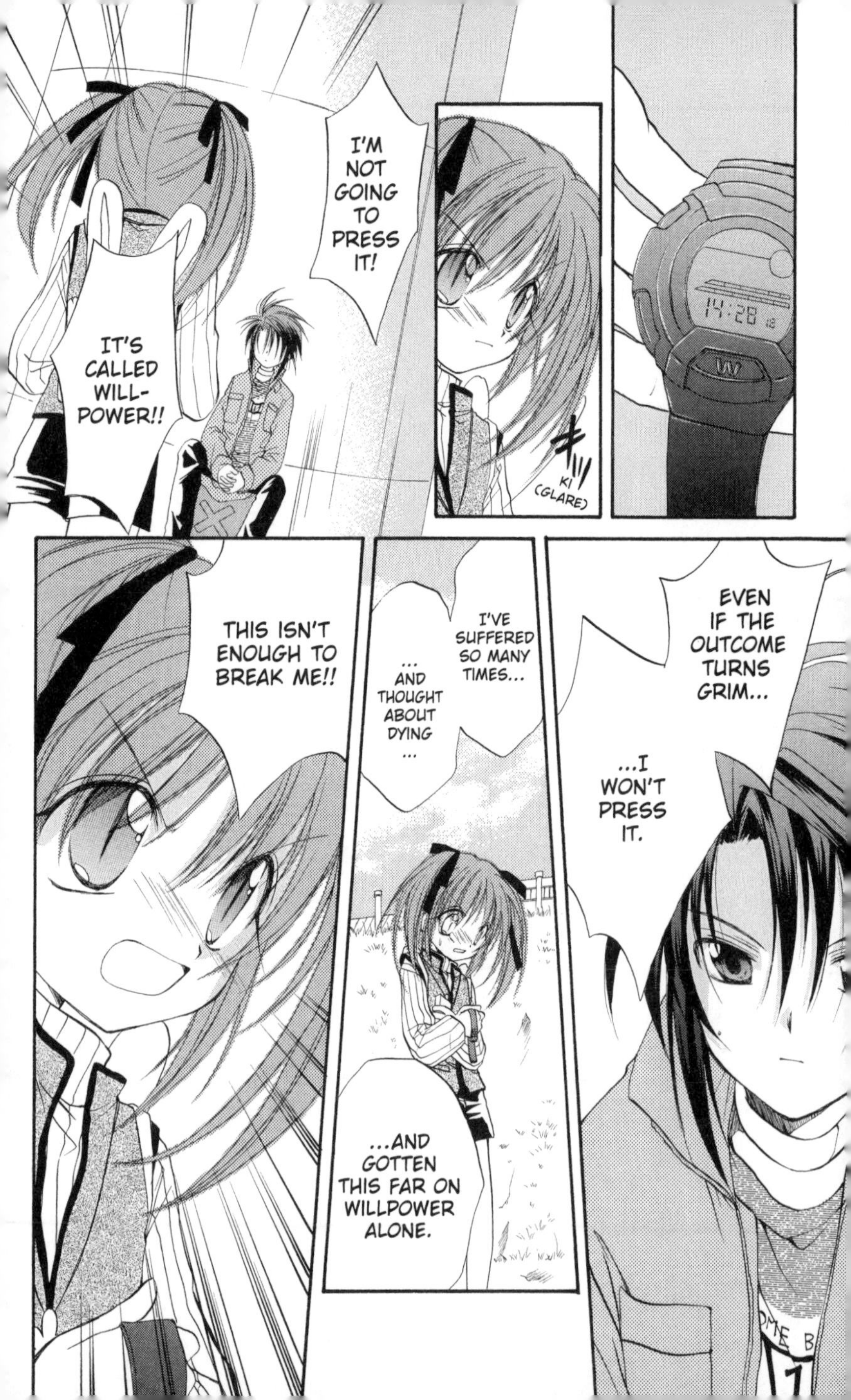
14:28 18
W
KI (GLARE)
I'M NOT GOING TO PRESS IT!
IT'S CALLED WILL-POWER!!
EVEN IF THE OUTCOME TURNS GRIM...
...I WON'T PRESS IT.
I'VE SUFFERED SO MANY TIMES...
...AND THOUGHT ABOUT DYING...
...AND GOTTEN THIS FAR ON WILLPOWER ALONE.
THIS ISN'T ENOUGH TO BREAK ME!!

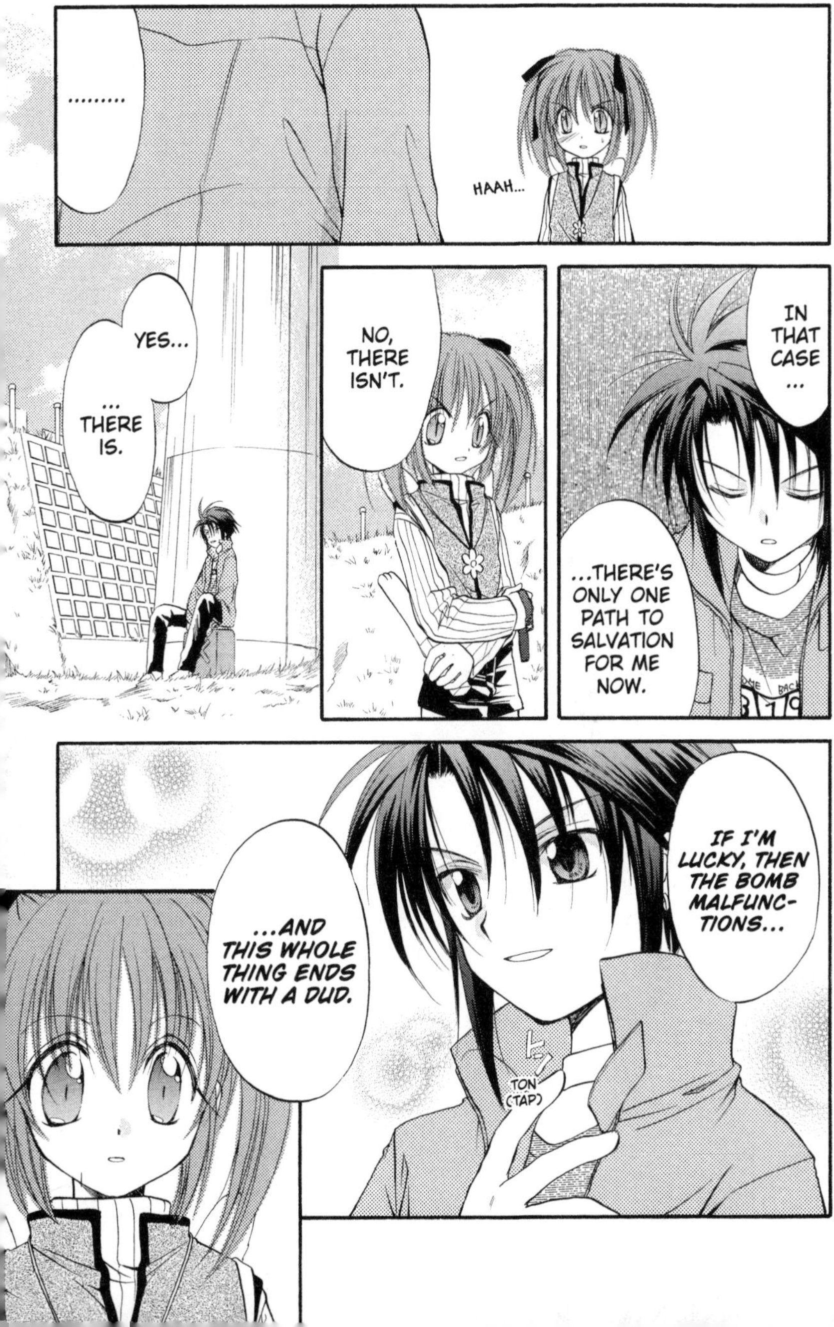
HAAH...
....
IN THAT CASE ...
...THERE'S ONLY ONE PATH TO SALVATION FOR ME NOW.
NO, THERE ISN'T.
YES...
... THERE IS.
IF I'M LUCKY, THEN THE BOMB MALFUNC-TIONS...
TON (TAP)
...AND THIS WHOLE THING ENDS WITH A DUD.

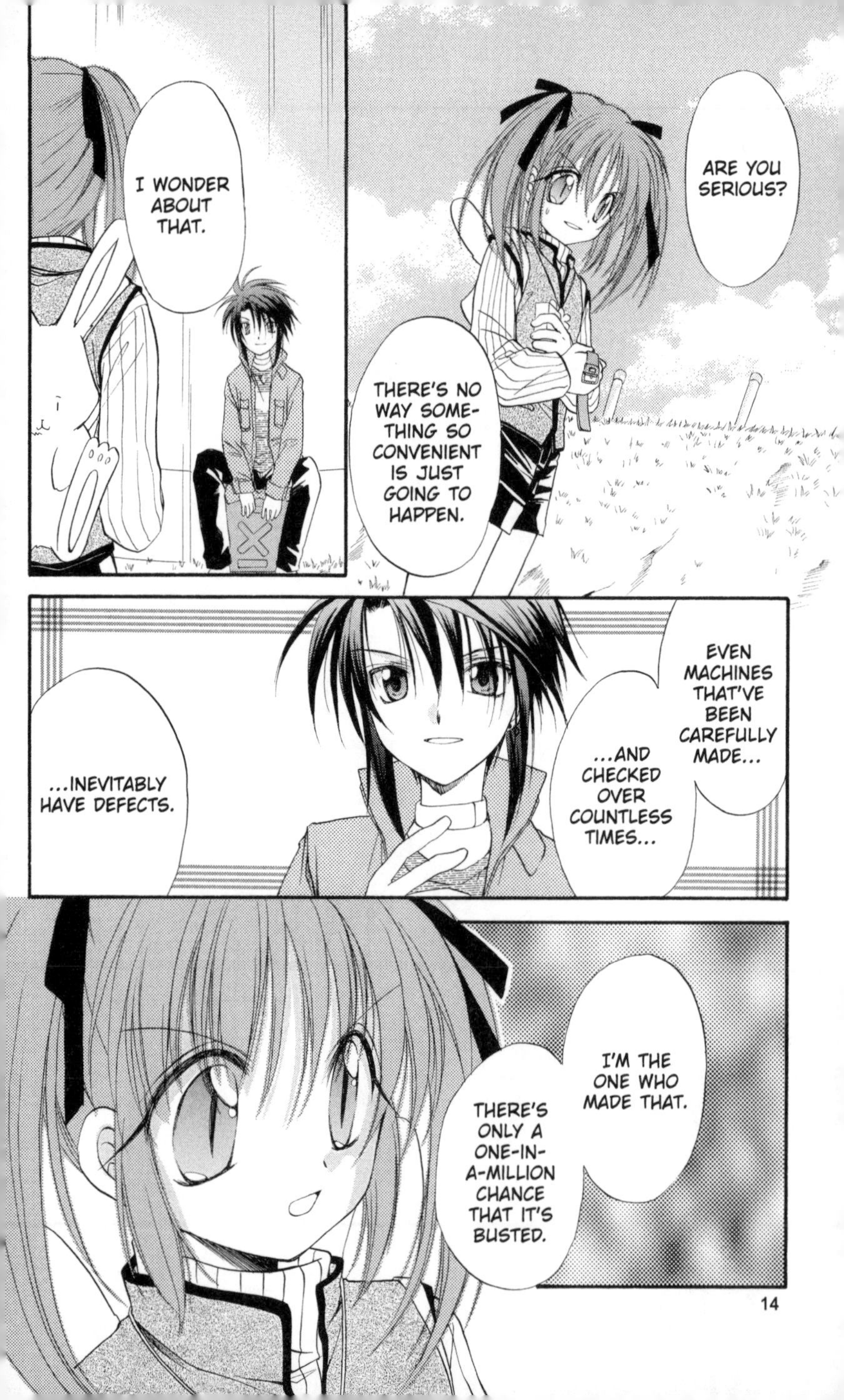
ARE YOU SERIOUS?
THERE'S NO WAY SOME-THING SO CONVENIENT IS JUST GOING TO HAPPEN.
I WONDER ABOUT THAT.
EVEN MACHINES THAT'VE BEEN CAREFULLY MADE...
...AND CHECKED OVER COUNTLESS TIMES...
...INEVITABLY HAVE DEFECTS.
I'M THE ONE WHO MADE THAT.
THERE'S ONLY A ONE-IN-A-MILLION CHANCE THAT IT'S BUSTED.

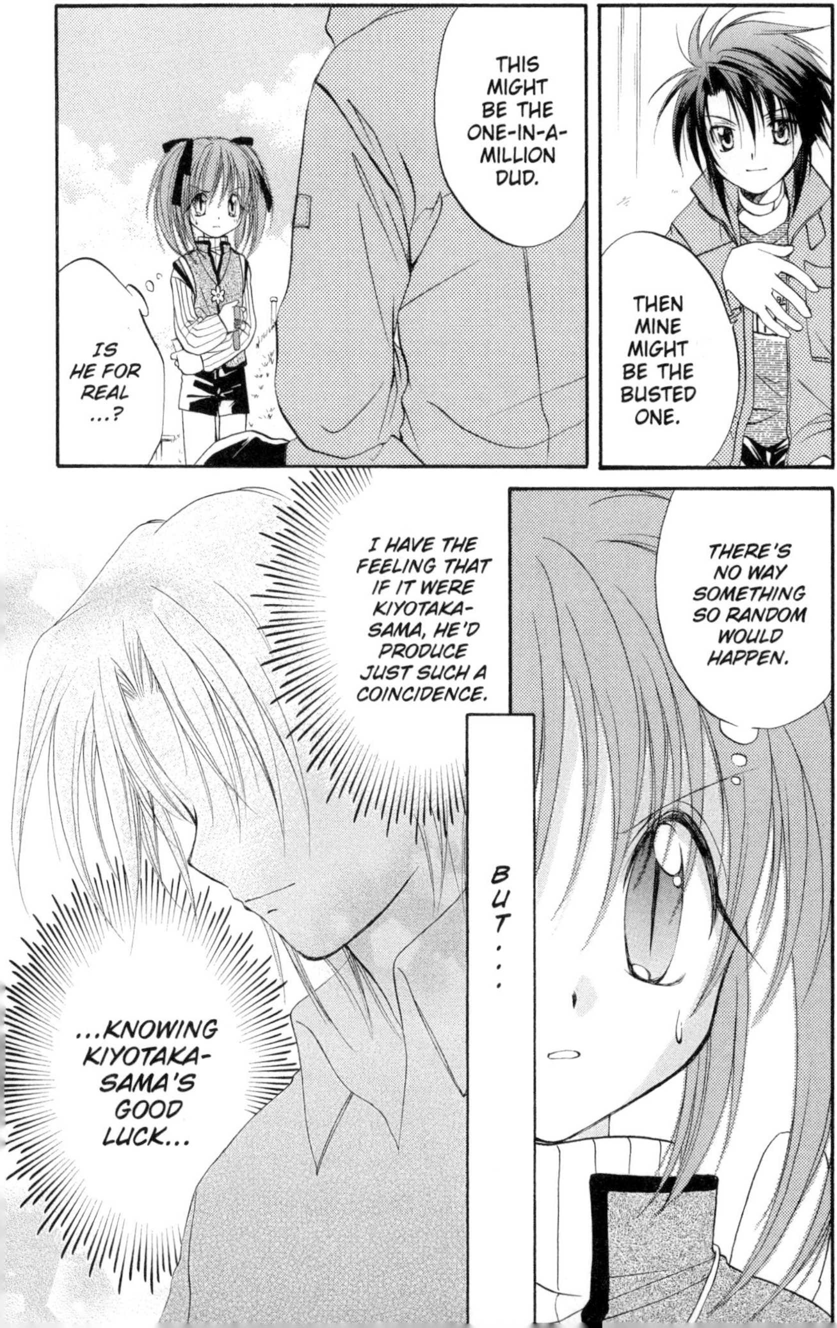
THEN MINE MIGHT BE THE BUSTED ONE.
THIS MIGHT BE THE ONE-IN-A-MILLION DUD.
IS HE FOR REAL ...?
THERE'S NO WAY SOMETHING SO RANDOM WOULD HAPPEN.
BUT...
I HAVE THE FEELING THAT IF IT WERE KIYOTAKA-SAMA, HE'D PRODUCE JUST SUCH A COINCIDENCE.
...KNOWING KIYOTAKA-SAMA'S GOOD LUCK...

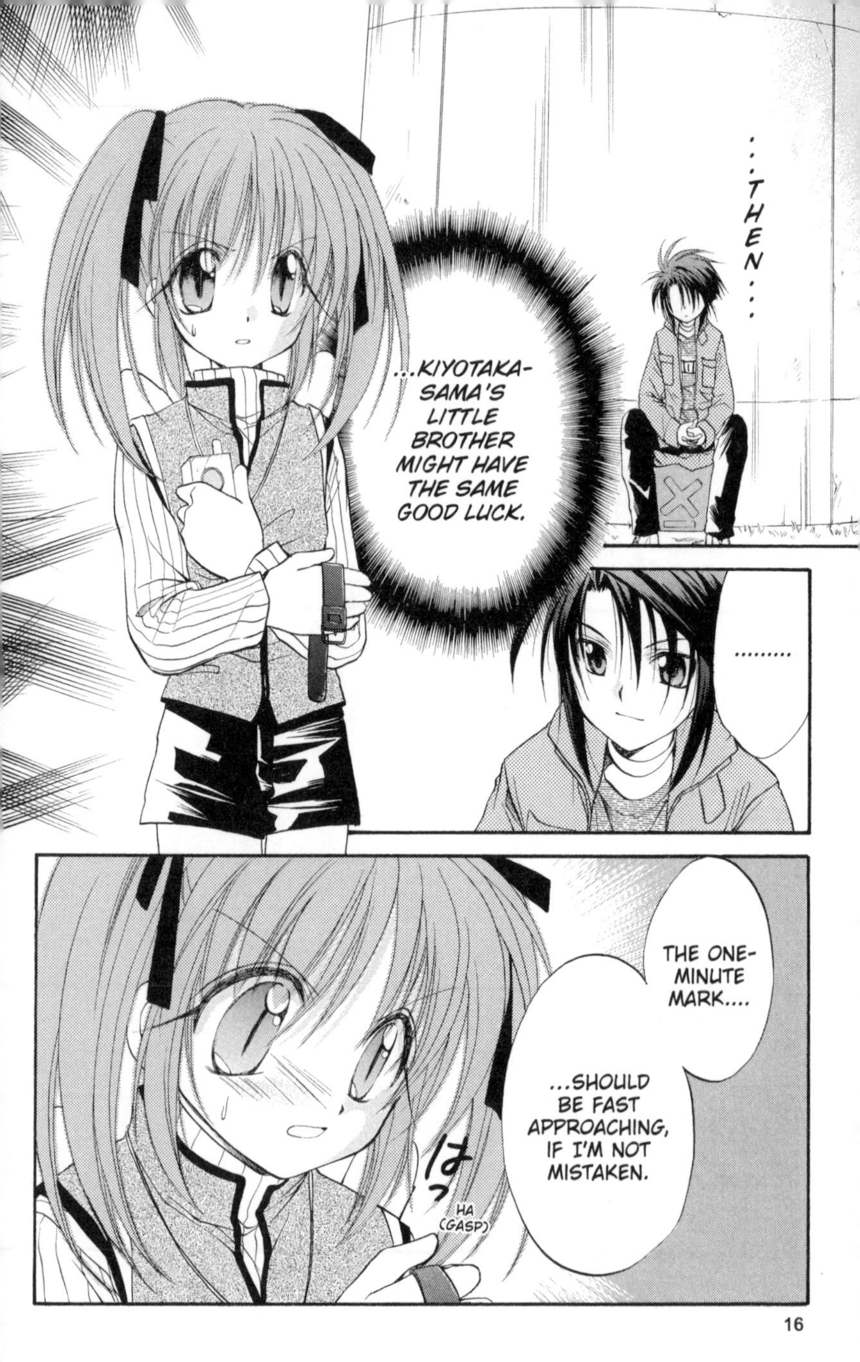
...THEN...
....
...KIYOTAKA-SAMA'S LITTLE BROTHER MIGHT HAVE THE SAME GOOD LUCK.
THE ONE-MINUTE MARK....
...SHOULD BE FAST APPROACHING, IF I'M NOT MISTAKEN.
HA (GASP)

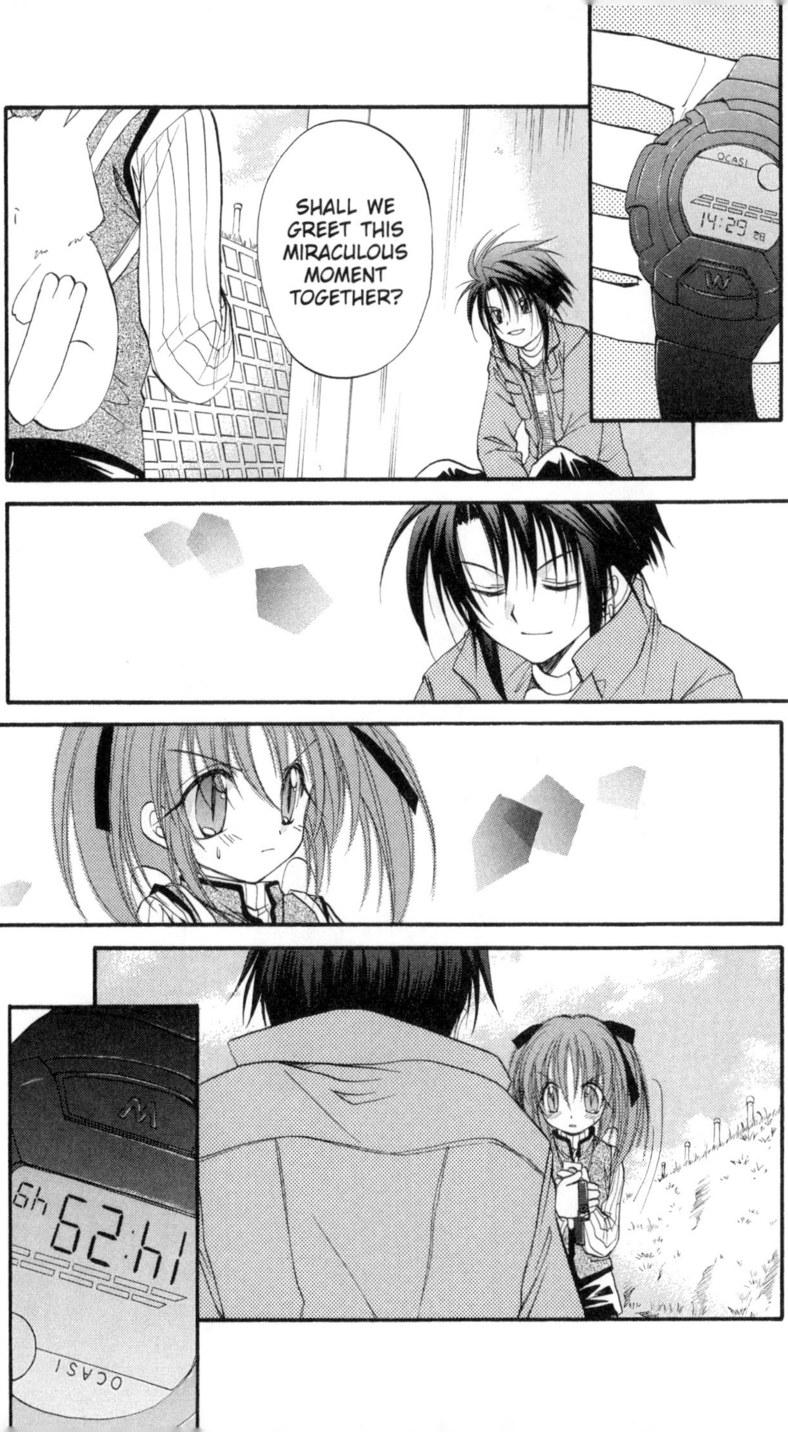
OCASI
14:29 28
SHALL WE GREET THIS MIRACULOUS MOMENT TOGETHER?

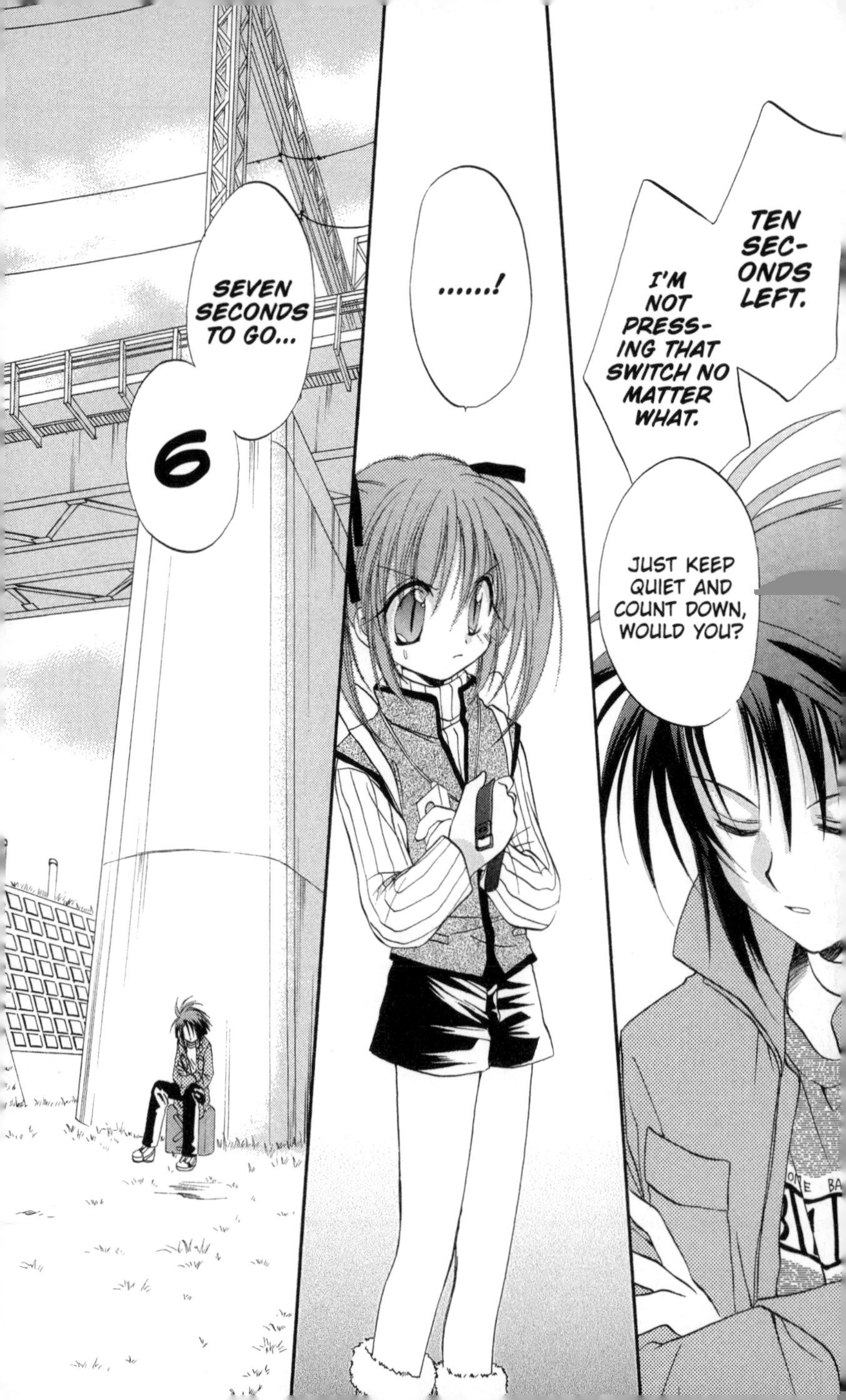
TEN SEC-ONDS LEFT.
I'M NOT PRESS-ING THAT SWITCH NO MATTER WHAT.
JUST KEEP QUIET AND COUNT DOWN, WOULD YOU?
......!
SEVEN SECONDS TO GO...
6

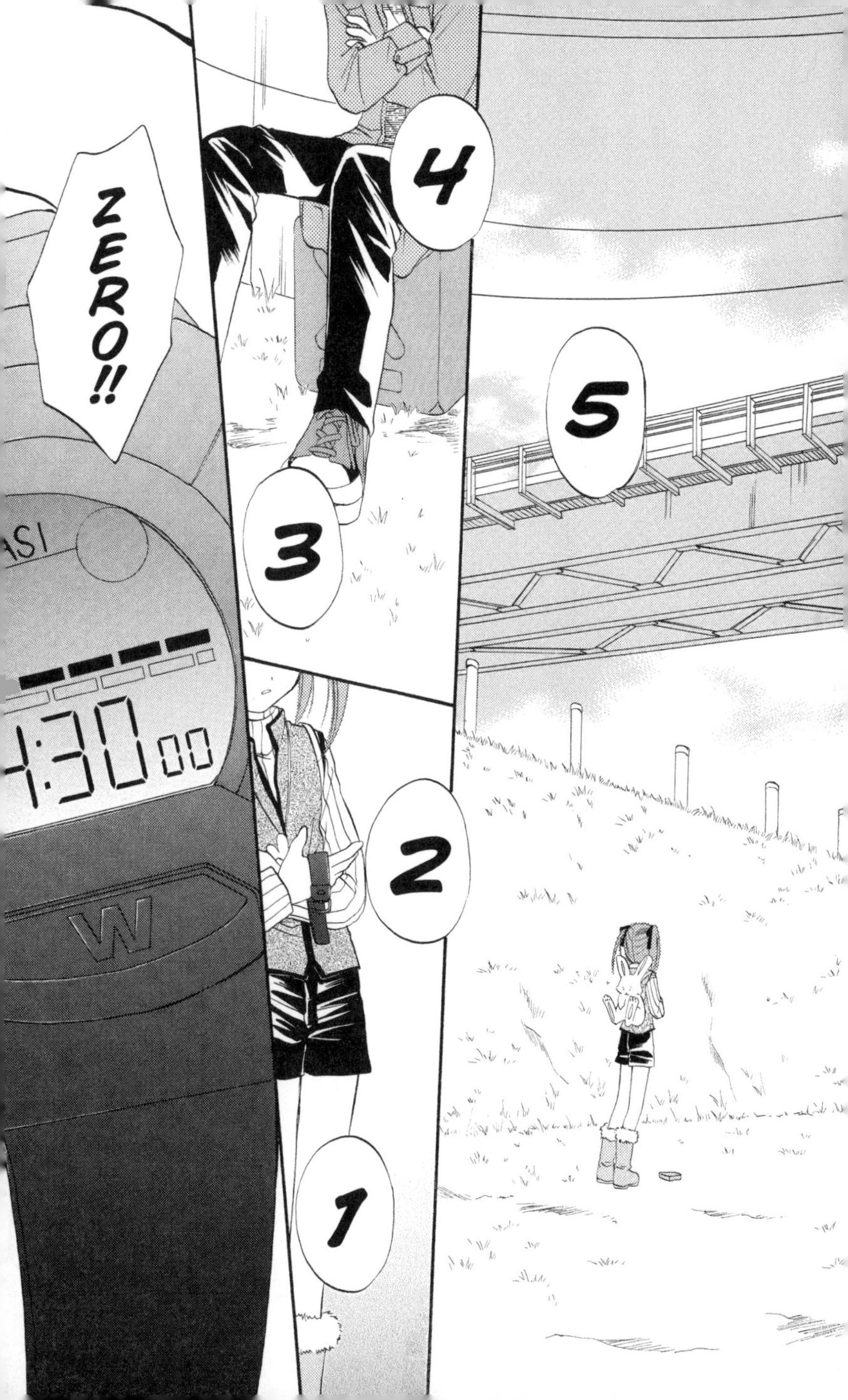
5
4
3
2
1
ZERO!!

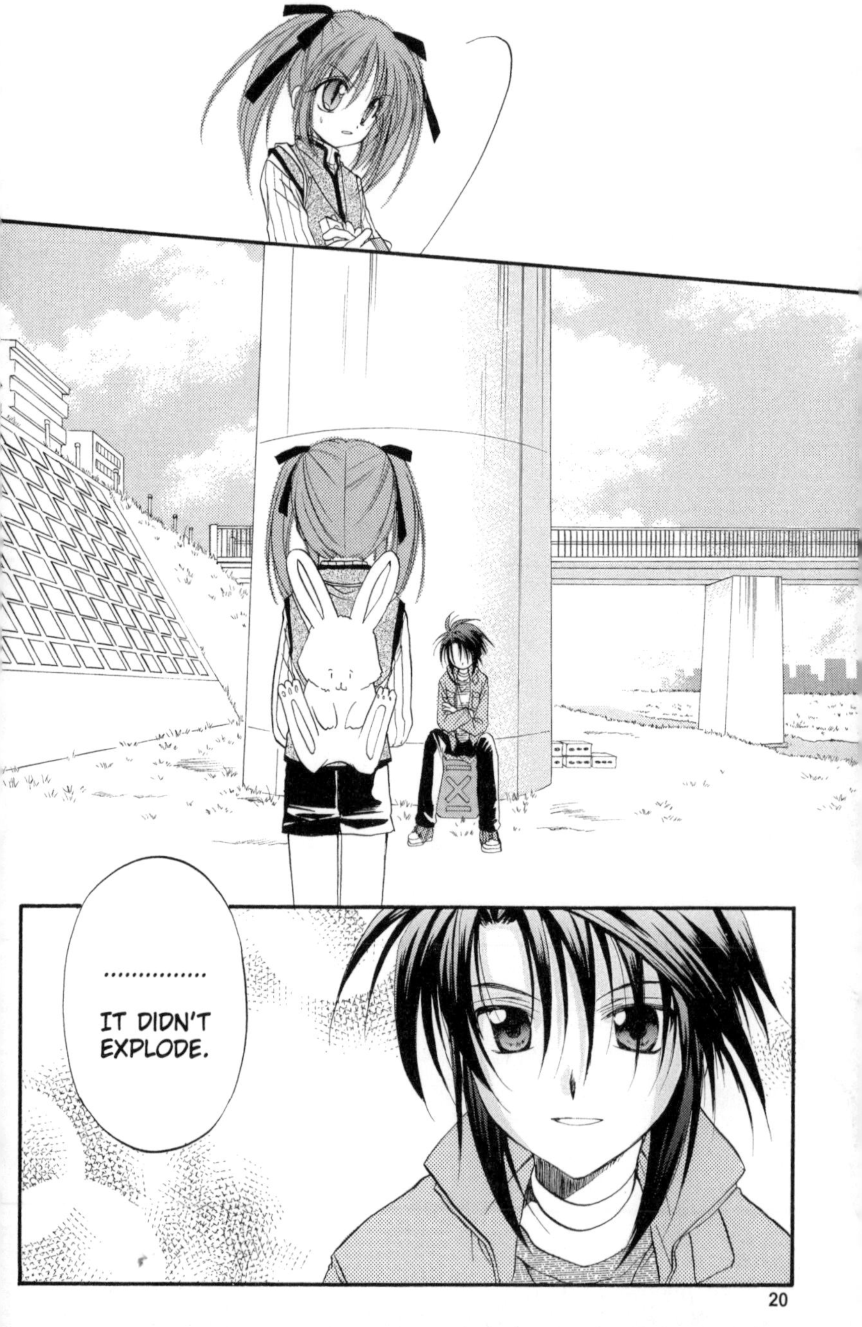
....
IT DIDN'T EXPLODE.

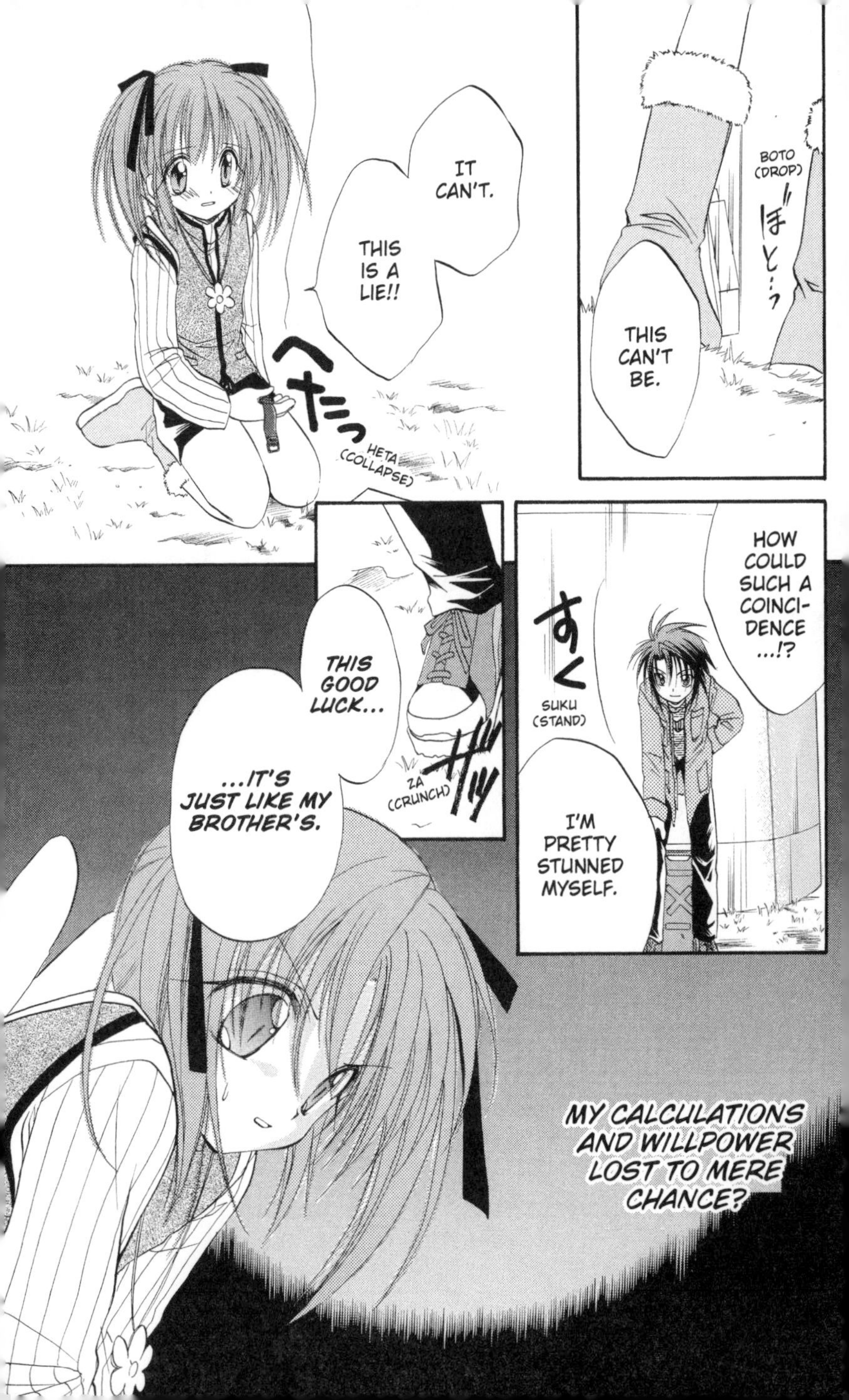
BOTO (DROP)
ぼと…
THIS CAN'T BE.
IT CAN'T.
THIS IS A LIE!!
へたっ
HETA (COLLAPSE)
HOW COULD SUCH A COINCIDENCE...!?
すく
SUKU (STAND)
I'M PRETTY STUNNED MYSELF.
ザッ
ZA (CRUNCH)
THIS GOOD LUCK...
...IT'S JUST LIKE MY BROTHER'S.
MY CALCULATIONS AND WILLPOWER LOST TO MERE CHANCE?

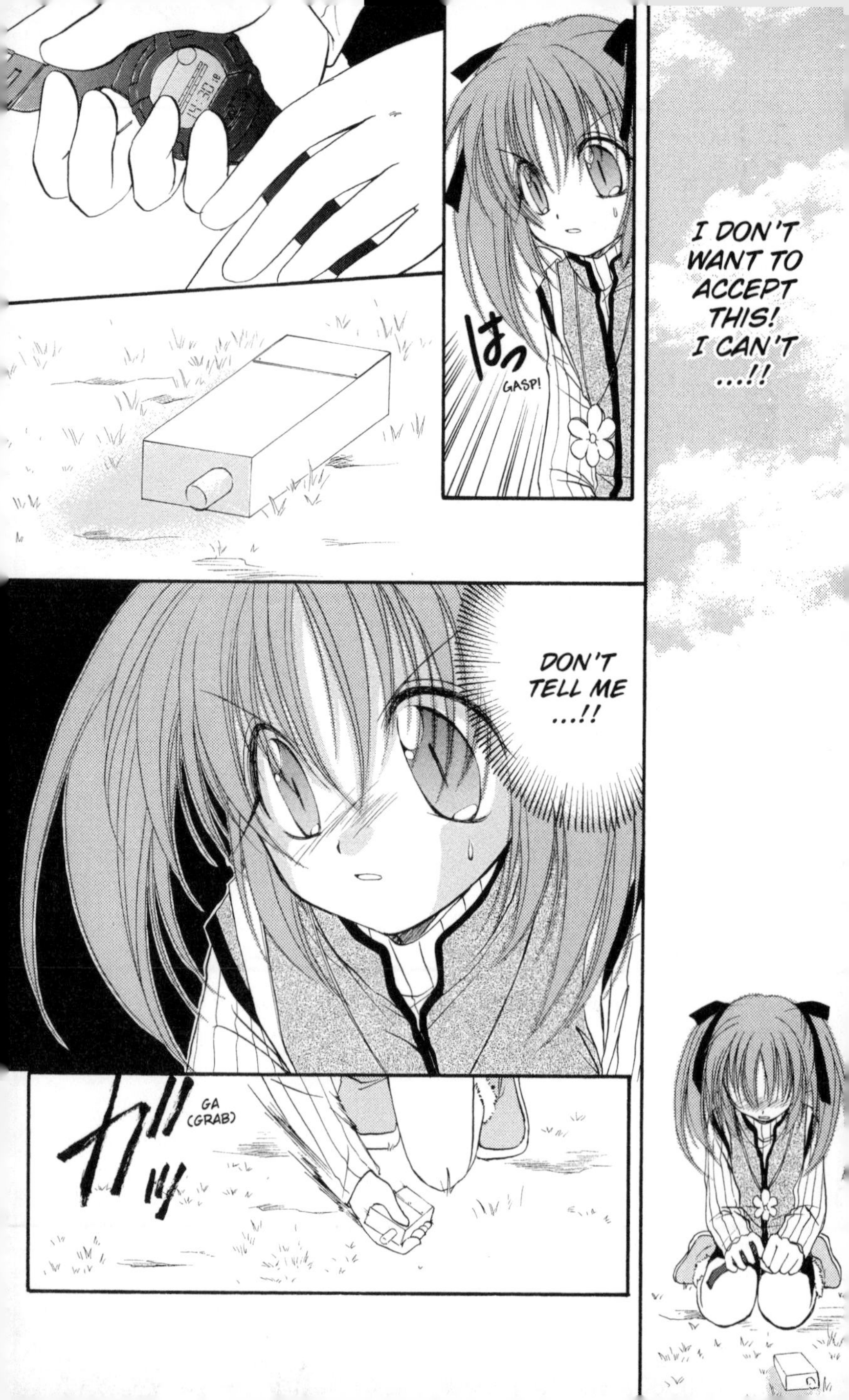
I DON'T WANT TO ACCEPT THIS! I CAN'T ...!!
はっ
GASP!
DON'T TELL ME ...!!
ガッ
GA (GRAB)

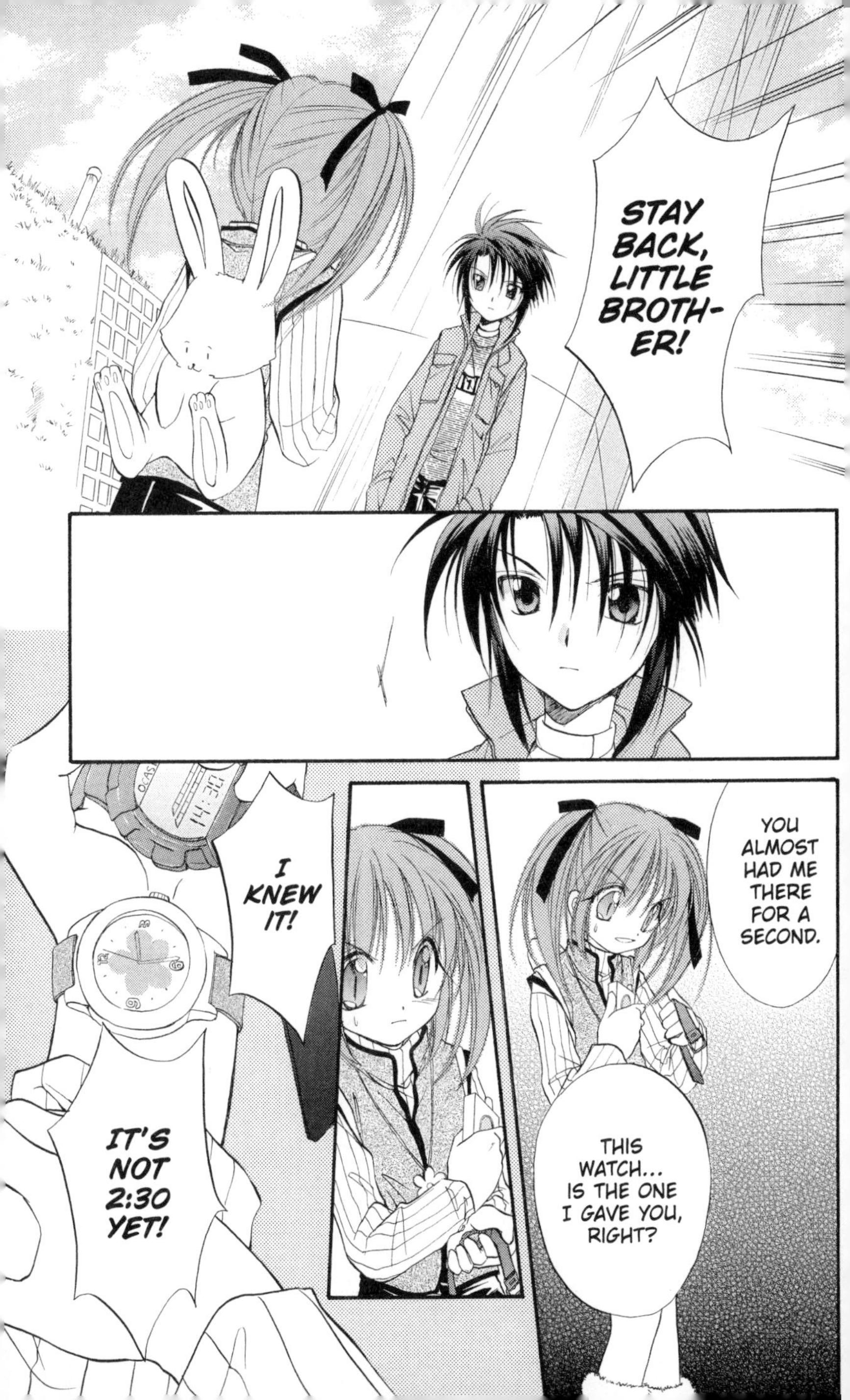
STAY BACK, LITTLE BROTH-ER!
YOU ALMOST HAD ME THERE FOR A SECOND.
THIS WATCH... IS THE ONE I GAVE YOU, RIGHT?
I KNEW IT!
IT'S NOT 2:30 YET!

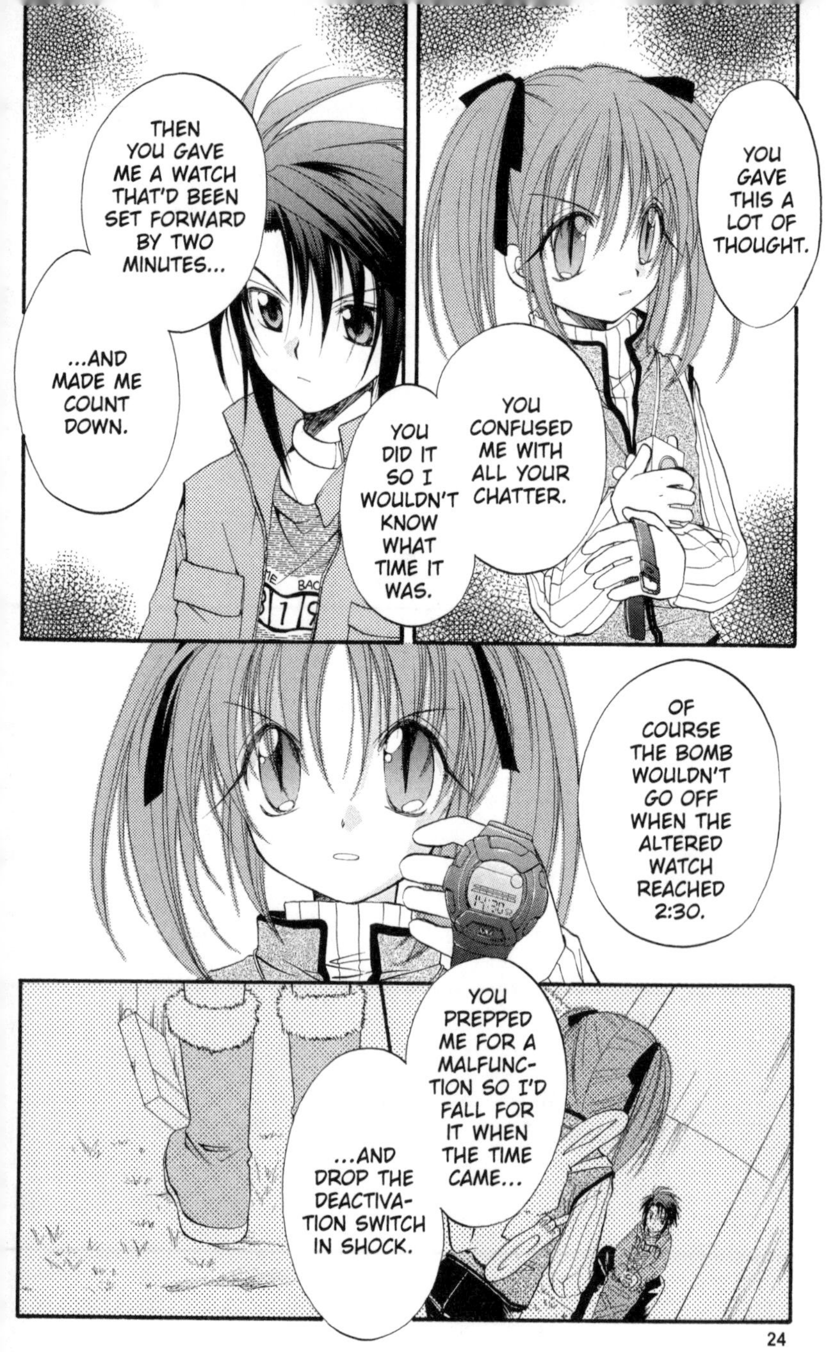
YOU GAVE THIS A LOT OF THOUGHT.
YOU CONFUSED ME WITH ALL YOUR CHATTER.
YOU DID IT SO I WOULDN'T KNOW WHAT TIME IT WAS.
THEN YOU GAVE ME A WATCH THAT'D BEEN SET FORWARD BY TWO MINUTES...
...AND MADE ME COUNT DOWN.
OF COURSE THE BOMB WOULDN'T GO OFF WHEN THE ALTERED WATCH REACHED 2:30.
YOU PREPPED ME FOR A MALFUNCTION SO I'D FALL FOR IT WHEN THE TIME CAME...
...AND DROP THE DEACTIVATION SWITCH IN SHOCK.

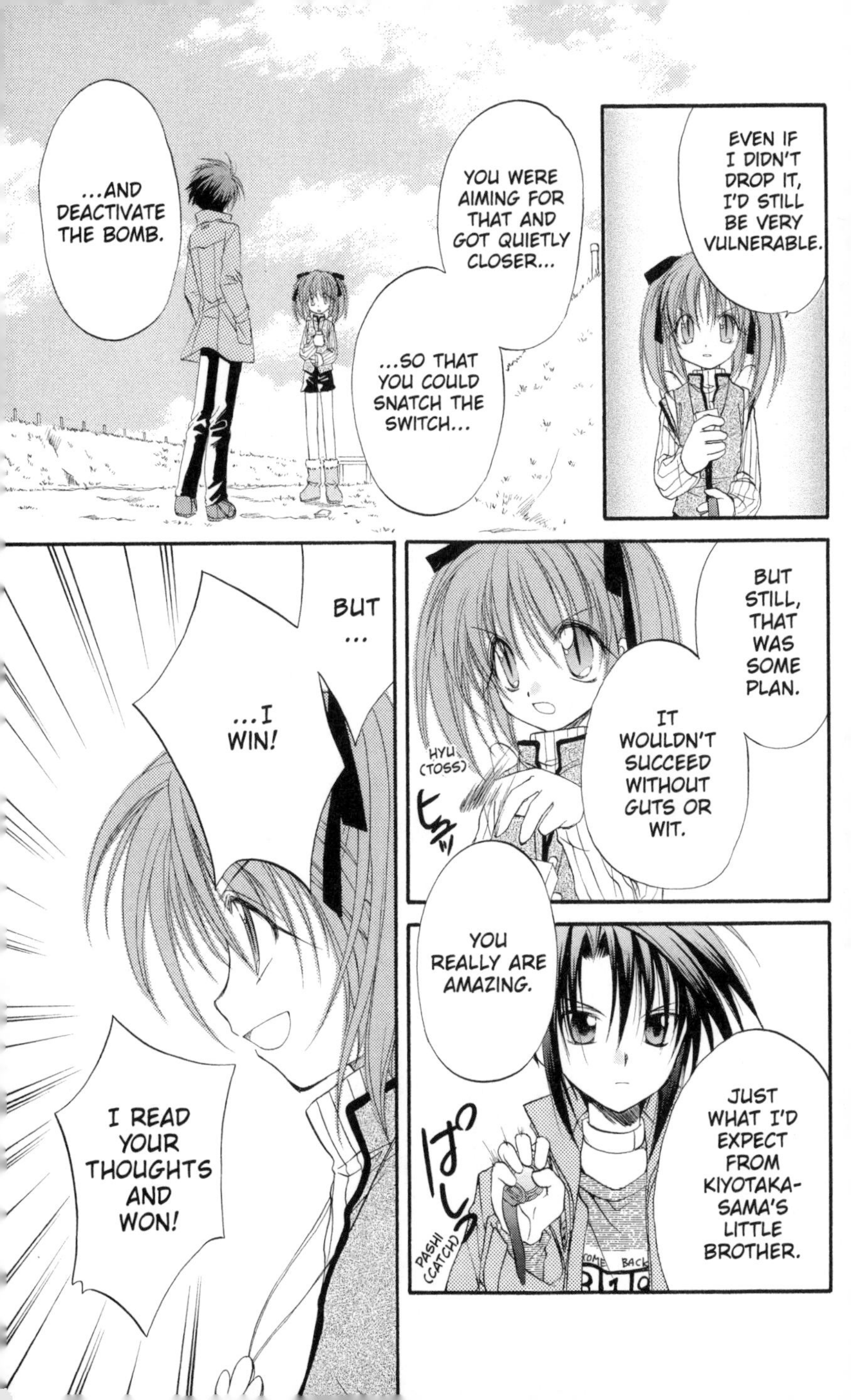
EVEN IF I DIDN'T DROP IT, I'D STILL BE VERY VULNERABLE.
YOU WERE AIMING FOR THAT AND GOT QUIETLY CLOSER...
...SO THAT YOU COULD SNATCH THE SWITCH...
...AND DEACTIVATE THE BOMB.
BUT STILL, THAT WAS SOME PLAN.
IT WOULDN'T SUCCEED WITHOUT GUTS OR WIT.
HYU (TOSS)
YOU REALLY ARE AMAZING.
JUST WHAT I'D EXPECT FROM KIYOTAKA-SAMA'S LITTLE BROTHER.
PASHI (CATCH)
COME BACK
BUT ...
...I WIN!
I READ YOUR THOUGHTS AND WON!

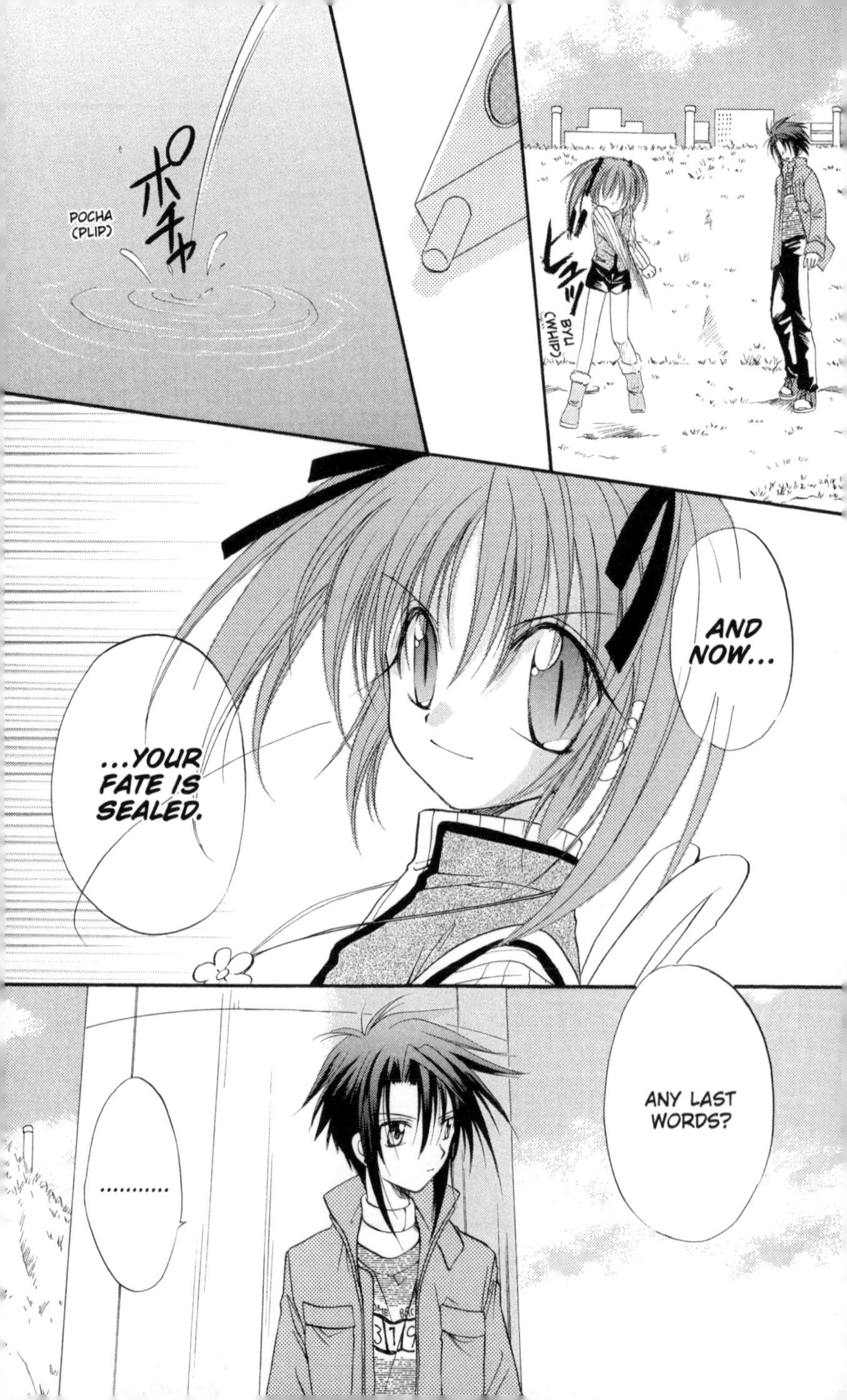
ヒュッ
BYU (WHIP)
ポチャ
POCHA (PLIP)
AND NOW...
...YOUR FATE IS SEALED.
ANY LAST WORDS?
....

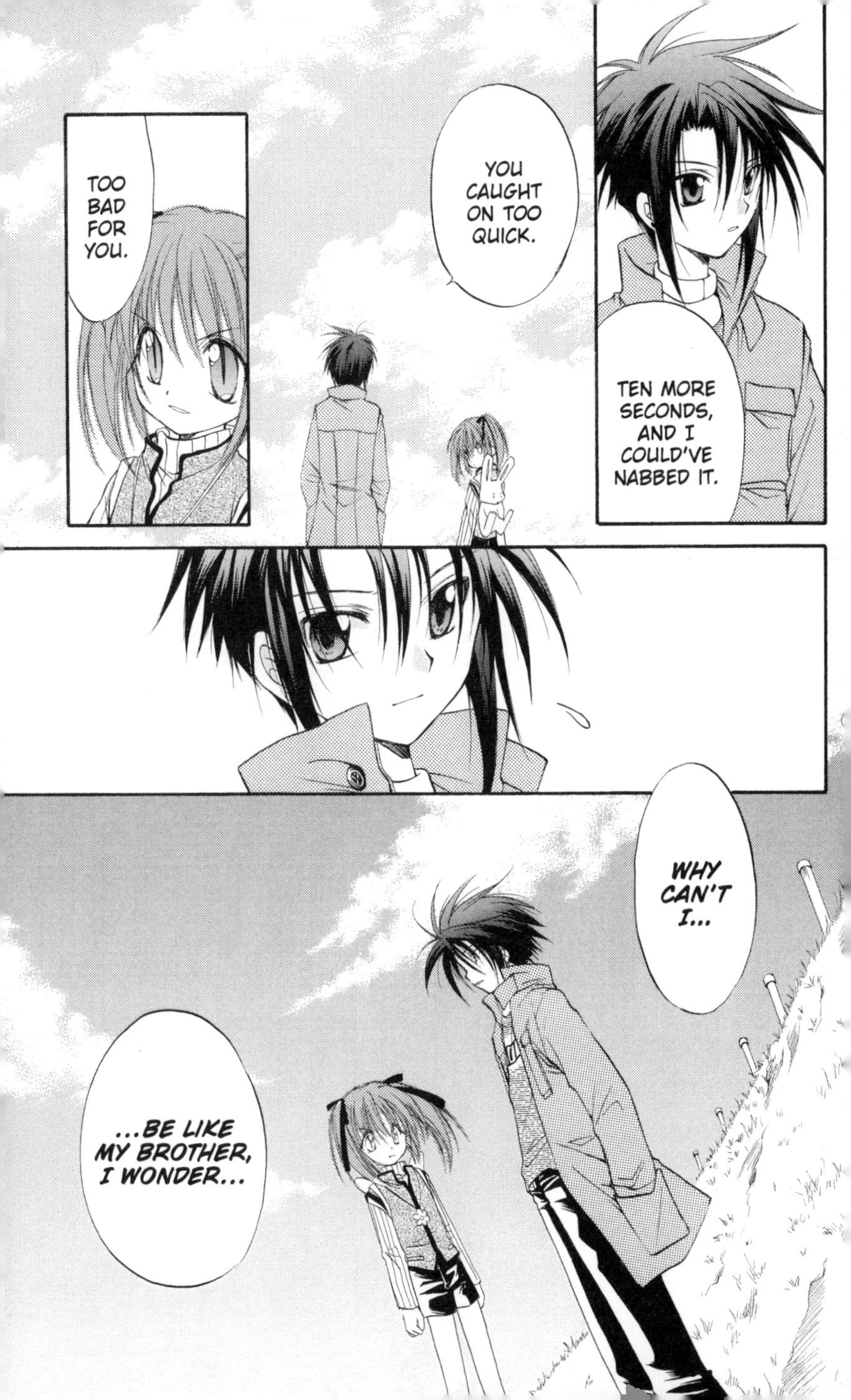
TEN MORE SECONDS, AND I COULD'VE NABBED IT.
YOU CAUGHT ON TOO QUICK.
TOO BAD FOR YOU.
WHY CAN'T I...
...BE LIKE MY BROTHER, I WONDER...

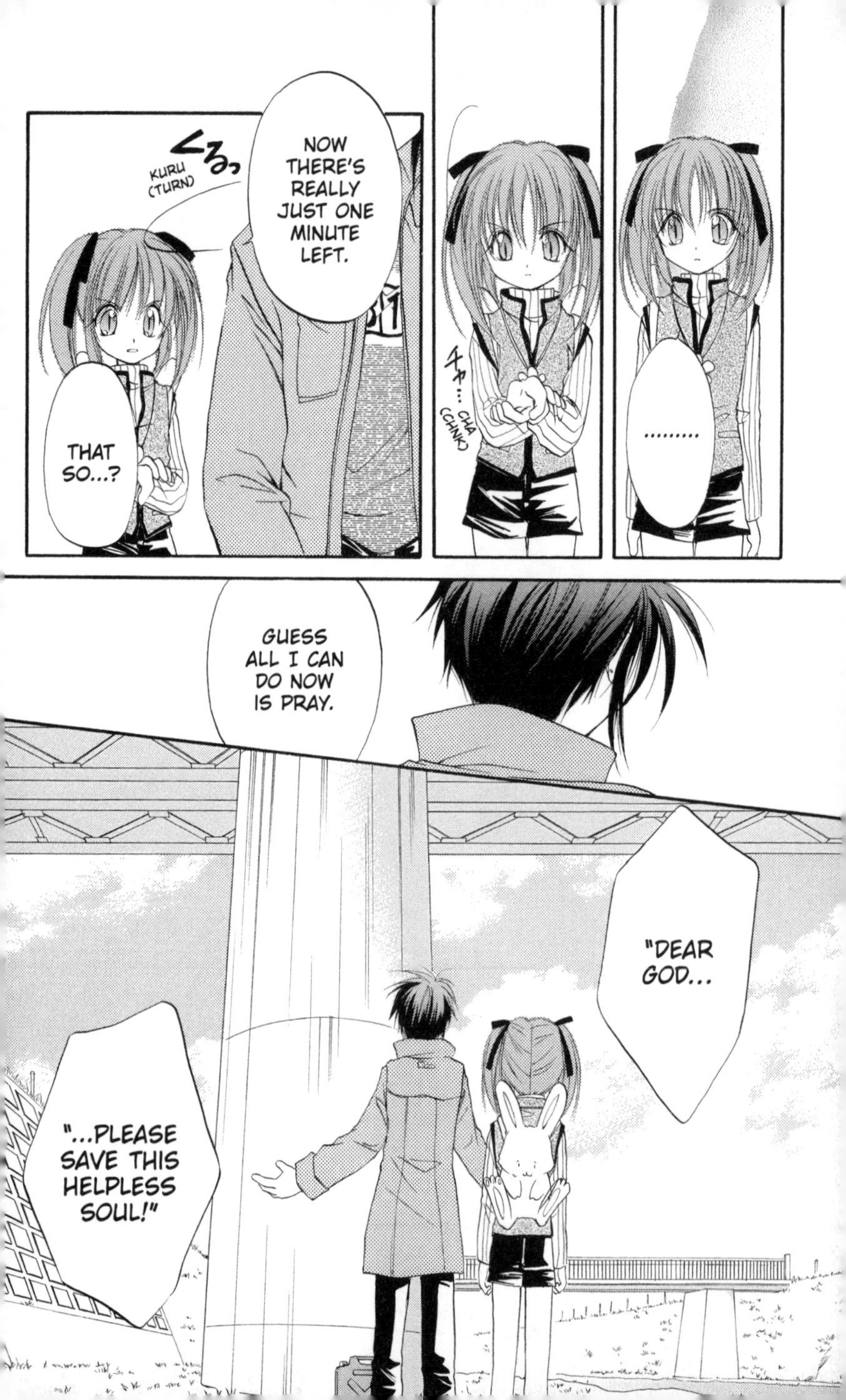
....
チャ… CHA (CHINK)
NOW THERE'S REALLY JUST ONE MINUTE LEFT.
くるっ KURU (TURN)
THAT SO...?
GUESS ALL I CAN DO NOW IS PRAY.
"DEAR GOD...
"...PLEASE SAVE THIS HELPLESS SOUL!"

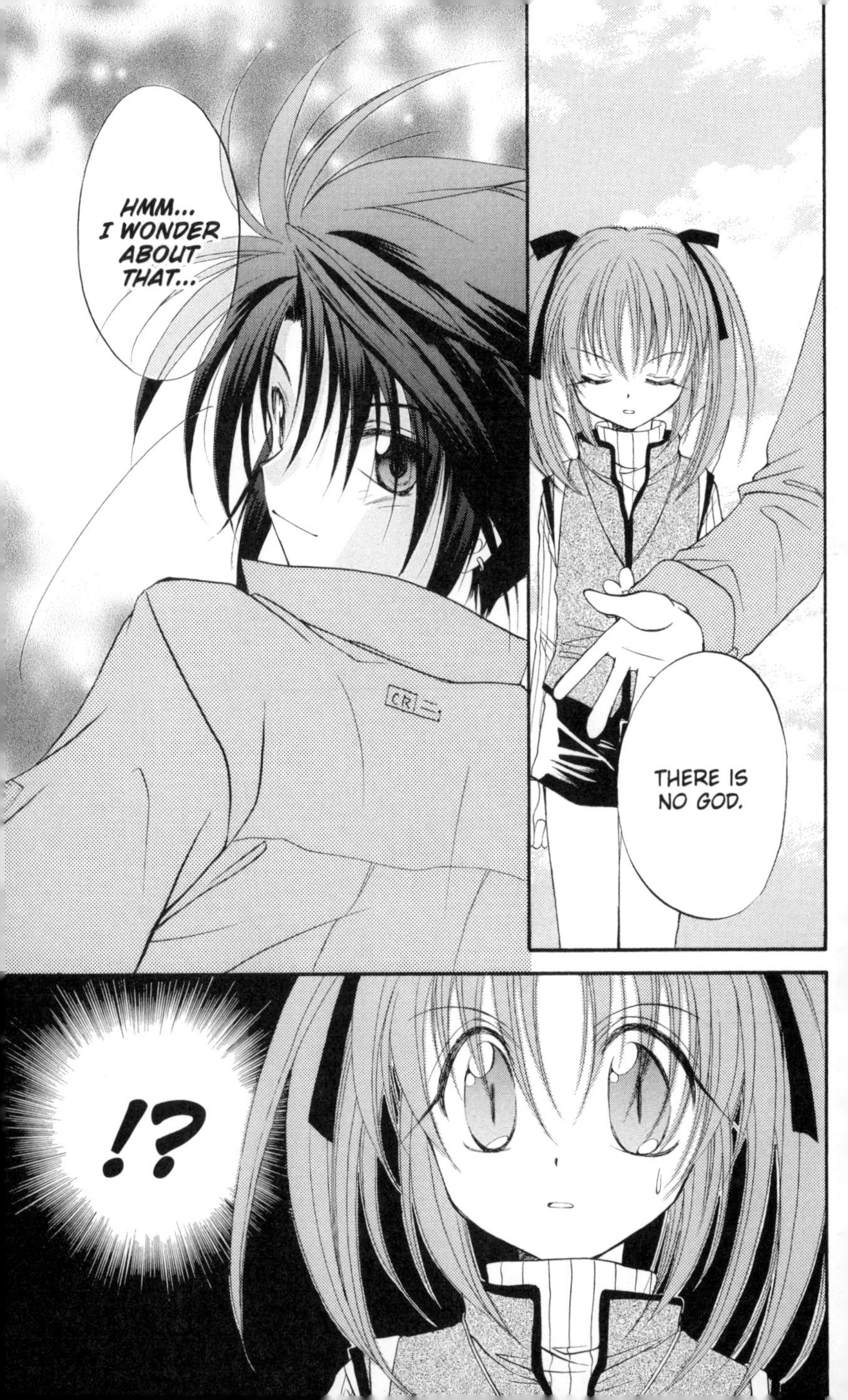
THERE IS NO GOD.
HMM... I WONDER ABOUT THAT...
!?

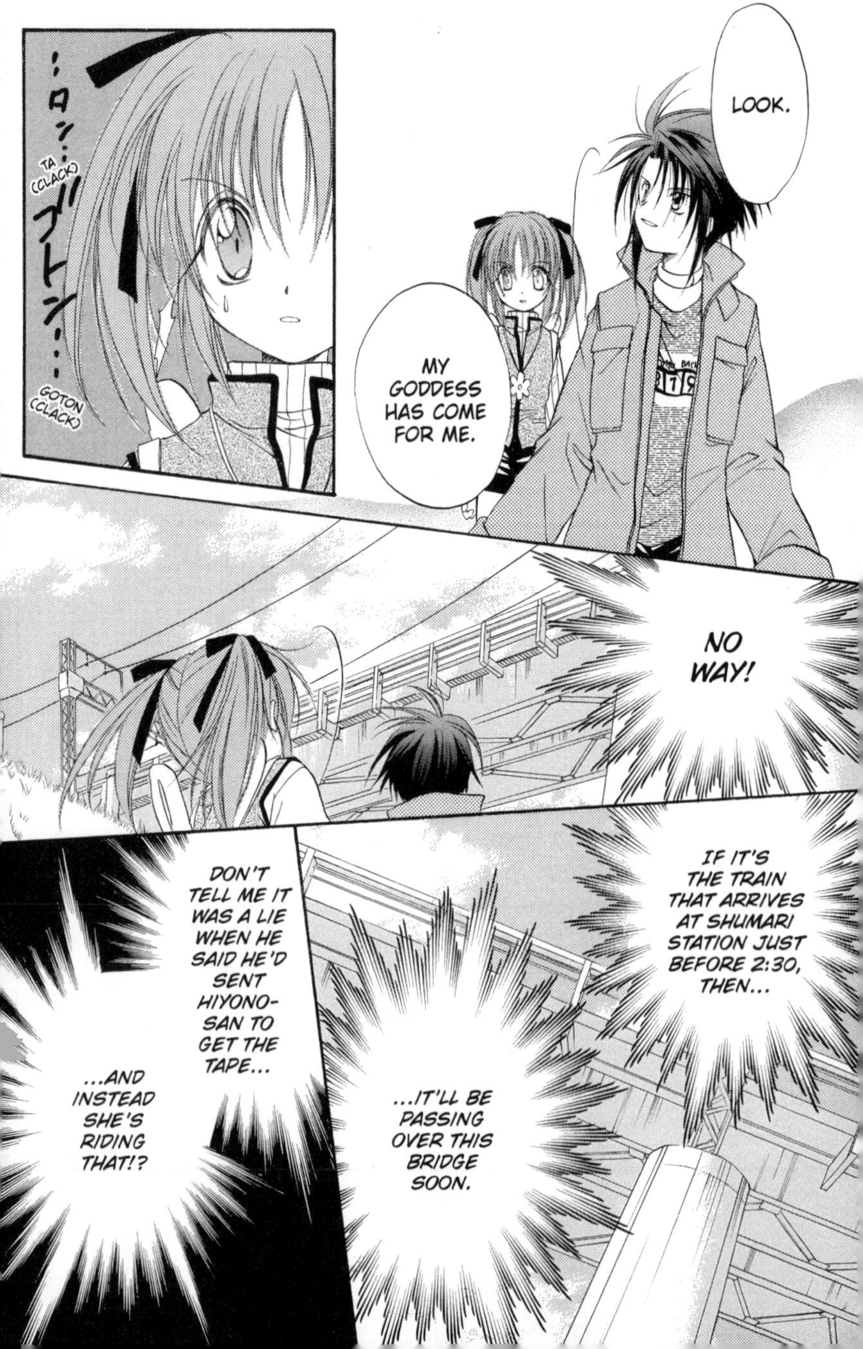
LOOK.
MY GODDESS HAS COME FOR ME.
タン…
TA (CLACK)
ゴトン…
GOTON (CLACK)
NO WAY!
IF IT'S THE TRAIN THAT ARRIVES AT SHUMARI STATION JUST BEFORE 2:30, THEN...
...IT'LL BE PASSING OVER THIS BRIDGE SOON.
DON'T TELL ME IT WAS A LIE WHEN HE SAID HE'D SENT HIYONO-SAN TO GET THE TAPE...
...AND INSTEAD SHE'S RIDING THAT!?

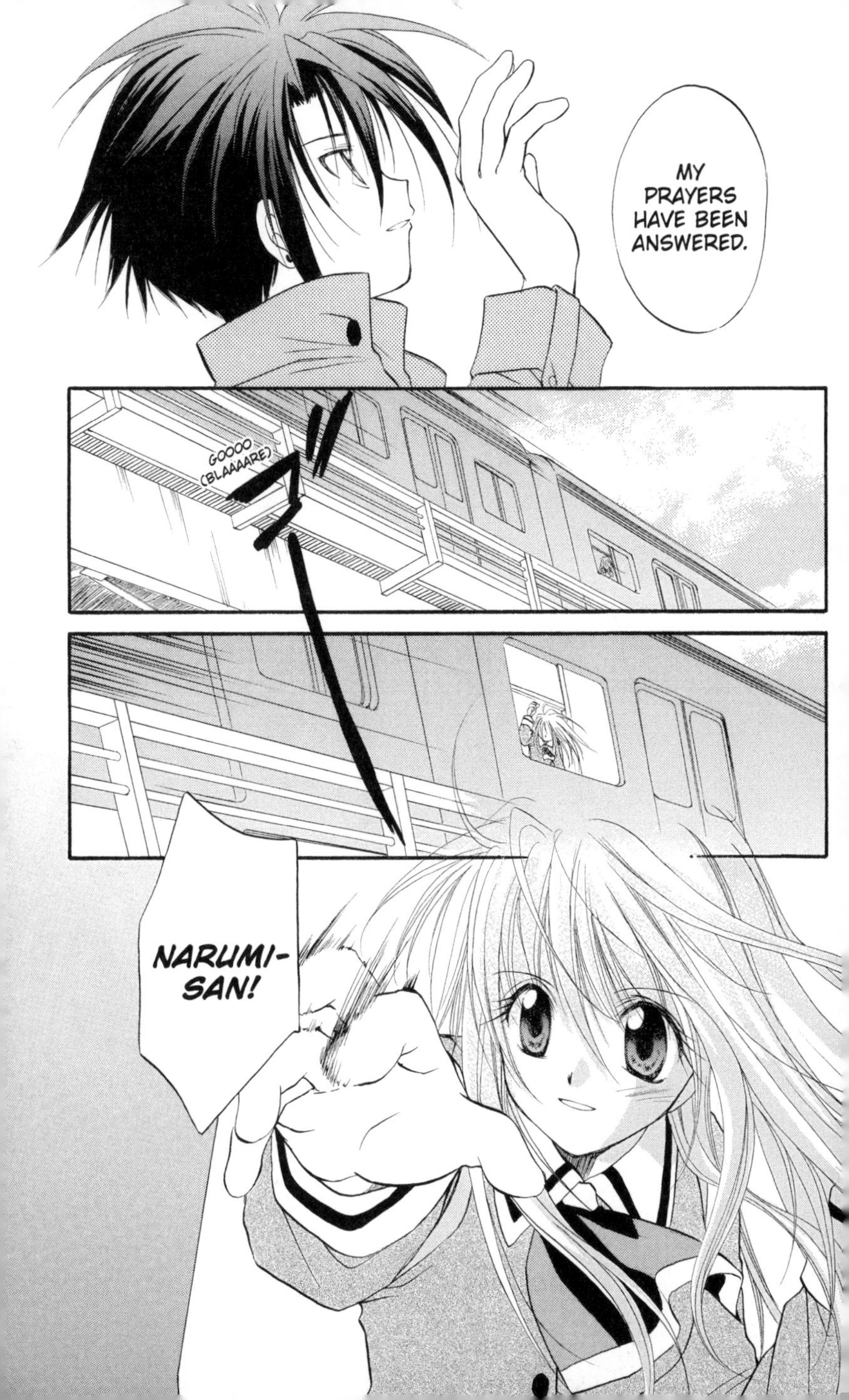
MY PRAYERS HAVE BEEN ANSWERED.
GOOOO (BLAAAARE)
NARUMI-SAN!

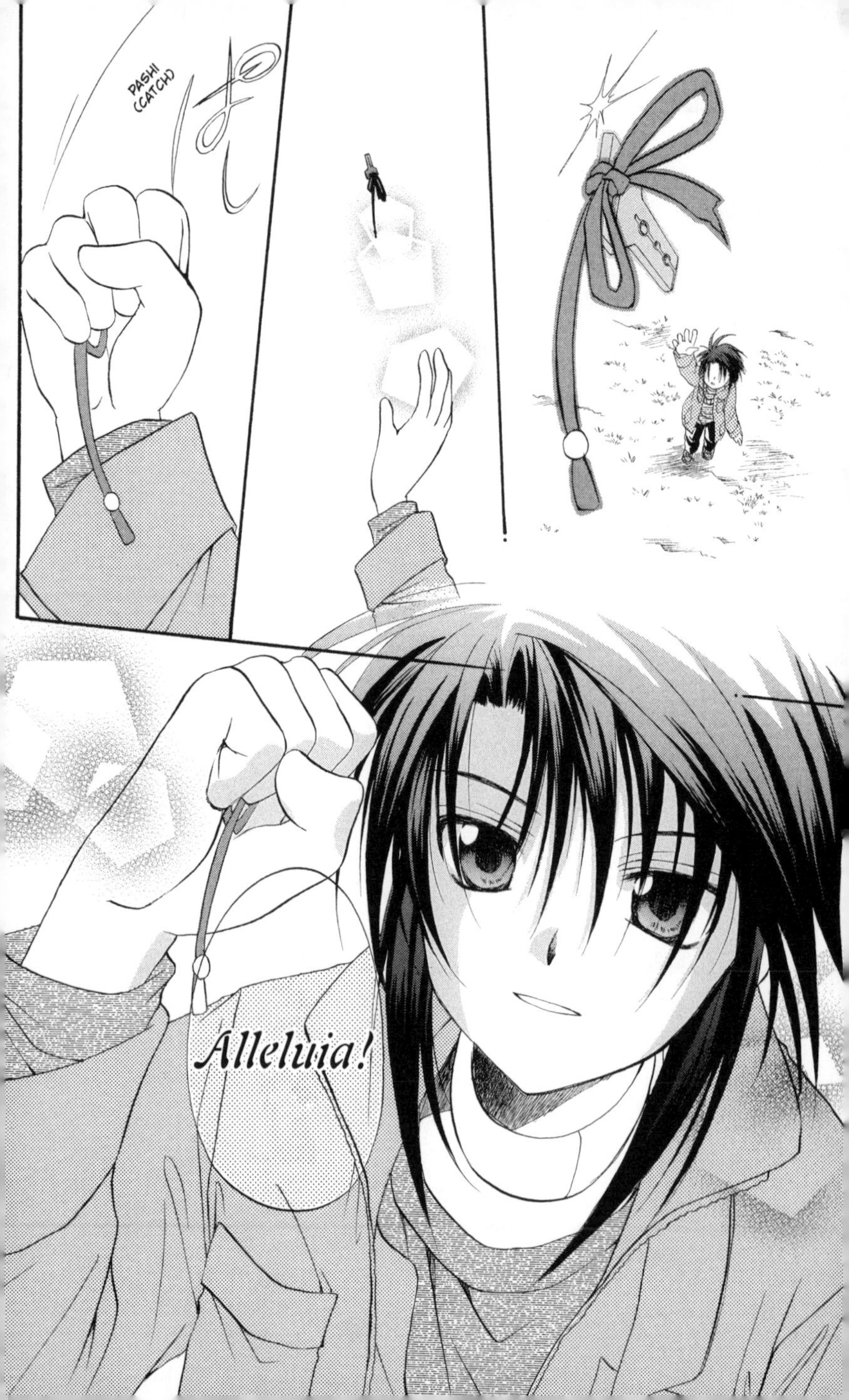
PASHI (CATCH)
Alleluia!

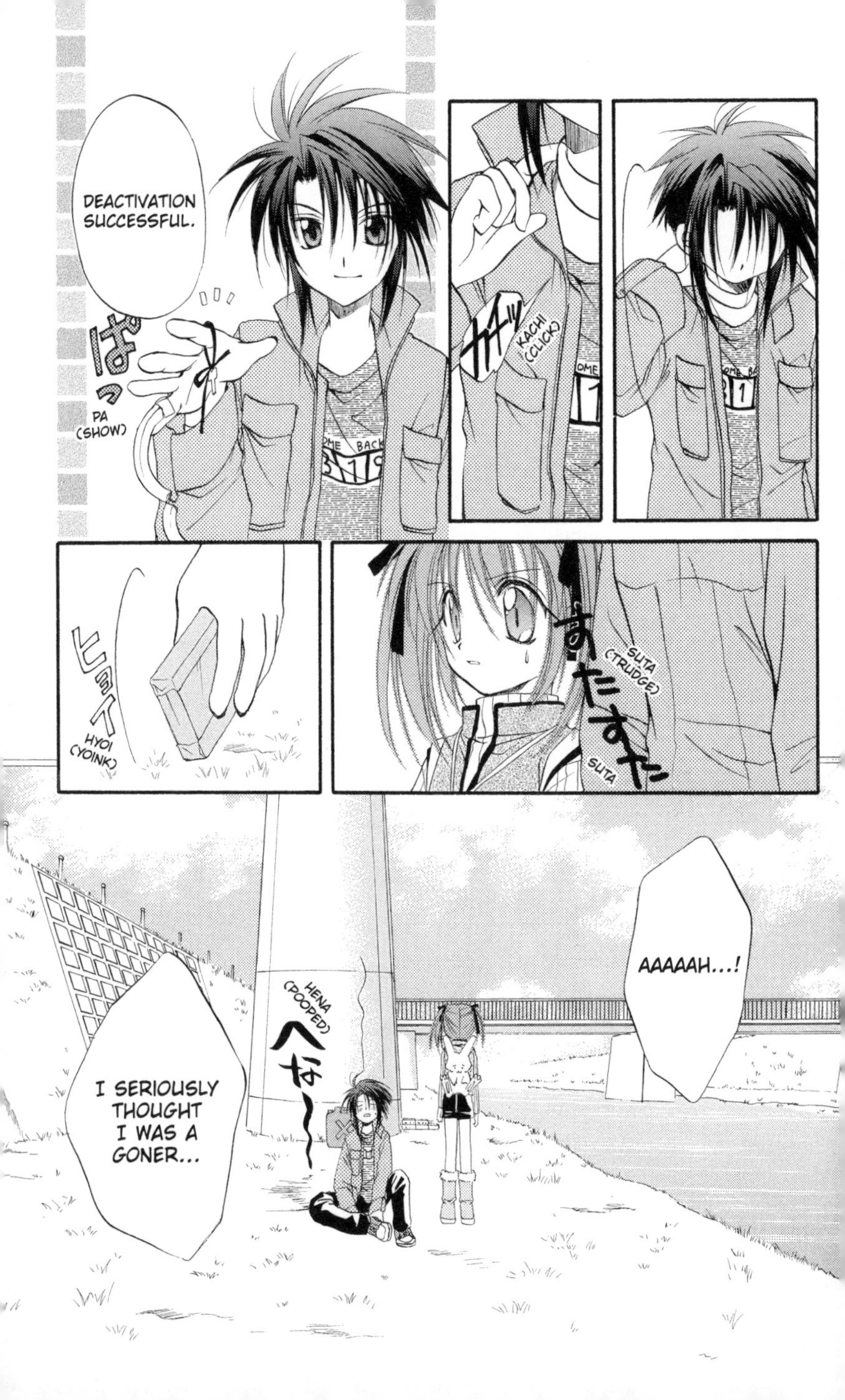

カチッ
KACHI (CLICK)
DEACTIVATION SUCCESSFUL.
ぱっ
PA (SHOW)
すたすた
SUTA (TRUDGE) SUTA
ヒョイ
HYOI (YOINK)
AAAAAH...!
へな〜
HENA (POOPED)
I SERIOUSLY THOUGHT I WAS A GONER...

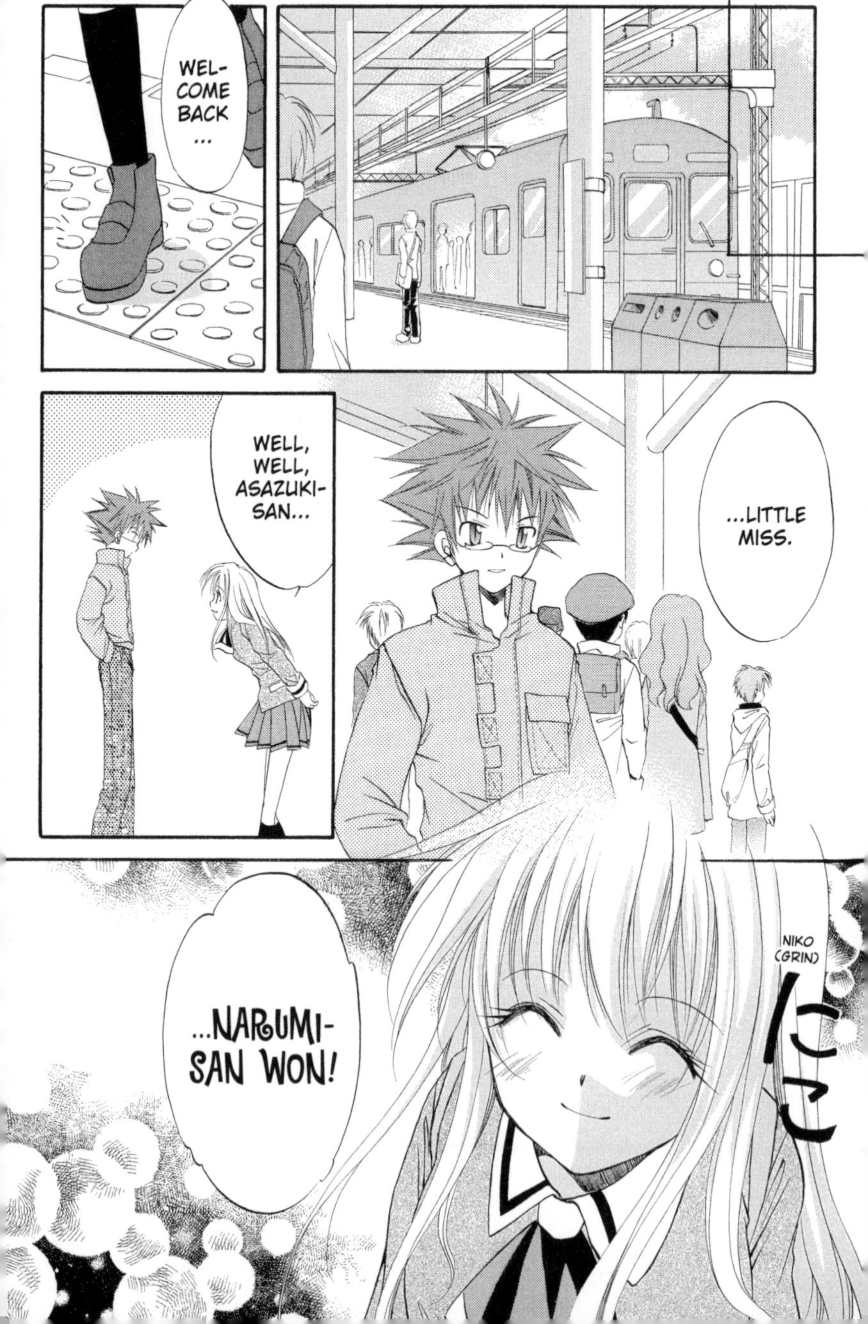
WEL-COME BACK...
...LITTLE MISS.
WELL, WELL, ASAZUKI-SAN...
にこ
NIKO (GRIN)
...NARUMI-SAN WON!

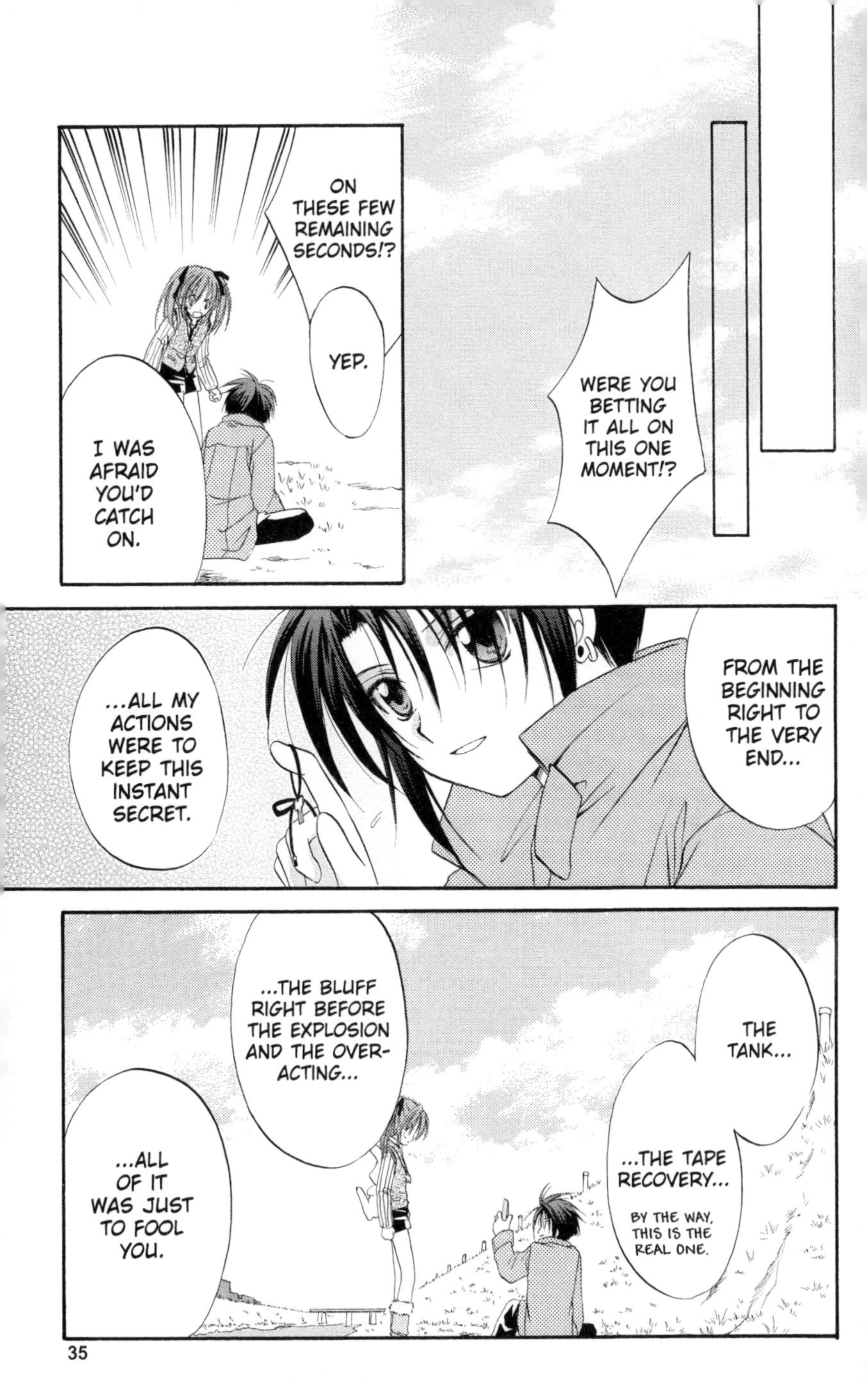
WERE YOU BETTING IT ALL ON THIS ONE MOMENT!?
ON THESE FEW REMAINING SECONDS!?
YEP.
I WAS AFRAID YOU'D CATCH ON.
FROM THE BEGINNING RIGHT TO THE VERY END...
...ALL MY ACTIONS WERE TO KEEP THIS INSTANT SECRET.
THE TANK...
...THE TAPE RECOVERY...
BY THE WAY, THIS IS THE REAL ONE.
...THE BLUFF RIGHT BEFORE THE EXPLOSION AND THE OVER-ACTING...
...ALL OF IT WAS JUST TO FOOL YOU.

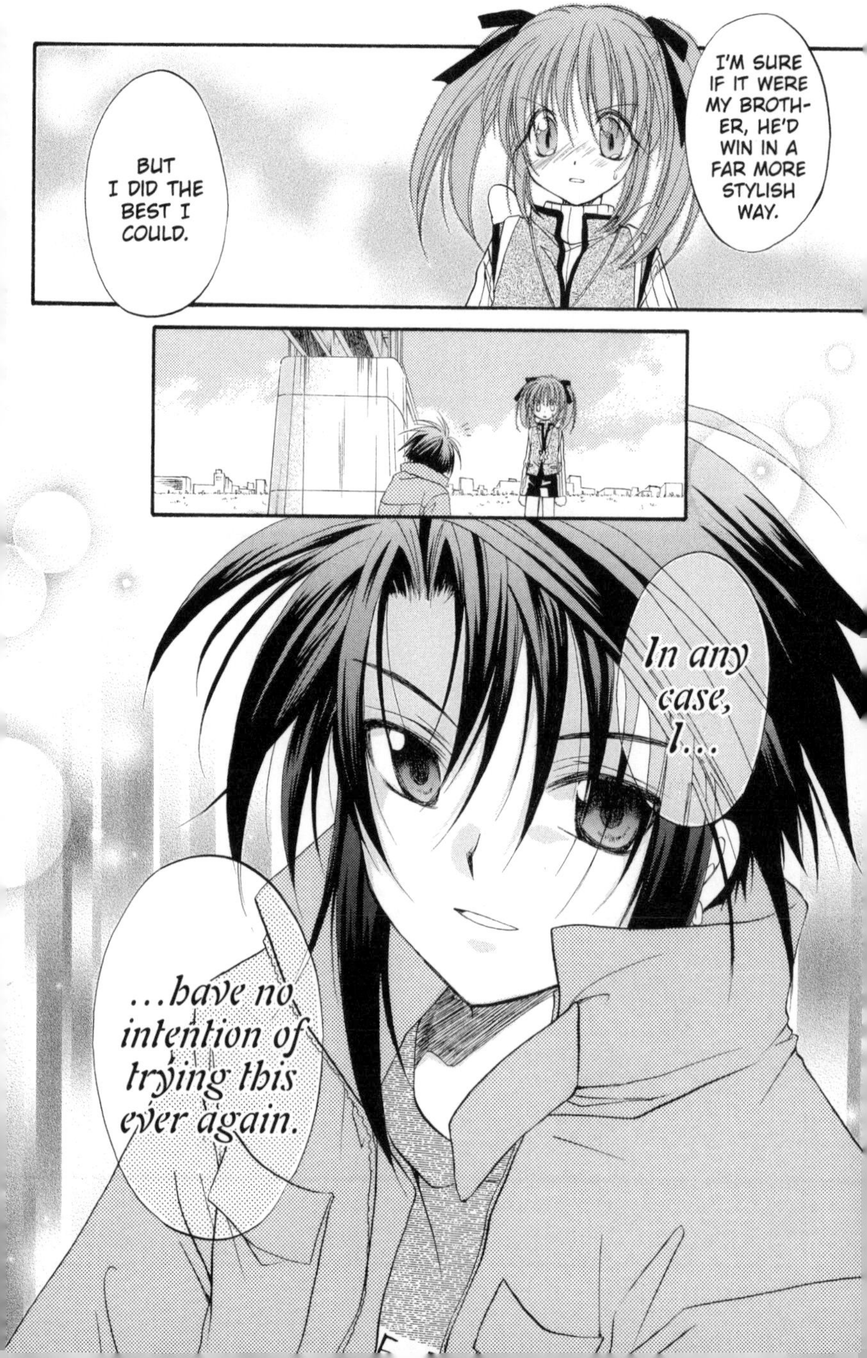
I'M SURE IF IT WERE MY BROTH-ER, HE'D WIN IN A FAR MORE STYLISH WAY.
BUT I DID THE BEST I COULD.
In any case, I...
...have no intention of trying this ever again.

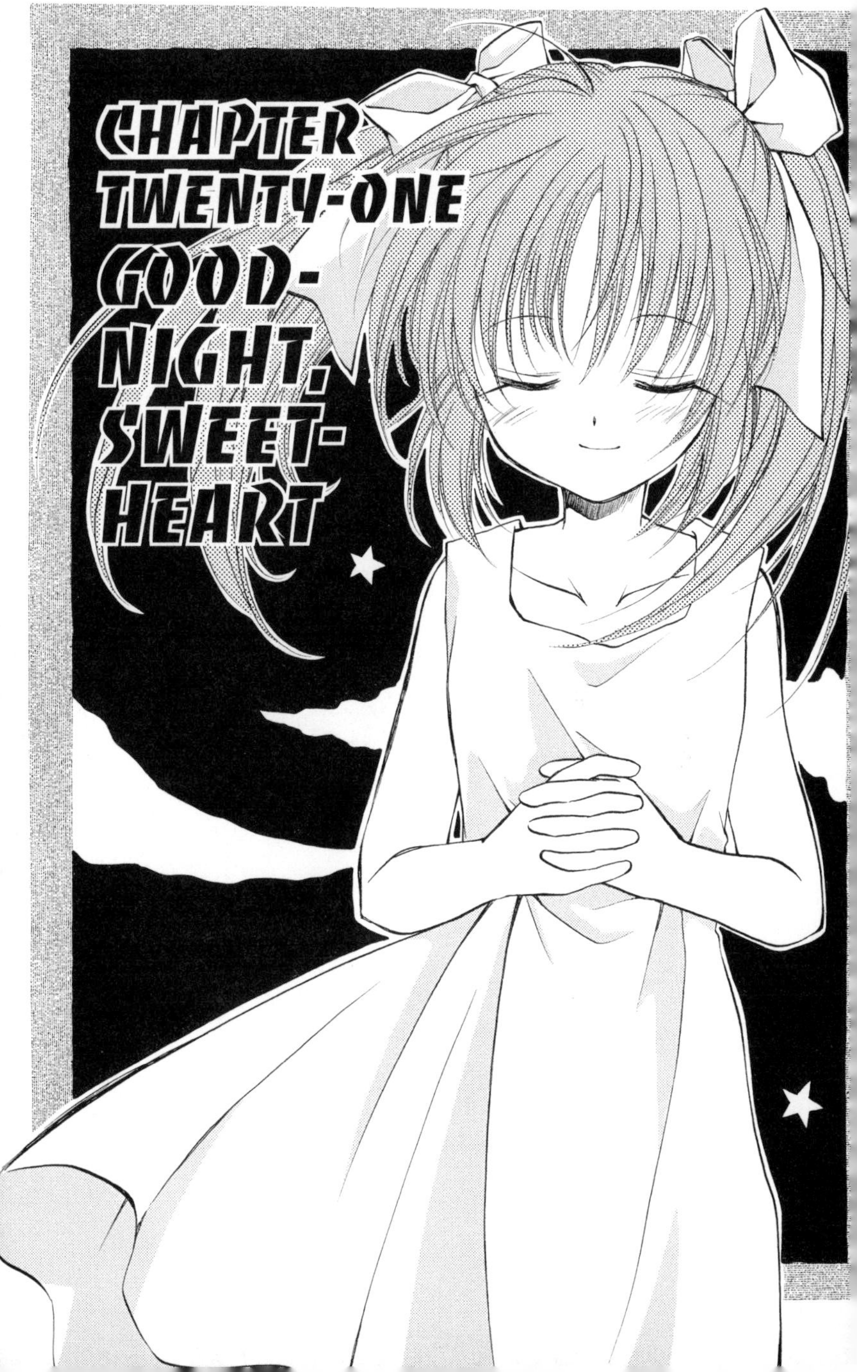
CHAPTER TWENTY-ONE
GOOD-NIGHT, SWEET-HEART

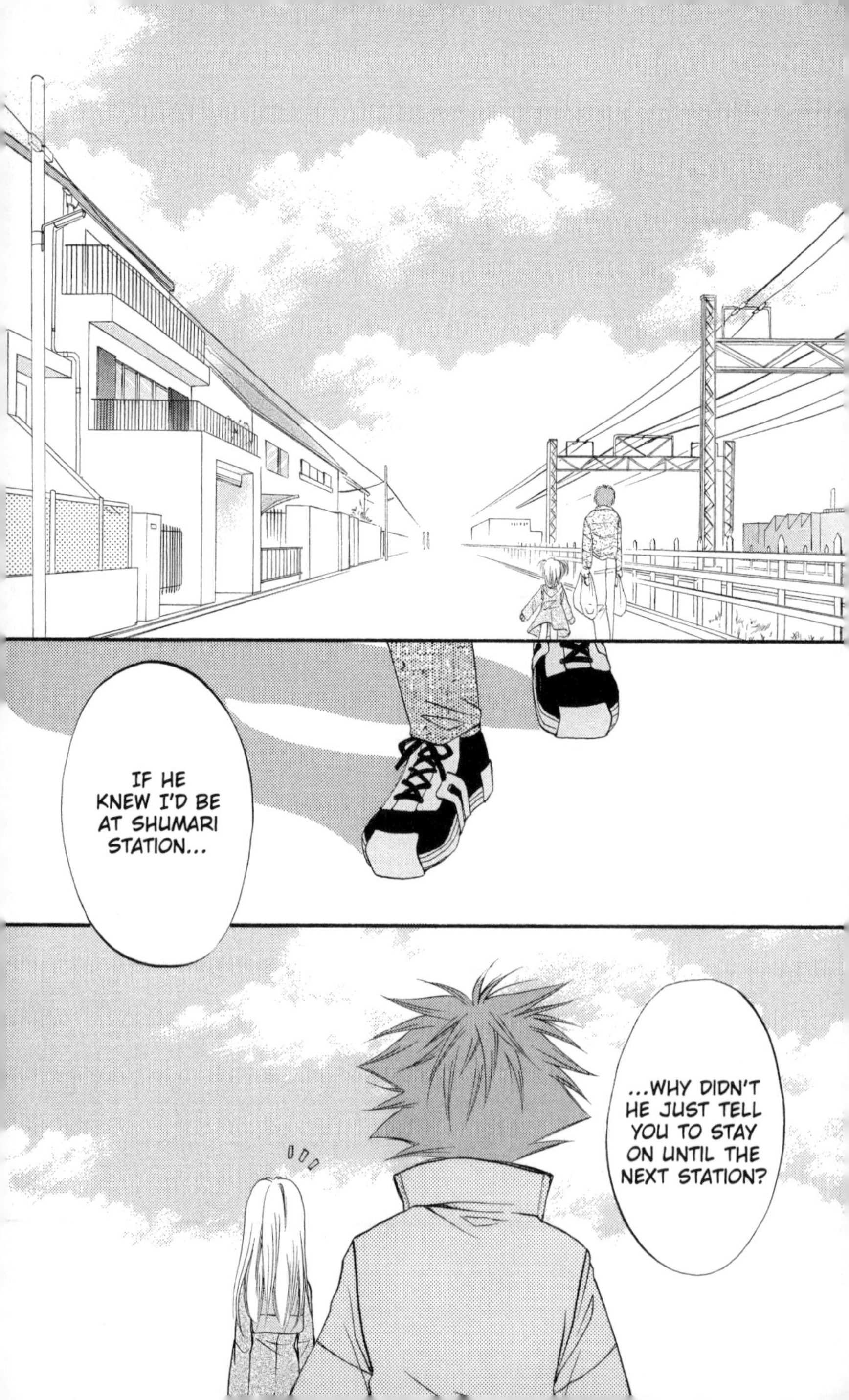
IF HE KNEW I'D BE AT SHUMARI STATION...
...WHY DIDN'T HE JUST TELL YOU TO STAY ON UNTIL THE NEXT STATION?

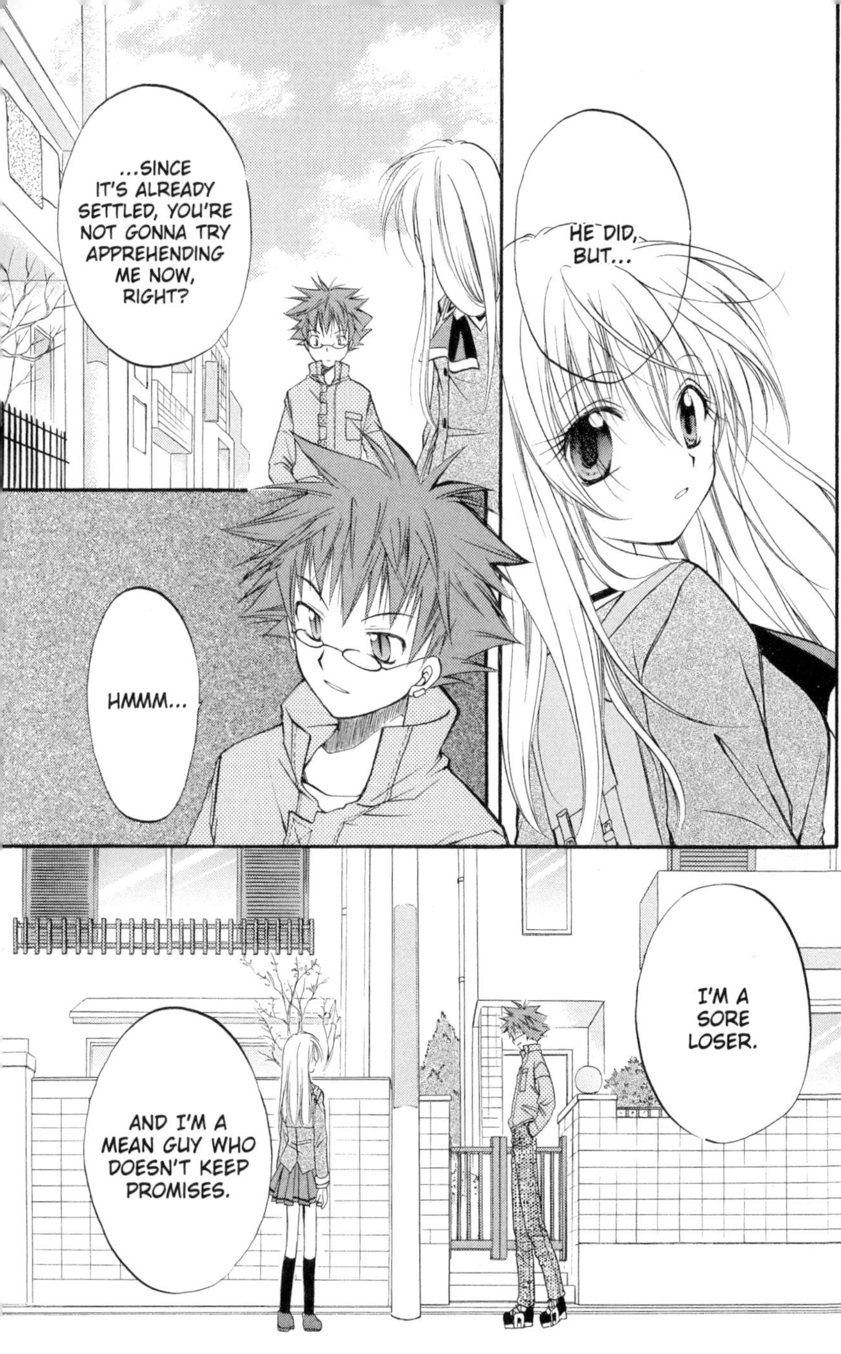
HE DID, BUT...
...SINCE IT'S ALREADY SETTLED, YOU'RE NOT GONNA TRY APPREHENDING ME NOW, RIGHT?
HMMM...
I'M A SORE LOSER.
AND I'M A MEAN GUY WHO DOESN'T KEEP PROMISES.

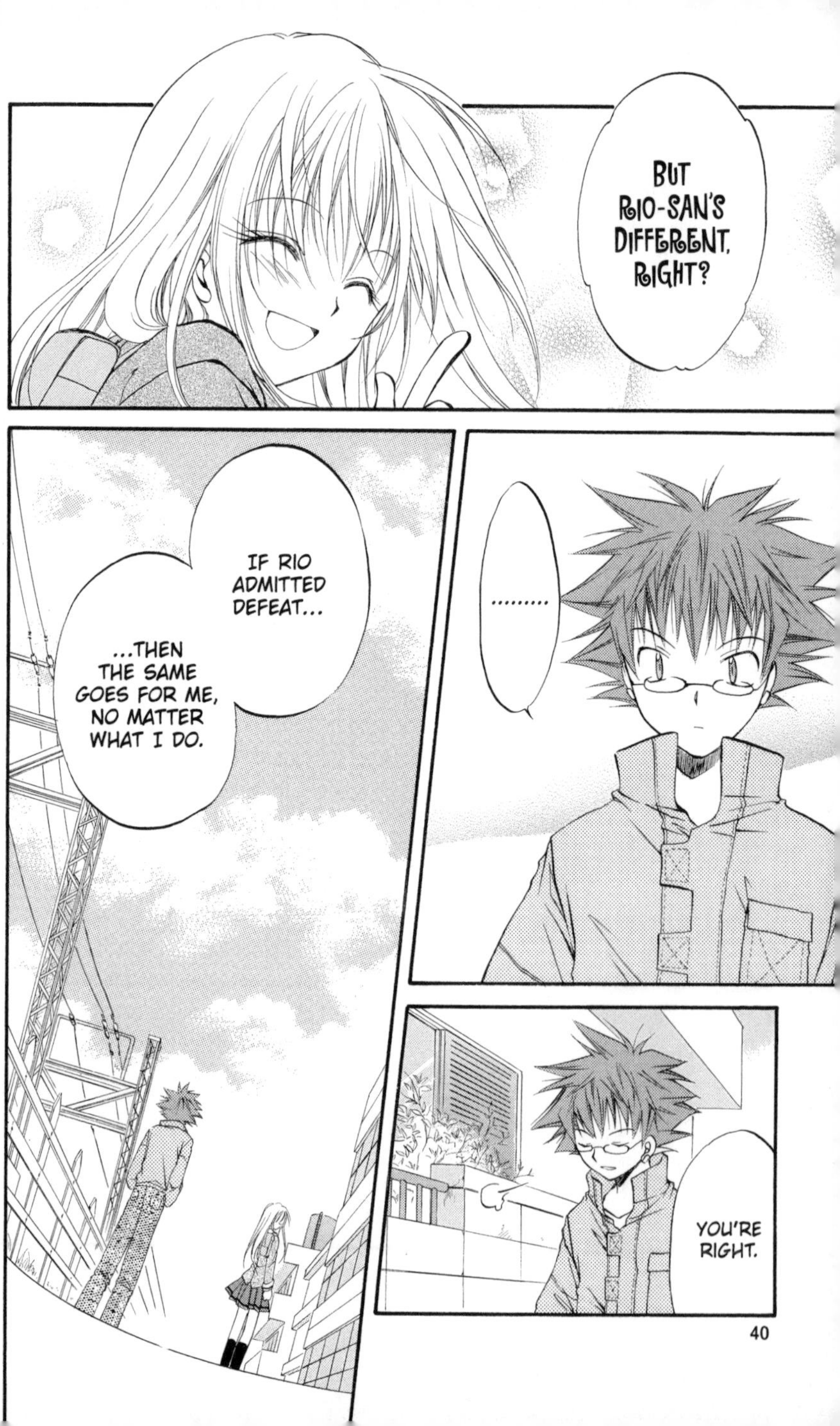
BUT RIO-SAN'S DIFFERENT, RIGHT?
....
YOU'RE RIGHT.
IF RIO ADMITTED DEFEAT...
...THEN THE SAME GOES FOR ME, NO MATTER WHAT I DO.

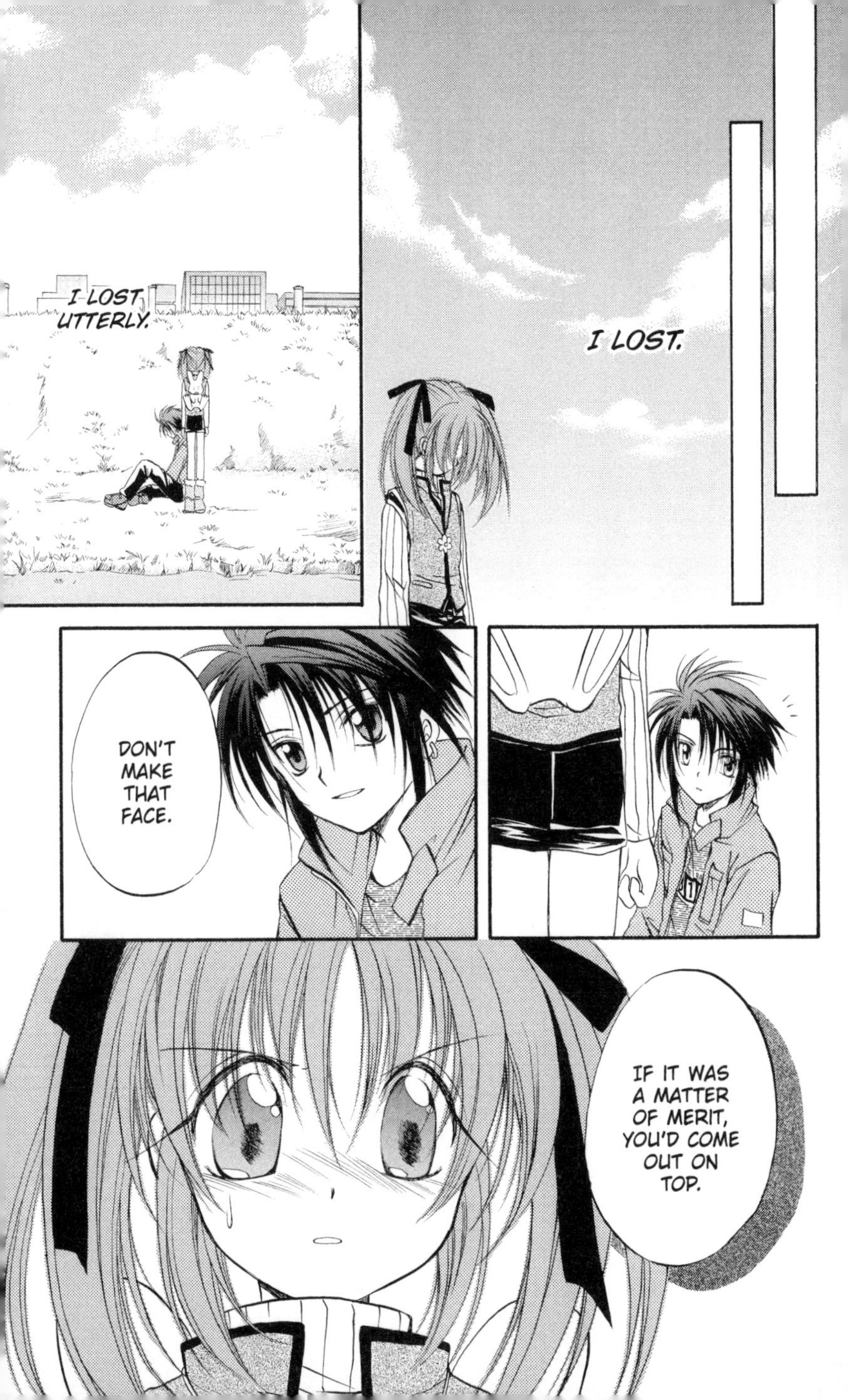
I LOST.
I LOST UTTERLY.
DON'T MAKE THAT FACE.
IF IT WAS A MATTER OF MERIT, YOU'D COME OUT ON TOP.

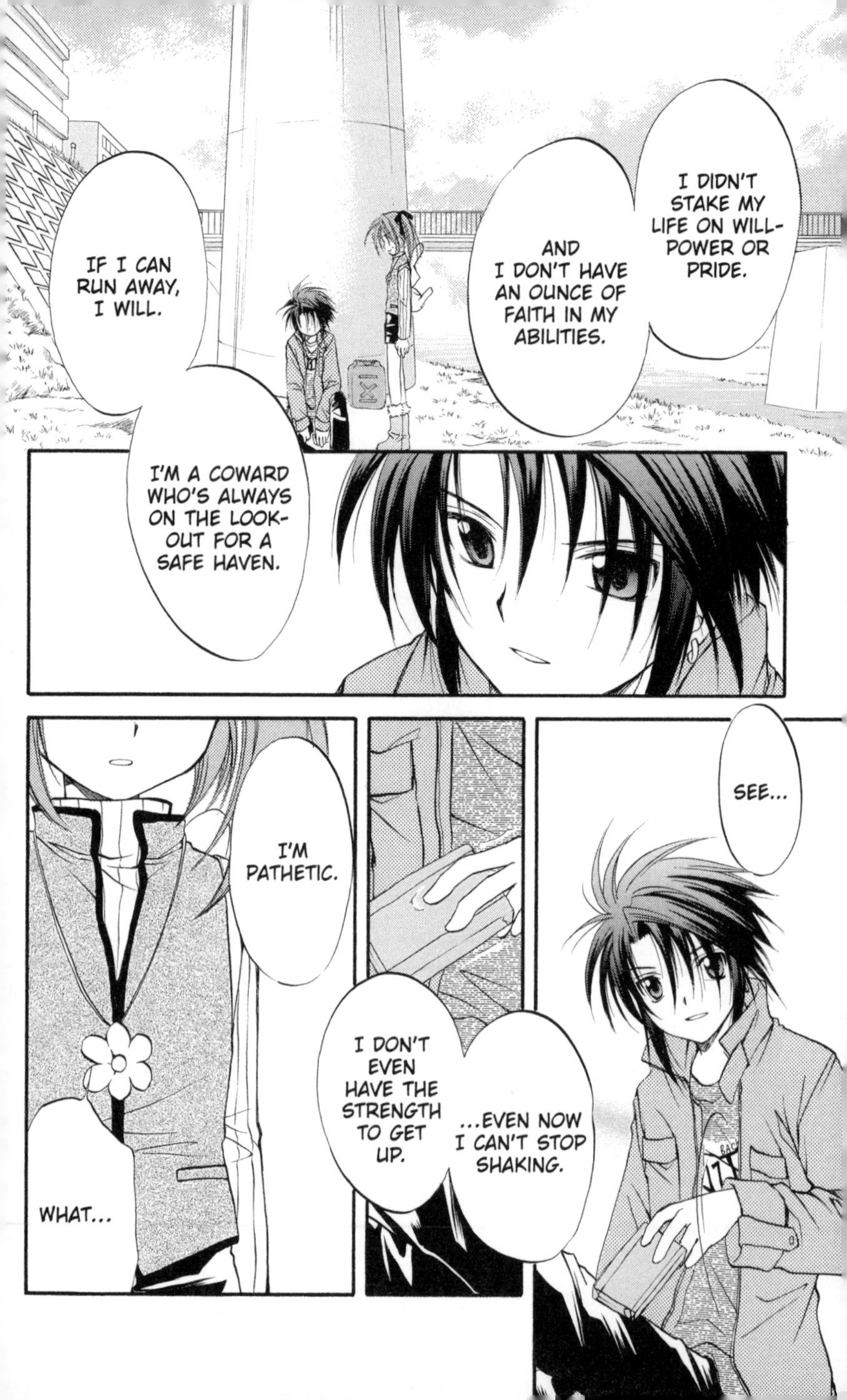
I DIDN'T STAKE MY LIFE ON WILL-POWER OR PRIDE.
AND I DON'T HAVE AN OUNCE OF FAITH IN MY ABILITIES.
IF I CAN RUN AWAY, I WILL.
I'M A COWARD WHO'S ALWAYS ON THE LOOK-OUT FOR A SAFE HAVEN.
SEE...
...EVEN NOW I CAN'T STOP SHAKING.
I DON'T EVEN HAVE THE STRENGTH TO GET UP.
I'M PATHETIC.
WHAT...

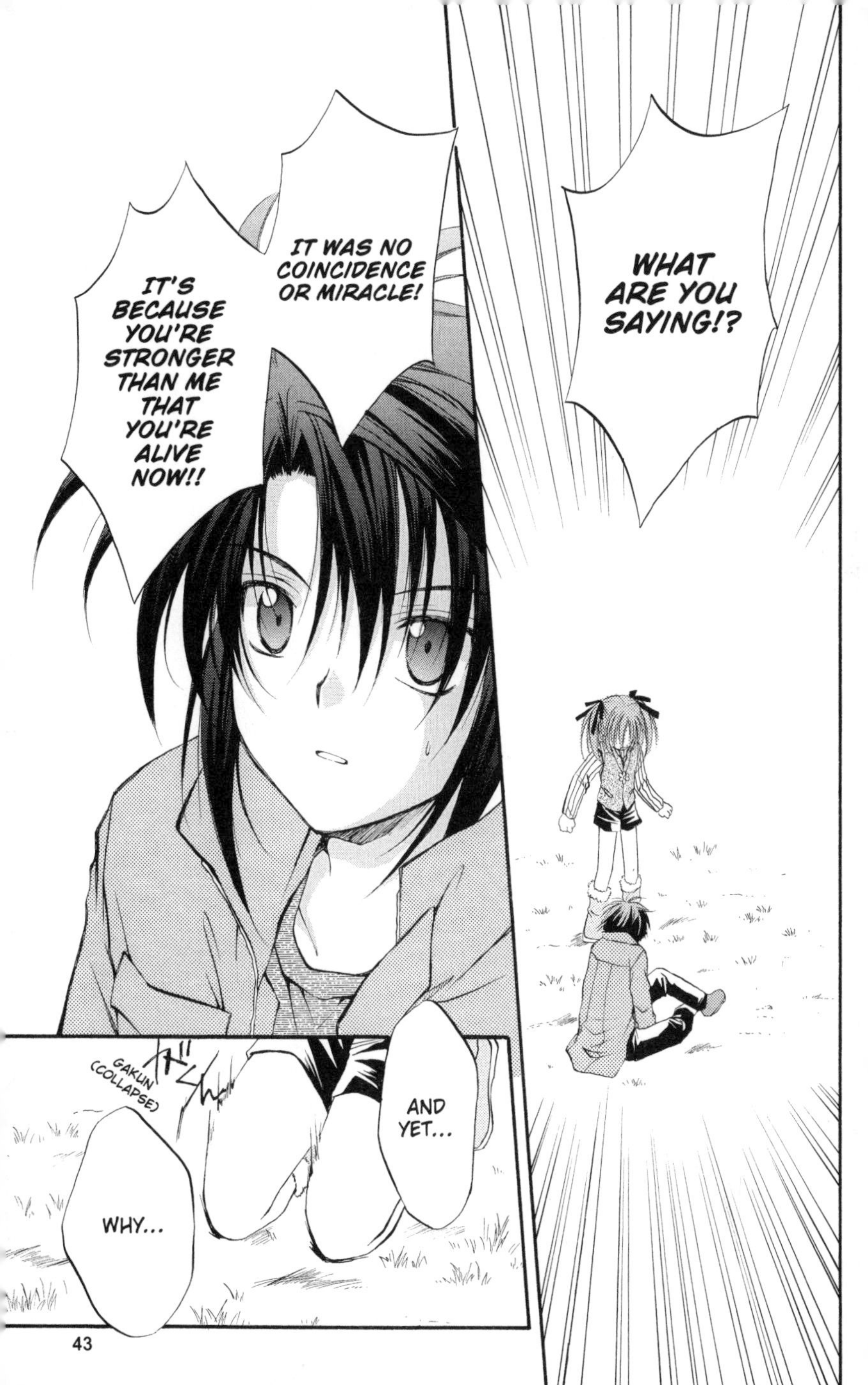
WHAT ARE YOU SAYING!?
IT WAS NO COINCIDENCE OR MIRACLE!
IT'S BECAUSE YOU'RE STRONGER THAN ME THAT YOU'RE ALIVE NOW!!
AND YET...
GAKUN (COLLAPSE)
WHY...

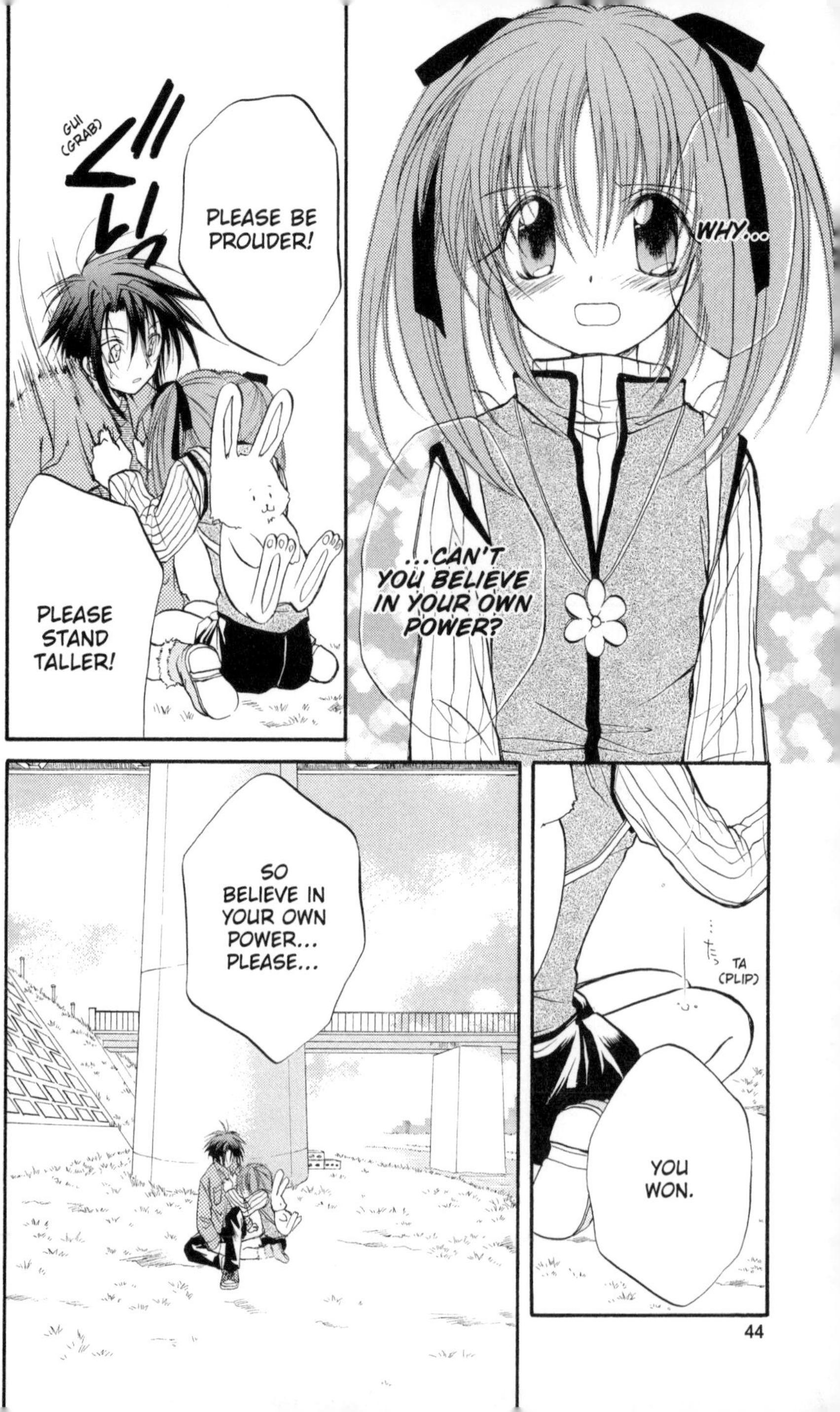
WHY...
...CAN'T YOU BELIEVE IN YOUR OWN POWER?
GUI (GRAB)
PLEASE BE PROUDER!
PLEASE STAND TALLER!
TA (PLIP)
YOU WON.
SO BELIEVE IN YOUR OWN POWER... PLEASE...

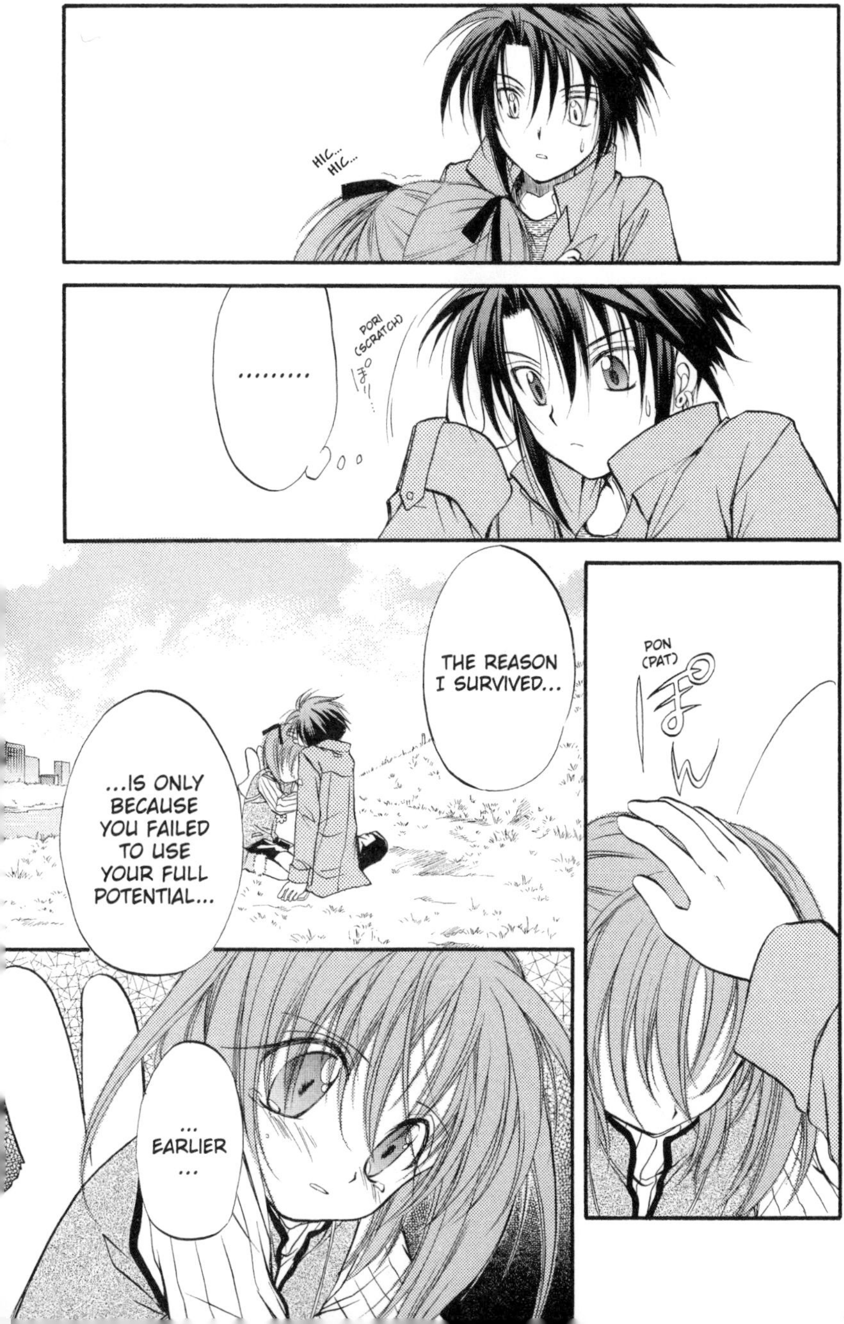
HIC... HIC...
PORI (SCRATCH)
ぽり…
....
PON (PAT)
ぽん
THE REASON I SURVIVED...
...IS ONLY BECAUSE YOU FAILED TO USE YOUR FULL POTENTIAL...
... EARLIER ...

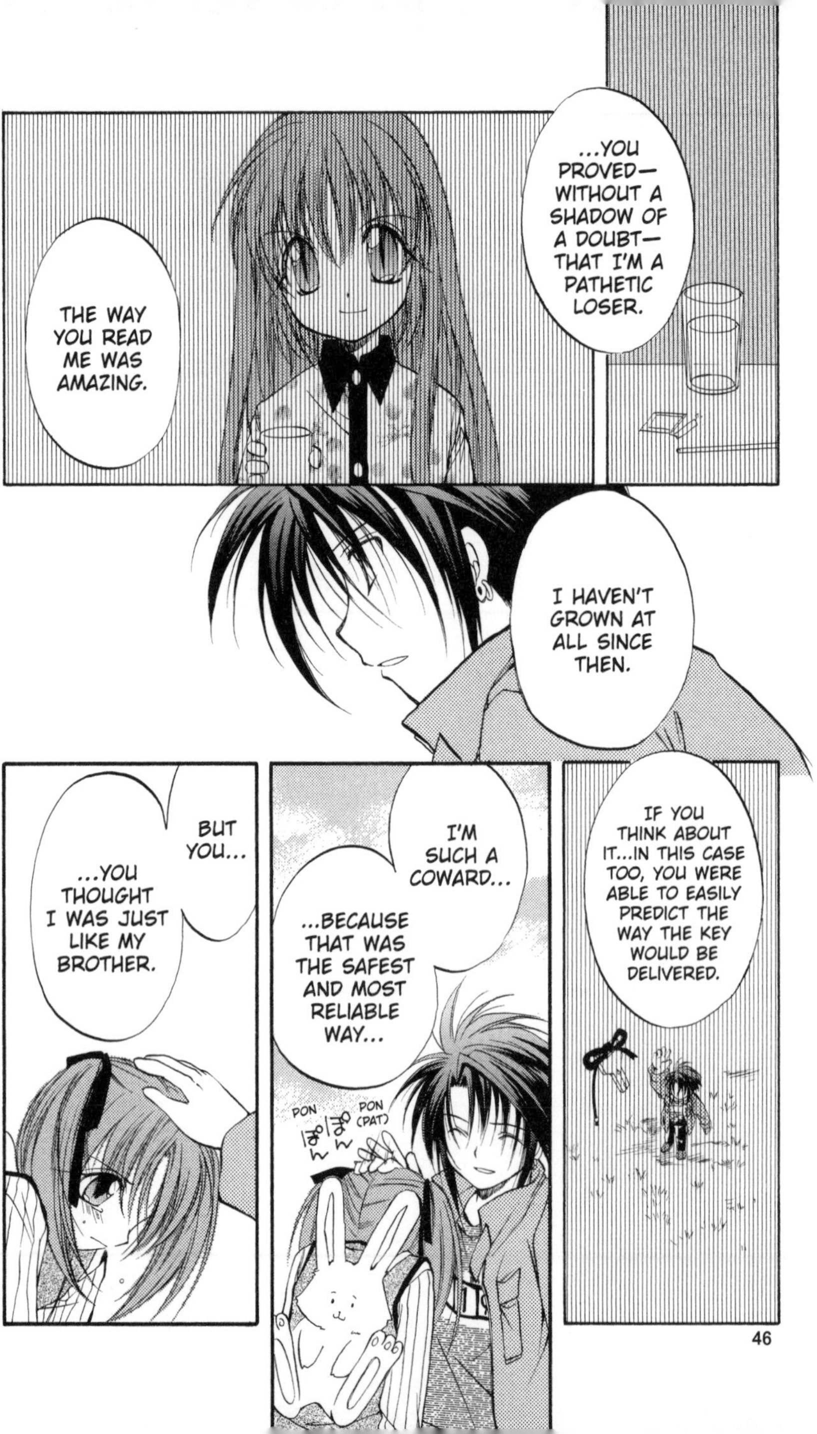
...YOU PROVED—WITHOUT A SHADOW OF A DOUBT—THAT I'M A PATHETIC LOSER.
THE WAY YOU READ ME WAS AMAZING.
I HAVEN'T GROWN AT ALL SINCE THEN.
IF YOU THINK ABOUT IT...IN THIS CASE TOO, YOU WERE ABLE TO EASILY PREDICT THE WAY THE KEY WOULD BE DELIVERED.
I'M SUCH A COWARD...
...BECAUSE THAT WAS THE SAFEST AND MOST RELIABLE WAY...
PON PON (PAT)
ぽん ぽん
BUT YOU...
...YOU THOUGHT I WAS JUST LIKE MY BROTHER.

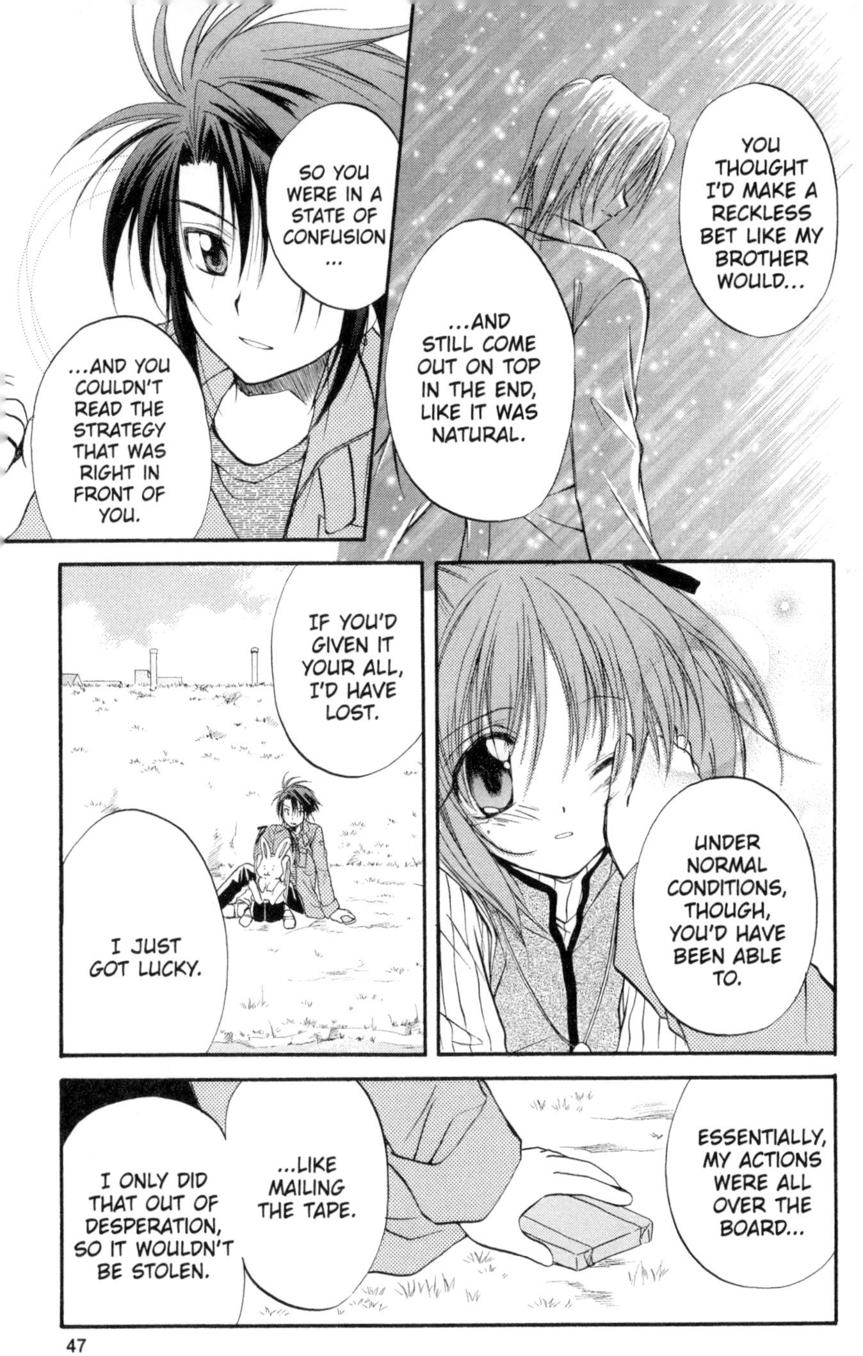
YOU THOUGHT I'D MAKE A RECKLESS BET LIKE MY BROTHER WOULD...
...AND STILL COME OUT ON TOP IN THE END, LIKE IT WAS NATURAL.
SO YOU WERE IN A STATE OF CONFUSION...
...AND YOU COULDN'T READ THE STRATEGY THAT WAS RIGHT IN FRONT OF YOU.
UNDER NORMAL CONDITIONS, THOUGH, YOU'D HAVE BEEN ABLE TO.
IF YOU'D GIVEN IT YOUR ALL, I'D HAVE LOST.
I JUST GOT LUCKY.
ESSENTIALLY, MY ACTIONS WERE ALL OVER THE BOARD...
...LIKE MAILING THE TAPE.
I ONLY DID THAT OUT OF DESPERATION, SO IT WOULDN'T BE STOLEN.

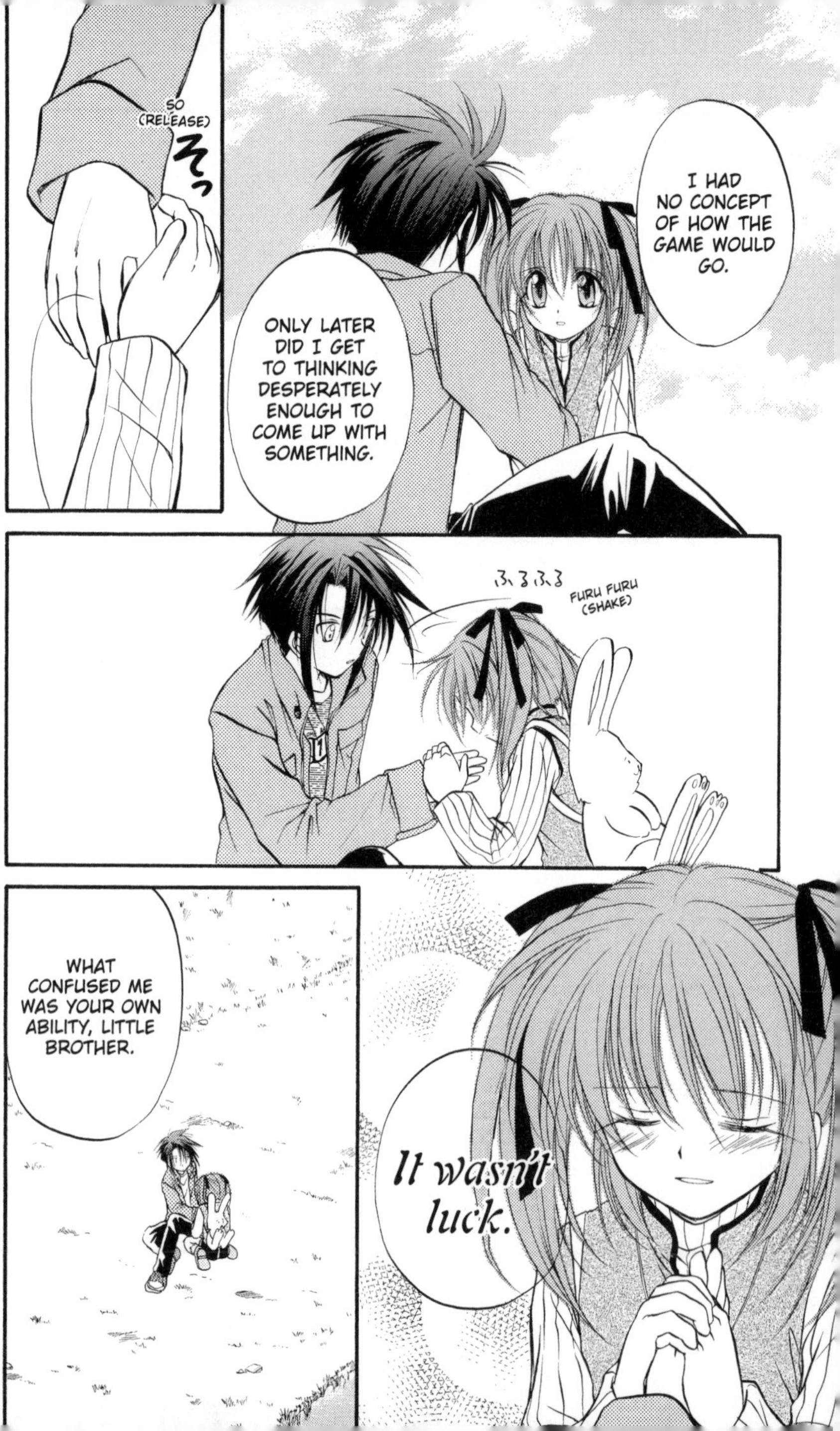
I HAD NO CONCEPT OF HOW THE GAME WOULD GO.
ONLY LATER DID I GET TO THINKING DESPERATELY ENOUGH TO COME UP WITH SOMETHING.
SO (RELEASE)
そっ
ふるふる
FURU FURU (SHAKE)
It wasn't luck.
WHAT CONFUSED ME WAS YOUR OWN ABILITY, LITTLE BROTHER.

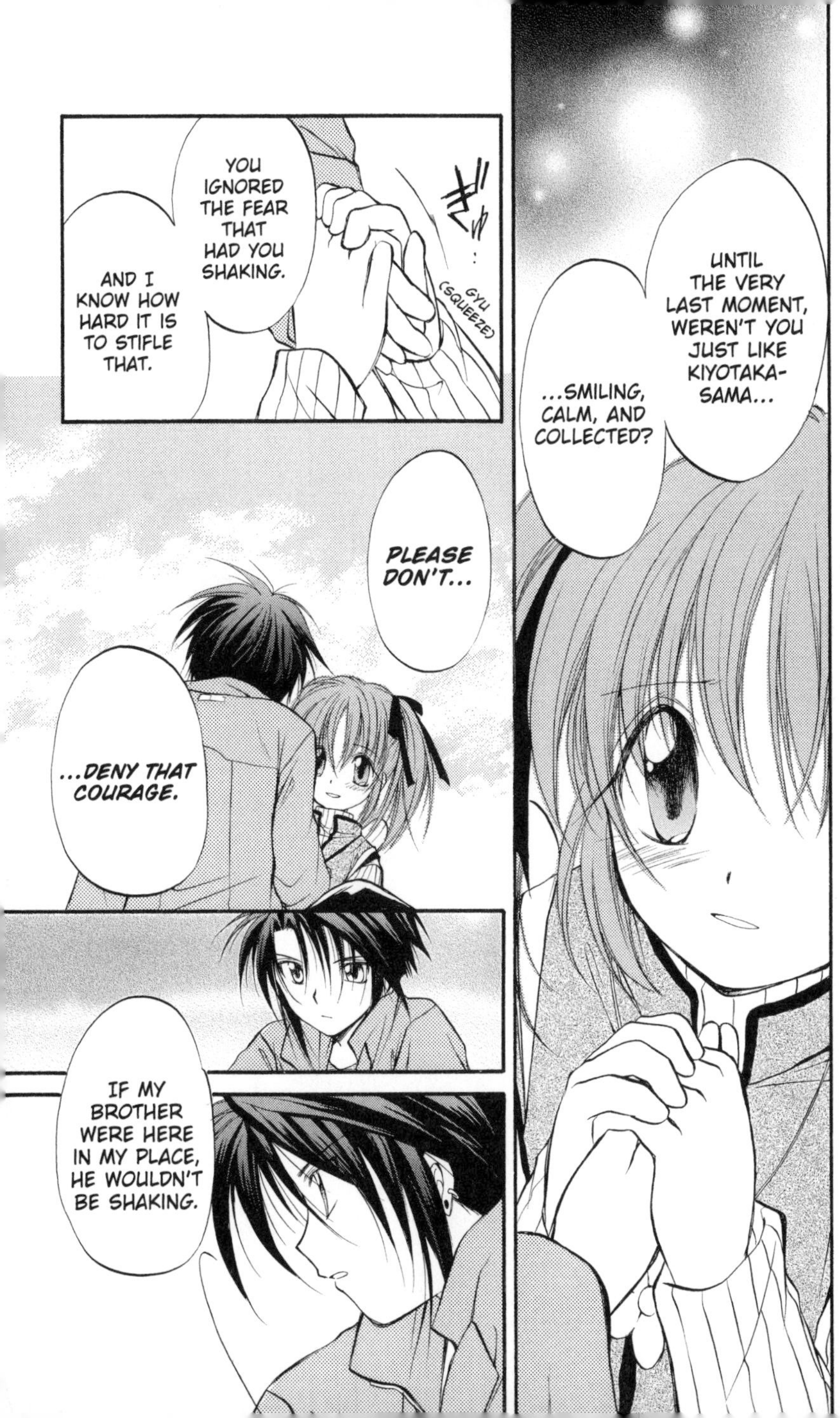
UNTIL THE VERY LAST MOMENT, WEREN'T YOU JUST LIKE KIYOTAKA-SAMA...
...SMILING, CALM, AND COLLECTED?
GYU (SQUEEZE)
YOU IGNORED THE FEAR THAT HAD YOU SHAKING.
AND I KNOW HOW HARD IT IS TO STIFLE THAT.
PLEASE DON'T...
...DENY THAT COURAGE.
IF MY BROTHER WERE HERE IN MY PLACE, HE WOULDN'T BE SHAKING.

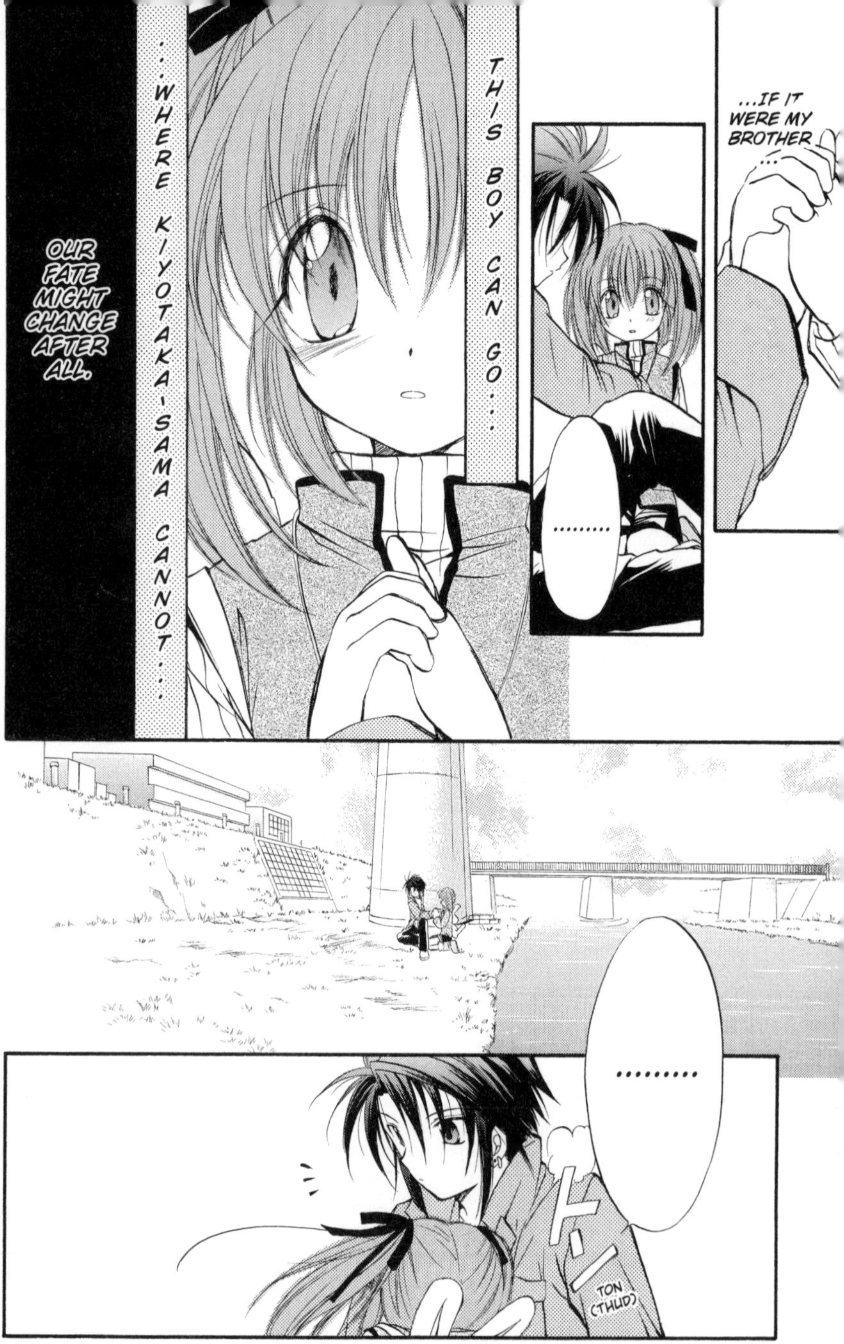
...IF IT WERE MY BROTHER ...
....
THIS BOY CAN GO...
...WHERE KIYOTAKA-SAMA CANNOT...
OUR FATE MIGHT CHANGE AFTER ALL.
....
TON (THUD)

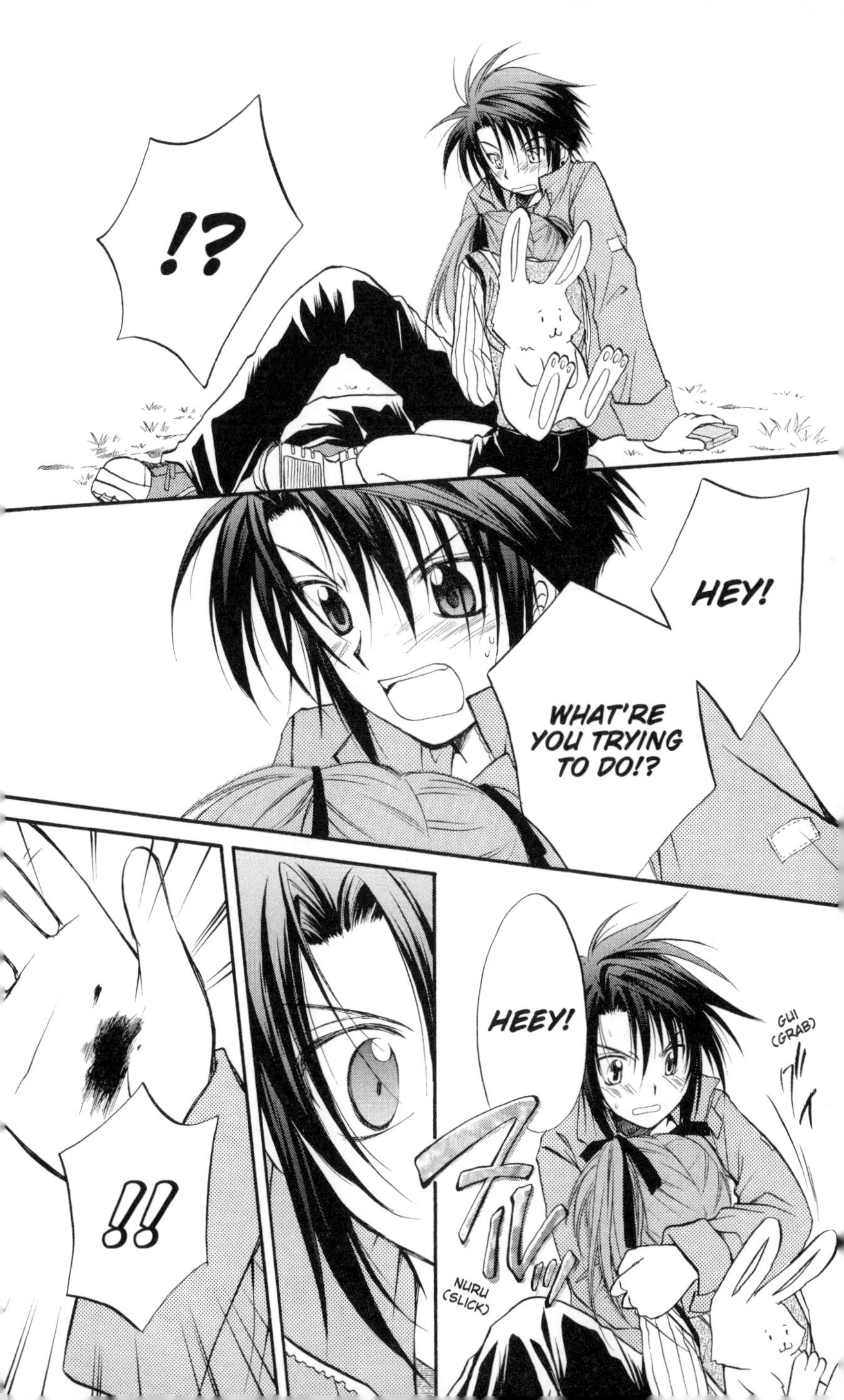
!?
HEY!
WHAT'RE YOU TRYING TO DO!?
HEEY!
GUI (GRAB)
NURU (SLICK)
!!

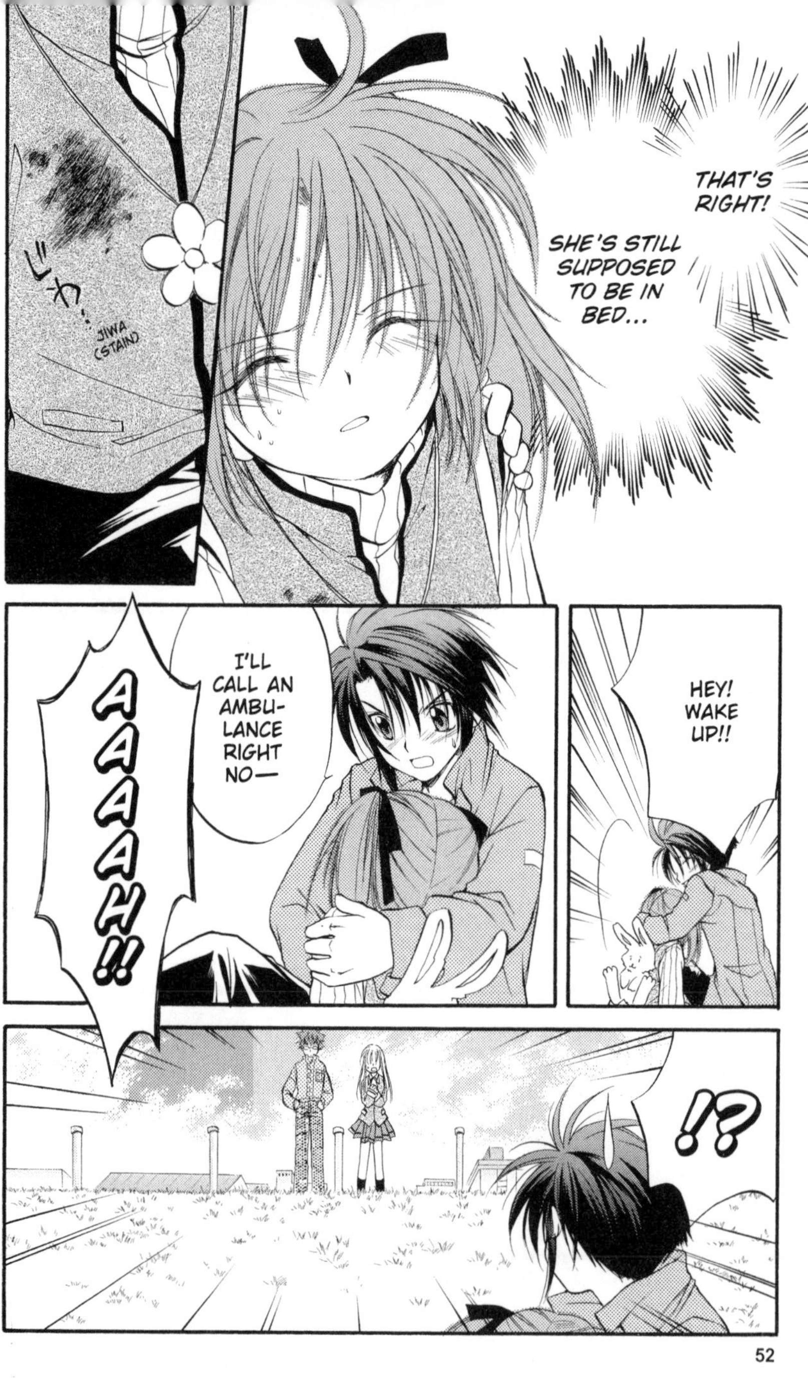
THAT'S RIGHT!
SHE'S STILL SUPPOSED TO BE IN BED...
じわ…
JIWA (STAIN)
HEY! WAKE UP!!
I'LL CALL AN AMBULANCE RIGHT NO—
AAAAH!!
!?

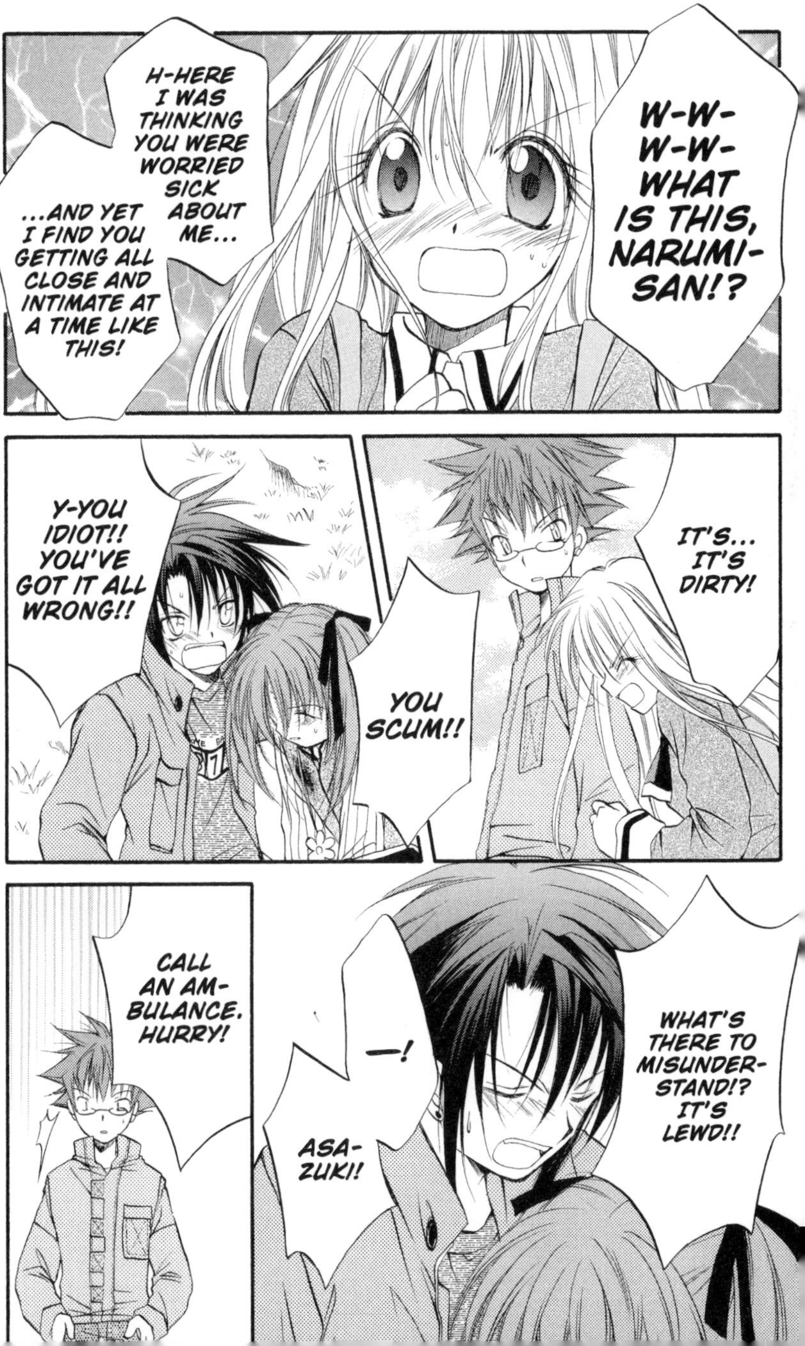
W-W-W-W-WHAT IS THIS, NARUMI-SAN!?
H-HERE I WAS THINKING YOU WERE WORRIED SICK ABOUT ME...
...AND YET I FIND YOU GETTING ALL CLOSE AND INTIMATE AT A TIME LIKE THIS!
IT'S... IT'S DIRTY!
YOU SCUM!!
Y-YOU IDIOT!! YOU'VE GOT IT ALL WRONG!!
WHAT'S THERE TO MISUNDERSTAND!? IT'S LEWD!!
—!
ASA-ZUKI!
CALL AN AM-BULANCE. HURRY!

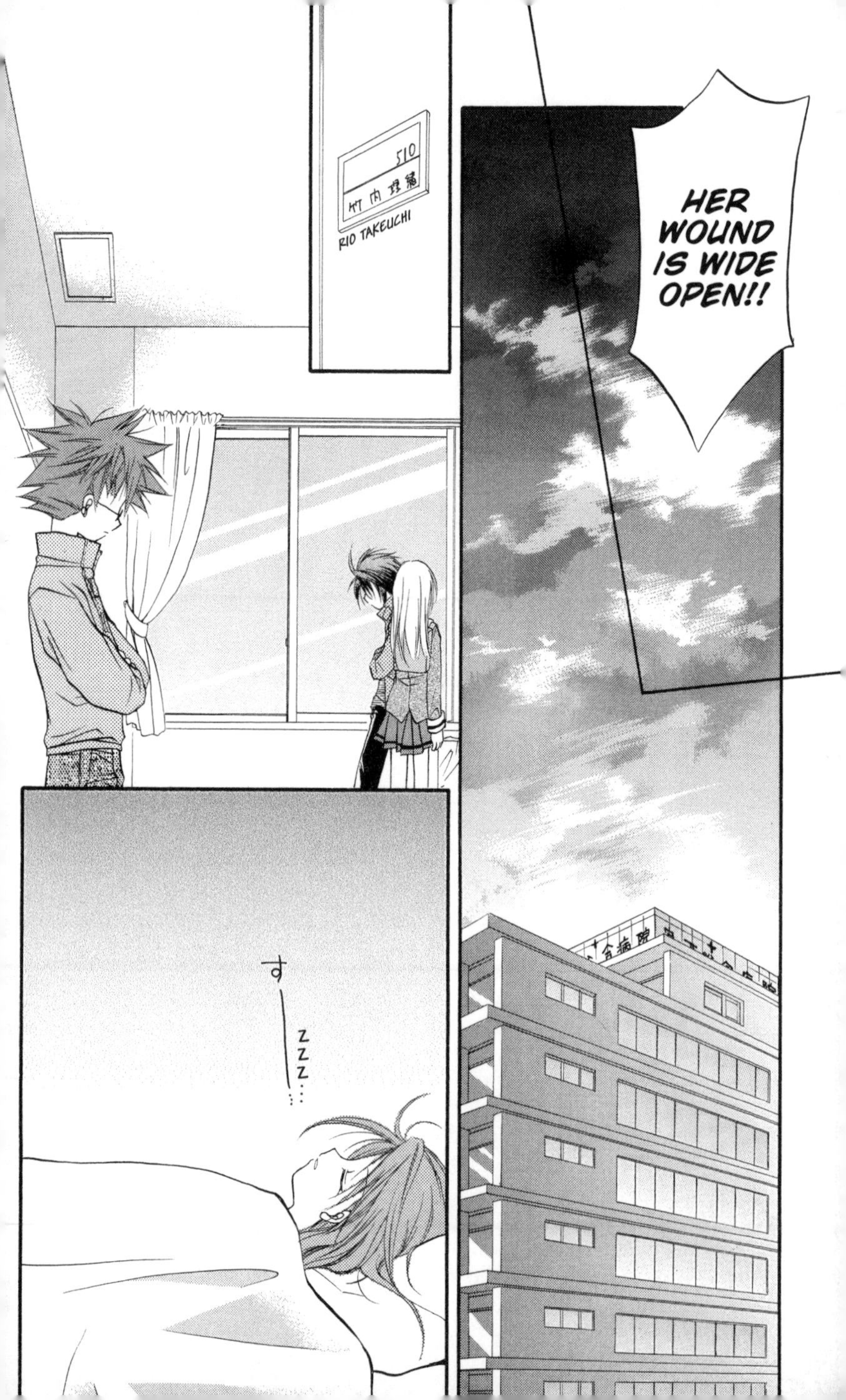
HER WOUND IS WIDE OPEN!!
510
RIO TAKEUCHI
す
ZZZ...

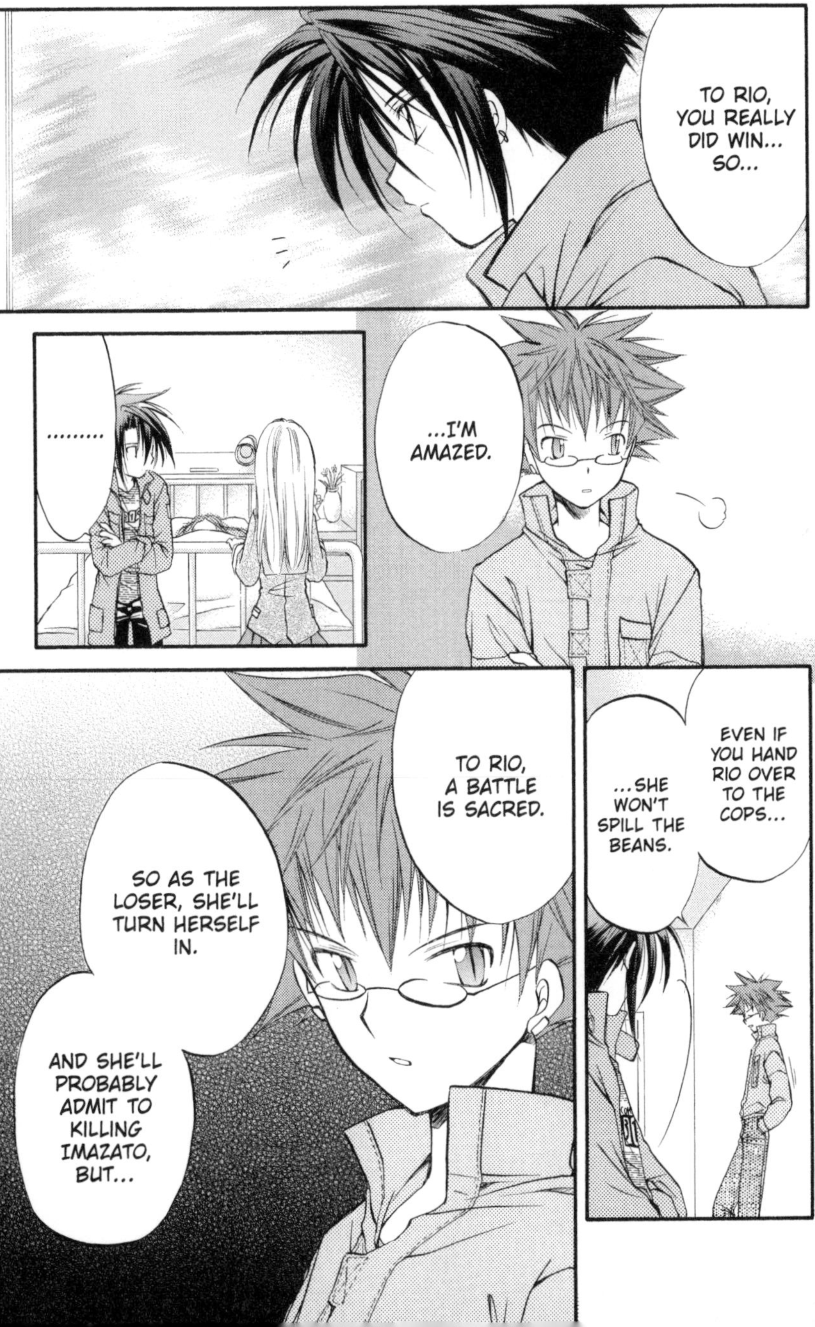
TO RIO, YOU REALLY DID WIN... SO...
...I'M AMAZED.
....
EVEN IF YOU HAND RIO OVER TO THE COPS...
...SHE WON'T SPILL THE BEANS.
TO RIO, A BATTLE IS SACRED.
SO AS THE LOSER, SHE'LL TURN HERSELF IN.
AND SHE'LL PROBABLY ADMIT TO KILLING IMAZATO, BUT...

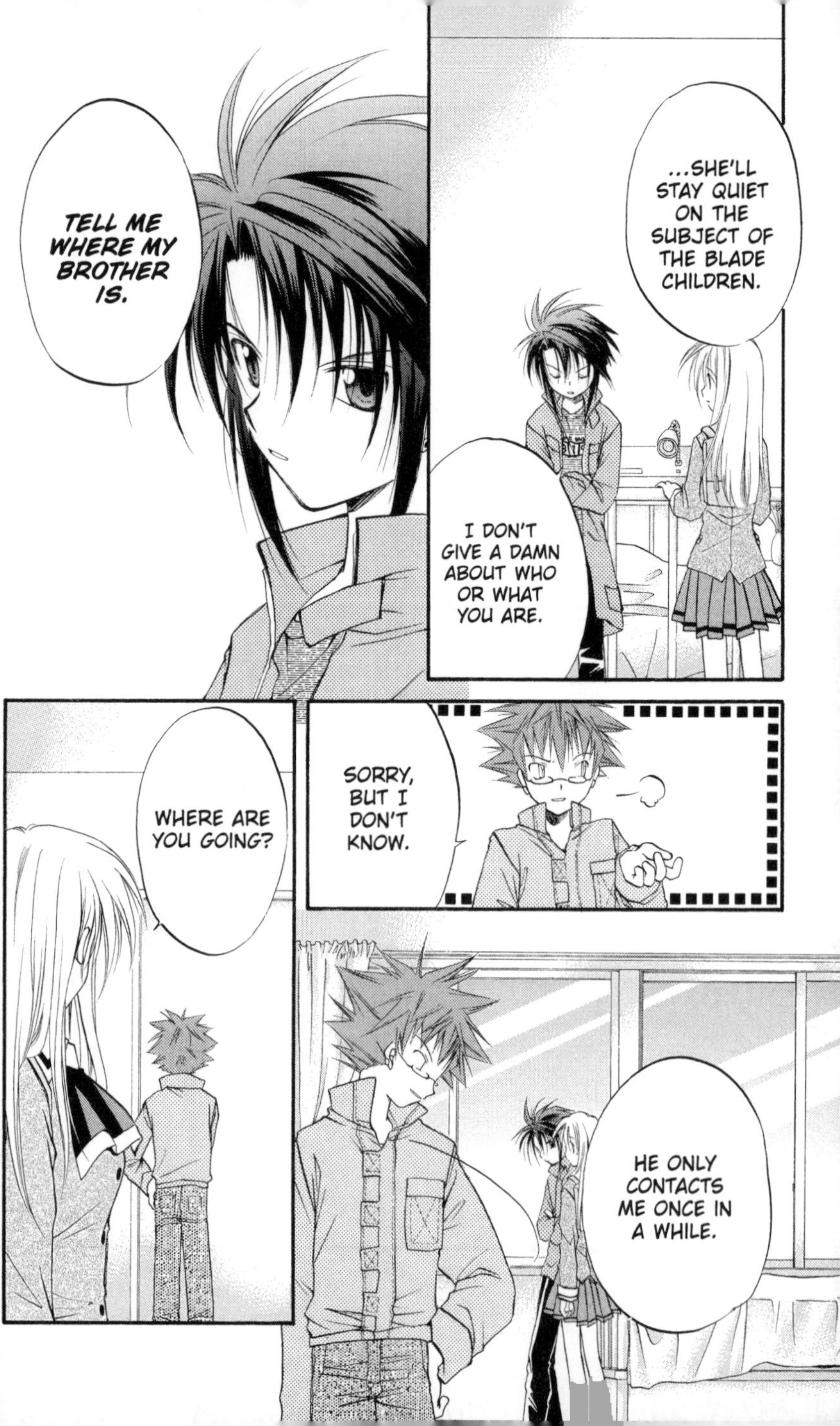
...SHE'LL STAY QUIET ON THE SUBJECT OF THE BLADE CHILDREN.
I DON'T GIVE A DAMN ABOUT WHO OR WHAT YOU ARE.
TELL ME WHERE MY BROTHER IS.
SORRY, BUT I DON'T KNOW.
HE ONLY CONTACTS ME ONCE IN A WHILE.
WHERE ARE YOU GOING?

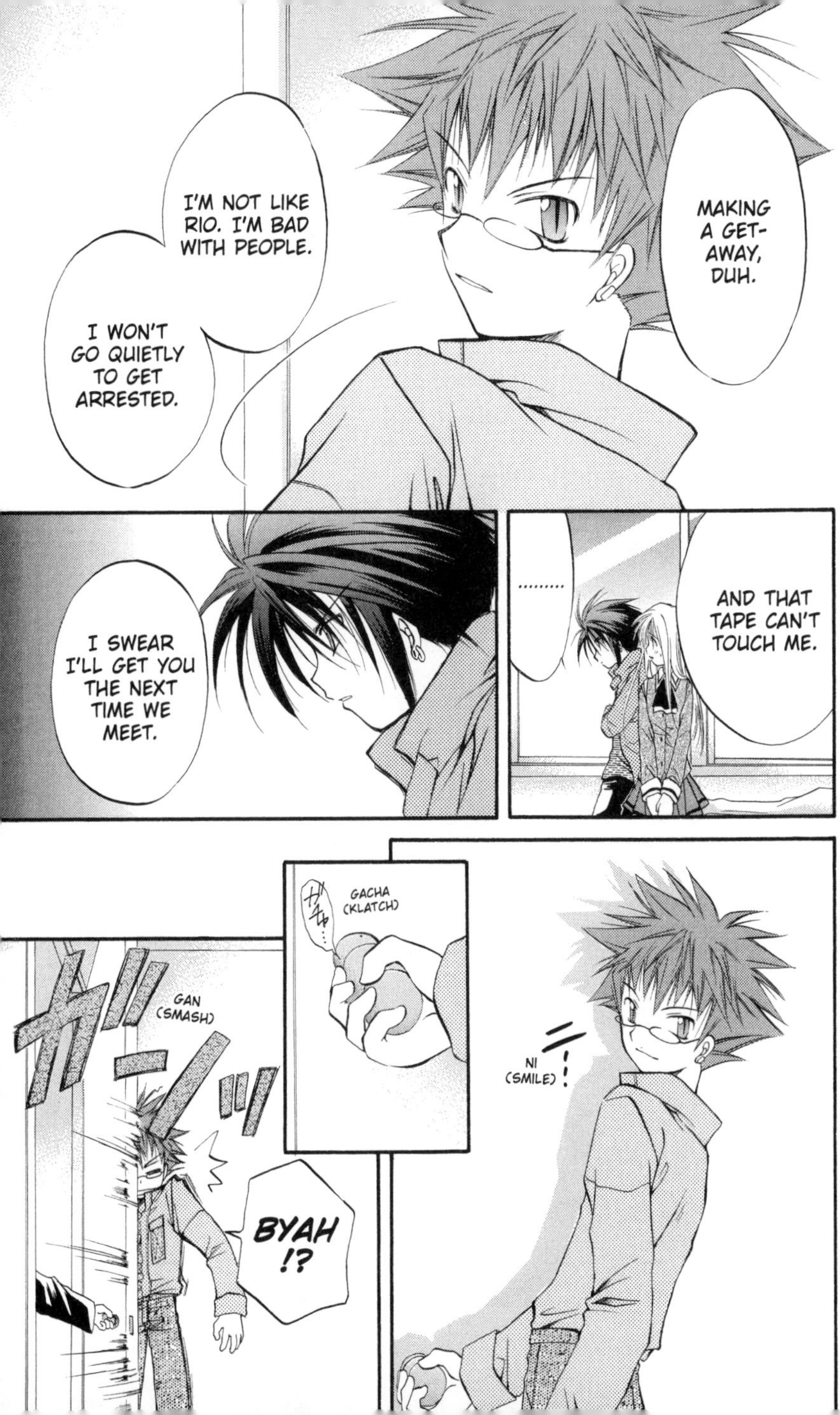
MAKING A GET-AWAY, DUH.
I'M NOT LIKE RIO. I'M BAD WITH PEOPLE.
I WON'T GO QUIETLY TO GET ARRESTED.
AND THAT TAPE CAN'T TOUCH ME.
....
I SWEAR I'LL GET YOU THE NEXT TIME WE MEET.
NI (SMILE)
GACHA (KLATCH)
GAN (SMASH)
BYAH !?

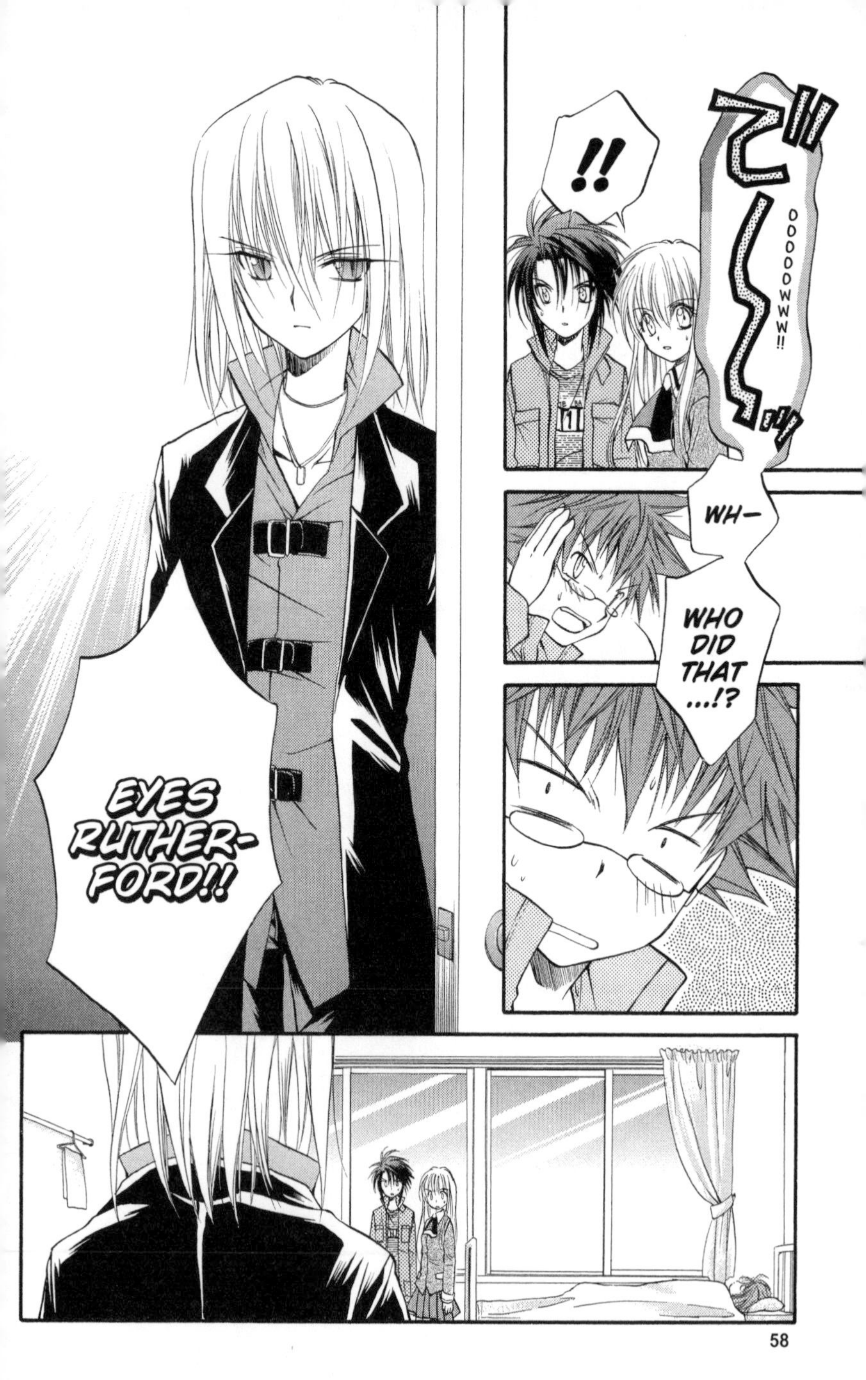
DOOOOOWWW!!
!!
WH—
WHO DID THAT ...!?
EYES RUTHER-FORD!!

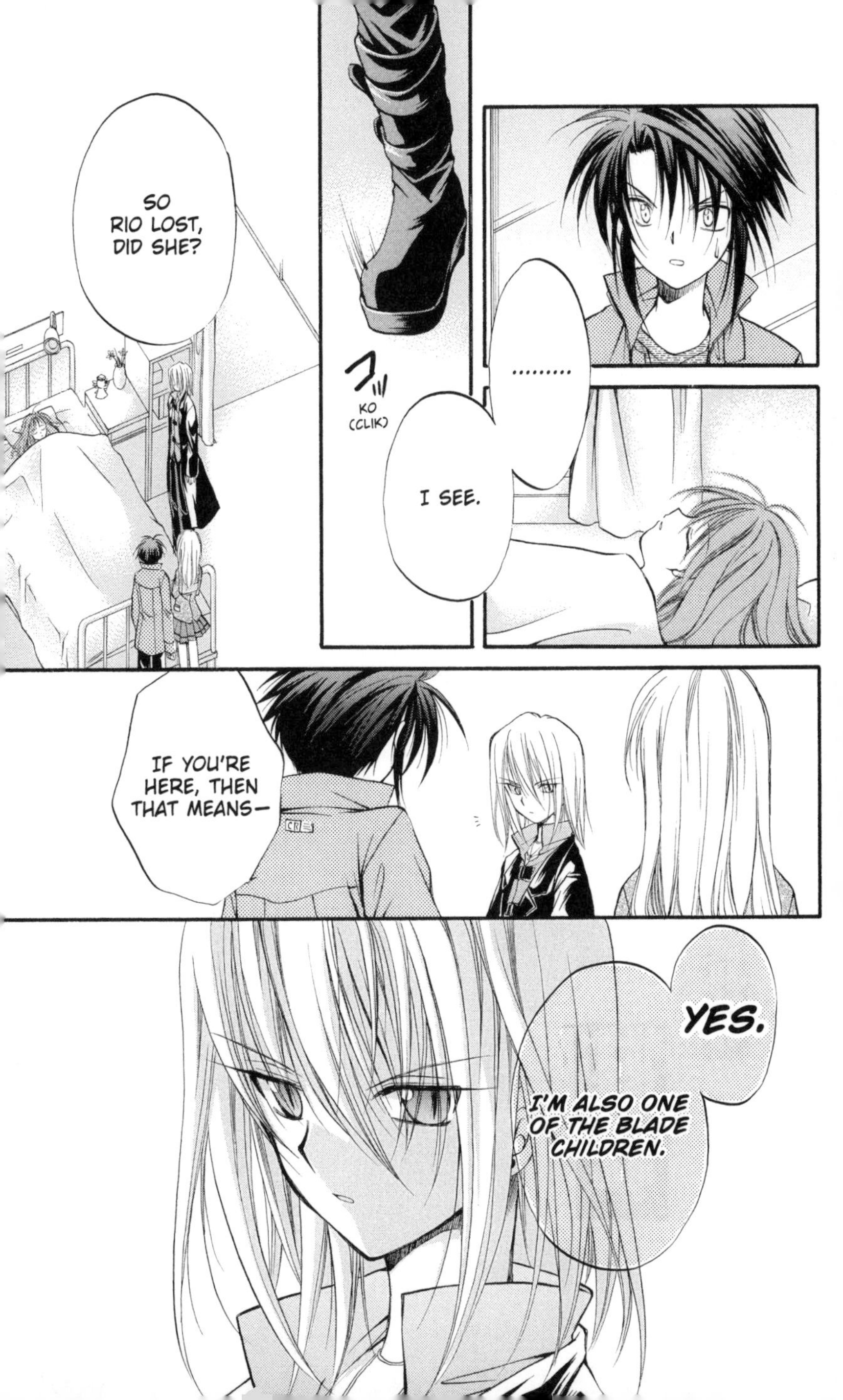
....
I SEE.
KO
(CLIK)
SO RIO LOST, DID SHE?
IF YOU'RE HERE, THEN THAT MEANS—
YES.
I'M ALSO ONE OF THE BLADE CHILDREN.

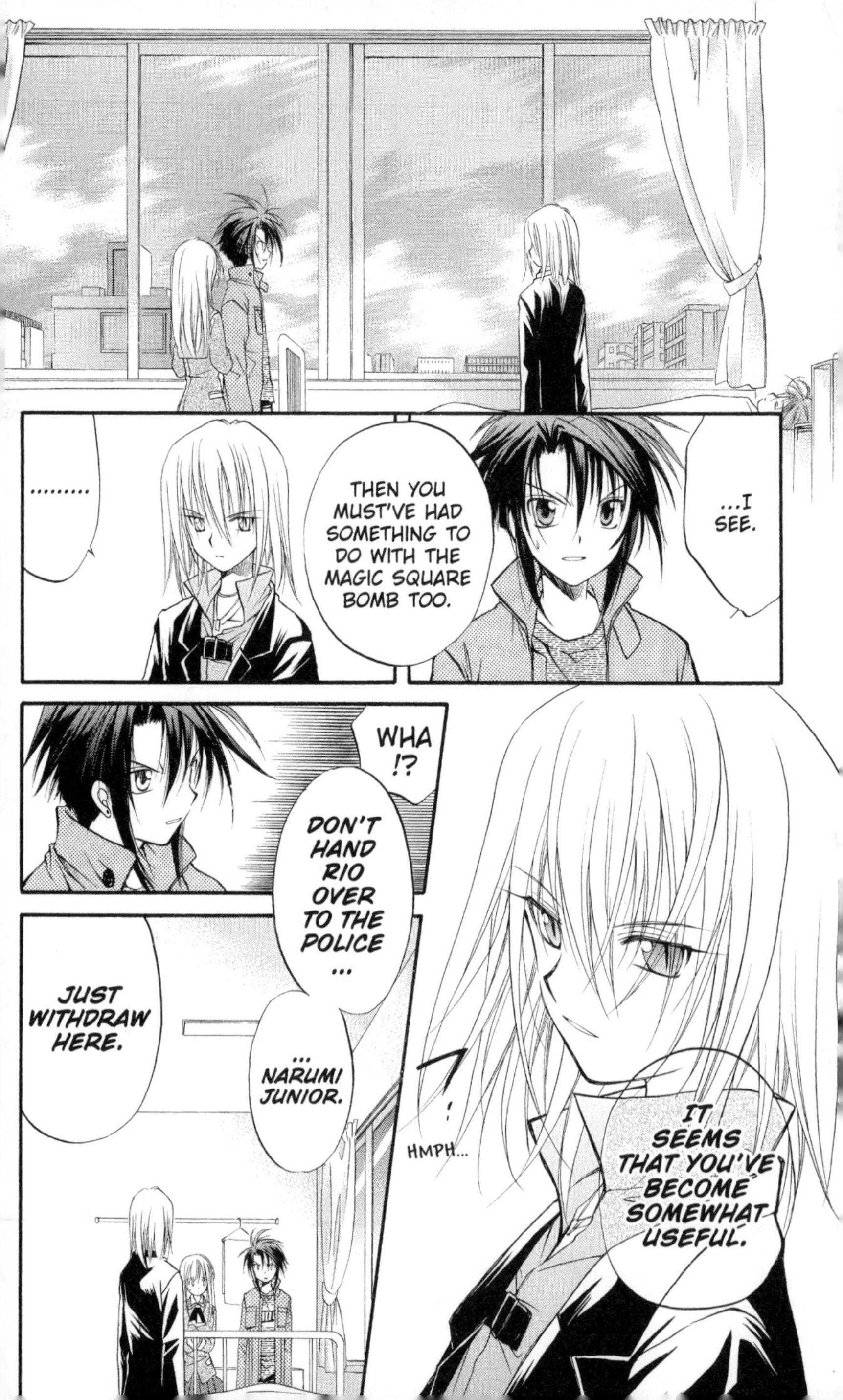
...I SEE.
THEN YOU MUST'VE HAD SOMETHING TO DO WITH THE MAGIC SQUARE BOMB TOO.
....
IT SEEMS THAT YOU'VE BECOME SOMEWHAT USEFUL.
HMPH...
WHA !?
DON'T HAND RIO OVER TO THE POLICE ...
... NARUMI JUNIOR.
JUST WITHDRAW HERE.

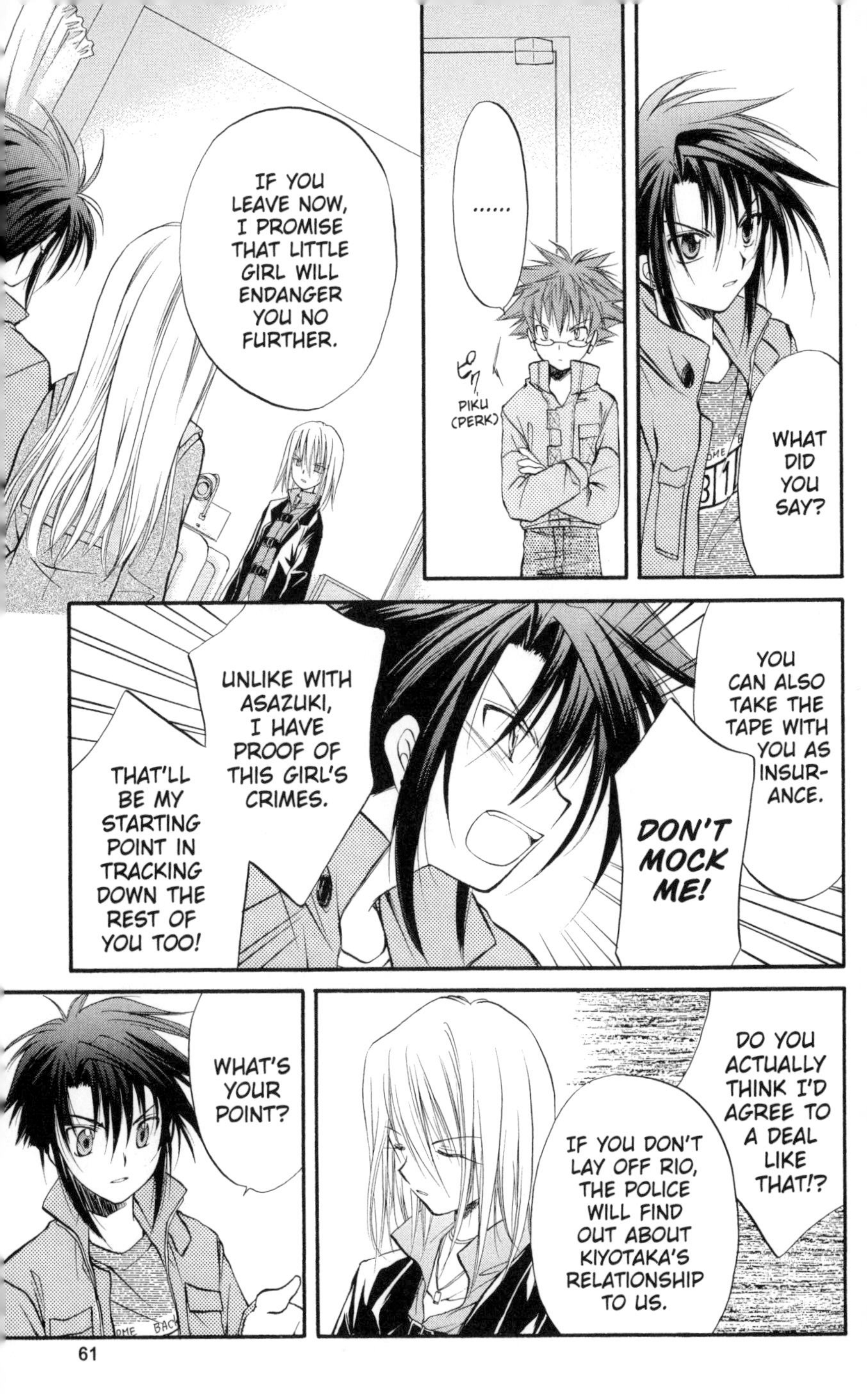
WHAT DID YOU SAY?
......
ピク
PIKU (PERK)
IF YOU LEAVE NOW, I PROMISE THAT LITTLE GIRL WILL ENDANGER YOU NO FURTHER.
YOU CAN ALSO TAKE THE TAPE WITH YOU AS INSUR-ANCE.
DON'T MOCK ME!
UNLIKE WITH ASAZUKI, I HAVE PROOF OF THIS GIRL'S CRIMES.
THAT'LL BE MY STARTING POINT IN TRACKING DOWN THE REST OF YOU TOO!
DO YOU ACTUALLY THINK I'D AGREE TO A DEAL LIKE THAT!?
IF YOU DON'T LAY OFF RIO, THE POLICE WILL FIND OUT ABOUT KIYOTAKA'S RELATIONSHIP TO US.
WHAT'S YOUR POINT?

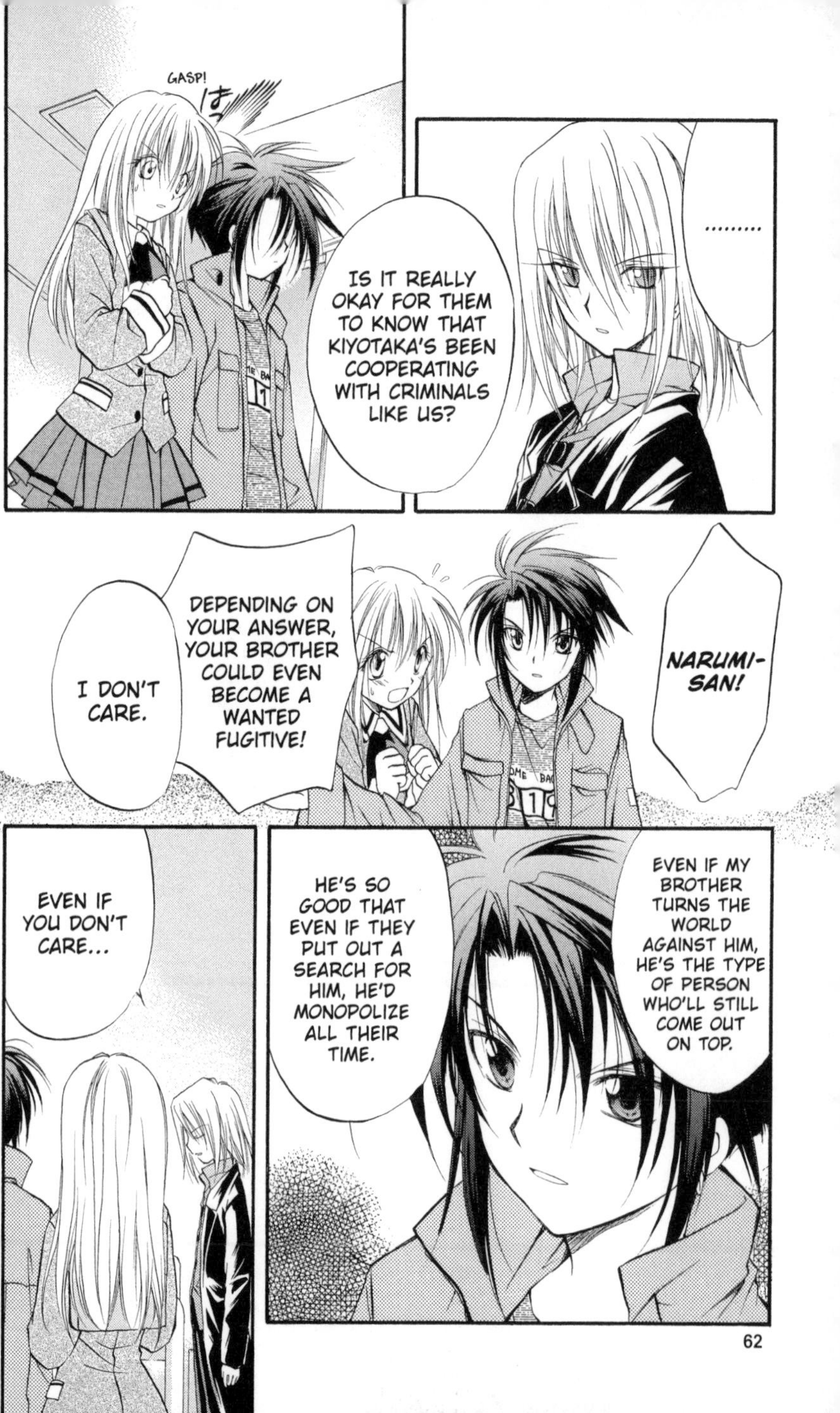
....
IS IT REALLY OKAY FOR THEM TO KNOW THAT KIYOTAKA'S BEEN COOPERATING WITH CRIMINALS LIKE US?
GASP!
はっ
NARUMI-SAN!
DEPENDING ON YOUR ANSWER, YOUR BROTHER COULD EVEN BECOME A WANTED FUGITIVE!
I DON'T CARE.
EVEN IF MY BROTHER TURNS THE WORLD AGAINST HIM, HE'S THE TYPE OF PERSON WHO'LL STILL COME OUT ON TOP.
HE'S SO GOOD THAT EVEN IF THEY PUT OUT A SEARCH FOR HIM, HE'D MONOPOLIZE ALL THEIR TIME.
EVEN IF YOU DON'T CARE...

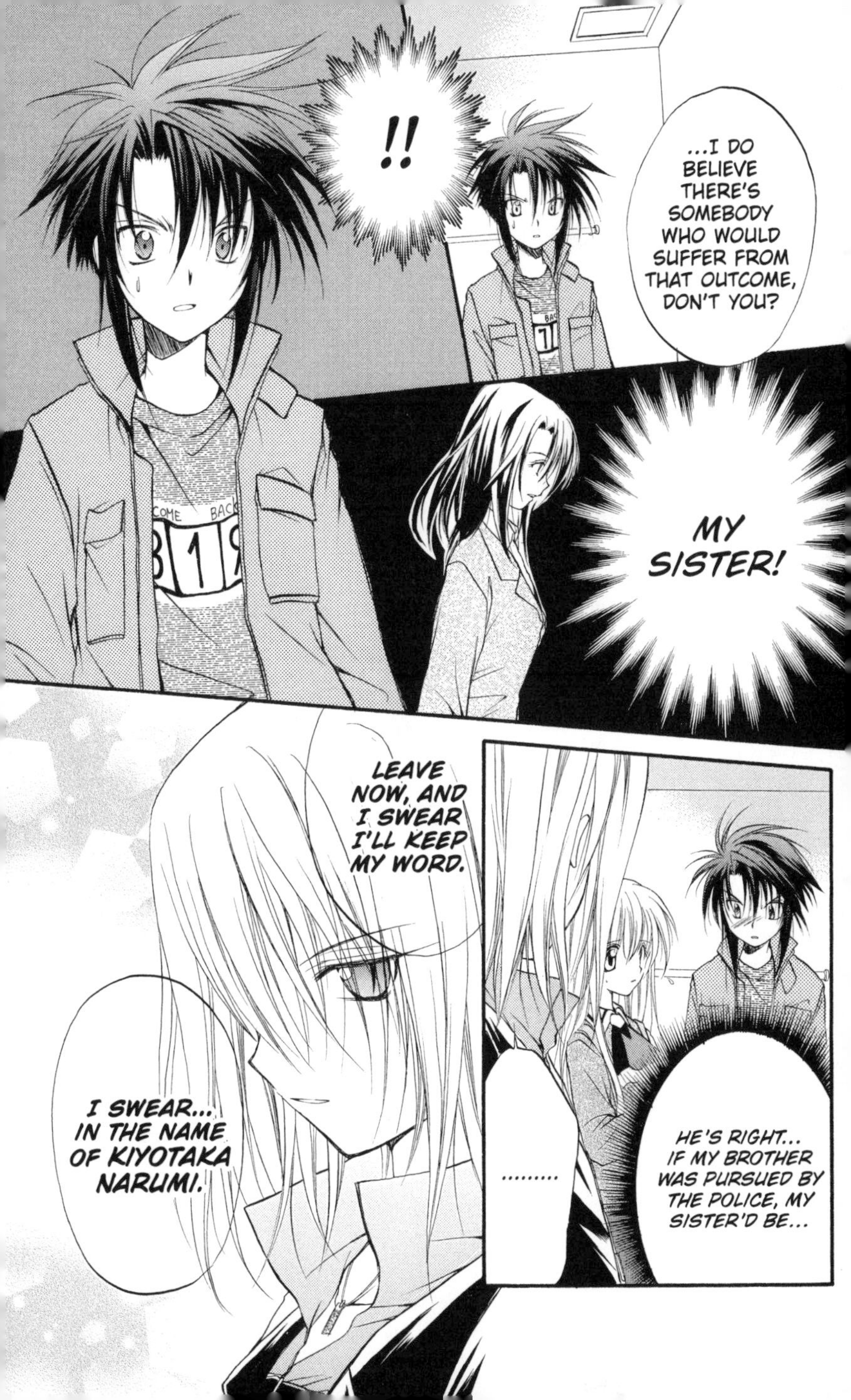
...I DO BELIEVE THERE'S SOMEBODY WHO WOULD SUFFER FROM THAT OUTCOME, DON'T YOU?
!!
MY SISTER!
HE'S RIGHT... IF MY BROTHER WAS PURSUED BY THE POLICE, MY SISTER'D BE...
....
LEAVE NOW, AND I SWEAR I'LL KEEP MY WORD.
I SWEAR... IN THE NAME OF KIYOTAKA NARUMI.

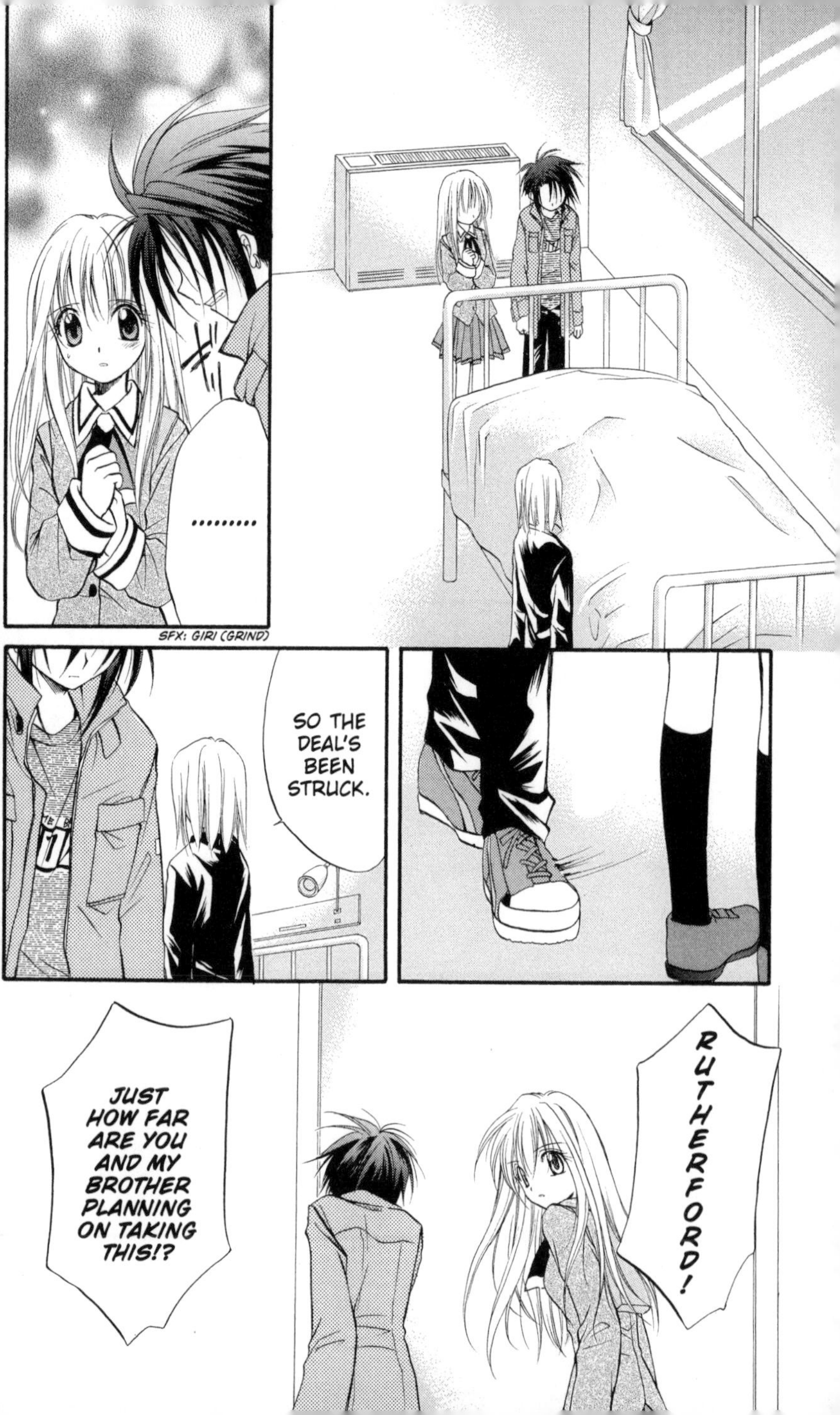
....
SFX: GIRI (GRIND)
SO THE DEAL'S BEEN STRUCK.
RUTHERFORD!
JUST HOW FAR ARE YOU AND MY BROTHER PLANNING ON TAKING THIS!?

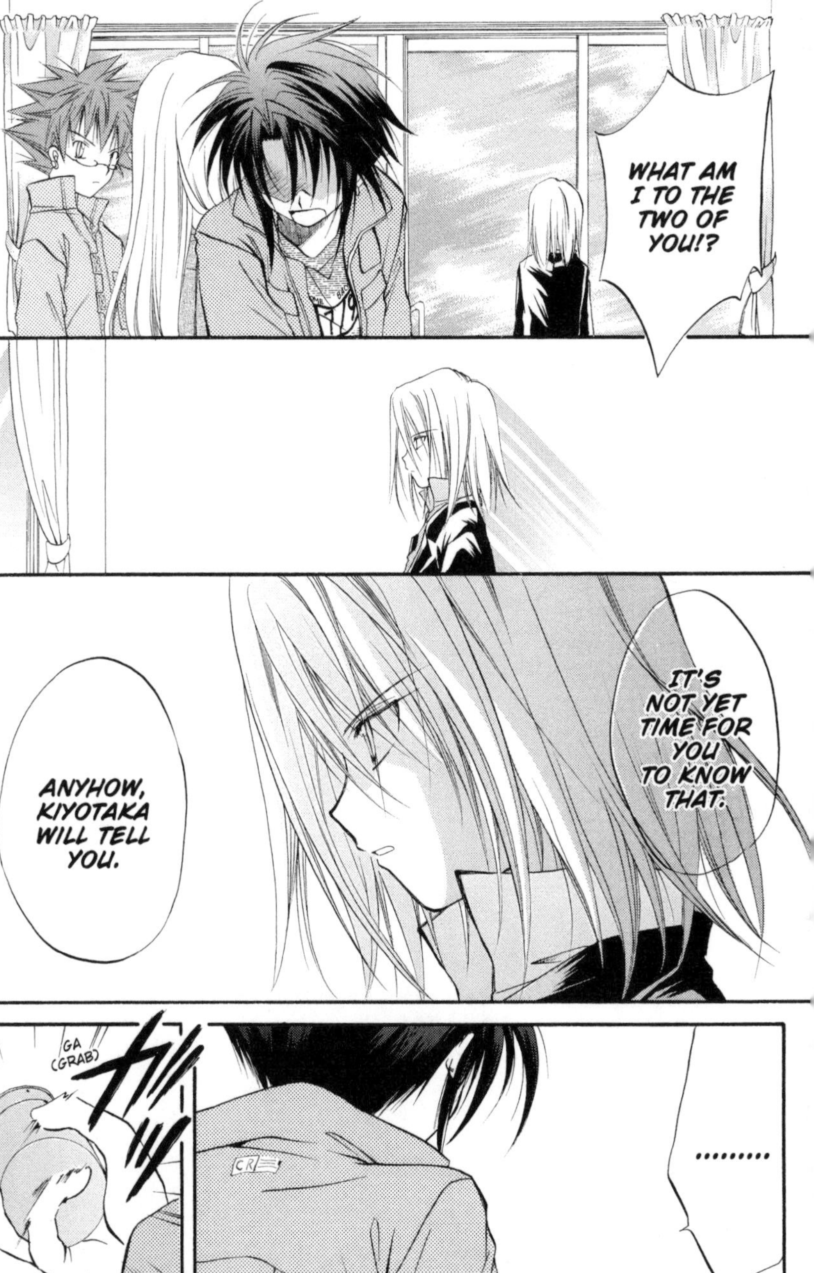
WHAT AM I TO THE TWO OF YOU!?
IT'S NOT YET TIME FOR YOU TO KNOW THAT.
ANYHOW, KIYOTAKA WILL TELL YOU.
....
GA (GRAB)

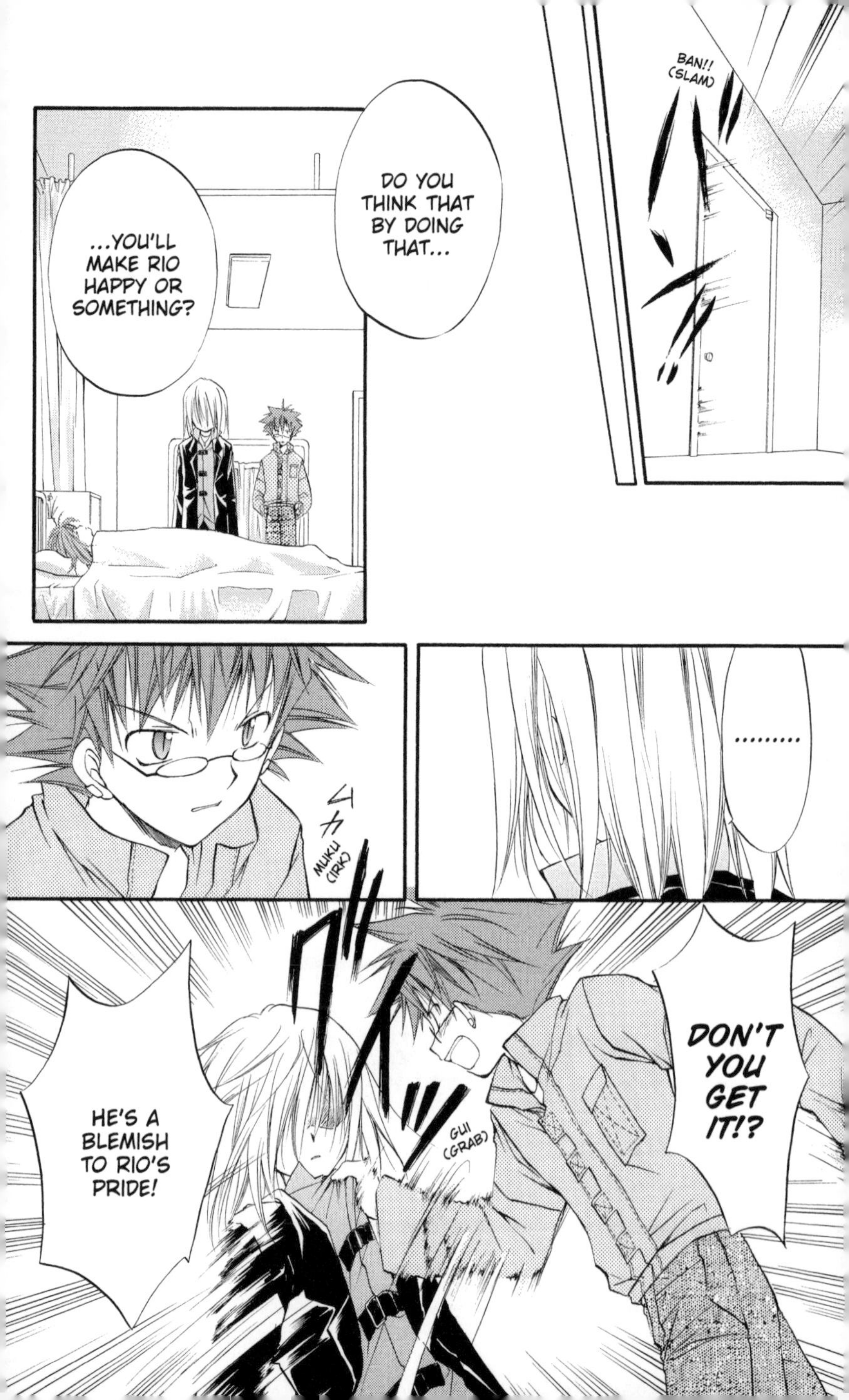
BAN!! (SLAM)
DO YOU THINK THAT BY DOING THAT...
...YOU'LL MAKE RIO HAPPY OR SOMETHING?
....
MUKU (IRK)
DON'T YOU GET IT!?
GUI (GRAB)
HE'S A BLEMISH TO RIO'S PRIDE!

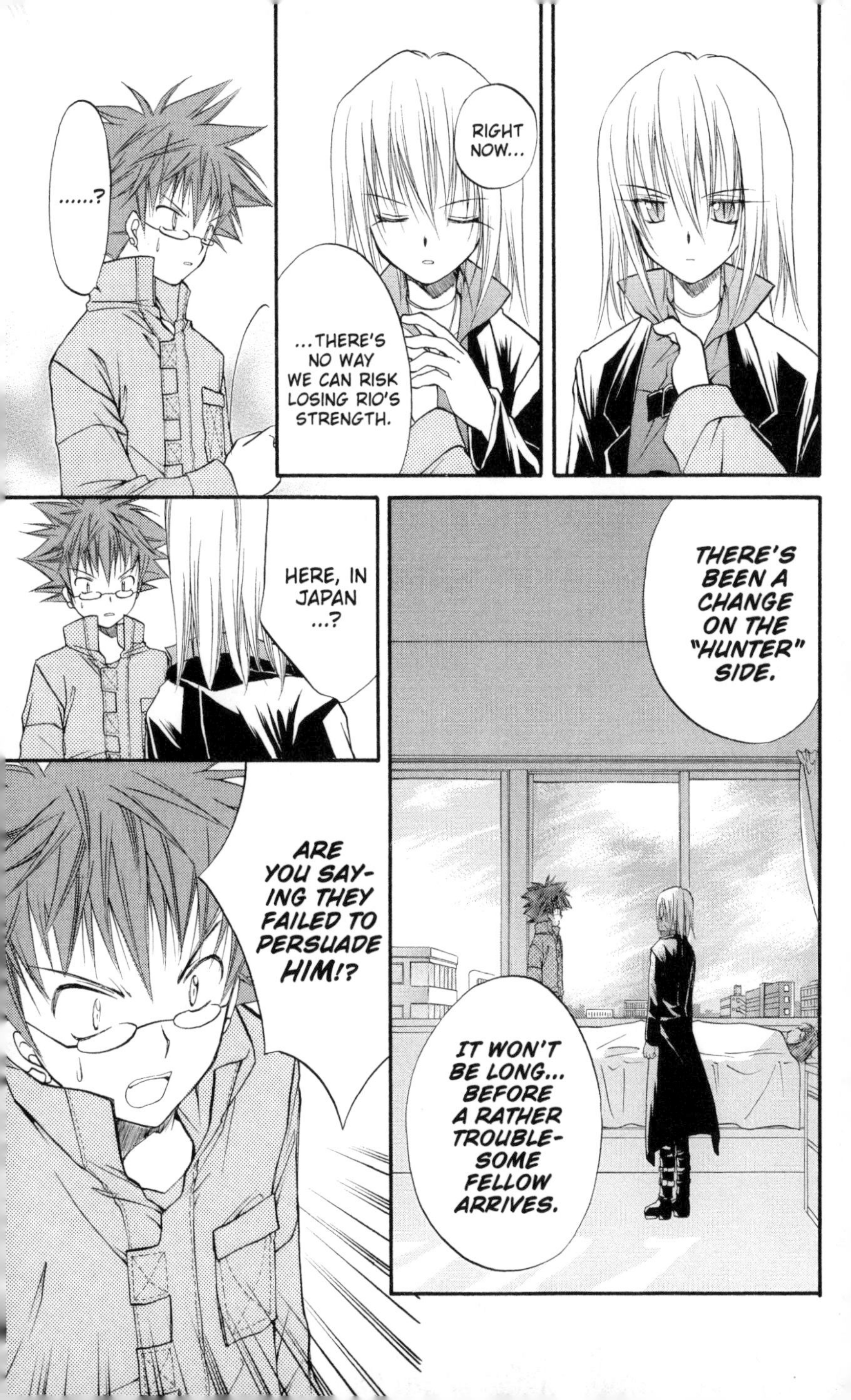
RIGHT NOW...
...THERE'S NO WAY WE CAN RISK LOSING RIO'S STRENGTH.
......?
THERE'S BEEN A CHANGE ON THE "HUNTER" SIDE.
IT WON'T BE LONG... BEFORE A RATHER TROUBLESOME FELLOW ARRIVES.
HERE, IN JAPAN ...?
ARE YOU SAYING THEY FAILED TO PERSUADE HIM!?

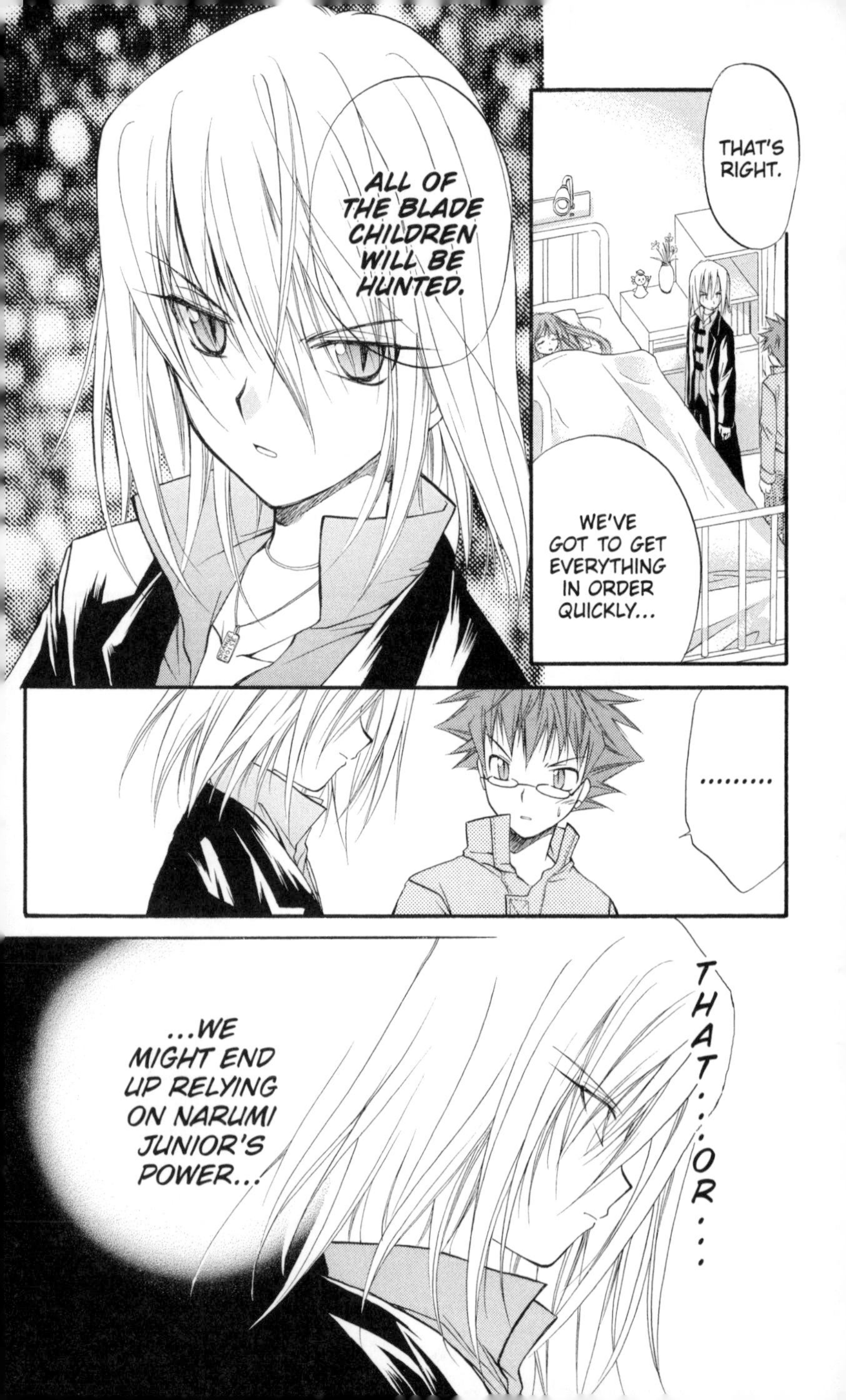
THAT'S RIGHT.
WE'VE GOT TO GET EVERYTHING IN ORDER QUICKLY...
ALL OF THE BLADE CHILDREN WILL BE HUNTED.
....
THAT... OR...
...WE MIGHT END UP RELYING ON NARUMI JUNIOR'S POWER...

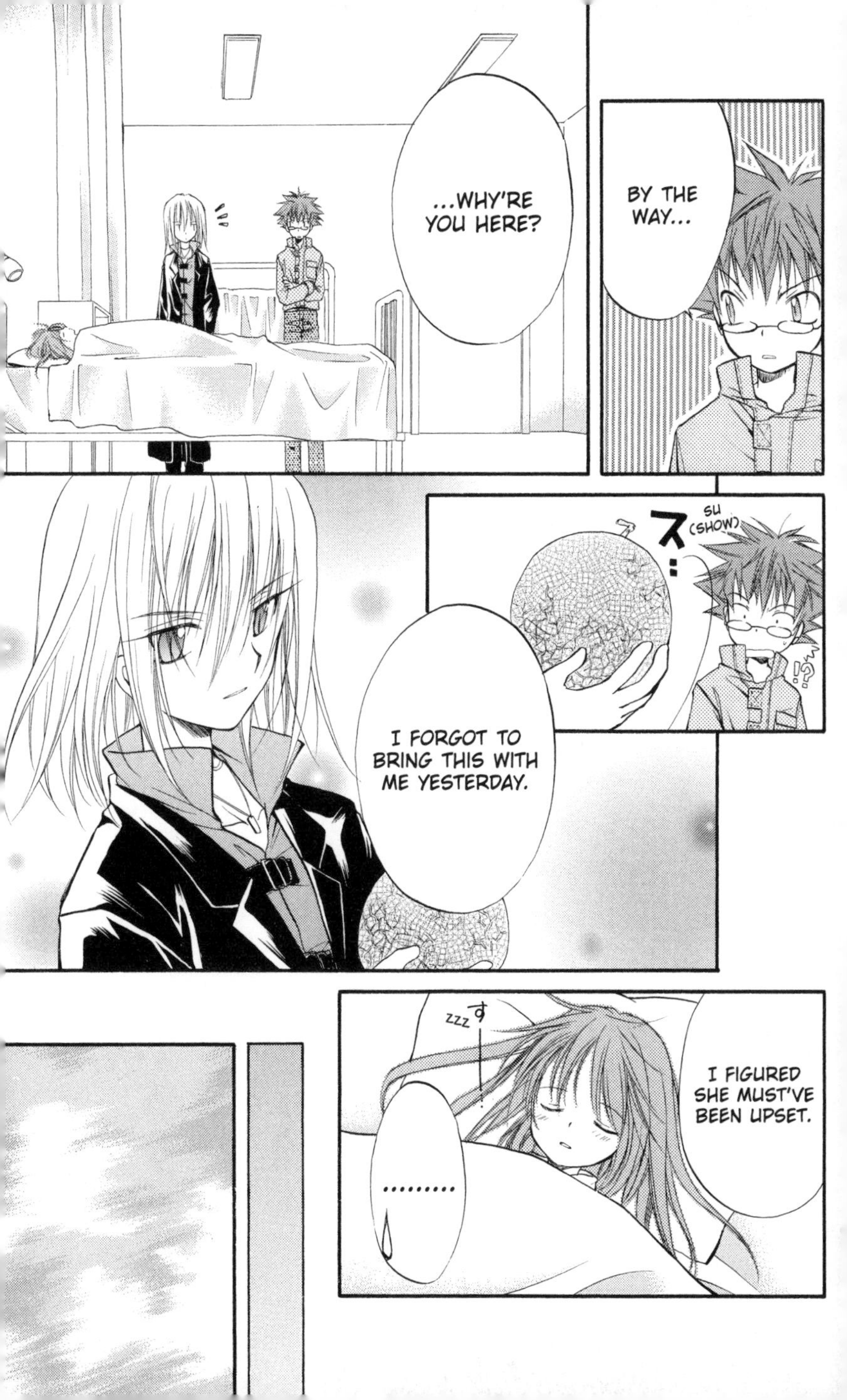
BY THE WAY...
...WHY'RE YOU HERE?
ス
SU (SHOW)
!?
I FORGOT TO BRING THIS WITH ME YESTERDAY.
I FIGURED SHE MUST'VE BEEN UPSET.
ZZZ す
....

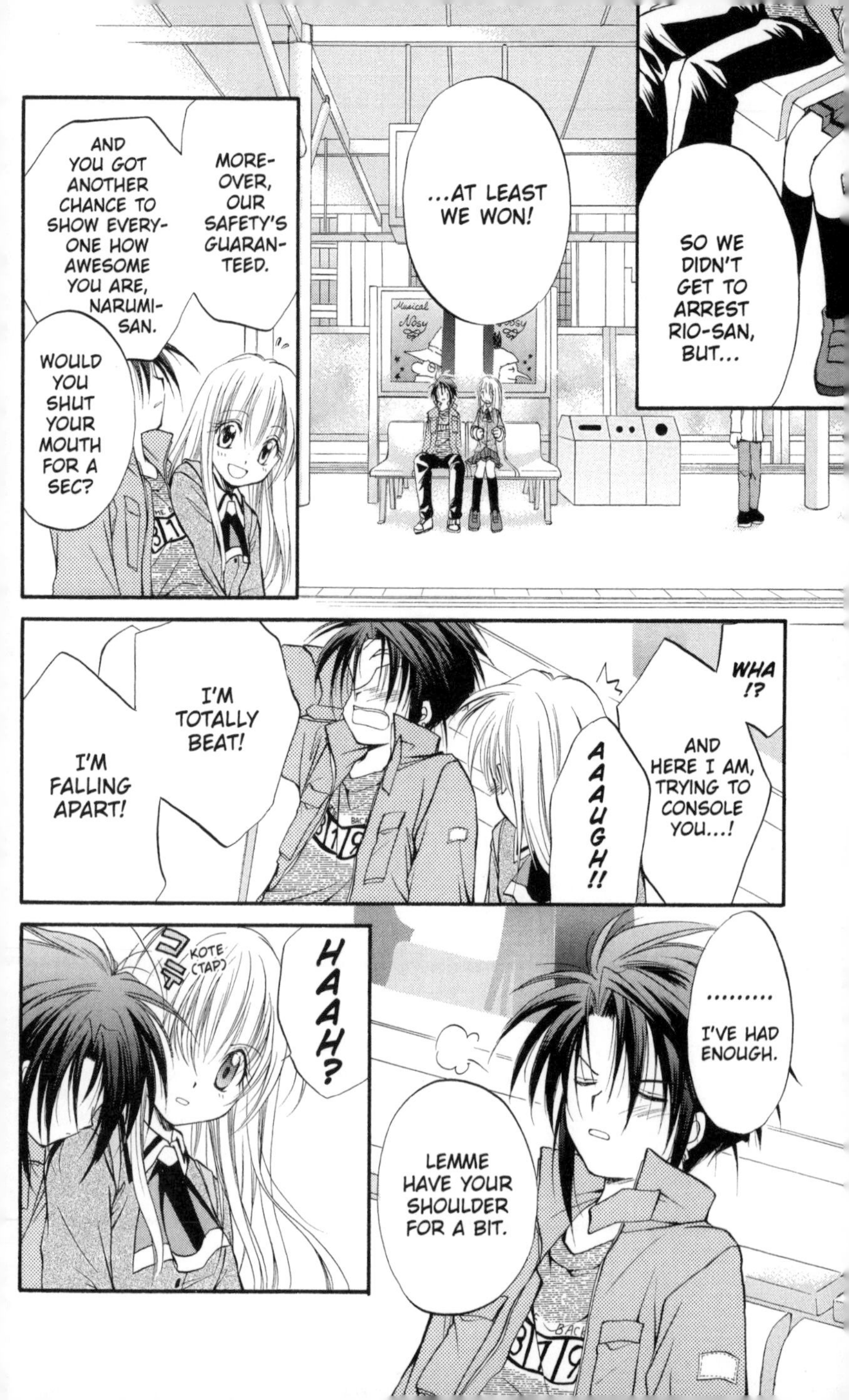
SO WE DIDN'T GET TO ARREST RIO-SAN, BUT...
...AT LEAST WE WON!
Musical Nosy
MORE-OVER, OUR SAFETY'S GUARAN-TEED.
AND YOU GOT ANOTHER CHANCE TO SHOW EVERY-ONE HOW AWESOME YOU ARE, NARUMI-SAN.
WOULD YOU SHUT YOUR MOUTH FOR A SEC?
WHA!?
AND HERE I AM, TRYING TO CONSOLE YOU...!
AAAAUGH!!
I'M TOTALLY BEAT!
I'M FALLING APART!
.... I'VE HAD ENOUGH.
LEMME HAVE YOUR SHOULDER FOR A BIT.
HAAAH?
KOTE (TAP)

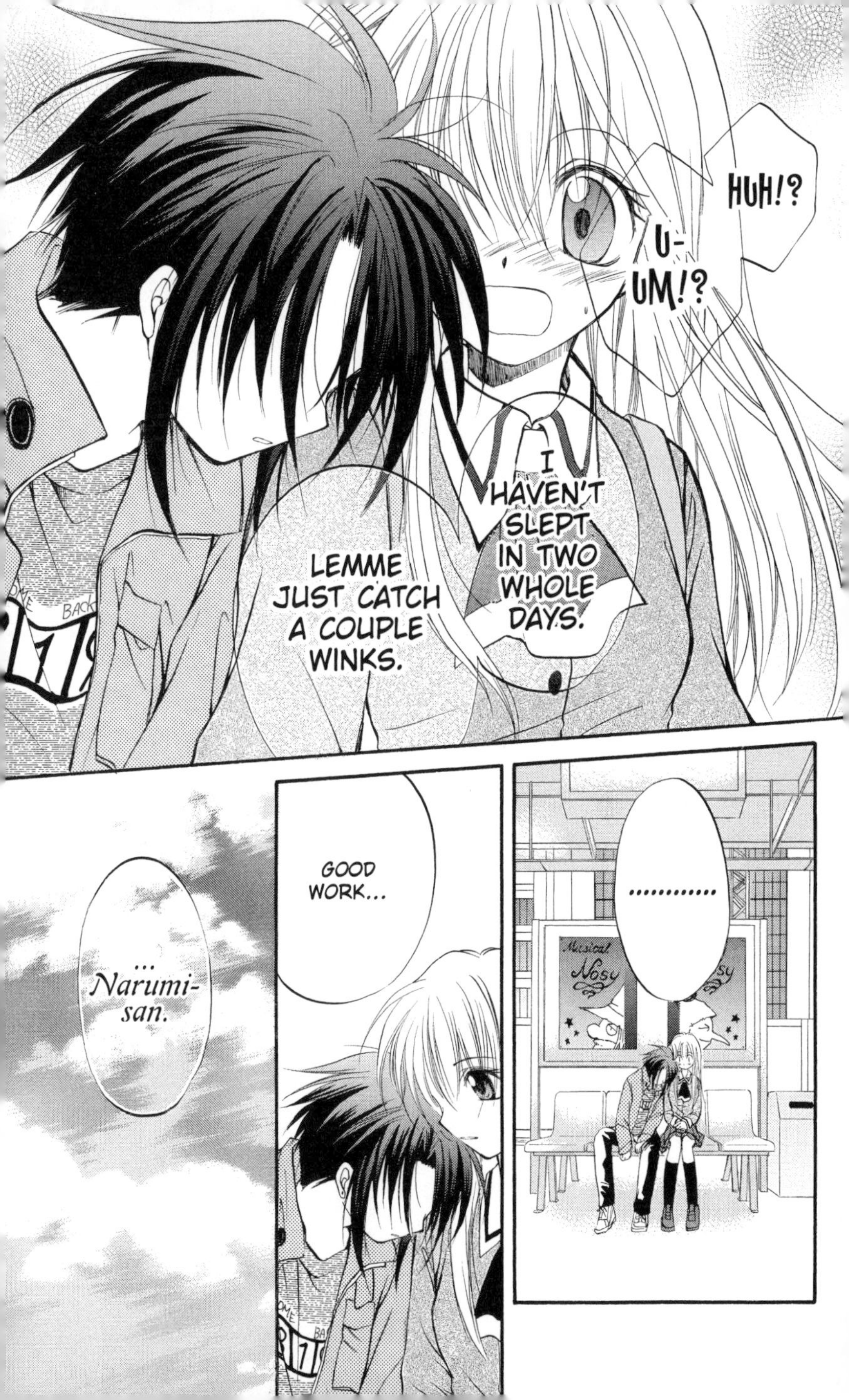
HUH!?
U-UM!?
I HAVEN'T SLEPT IN TWO WHOLE DAYS.
LEMME JUST CATCH A COUPLE WINKS.
....
Musical Nosy
GOOD WORK...
... Narumi-san.

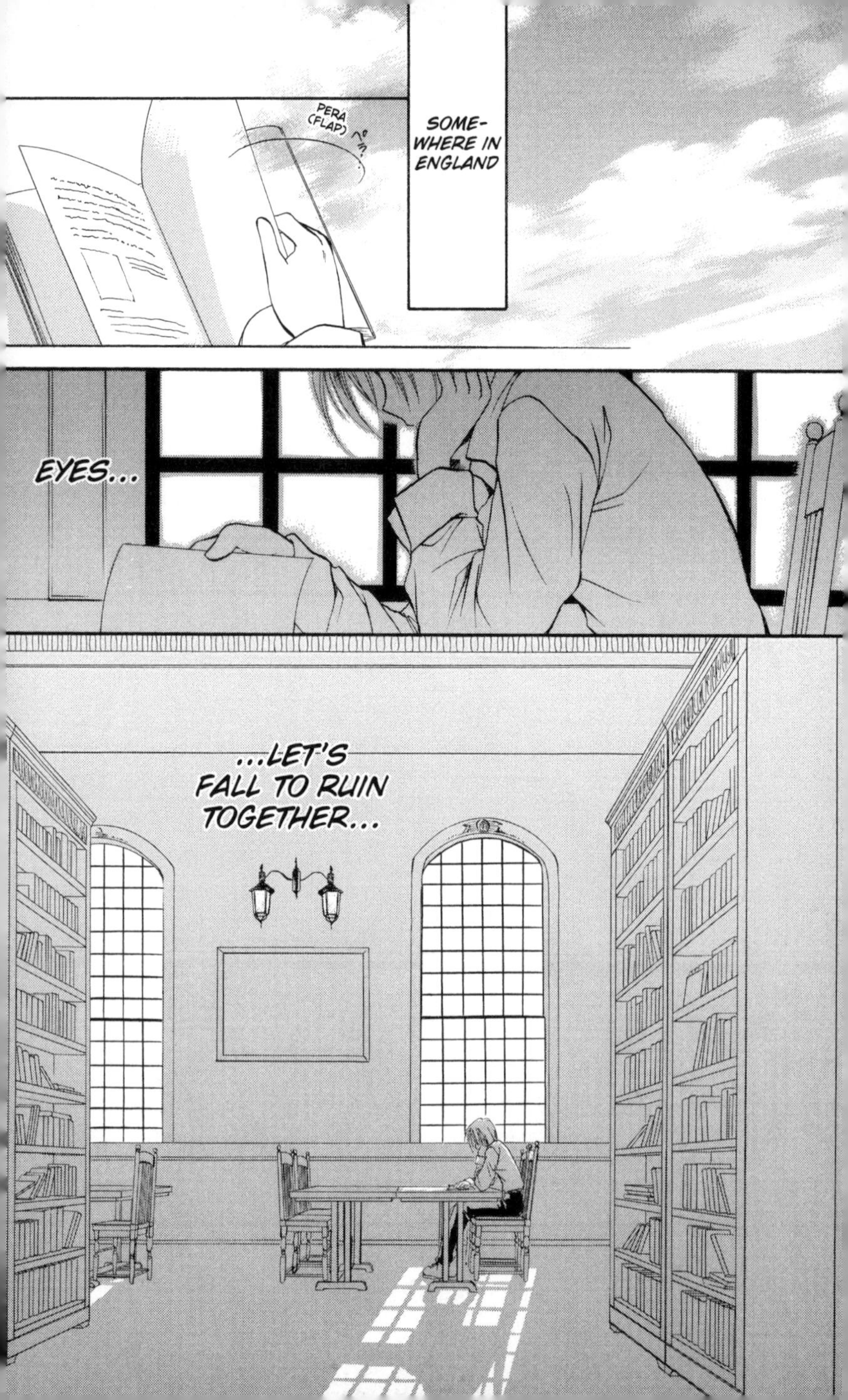
SOME-WHERE IN ENGLAND
PERA (FLAP)
EYES...
...LET'S FALL TO RUIN TOGETHER...

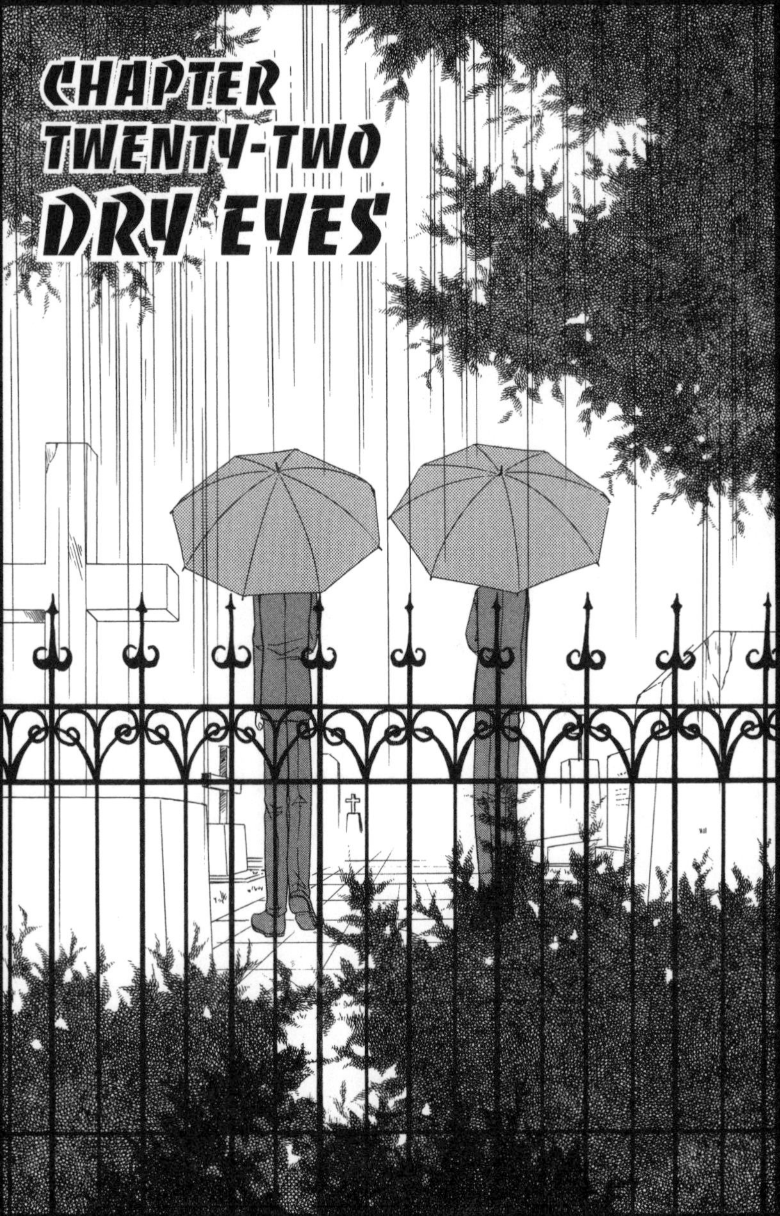
CHAPTER TWENTY-TWO
DRY EYES

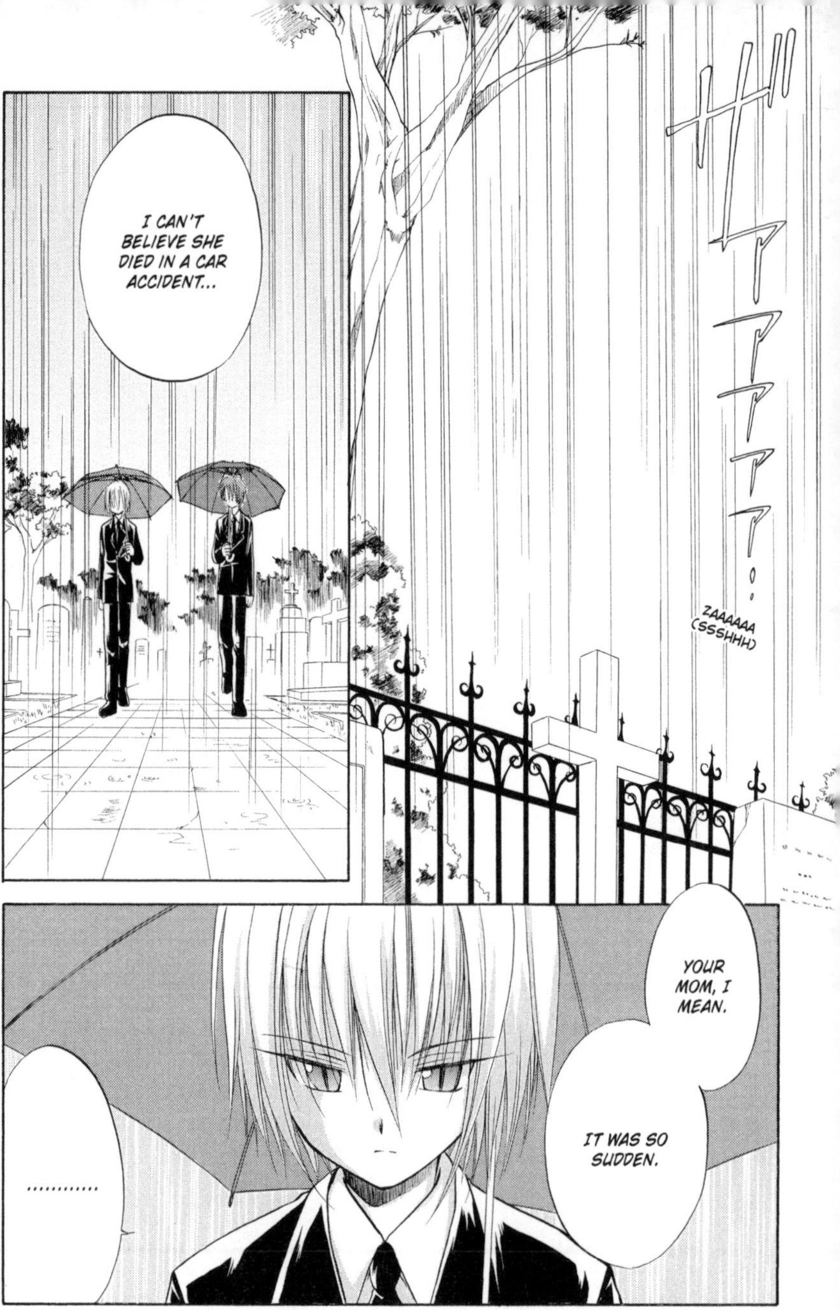
ZAAAAAA (SSSHHH)
I CAN'T BELIEVE SHE DIED IN A CAR ACCIDENT...
YOUR MOM, I MEAN.
IT WAS SO SUDDEN.
....

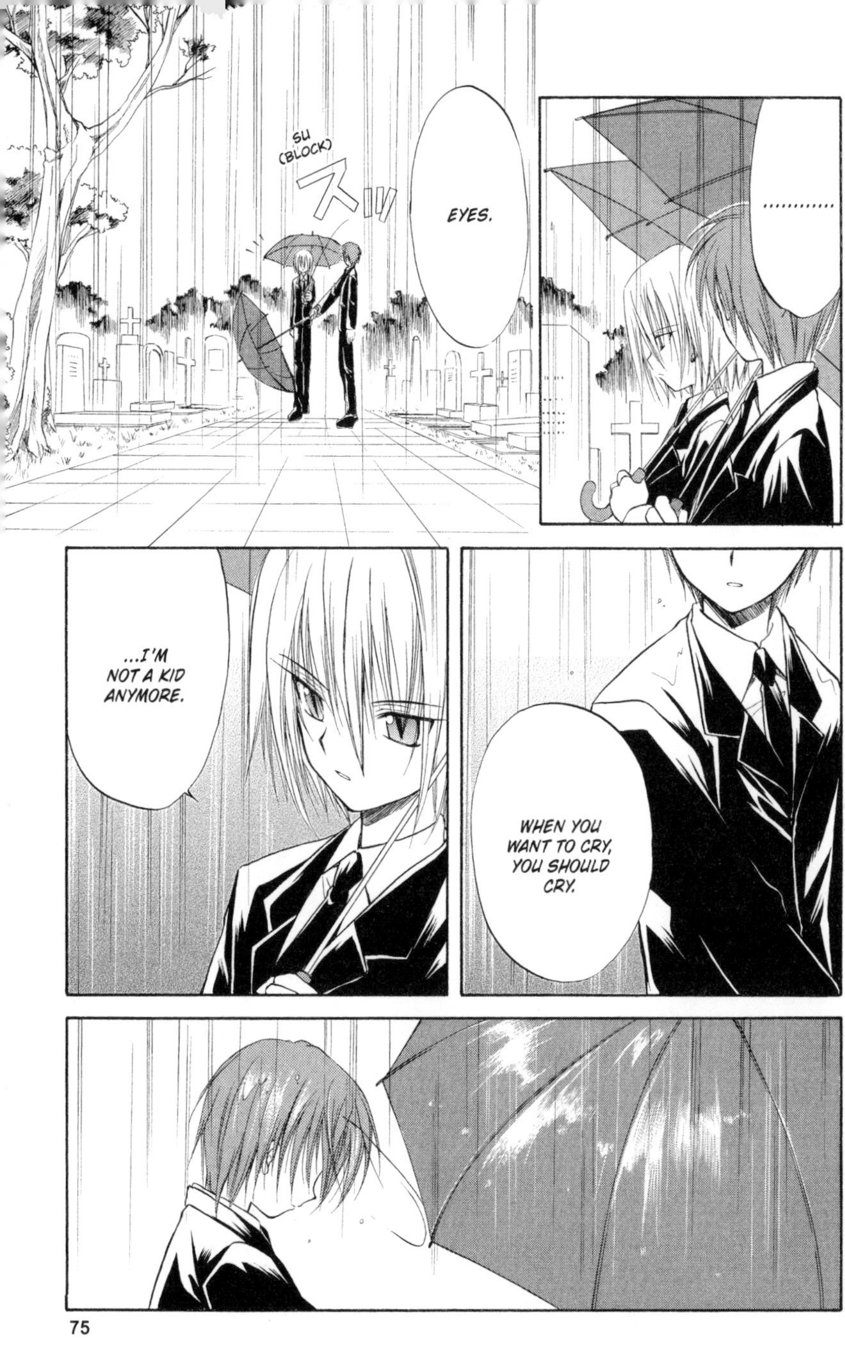
....
EYES.
SU (BLOCK)
スッ
WHEN YOU WANT TO CRY, YOU SHOULD CRY.
...I'M NOT A KID ANYMORE.

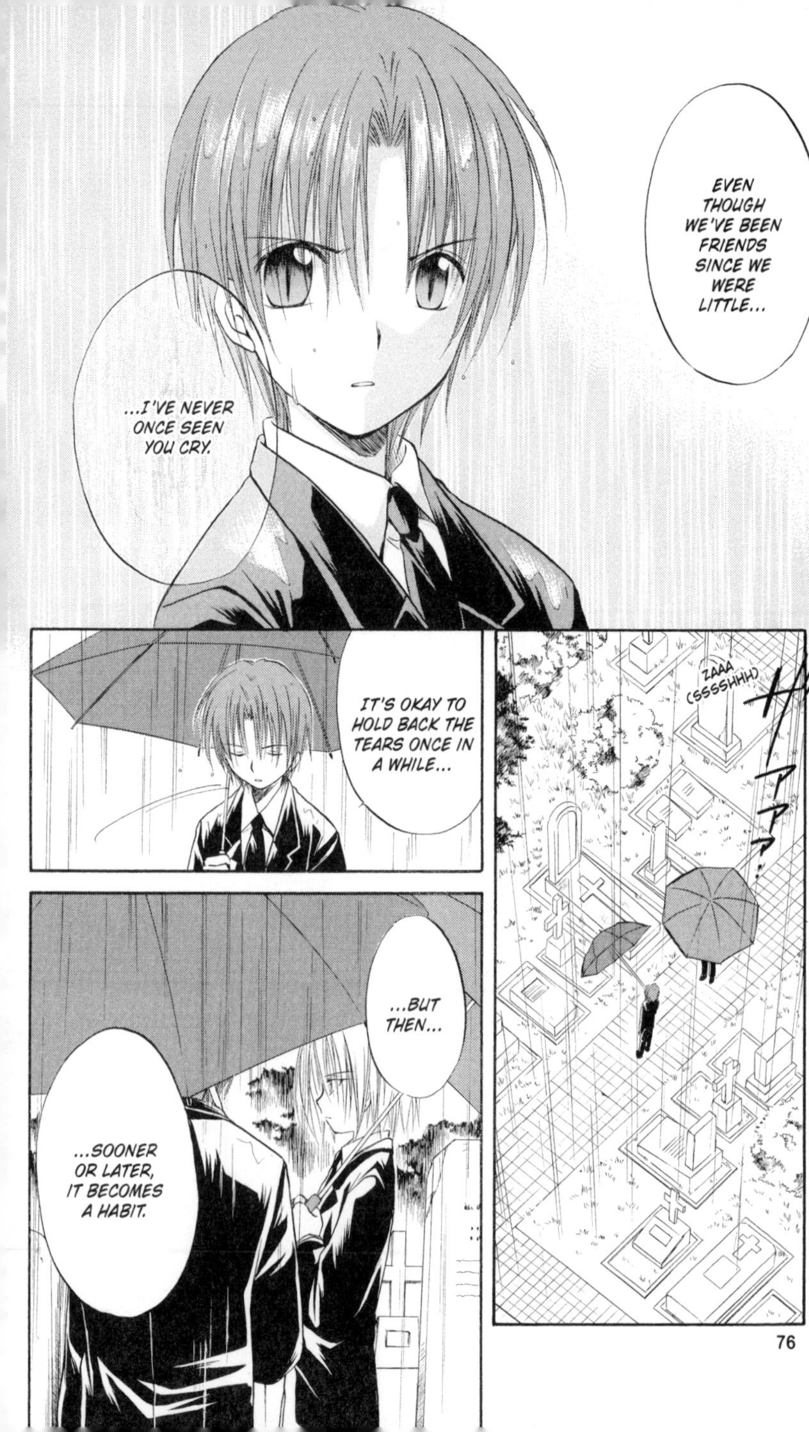
EVEN THOUGH WE'VE BEEN FRIENDS SINCE WE WERE LITTLE...
...I'VE NEVER ONCE SEEN YOU CRY.
ZAAA (SSSSHHH)
IT'S OKAY TO HOLD BACK THE TEARS ONCE IN A WHILE...
...BUT THEN...
...SOONER OR LATER, IT BECOMES A HABIT.

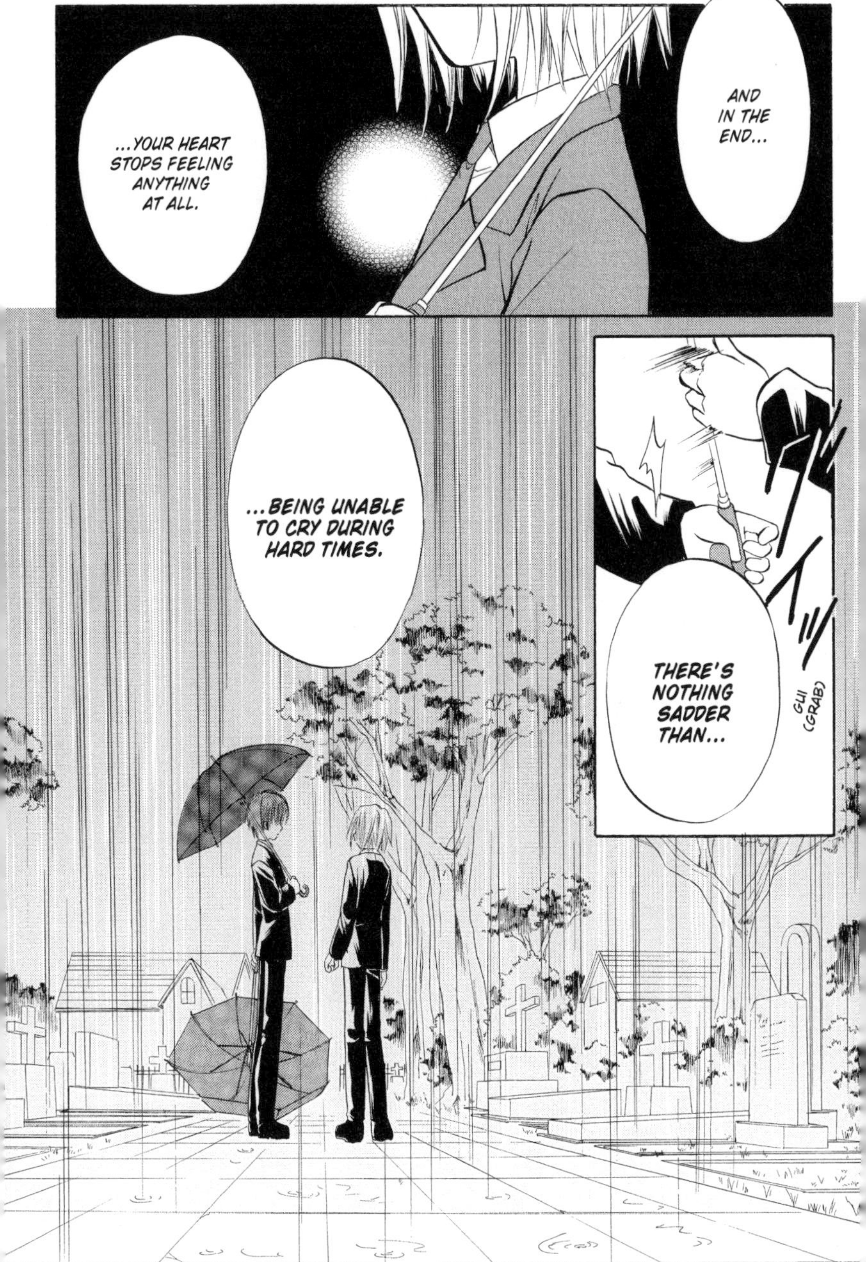
AND IN THE END...
...YOUR HEART STOPS FEELING ANYTHING AT ALL.
THERE'S NOTHING SADDER THAN...
GUI (GRAB)
...BEING UNABLE TO CRY DURING HARD TIMES.

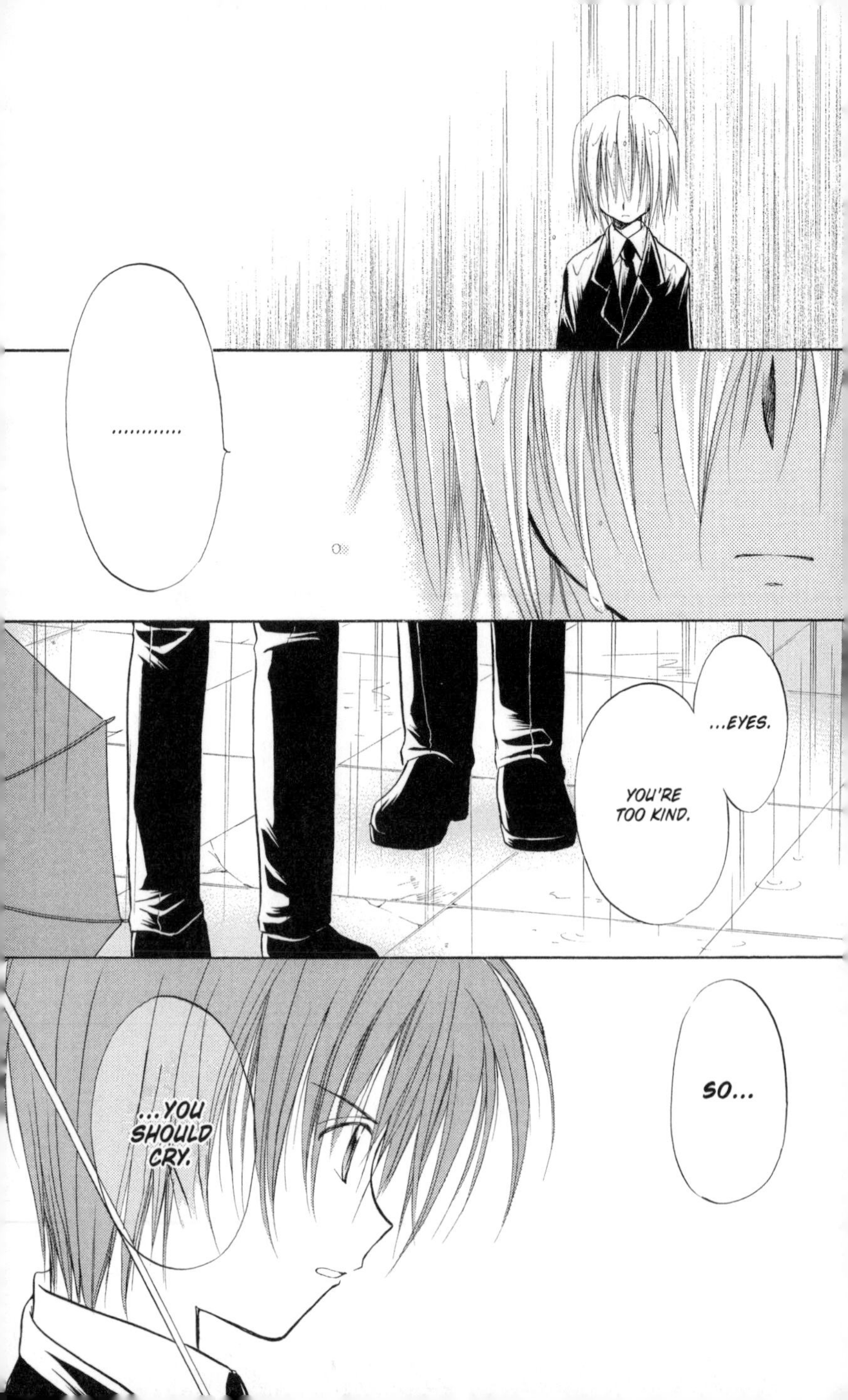
....
...EYES.
YOU'RE TOO KIND.
SO...
...YOU SHOULD CRY.

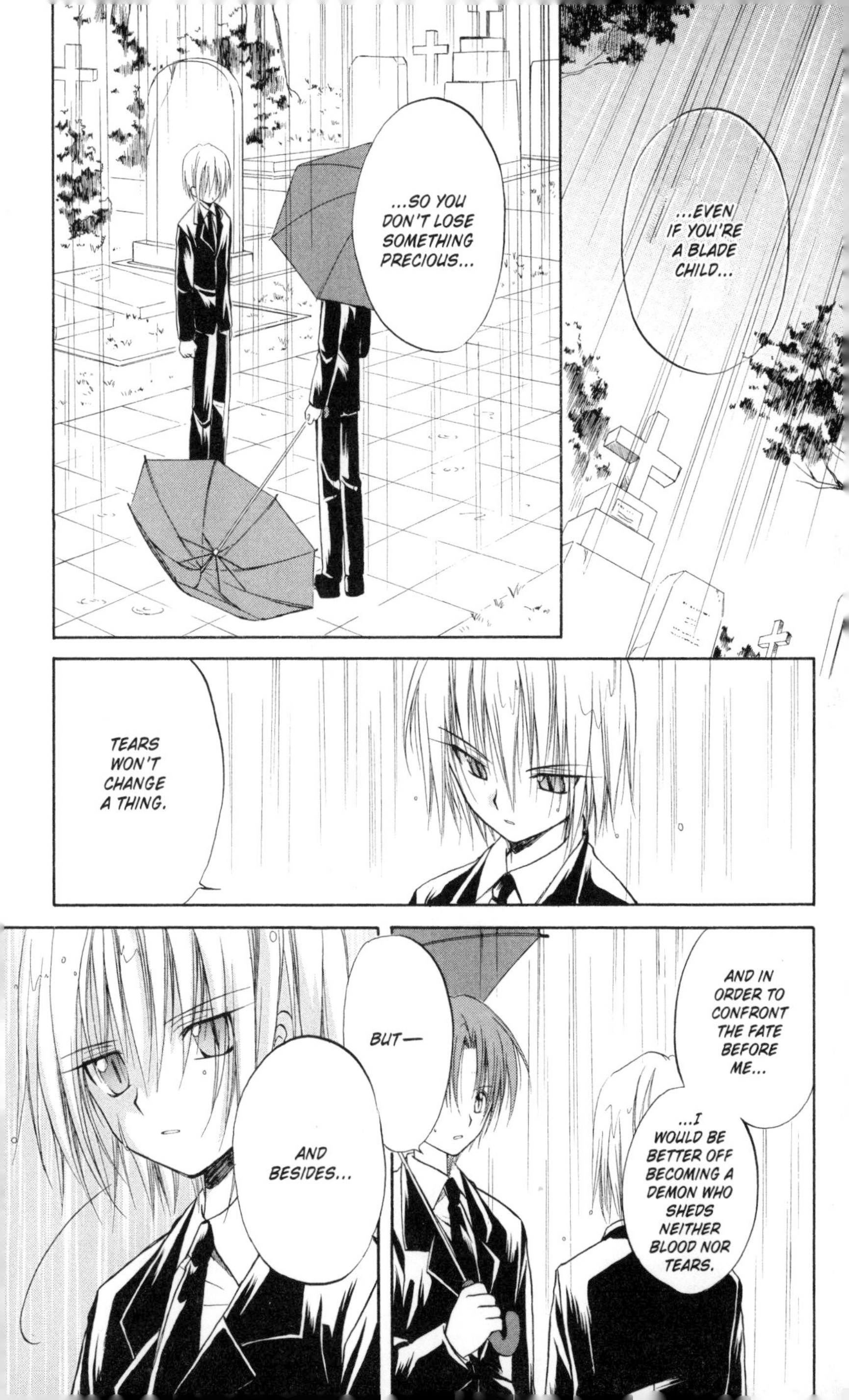
...EVEN IF YOU'RE A BLADE CHILD...
...SO YOU DON'T LOSE SOMETHING PRECIOUS...
TEARS WON'T CHANGE A THING.
AND IN ORDER TO CONFRONT THE FATE BEFORE ME...
...I WOULD BE BETTER OFF BECOMING A DEMON WHO SHEDS NEITHER BLOOD NOR TEARS.
BUT—
AND BESIDES...

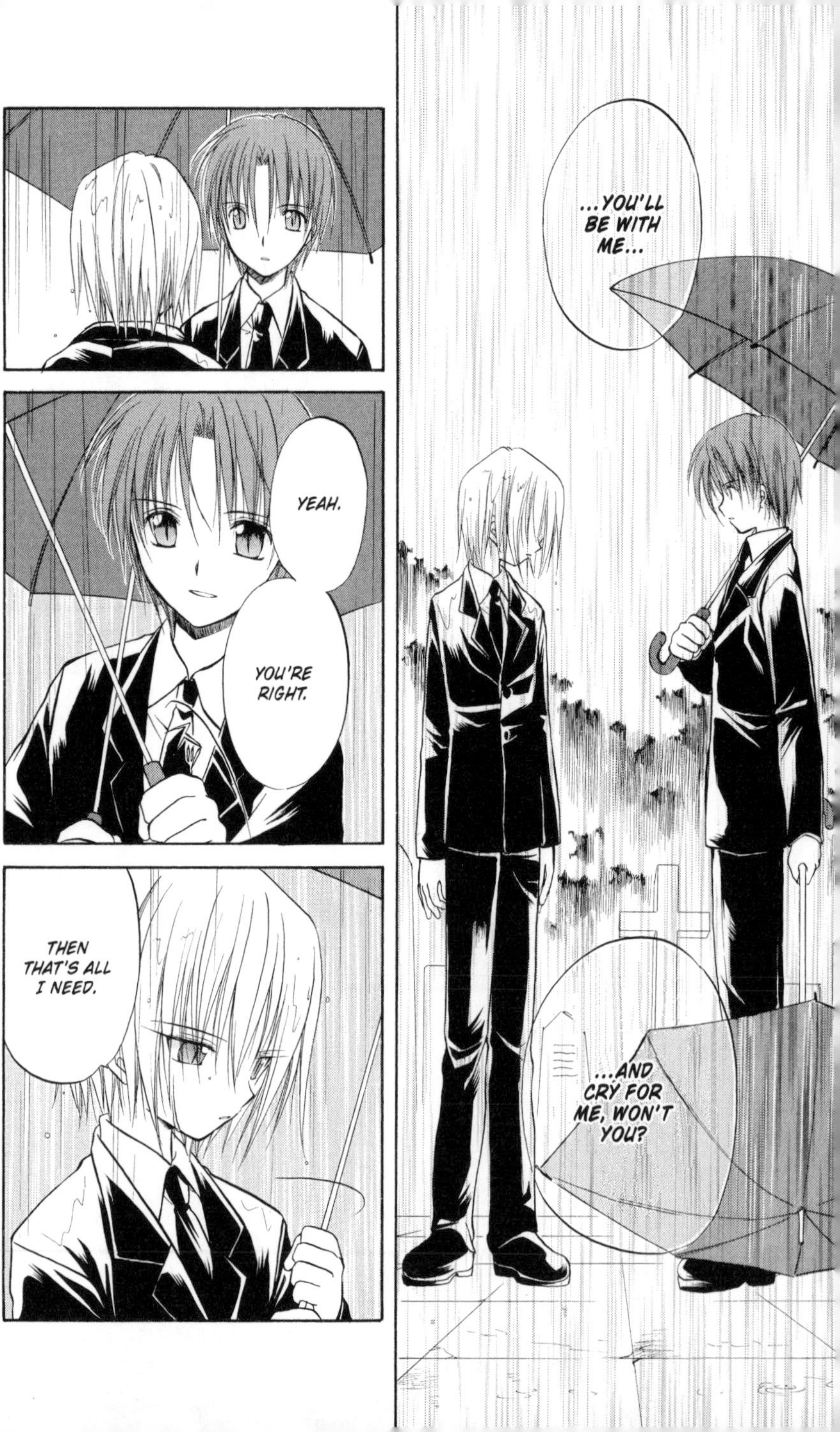
...YOU'LL BE WITH ME...
...AND CRY FOR ME, WON'T YOU?
YEAH.
YOU'RE RIGHT.
THEN THAT'S ALL I NEED.

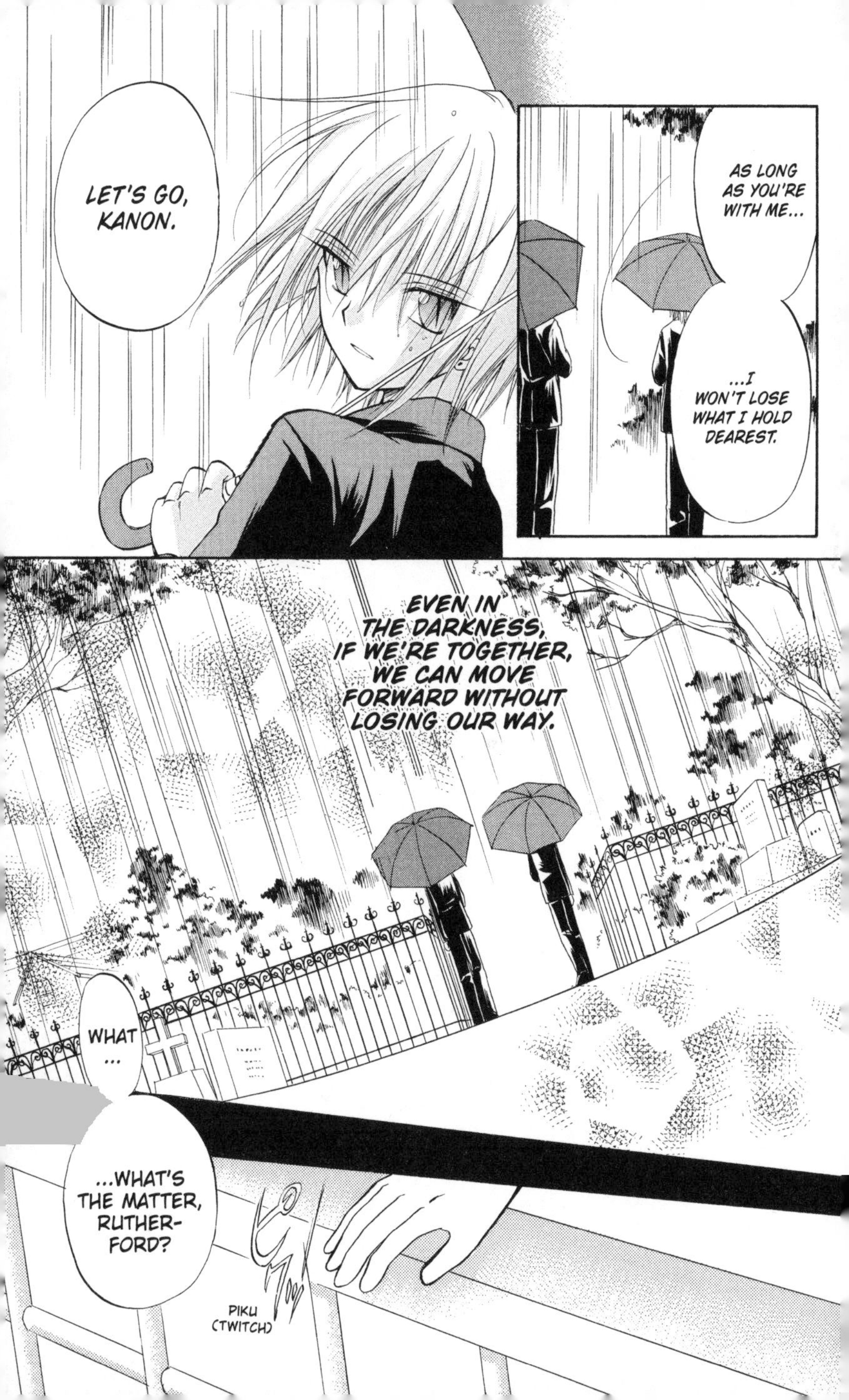
AS LONG AS YOU'RE WITH ME...
...I WON'T LOSE WHAT I HOLD DEAREST.
LET'S GO, KANON.
EVEN IN THE DARKNESS, IF WE'RE TOGETHER, WE CAN MOVE FORWARD WITHOUT LOSING OUR WAY.
WHAT...
...WHAT'S THE MATTER, RUTHER-FORD?
PIKU (TWITCH)

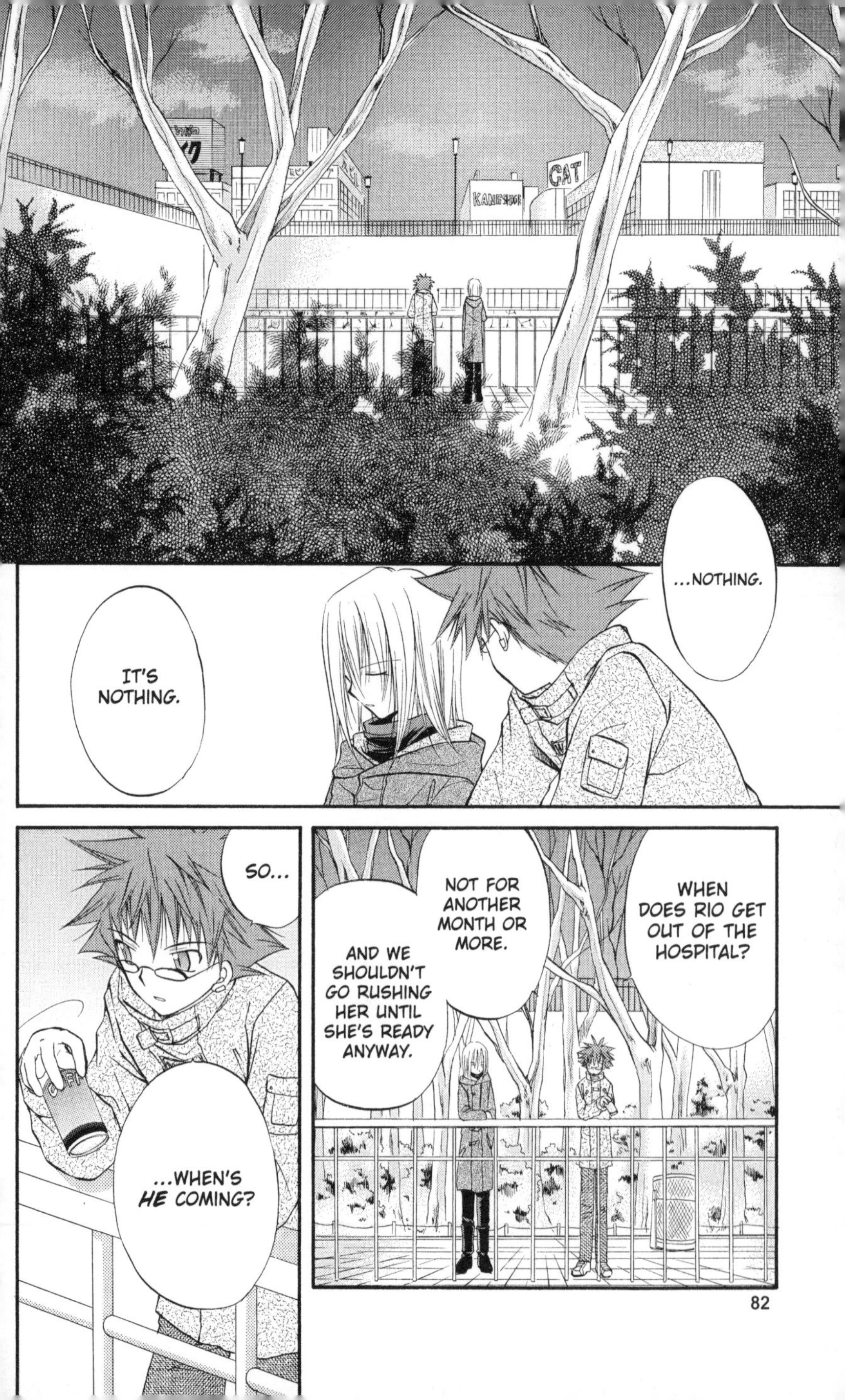
KANESHIGE
CAT
...NOTHING.
IT'S NOTHING.
WHEN DOES RIO GET OUT OF THE HOSPITAL?
NOT FOR ANOTHER MONTH OR MORE.
AND WE SHOULDN'T GO RUSHING HER UNTIL SHE'S READY ANYWAY.
SO...
...WHEN'S *HE* COMING?

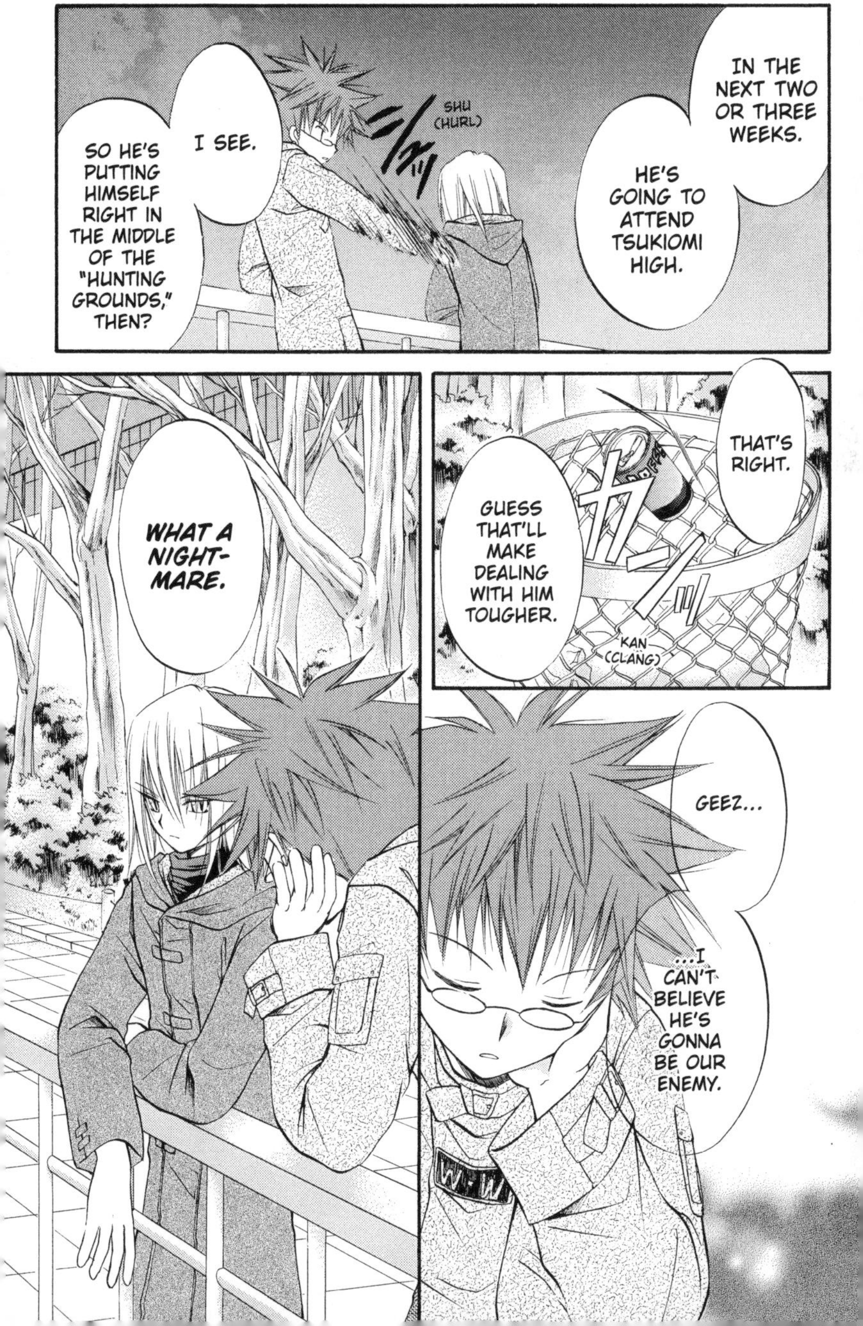
IN THE NEXT TWO OR THREE WEEKS.
HE'S GOING TO ATTEND TSUKIOMI HIGH.
SHU (HURL)
I SEE.
SO HE'S PUTTING HIMSELF RIGHT IN THE MIDDLE OF THE "HUNTING GROUNDS," THEN?
THAT'S RIGHT.
GUESS THAT'LL MAKE DEALING WITH HIM TOUGHER.
KAN (CLANG)
GEEZ...
...I CAN'T BELIEVE HE'S GONNA BE OUR ENEMY.
WHAT A NIGHT-MARE.

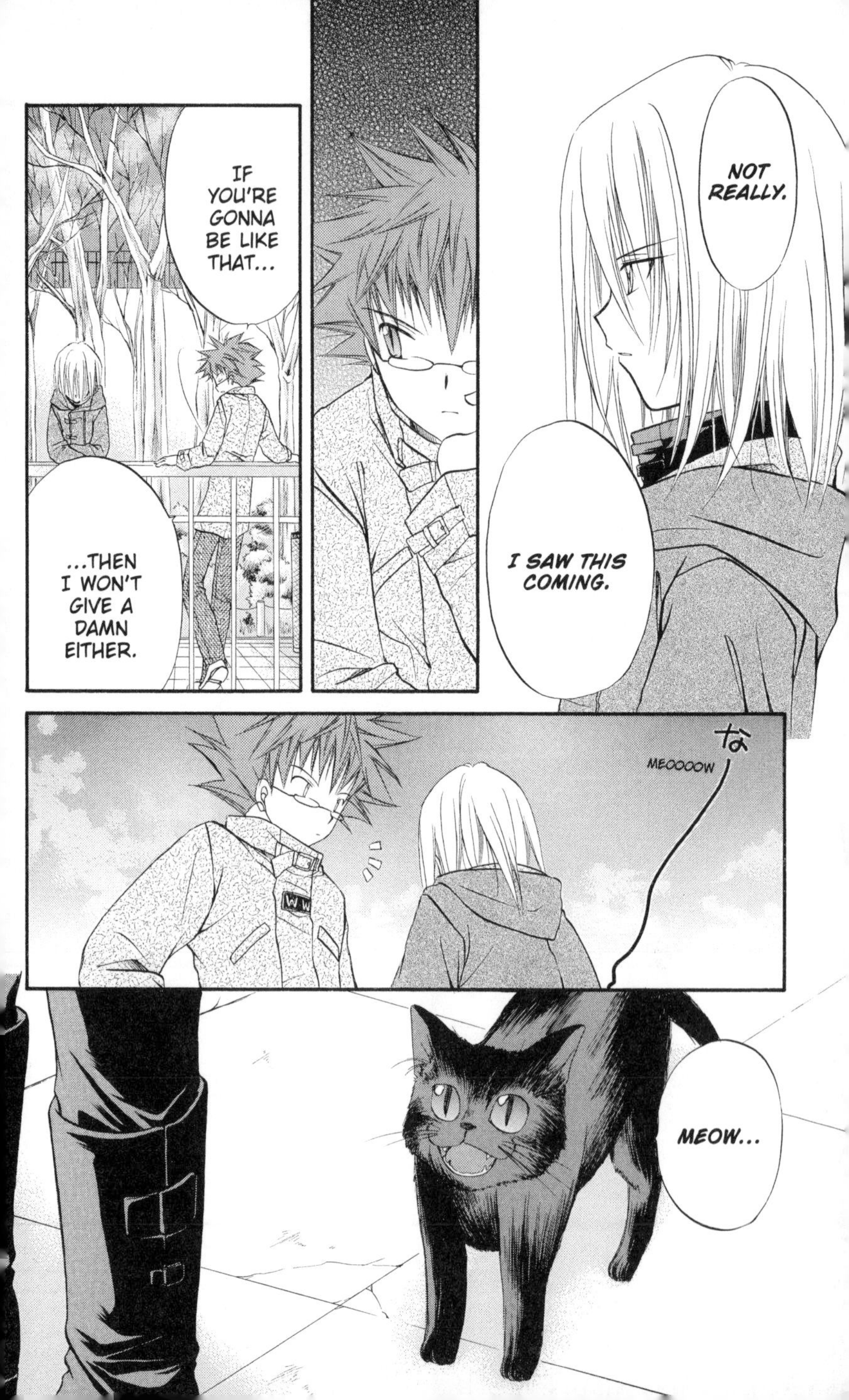
NOT REALLY.
I SAW THIS COMING.
IF YOU'RE GONNA BE LIKE THAT...
...THEN I WON'T GIVE A DAMN EITHER.
な
MEOOOOW
MEOW...

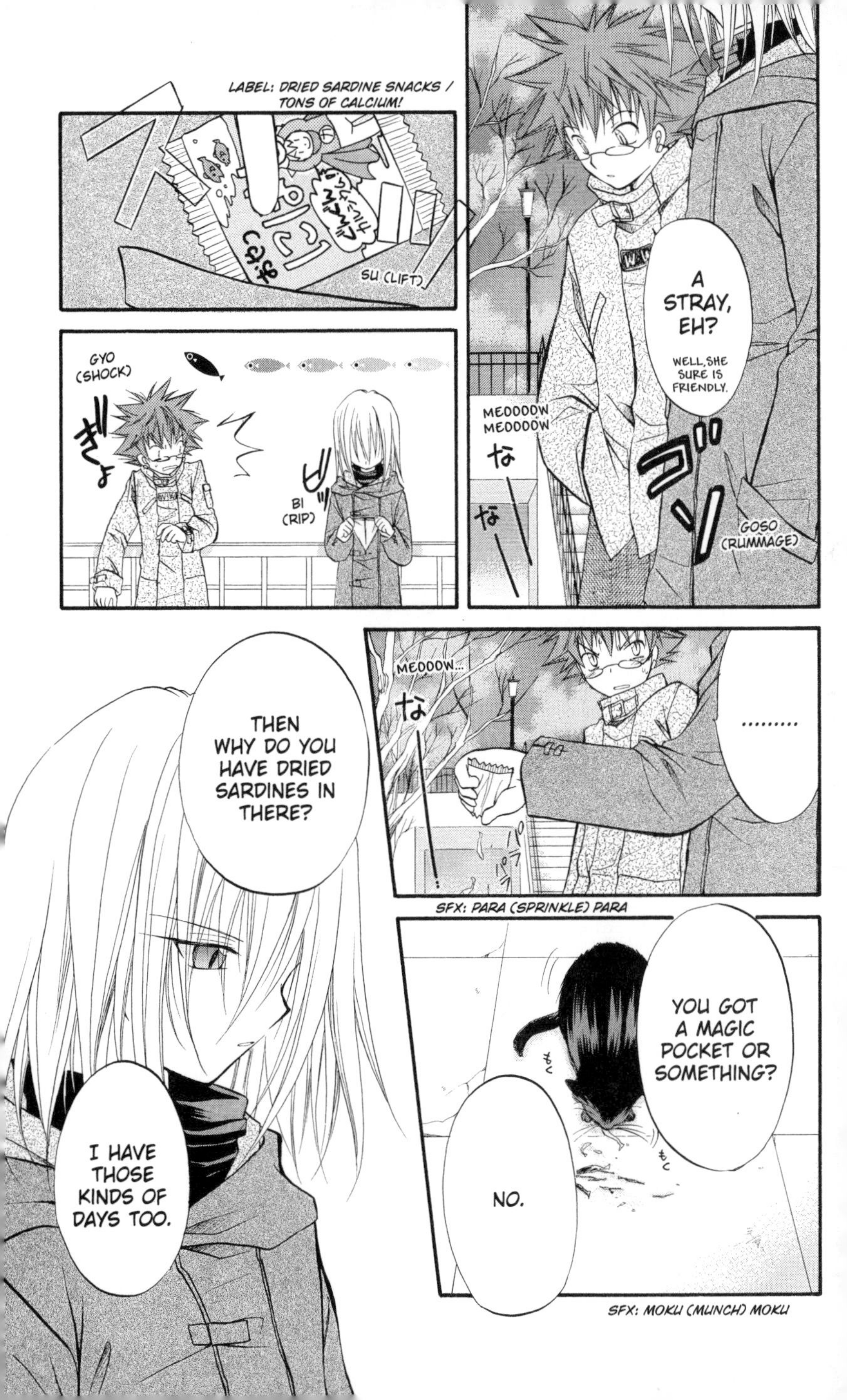
A STRAY, EH?
WELL, SHE SURE IS FRIENDLY.
MEOOOOW MEOOOOW
GOSO (RUMMAGE)
LABEL: DRIED SARDINE SNACKS / TONS OF CALCIUM!
SU (LIFT)
BI (RIP)
GYO (SHOCK)
....
MEOOOW...
SFX: PARA (SPRINKLE) PARA
THEN WHY DO YOU HAVE DRIED SARDINES IN THERE?
YOU GOT A MAGIC POCKET OR SOMETHING?
NO.
SFX: MOKU (MUNCH) MOKU
I HAVE THOSE KINDS OF DAYS TOO.

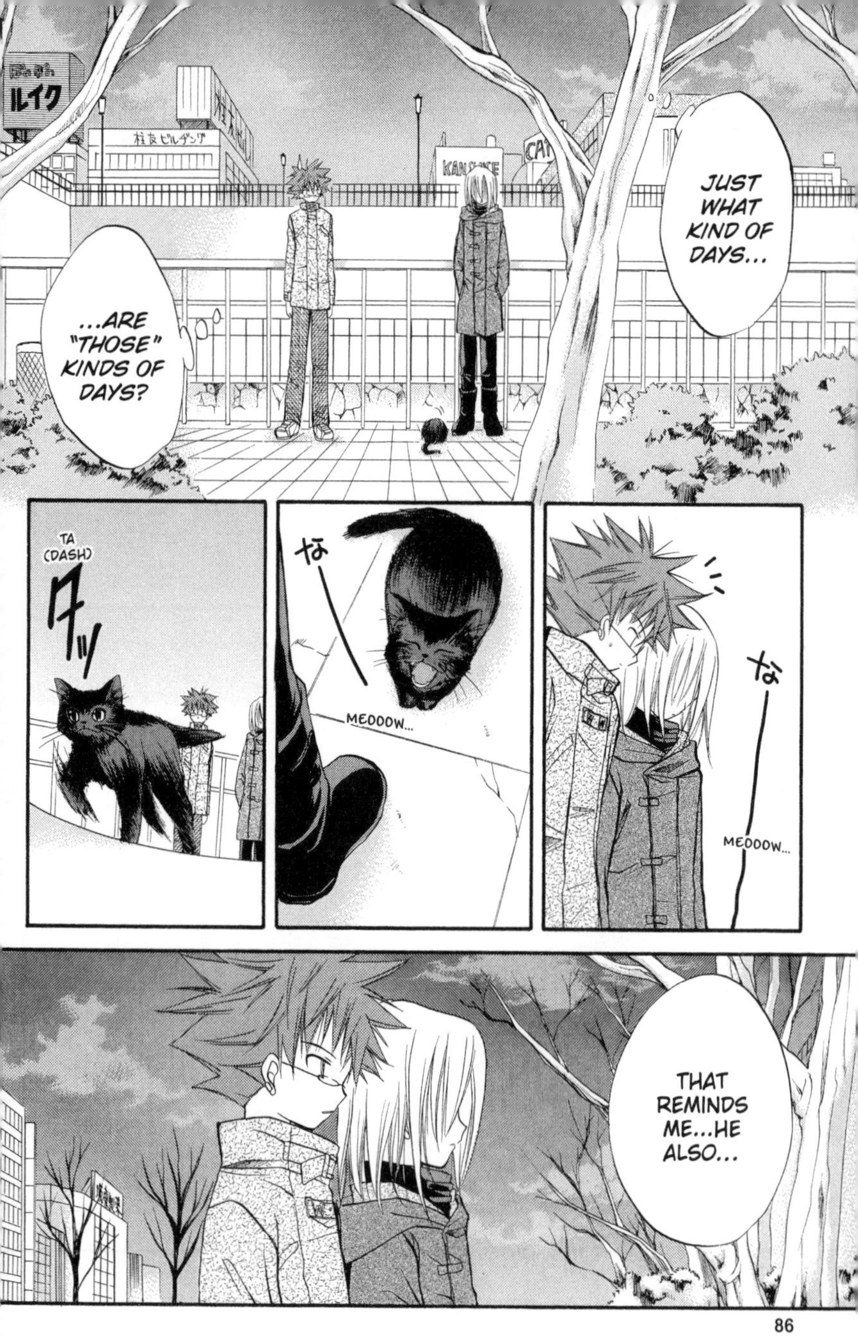
JUST WHAT KIND OF DAYS...
..."ARE "THOSE" KINDS OF DAYS?
な
MEOOOW...
な
MEOOOW...
TA (DASH)
タッ
THAT REMINDS ME...HE ALSO...

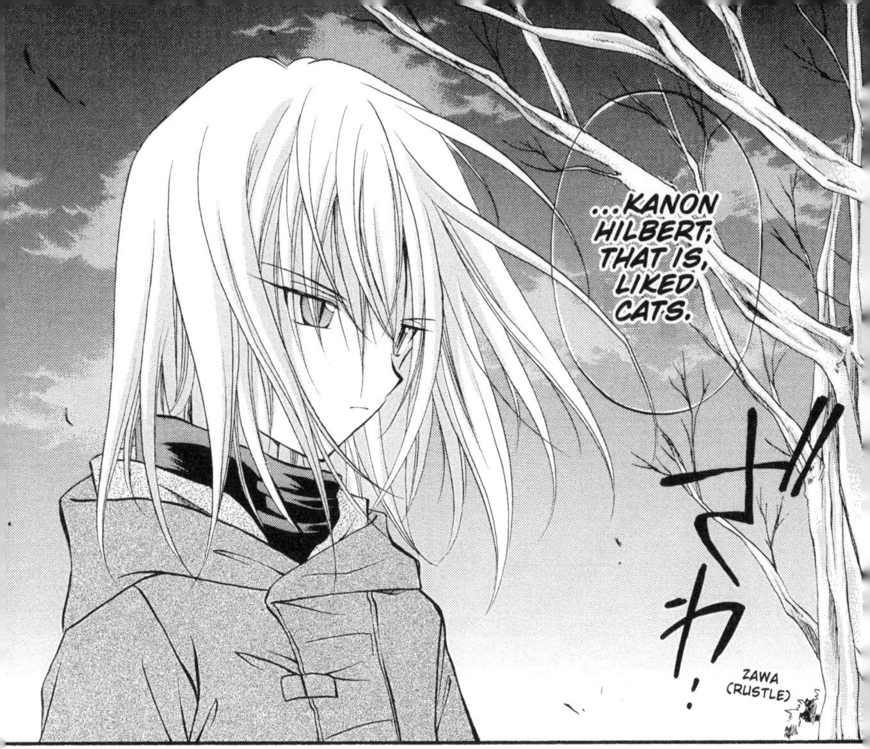
...KANON HILBERT, THAT IS, LIKED CATS.
ザワ!
ZAWA (RUSTLE)

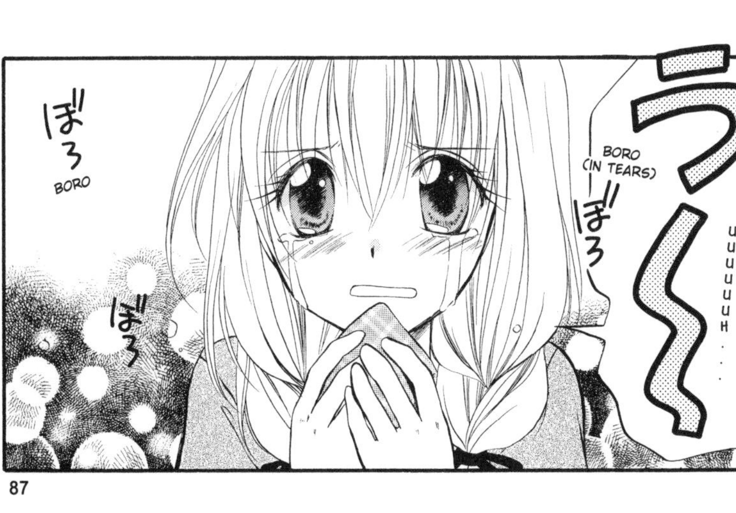
う〜
UUUUUUH . . .
ぼろ
BORO (IN TEARS)
ぼろ
BORO
ぼろ

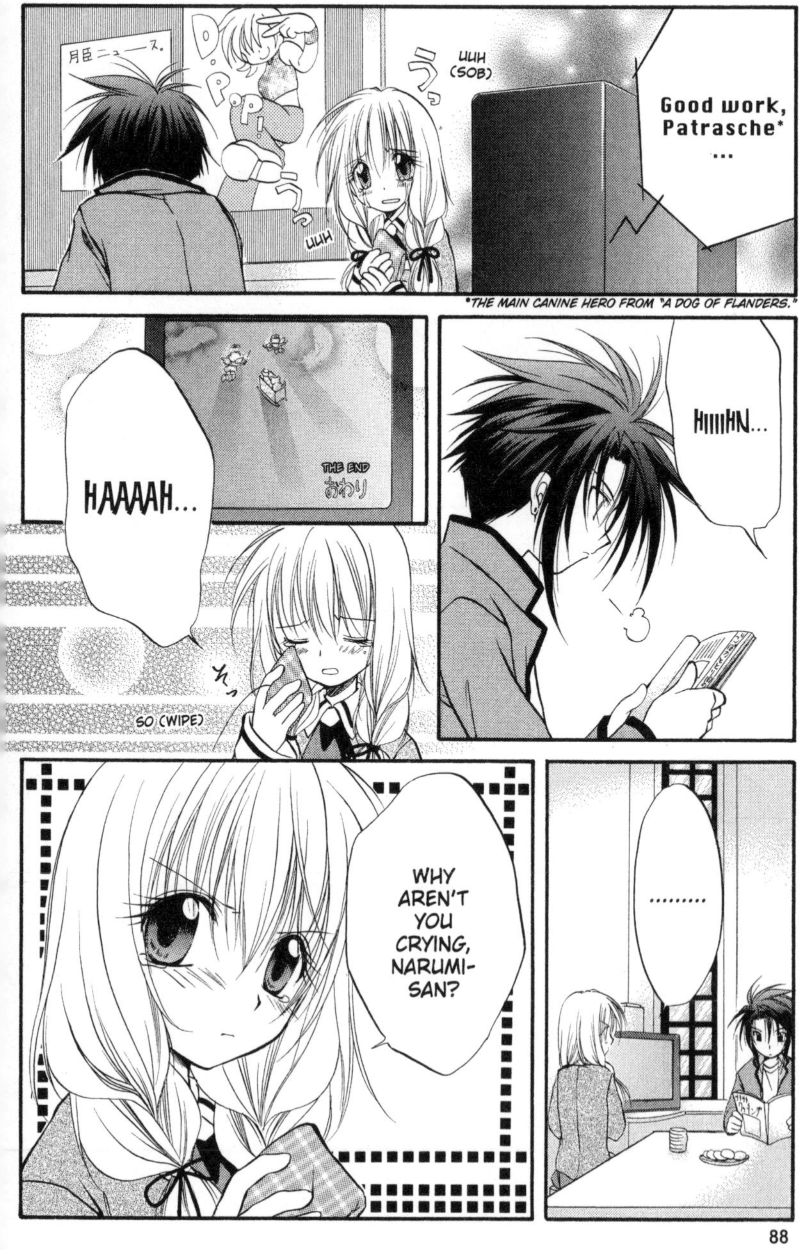
Good work, Patrasche* ...
UUH (SOB)
UUH
HIIIIHN...
HAAAAH...
THE END
おわり
SO (WIPE)
....
WHY AREN'T YOU CRYING, NARUMI-SAN?

*THE MAIN CANINE HERO FROM "A DOG OF FLANDERS."

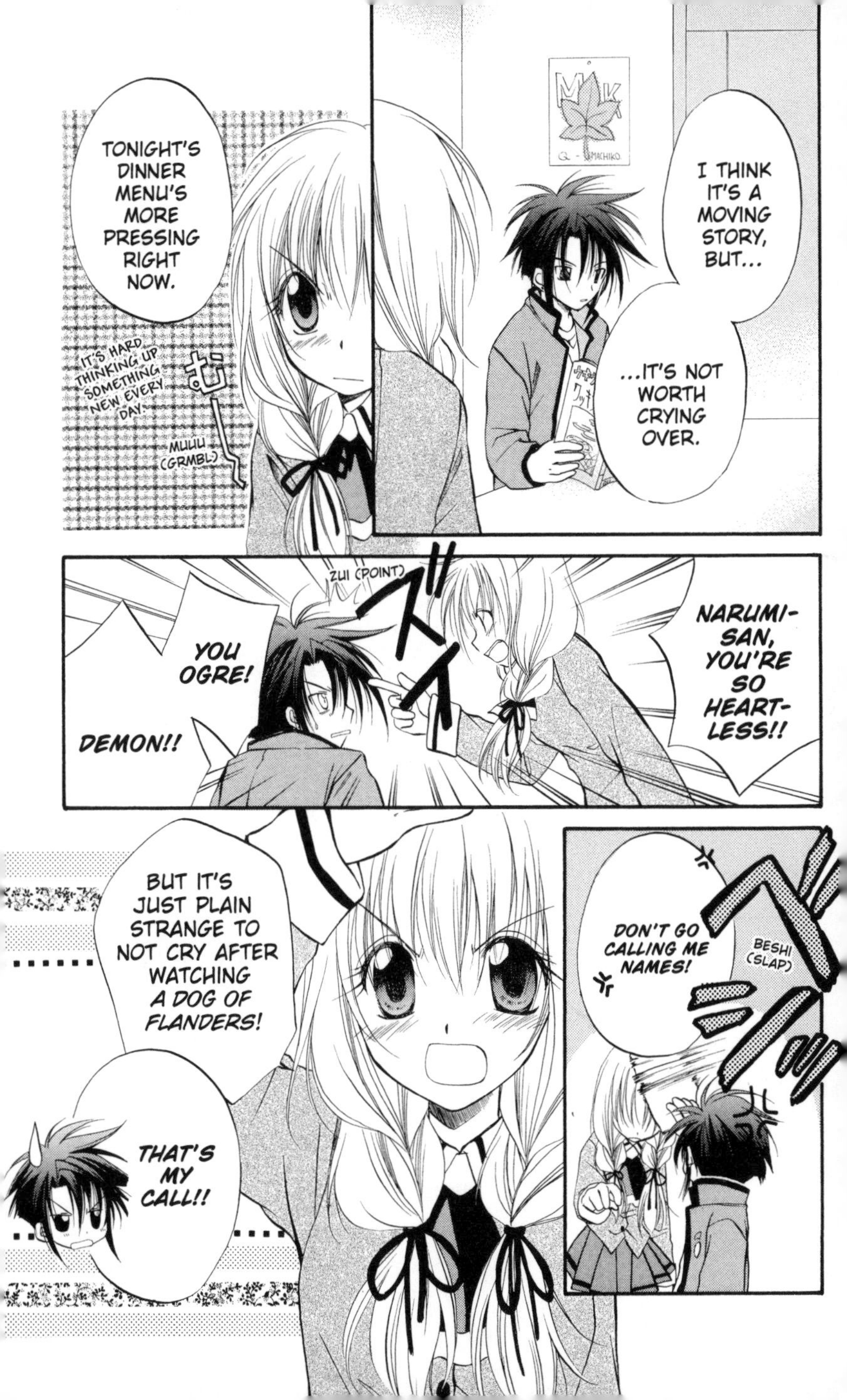
I THINK IT'S A MOVING STORY, BUT...
...IT'S NOT WORTH CRYING OVER.
TONIGHT'S DINNER MENU'S MORE PRESSING RIGHT NOW.
IT'S HARD THINKING UP SOMETHING NEW EVERY DAY.
MUUU (GRMBL)
NARUMI-SAN, YOU'RE SO HEARTLESS!!
ZUI (POINT)
YOU OGRE!
DEMON!!
DON'T GO CALLING ME NAMES!
BESHI (SLAP)
BUT IT'S JUST PLAIN STRANGE TO NOT CRY AFTER WATCHING A DOG OF FLANDERS!
THAT'S MY CALL!!

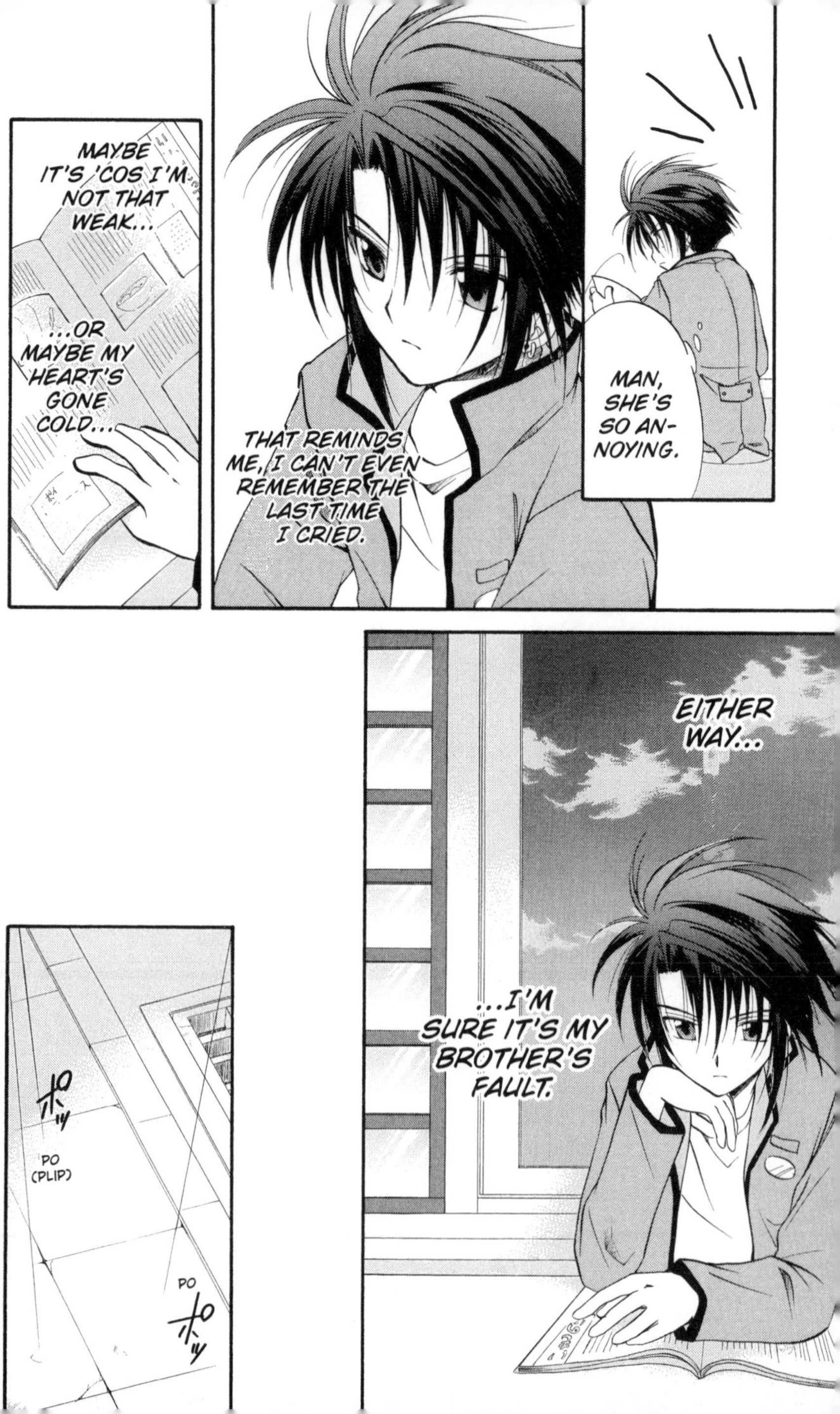
MAN, SHE'S SO AN-NOYING.
THAT REMINDS ME, I CAN'T EVEN REMEMBER THE LAST TIME I CRIED.
MAYBE IT'S 'COS I'M NOT THAT WEAK...
...OR MAYBE MY HEART'S GONE COLD...
EITHER WAY...
...I'M SURE IT'S MY BROTHER'S FAULT.
ポッ
PO (PLIP)
PO
ポッ

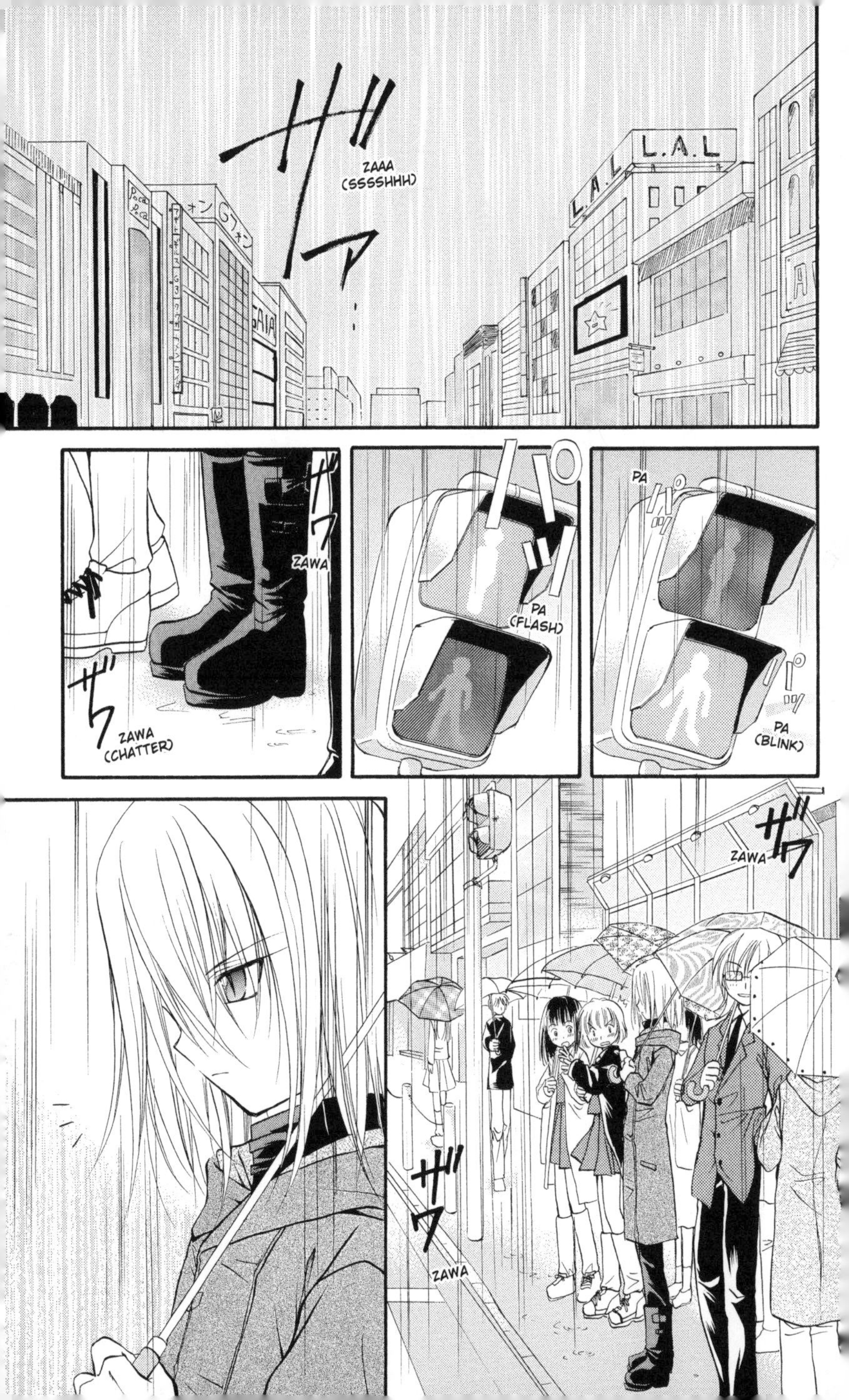
ZAAA (SSSSHHH)
PA
PA (BLINK)
PA (FLASH)
ZAWA
ZAWA (CHATTER)
ZAWA
ZAWA

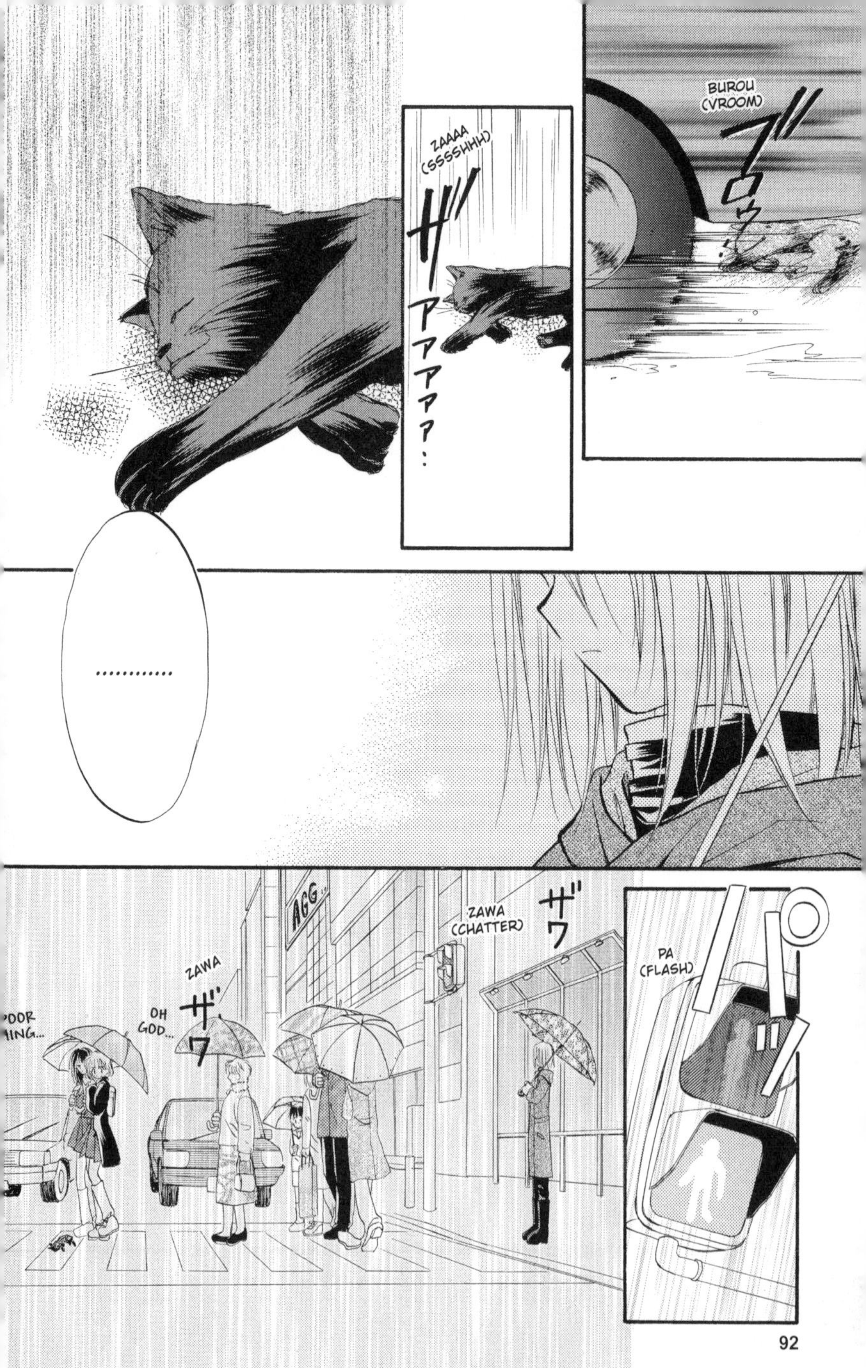

BUROU (VROOM)
ブロロウ…
ZAAAA (SSSSHHH)
ザアアアアア…
....
PA (FLASH)
パッ
ZAWA (CHATTER)
ザワ
ZAWA
ザワ
OH GOD...
POOR
ING...

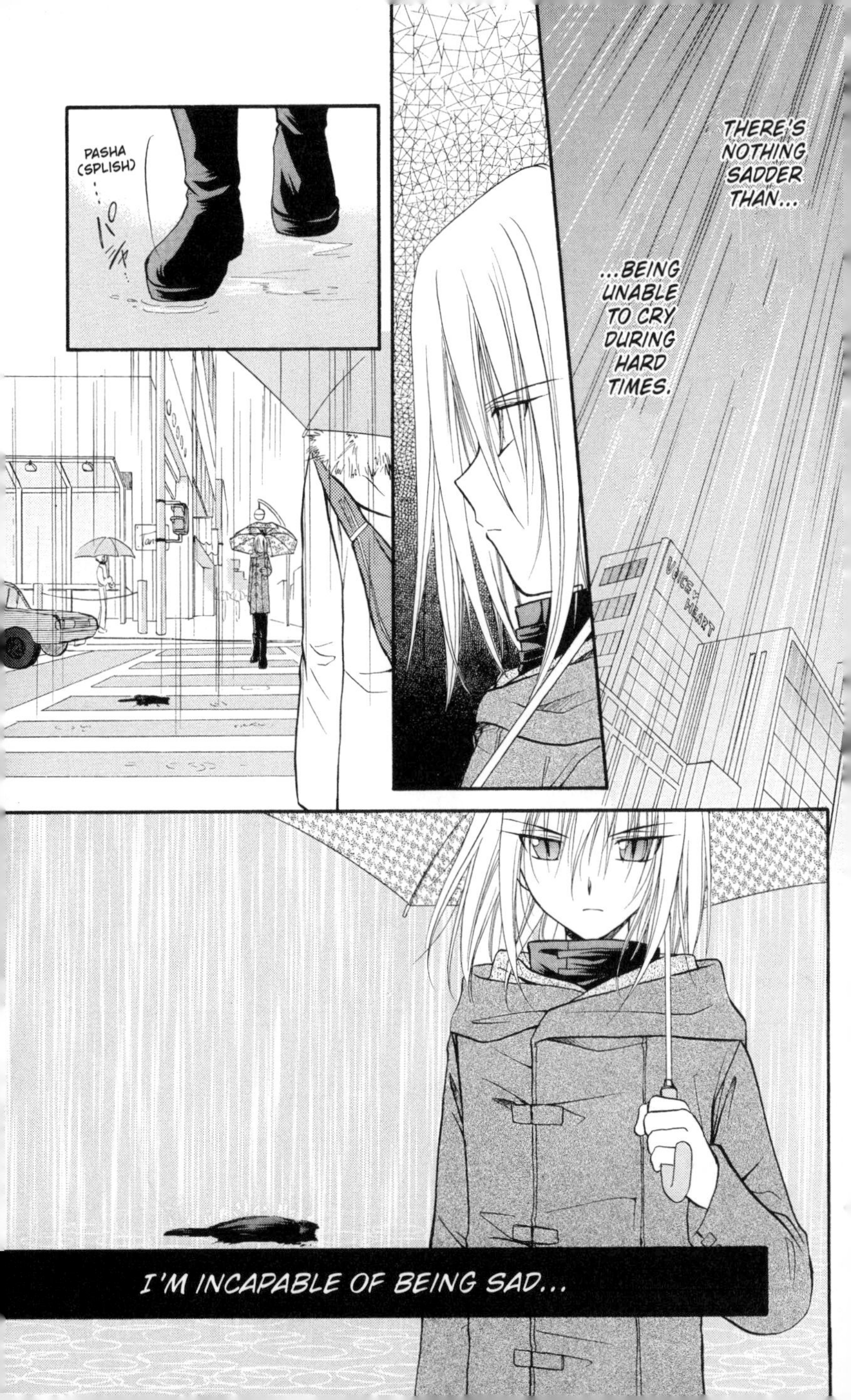
THERE'S NOTHING SADDER THAN...
...BEING UNABLE TO CRY DURING HARD TIMES.
PASHA (SPLISH)
I'M INCAPABLE OF BEING SAD...

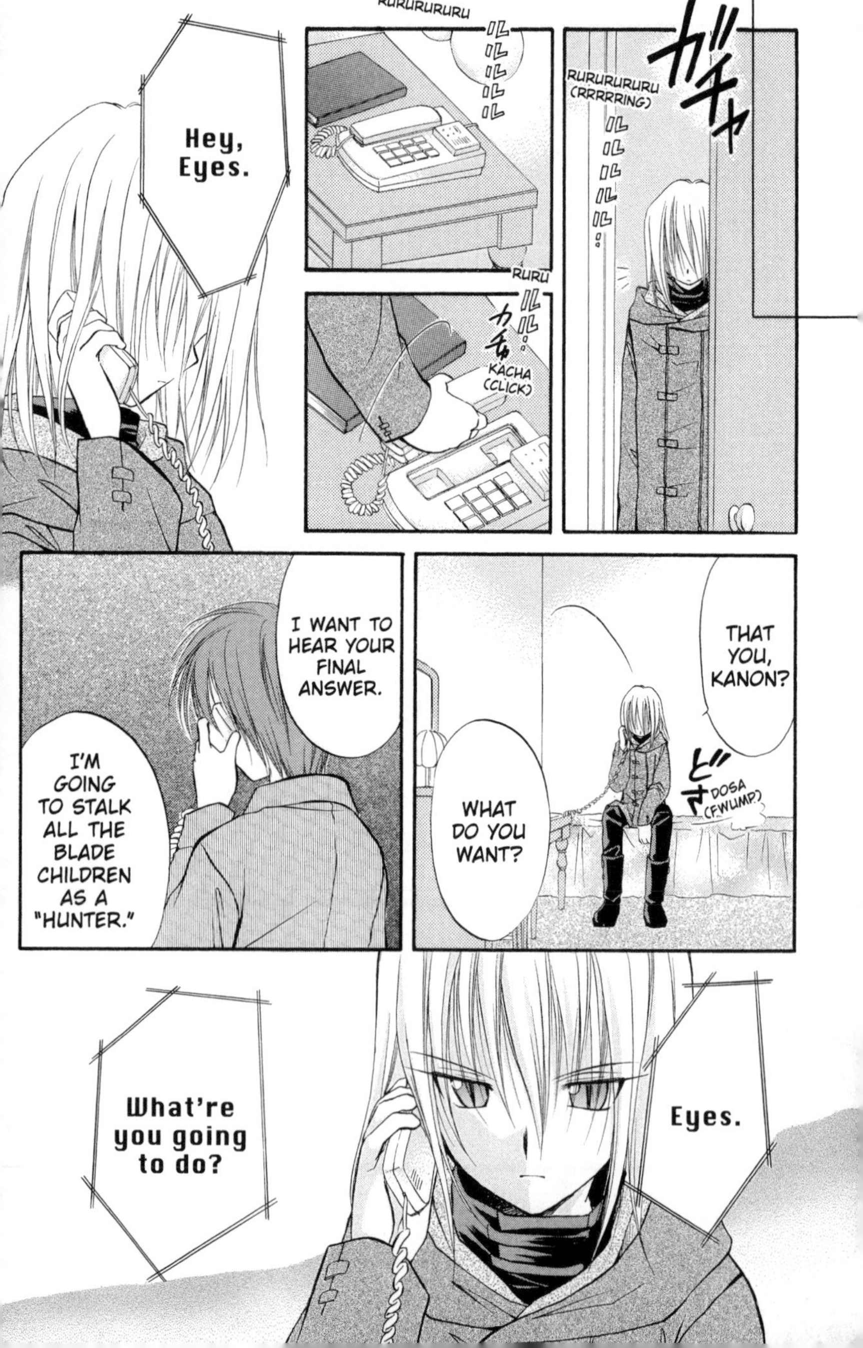
ガチャ
RURURURURU (RRRRRING)
ルルルルル!
RURURURURU
ルルルルル
RURU
ルル!
カチャ
KACHA (CLICK)
Hey, Eyes.
THAT YOU, KANON?
どさ
DOSA (FWUMP)
WHAT DO YOU WANT?
I WANT TO HEAR YOUR FINAL ANSWER.
I'M GOING TO STALK ALL THE BLADE CHILDREN AS A "HUNTER."
Eyes.
What're you going to do?

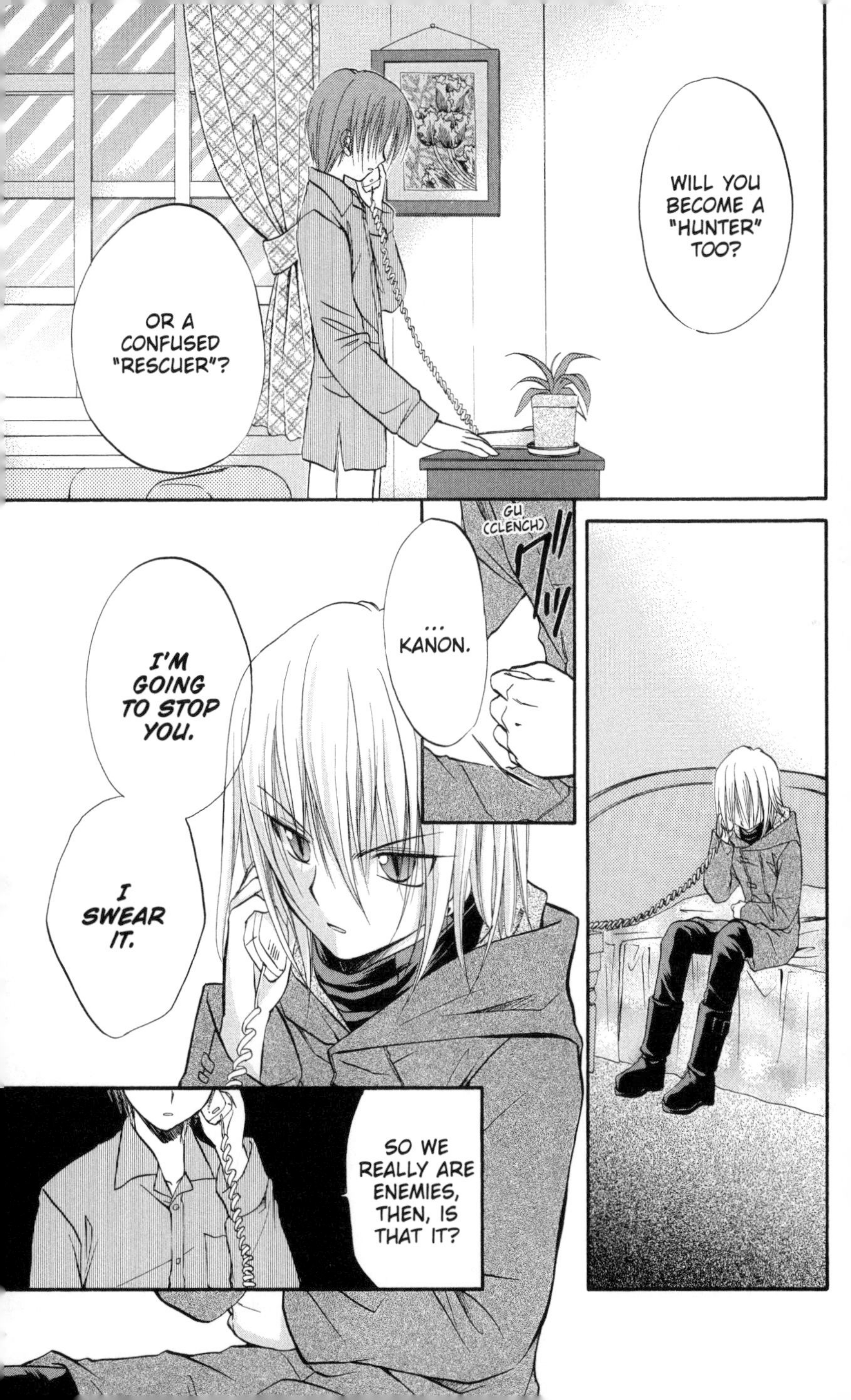
WILL YOU BECOME A "HUNTER" TOO?
OR A CONFUSED "RESCUER"?
GU (CLENCH)
... KANON.
I'M GOING TO STOP YOU.
I SWEAR IT.
SO WE REALLY ARE ENEMIES, THEN, IS THAT IT?

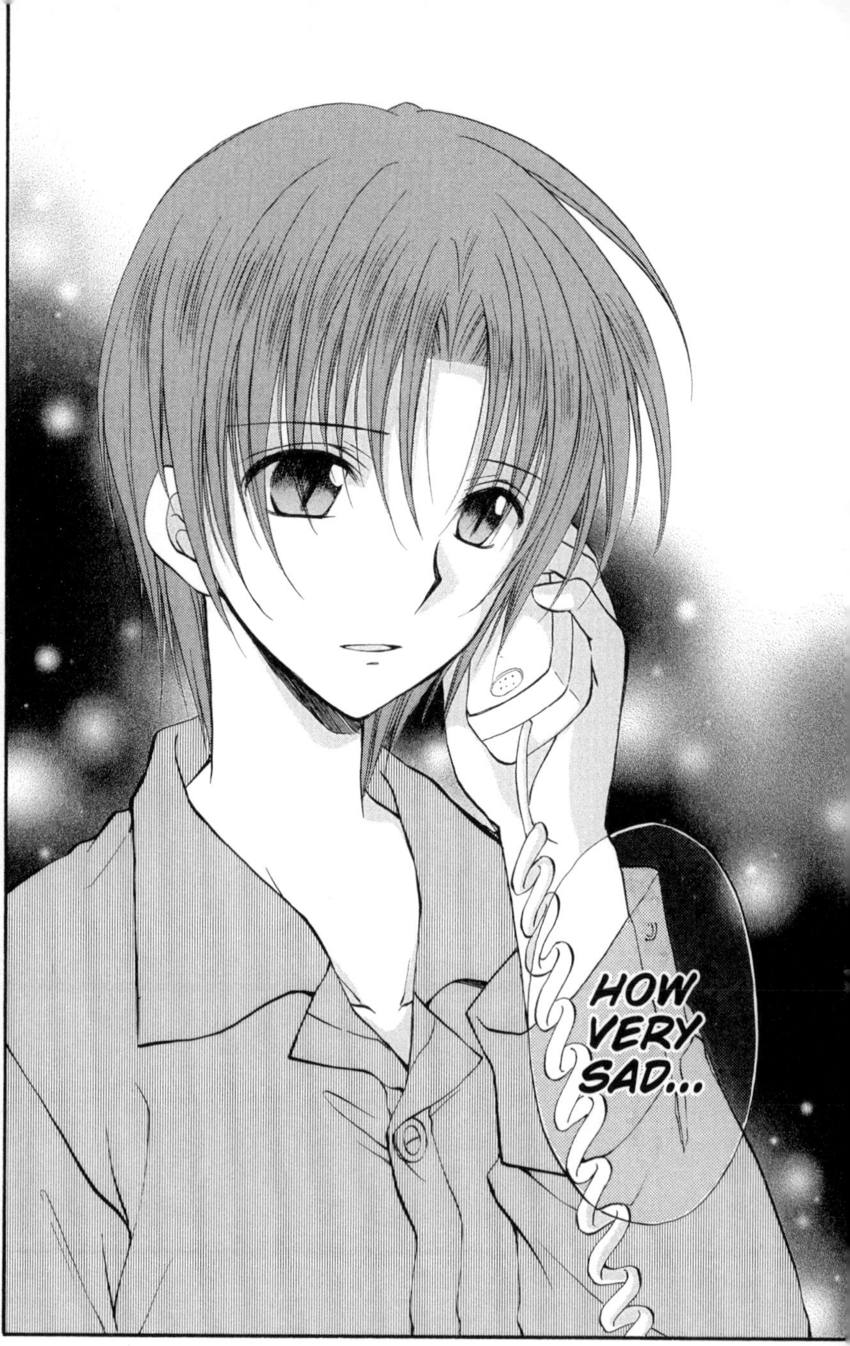
HOW VERY SAD...

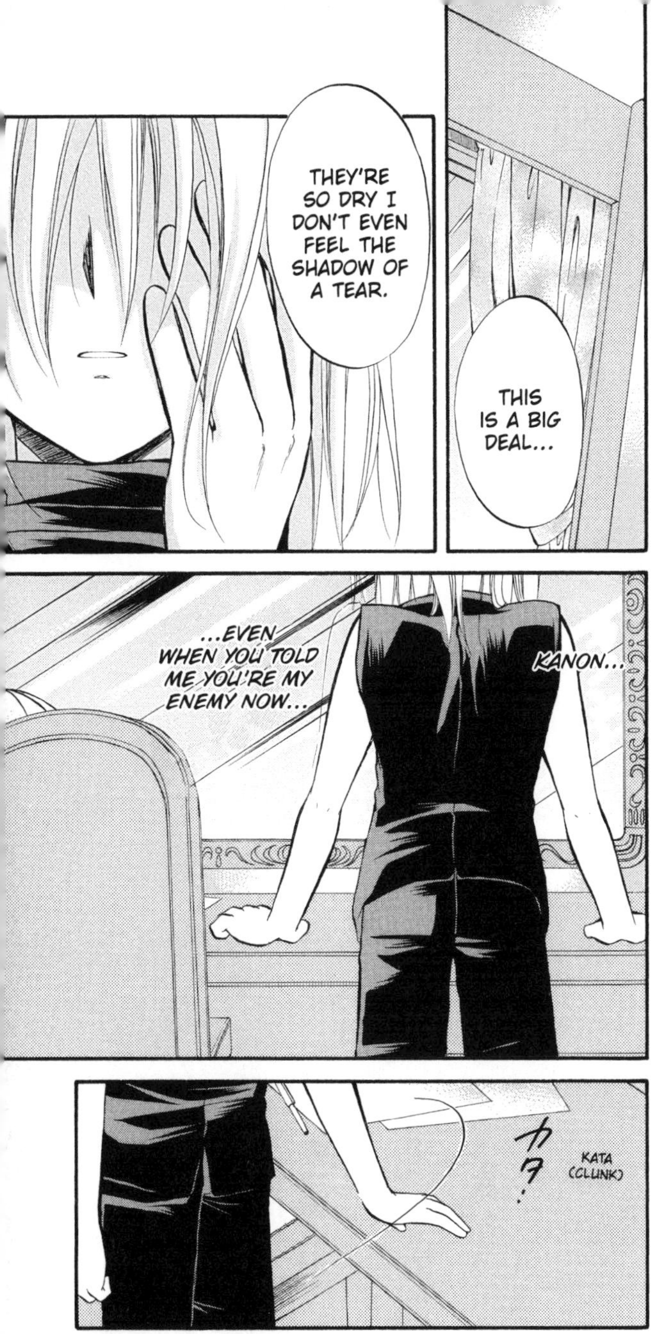
THIS IS A BIG DEAL...
THEY'RE SO DRY I DON'T EVEN FEEL THE SHADOW OF A TEAR.
KANON...
...EVEN WHEN YOU TOLD ME YOU'RE MY ENEMY NOW...
カタ
KATA (CLUNK)

WHEN DID I STOP LETTING THE TEARS FLOW?

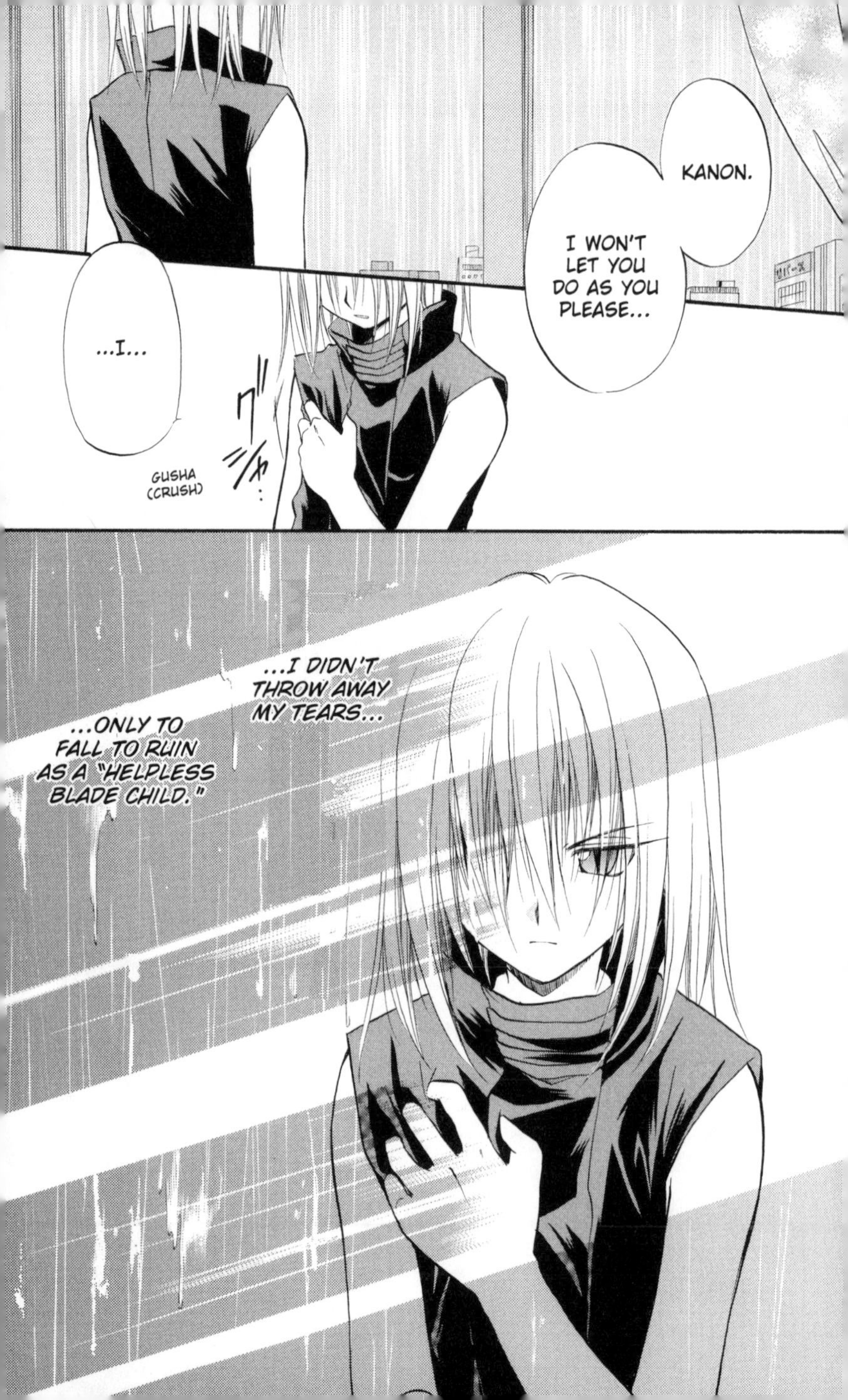
KANON.
I WON'T LET YOU DO AS YOU PLEASE...
...I...
GUSHA (CRUSH)
...I DIDN'T THROW AWAY MY TEARS...
...ONLY TO FALL TO RUIN AS A "HELPLESS BLADE CHILD."

CHAPTER TWENTY-THREE NIGHT FALLS AGAIN

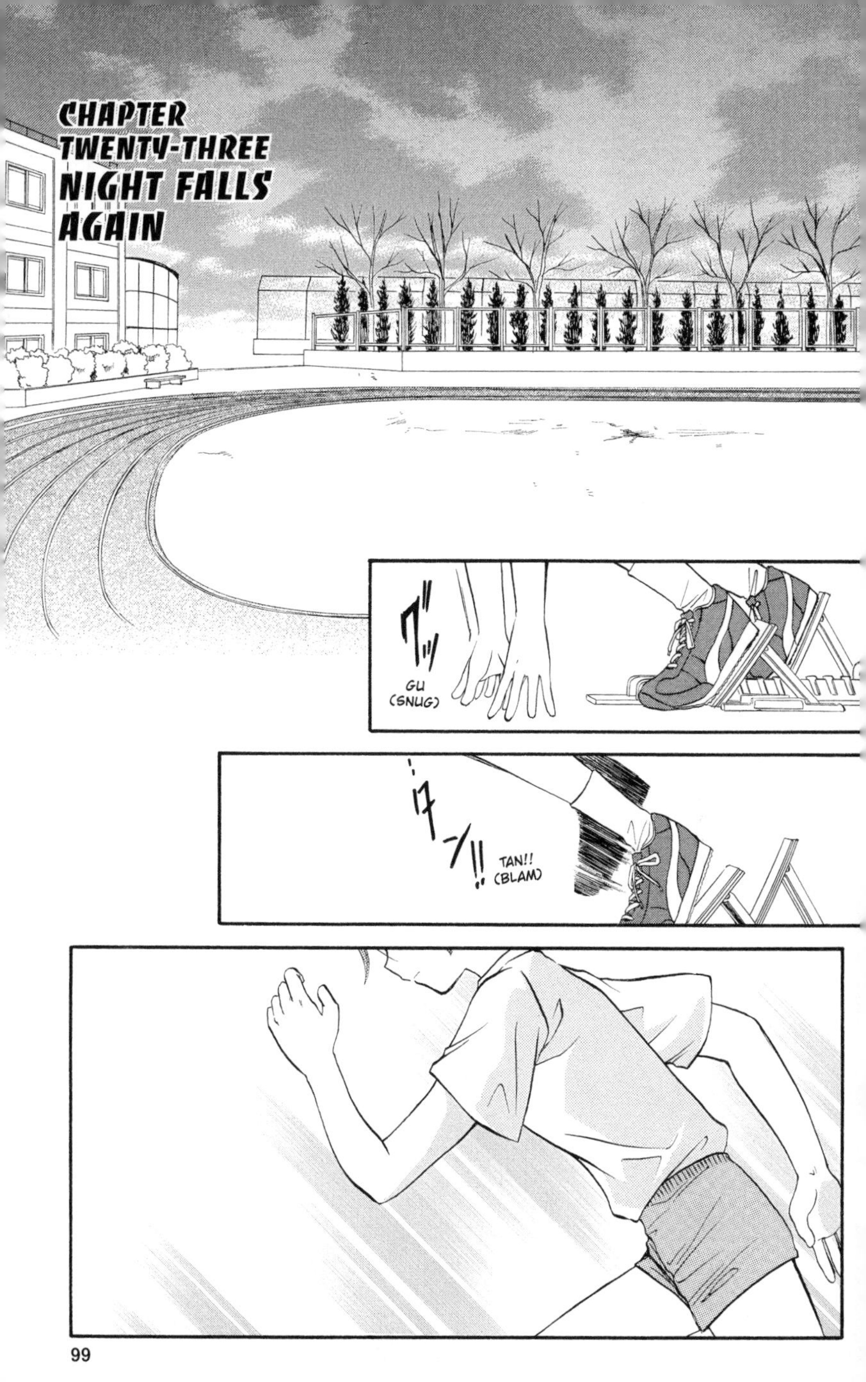
グッ
GU (SNUG)
ターン!!
TAN!! (BLAM)

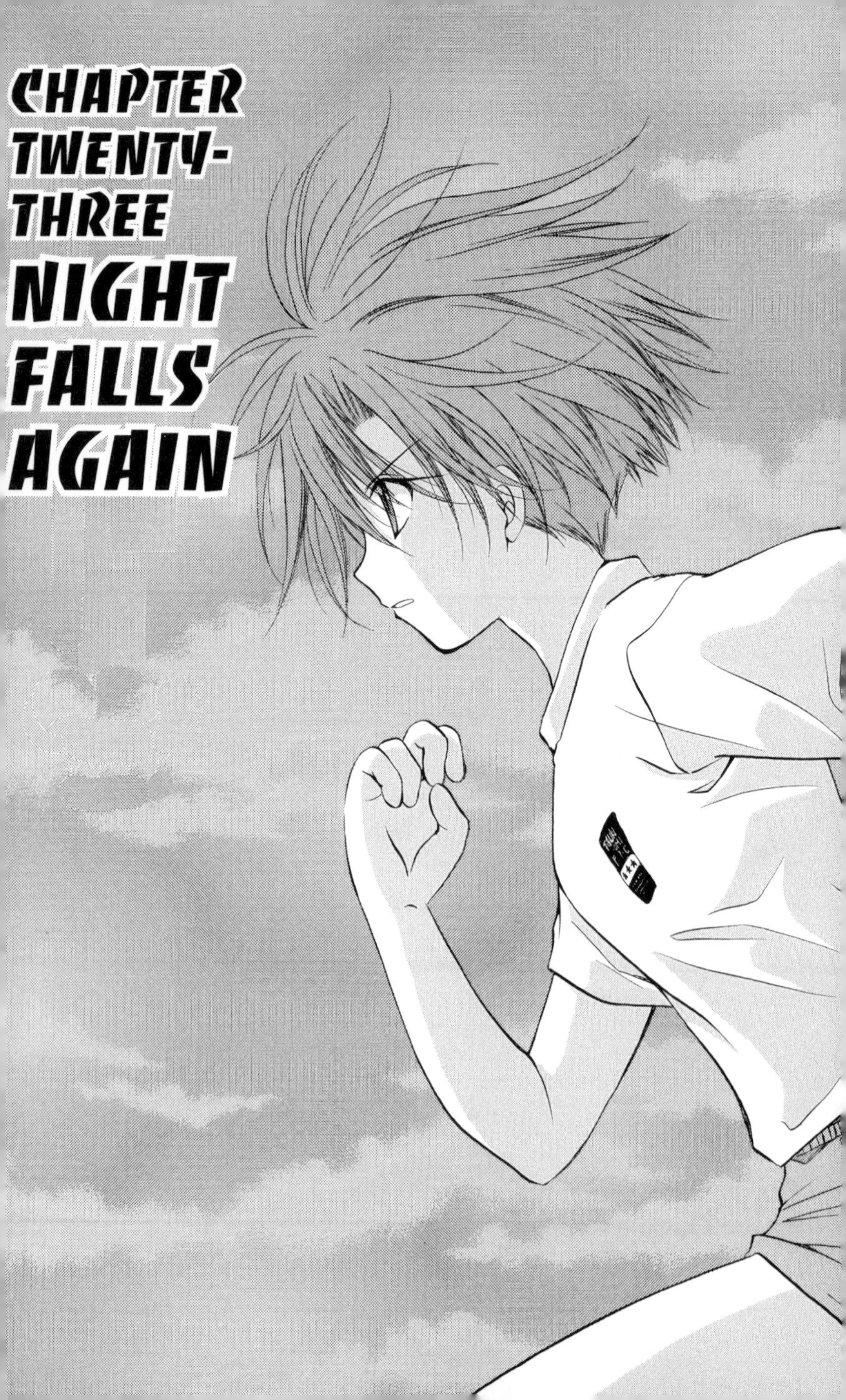
CHAPTER TWENTY-THREE
NIGHT FALLS AGAIN

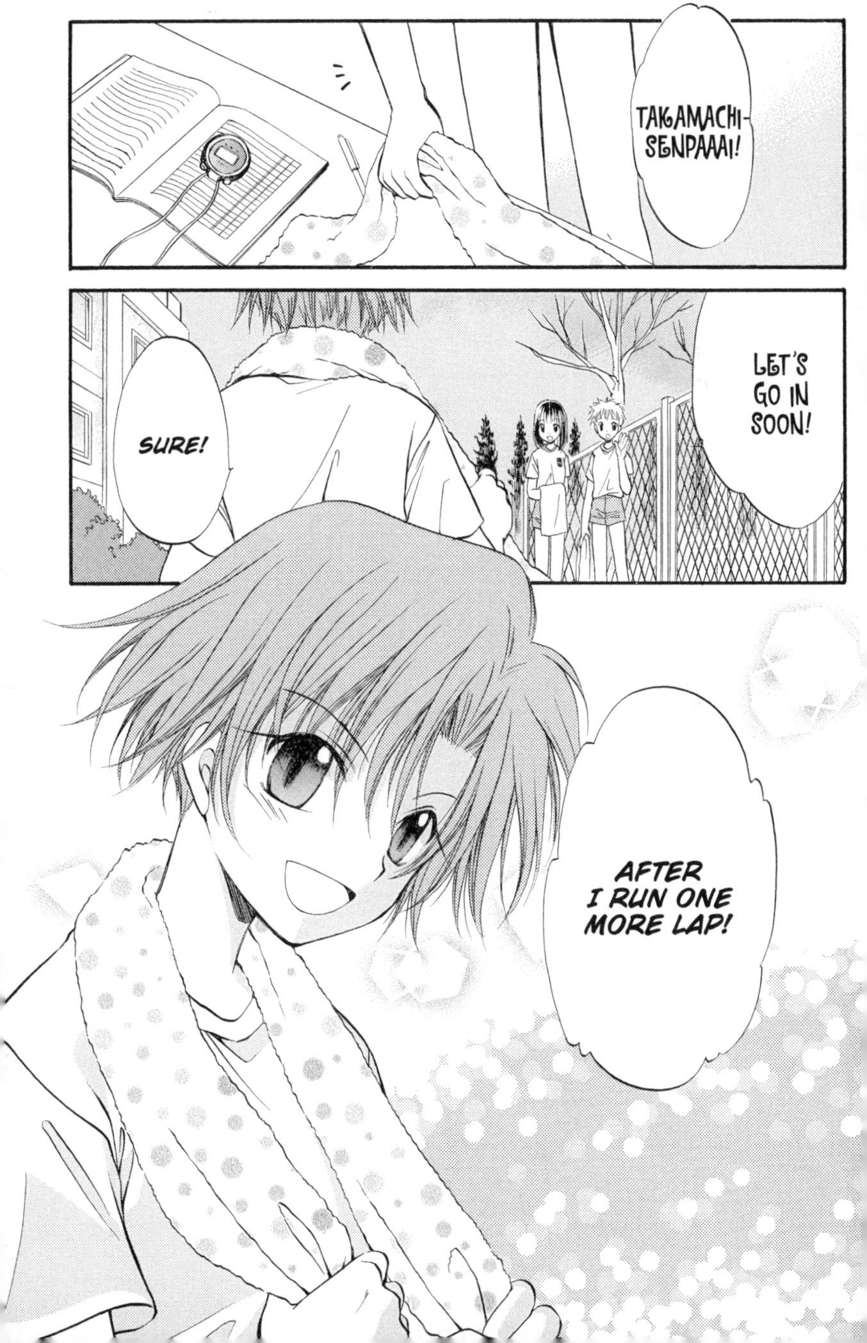
TAKAMACHI-SENPAAAI!
LET'S GO IN SOON!
SURE!
AFTER I RUN ONE MORE LAP!

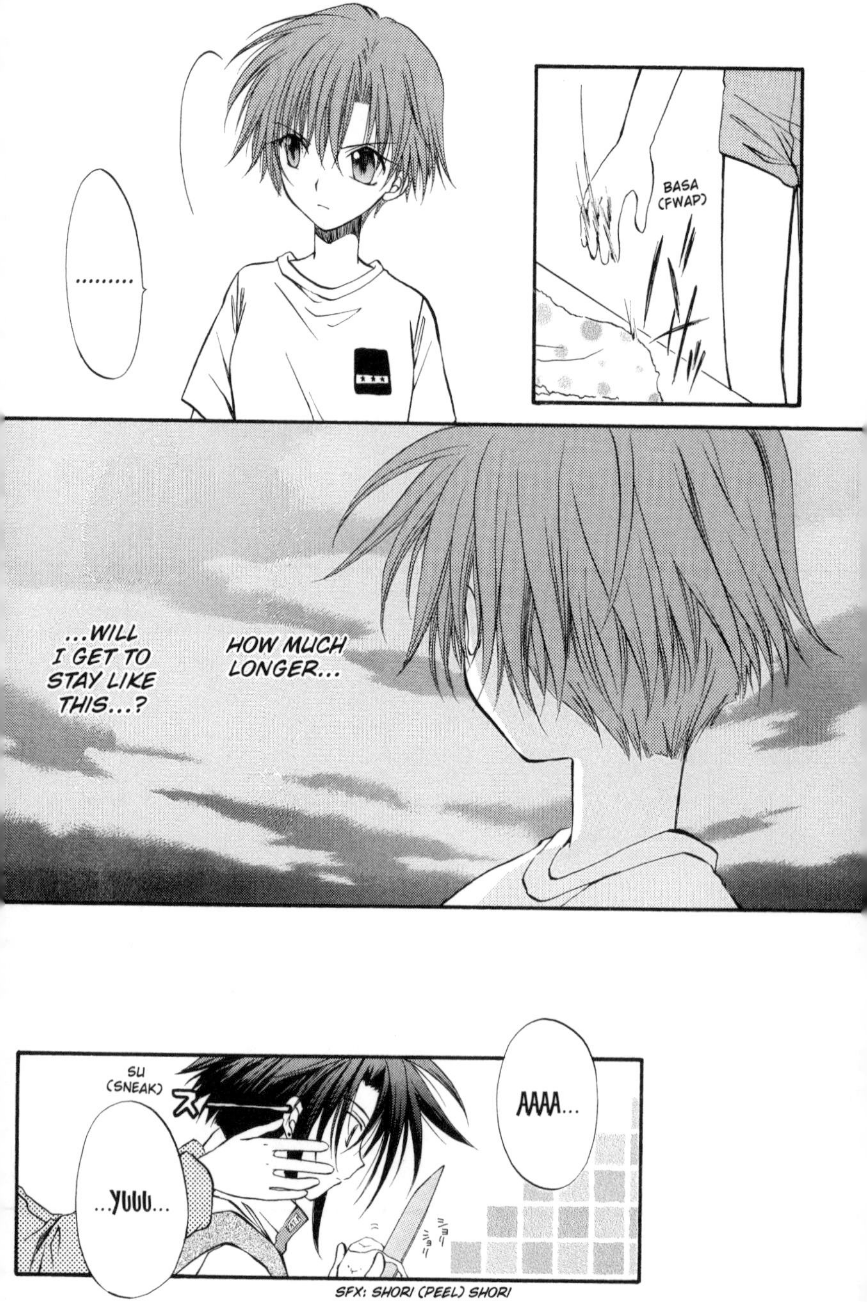
BASA (FWAP)
....
HOW MUCH LONGER...
...WILL I GET TO STAY LIKE THIS...?
AAAA...
SU (SNEAK)
...YUUU...
SFX: SHORI (PEEL) SHORI

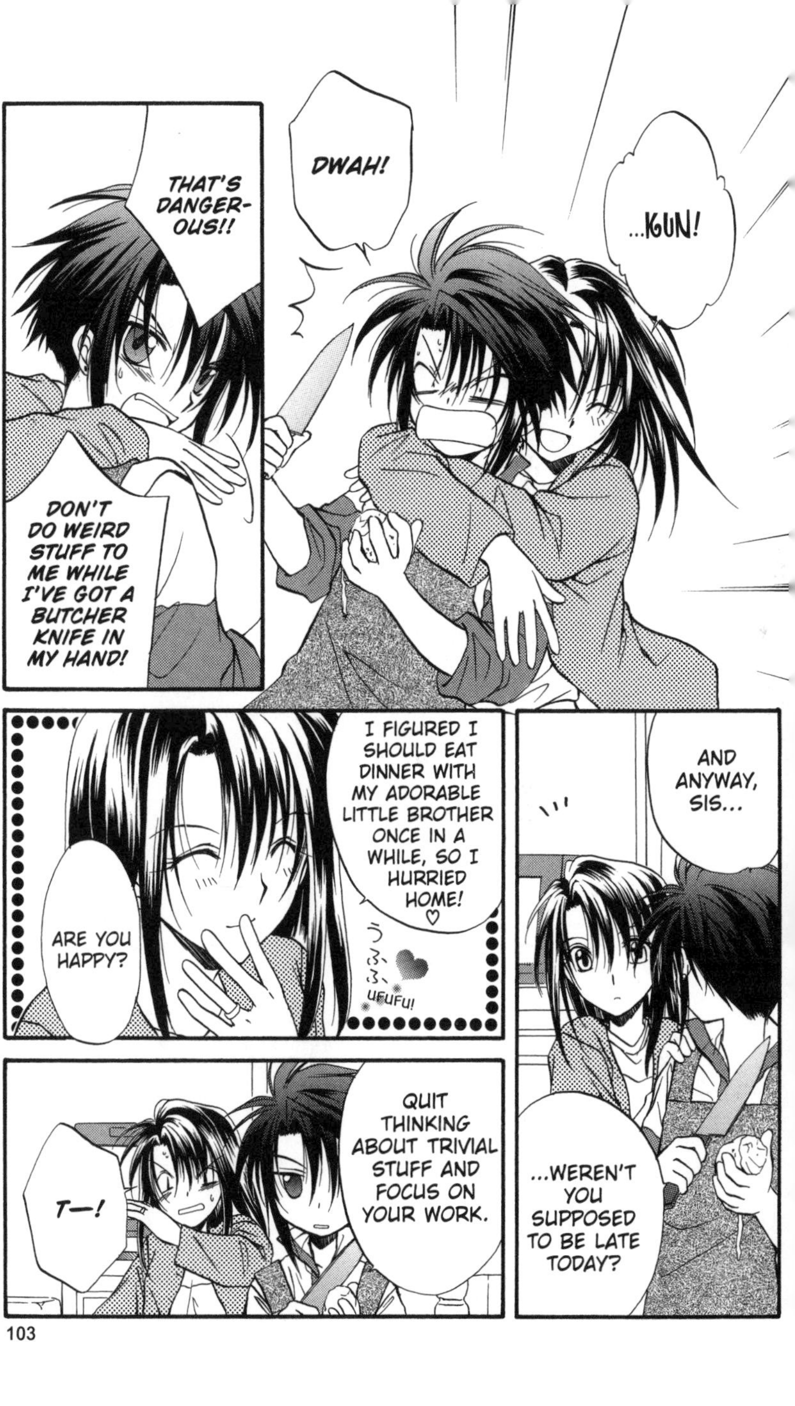
...KUN!
DWAH!
THAT'S DANGER-OUS!!
DON'T DO WEIRD STUFF TO ME WHILE I'VE GOT A BUTCHER KNIFE IN MY HAND!
AND ANYWAY, SIS...
...WEREN'T YOU SUPPOSED TO BE LATE TODAY?
I FIGURED I SHOULD EAT DINNER WITH MY ADORABLE LITTLE BROTHER ONCE IN A WHILE, SO I HURRIED HOME! ♡
うふふ
UFUFU!
ARE YOU HAPPY?
QUIT THINKING ABOUT TRIVIAL STUFF AND FOCUS ON YOUR WORK.
T—!

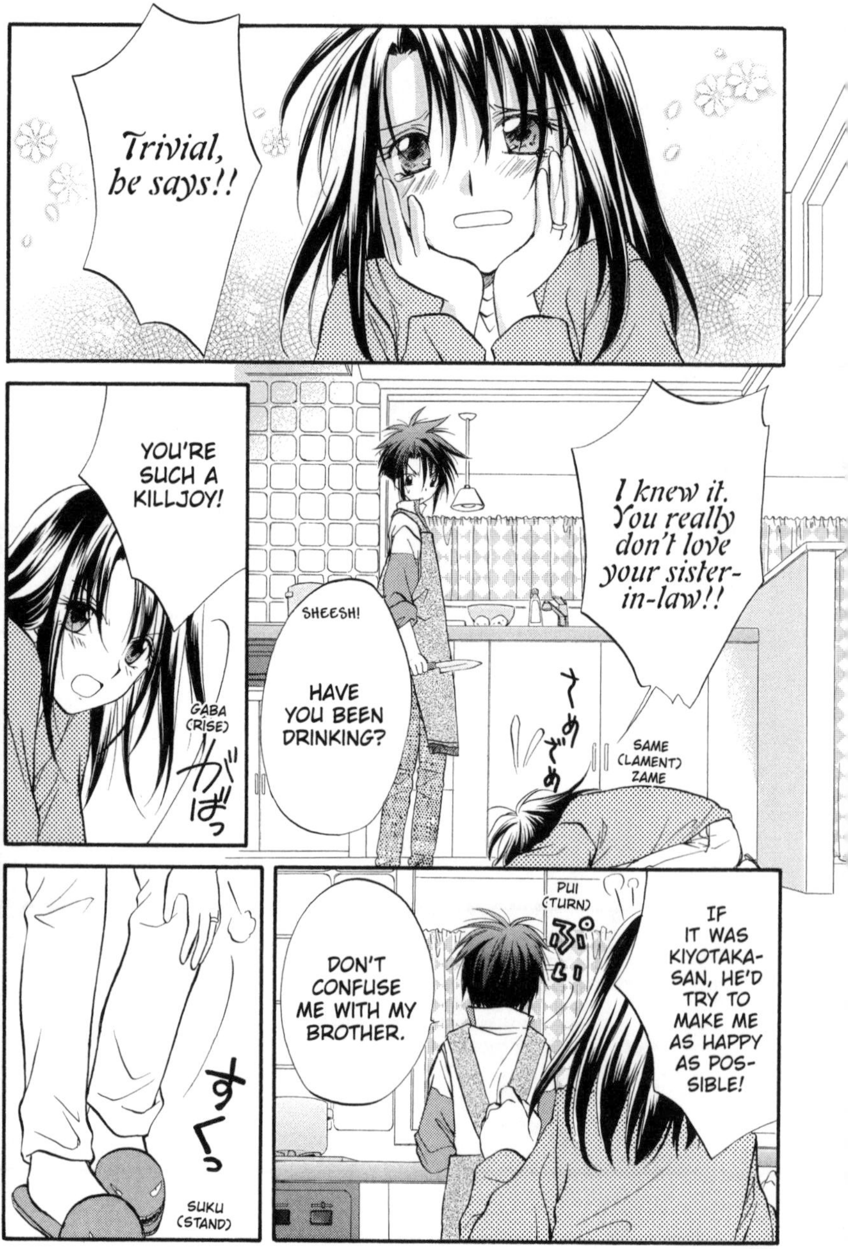
Trivial, he says!!
I knew it. You really don't love your sister-in-law!!
さめざめ
SAME (LAMENT) ZAME
SHEESH!
HAVE YOU BEEN DRINKING?
YOU'RE SUCH A KILLJOY!
GABA (RISE)
がばっ
IF IT WAS KIYOTAKA-SAN, HE'D TRY TO MAKE ME AS HAPPY AS POS-SIBLE!
PUI (TURN)
ぷい
DON'T CONFUSE ME WITH MY BROTHER.
すくっ
SUKU (STAND)

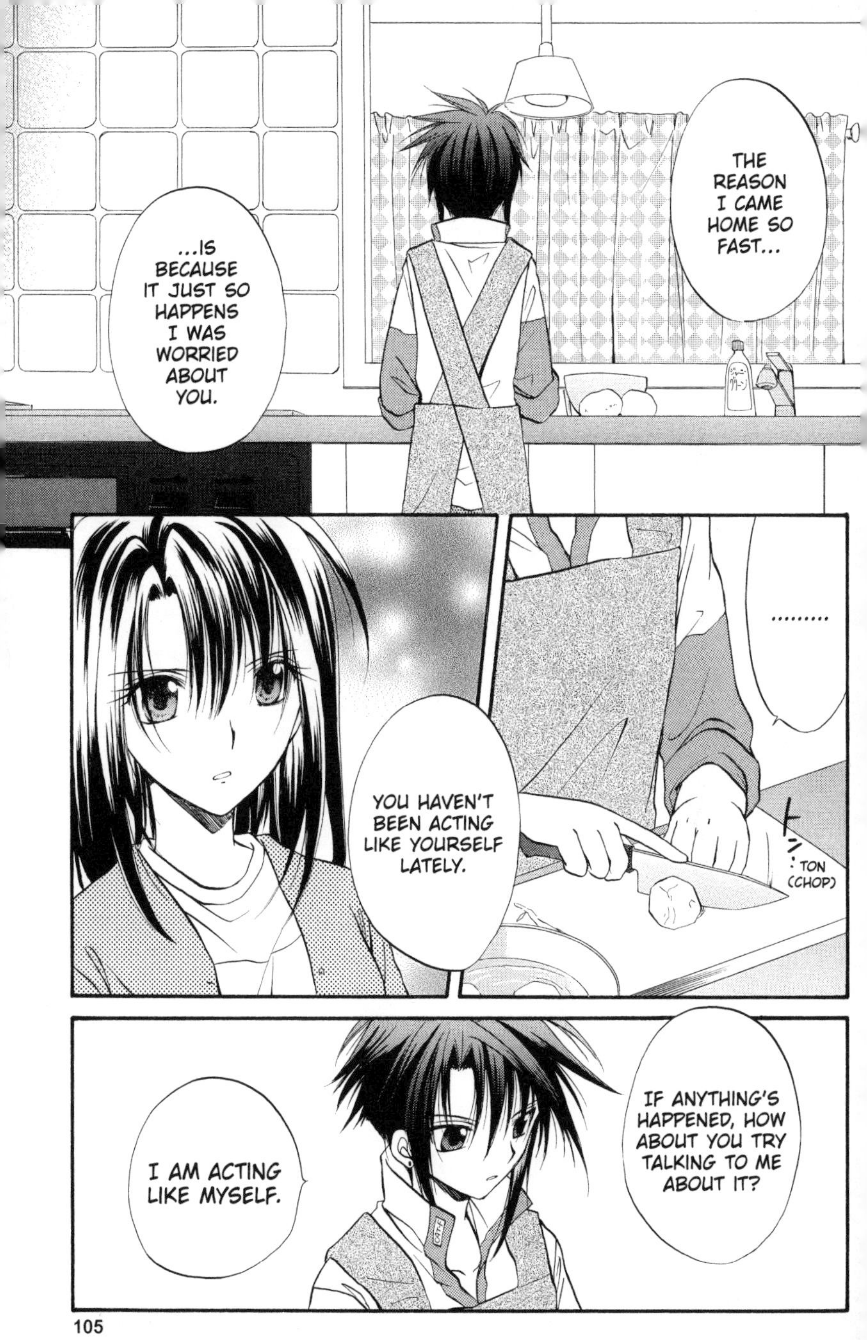
THE REASON I CAME HOME SO FAST...
...IS BECAUSE IT JUST SO HAPPENS I WAS WORRIED ABOUT YOU.
....
TON (CHOP)
YOU HAVEN'T BEEN ACTING LIKE YOURSELF LATELY.
IF ANYTHING'S HAPPENED, HOW ABOUT YOU TRY TALKING TO ME ABOUT IT?
I AM ACTING LIKE MYSELF.

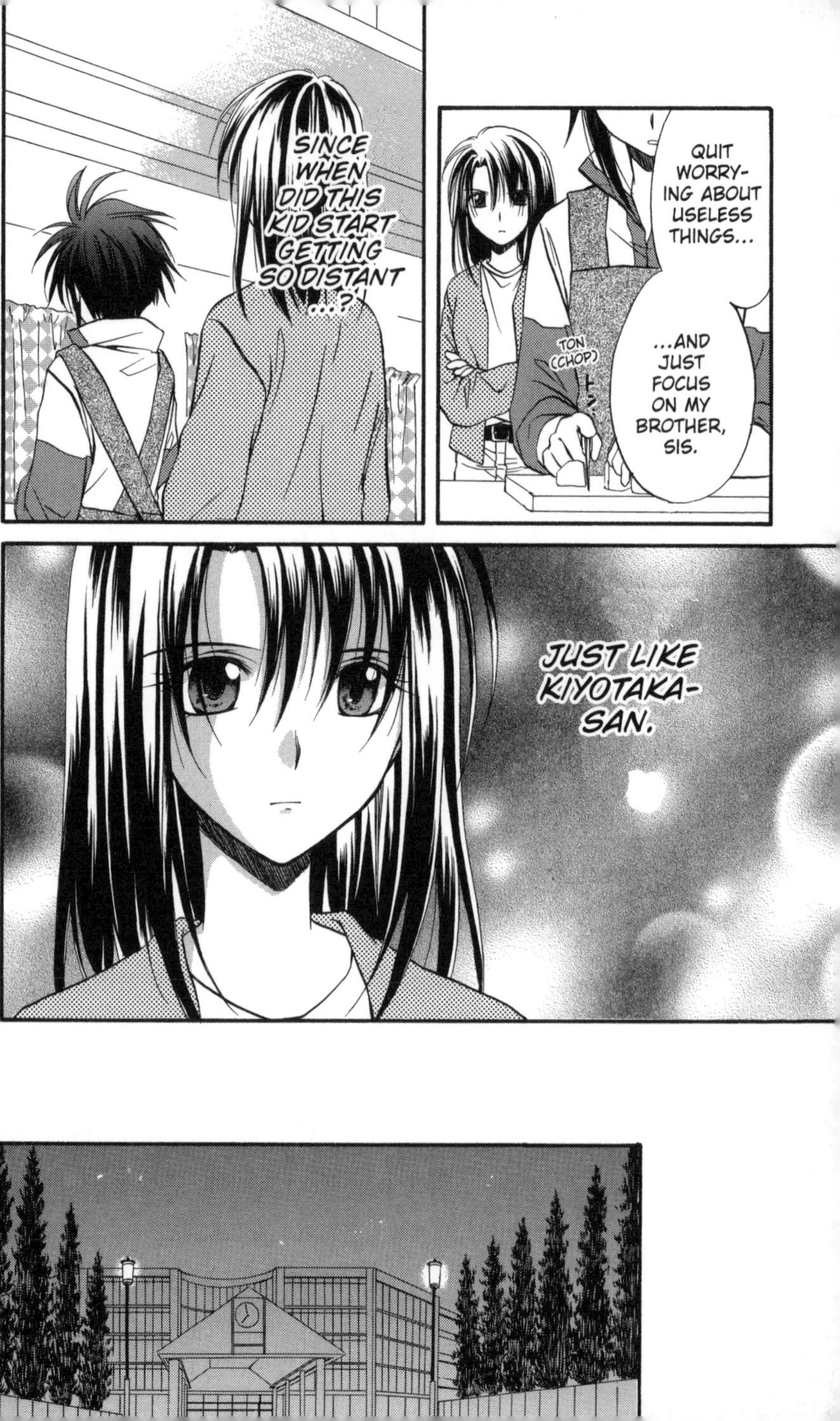
QUIT WORRYING ABOUT USELESS THINGS...
TON (CHOP)
...AND JUST FOCUS ON MY BROTHER, SIS.
SINCE WHEN DID THIS KID START GETTING SO DISTANT...?
JUST LIKE KIYOTAKA-SAN.

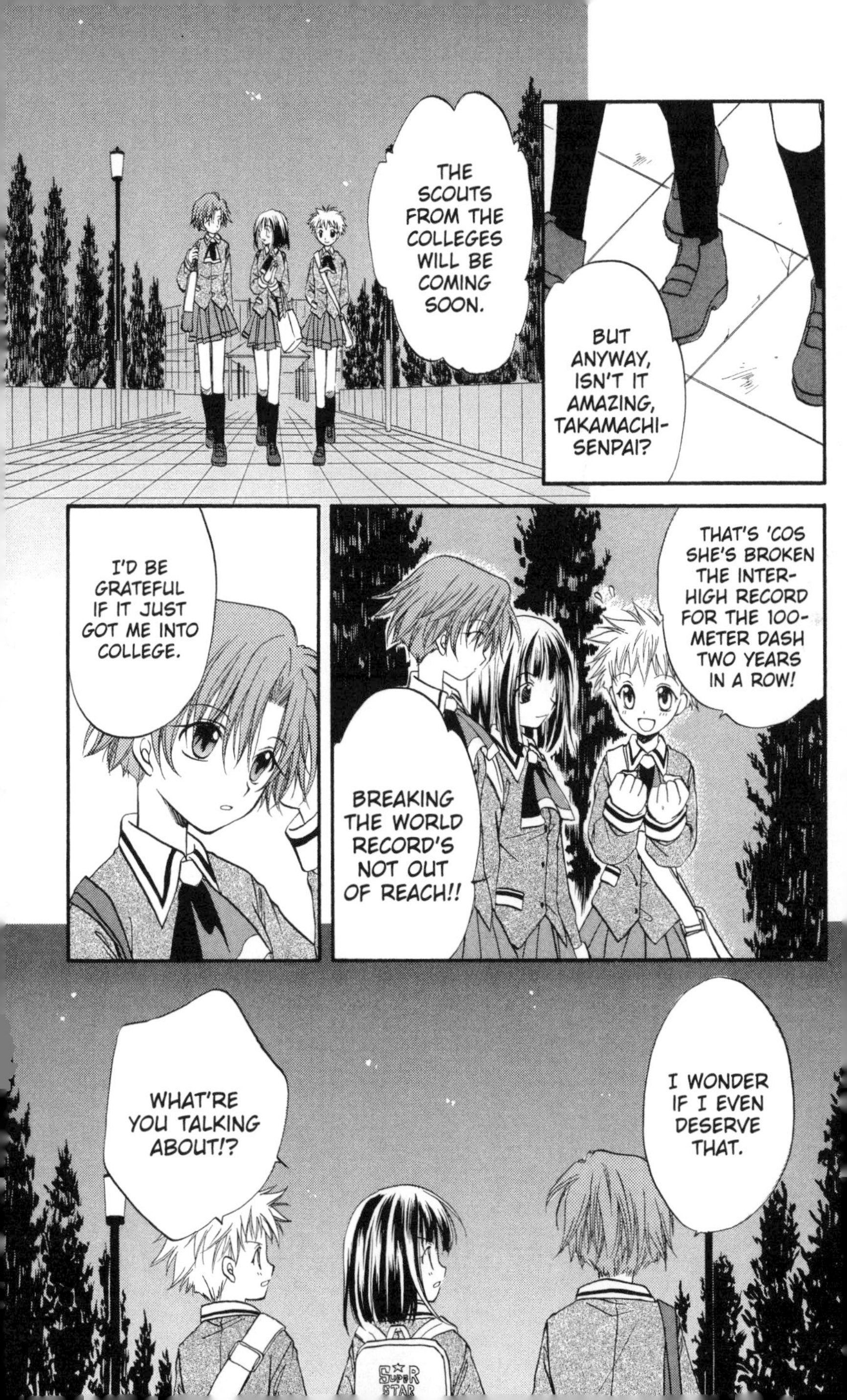
THE SCOUTS FROM THE COLLEGES WILL BE COMING SOON.
BUT ANYWAY, ISN'T IT AMAZING, TAKAMACHI-SENPAI?
THAT'S 'COS SHE'S BROKEN THE INTER-HIGH RECORD FOR THE 100-METER DASH TWO YEARS IN A ROW!
BREAKING THE WORLD RECORD'S NOT OUT OF REACH!!
I'D BE GRATEFUL IF IT JUST GOT ME INTO COLLEGE.
I WONDER IF I EVEN DESERVE THAT.
WHAT'RE YOU TALKING ABOUT!?
SUPER STAR

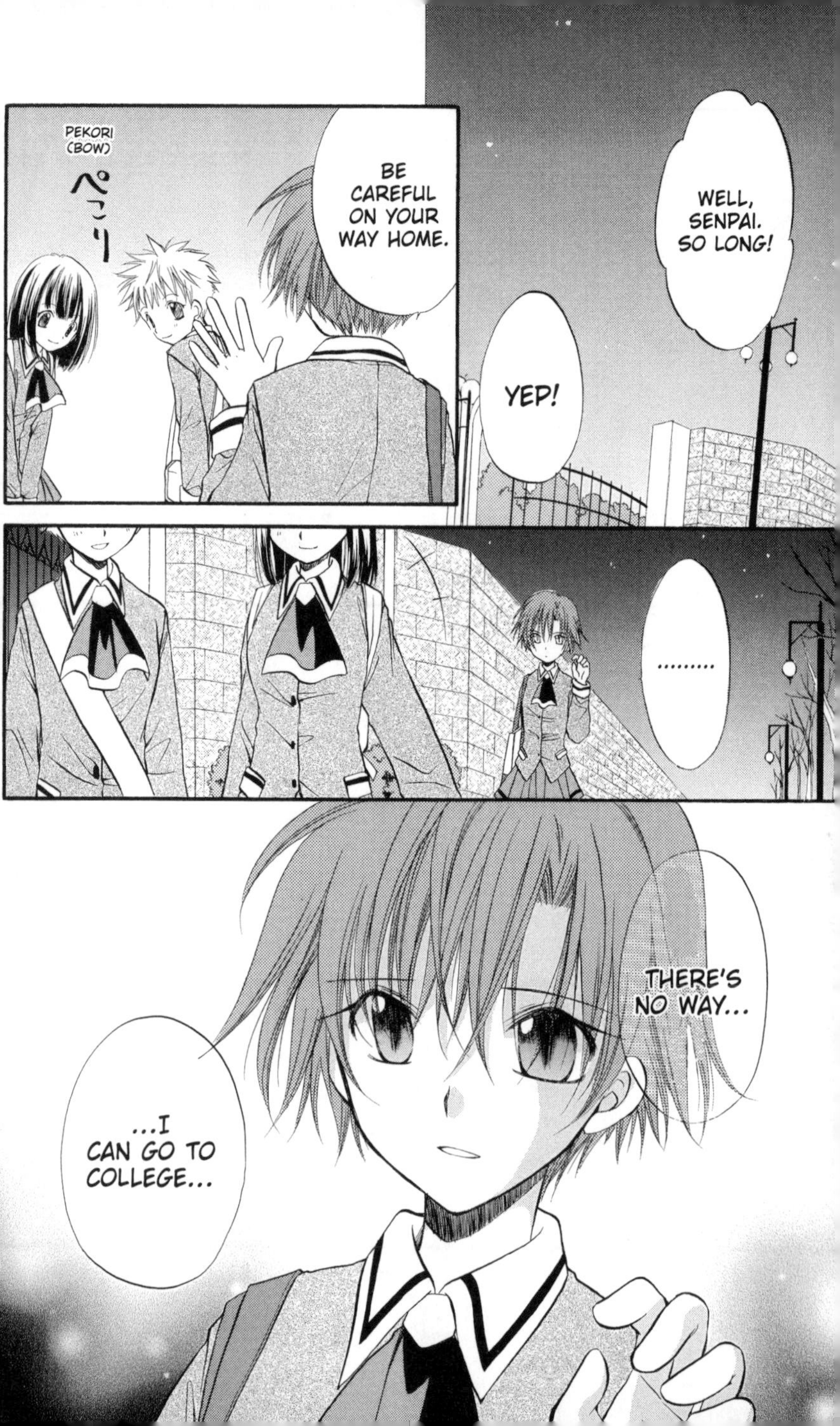

WELL, SENPAI. SO LONG!
YEP!
BE CAREFUL ON YOUR WAY HOME.
PEKORI (BOW)
ぺこり
....
THERE'S NO WAY...
...I CAN GO TO COLLEGE...

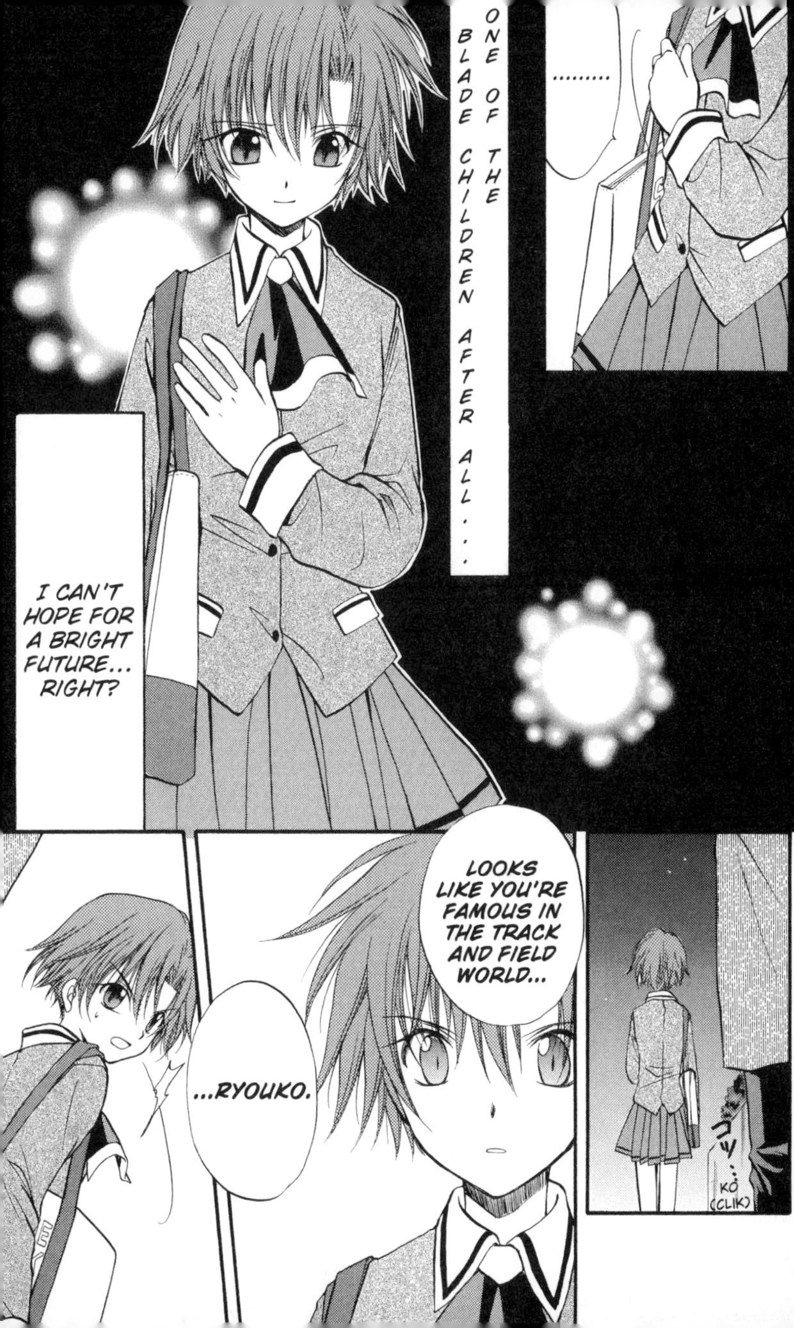
....
ONE OF THE BLADE CHILDREN AFTER ALL...
I CAN'T HOPE FOR A BRIGHT FUTURE... RIGHT?
KO (CLIK)
LOOKS LIKE YOU'RE FAMOUS IN THE TRACK AND FIELD WORLD...
...RYOUKO.

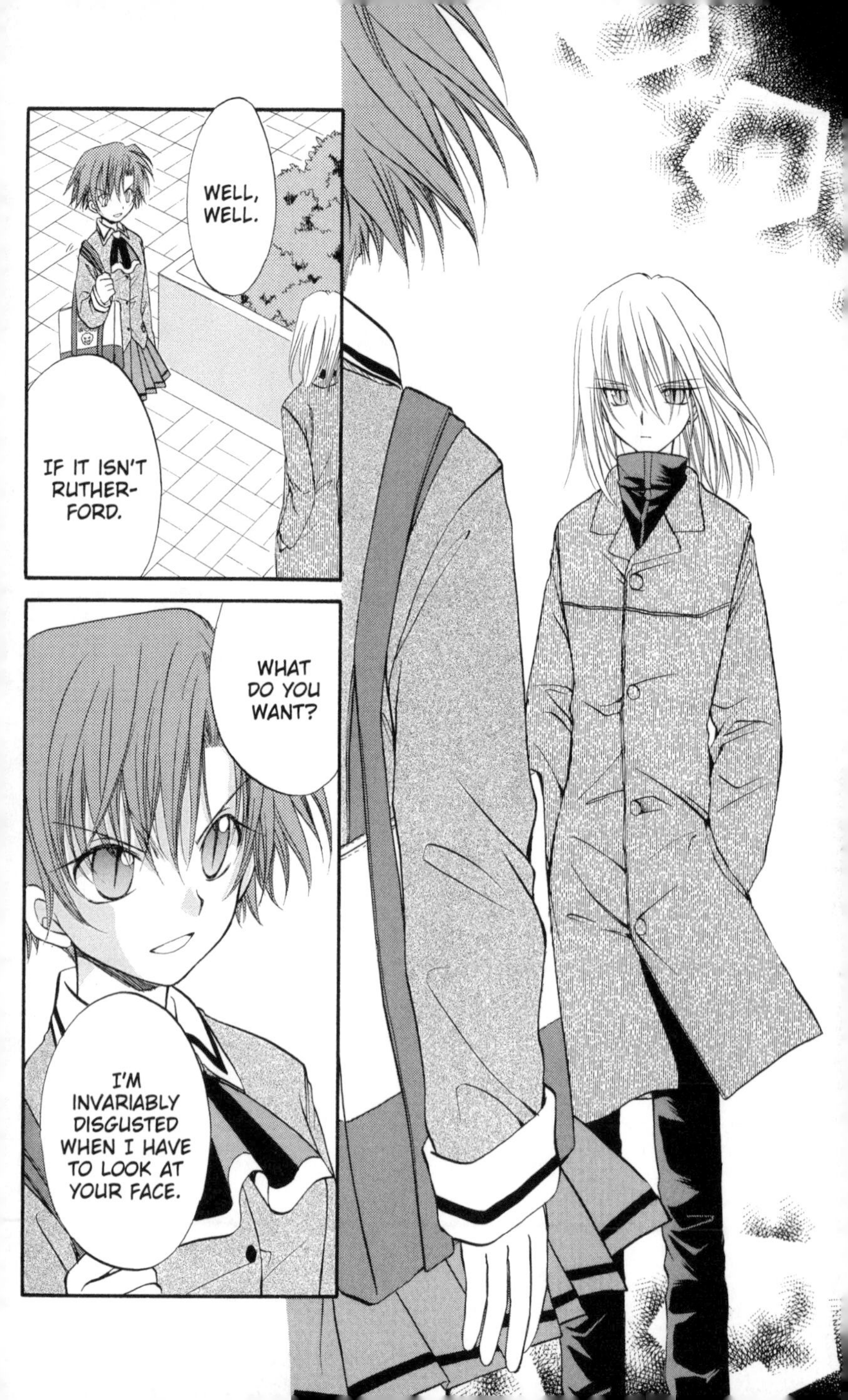
WELL, WELL.
IF IT ISN'T RUTHER-FORD.
WHAT DO YOU WANT?
I'M INVARIABLY DISGUSTED WHEN I HAVE TO LOOK AT YOUR FACE.

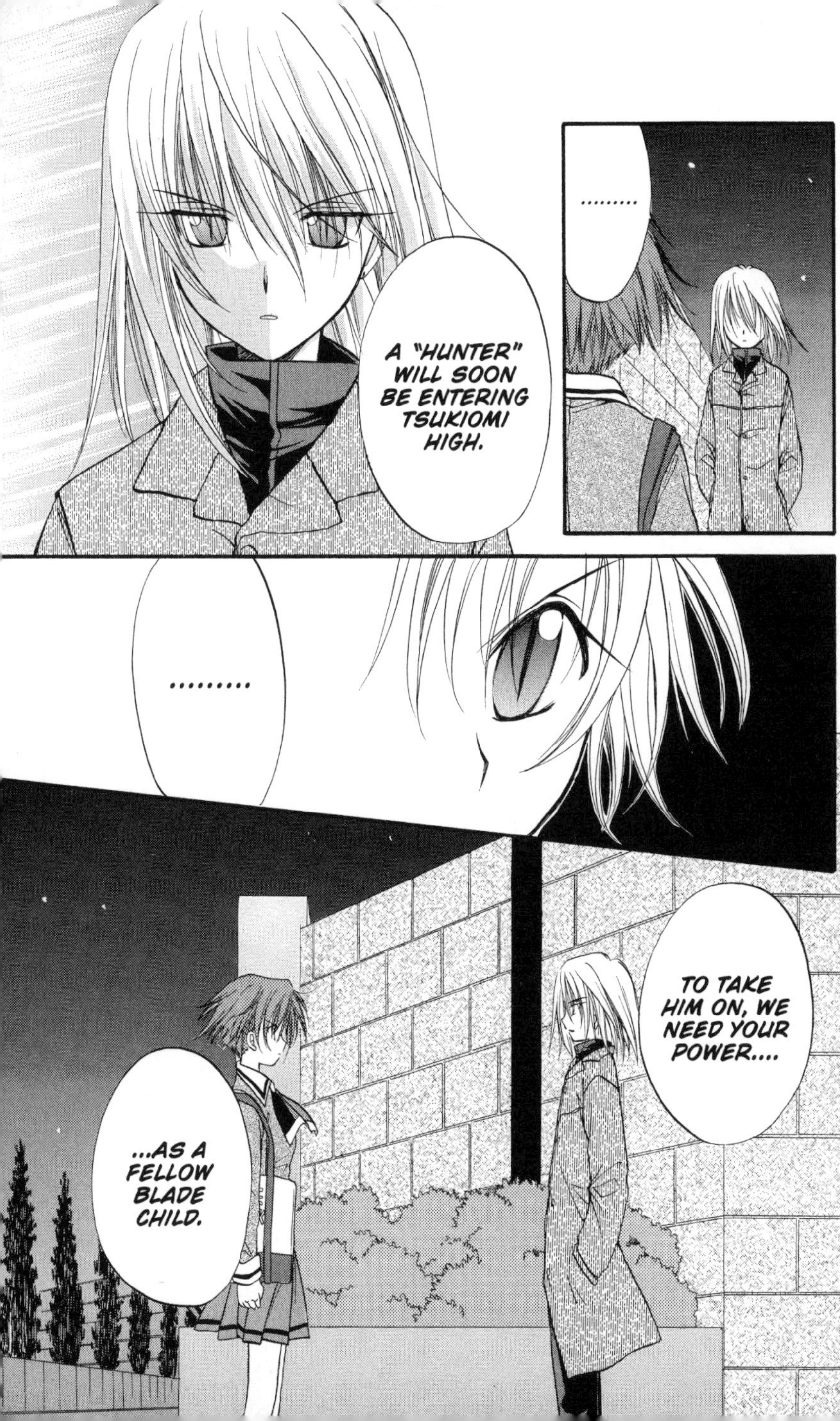
....
A "HUNTER" WILL SOON BE ENTERING TSUKIOMI HIGH.
....
TO TAKE HIM ON, WE NEED YOUR POWER....
...AS A FELLOW BLADE CHILD.

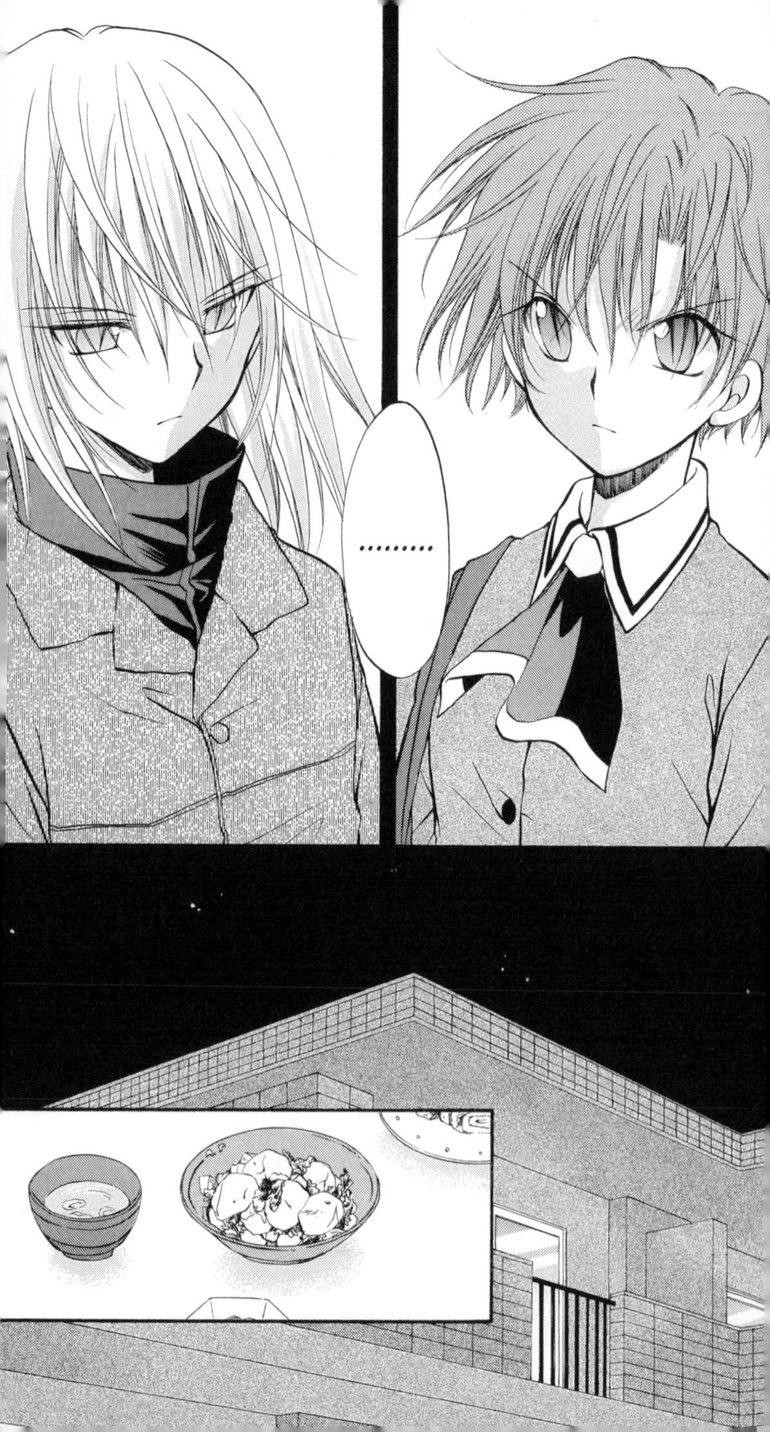
....

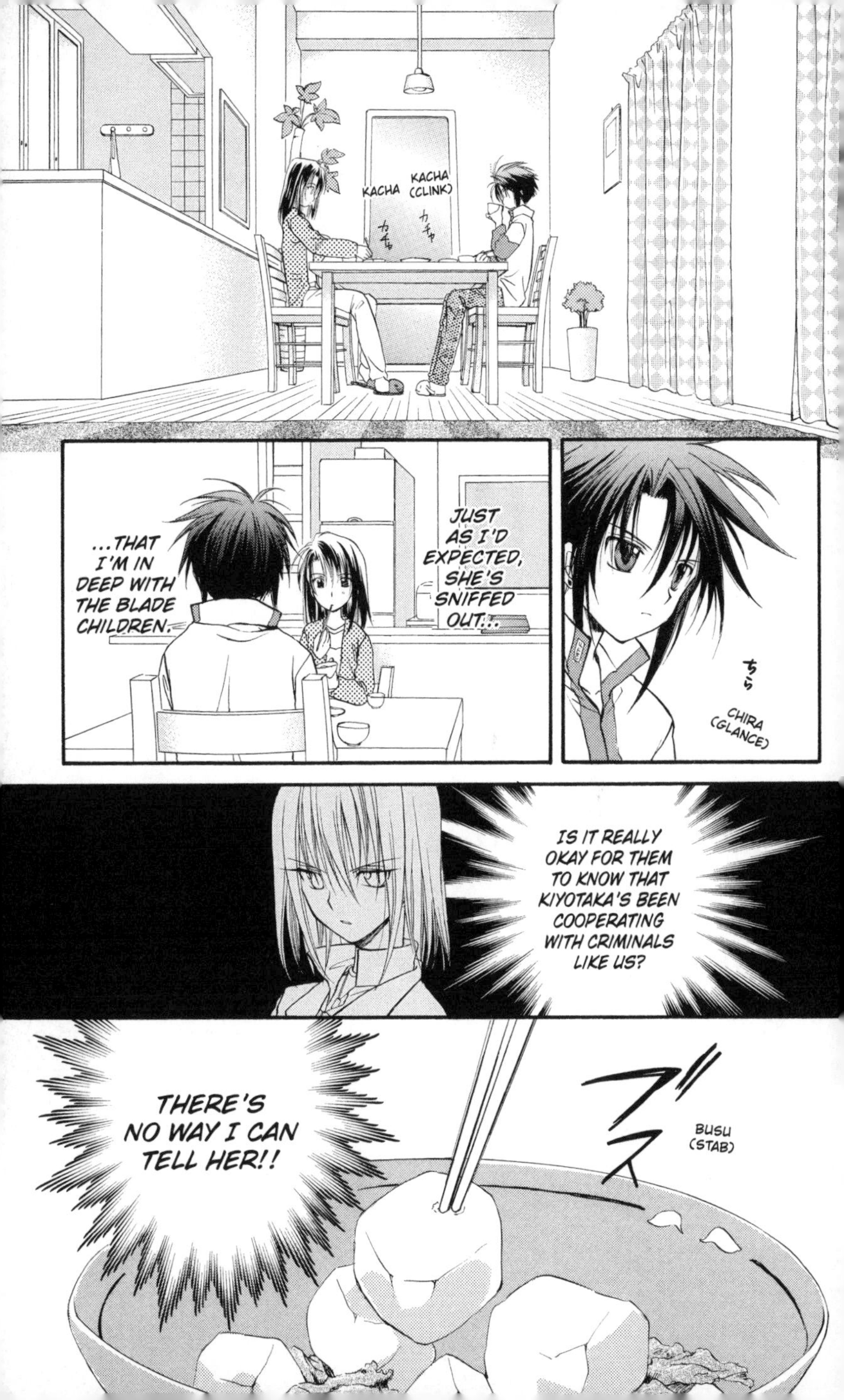
KACHA
KACHA (CLINK)
カチャ
カチャ
ちら
CHIRA (GLANCE)
JUST AS I'D EXPECTED, SHE'S SNIFFED OUT...
...THAT I'M IN DEEP WITH THE BLADE CHILDREN.
IS IT REALLY OKAY FOR THEM TO KNOW THAT KIYOTAKA'S BEEN COOPERATING WITH CRIMINALS LIKE US?
ブス
BUSU (STAB)
THERE'S NO WAY I CAN TELL HER!!

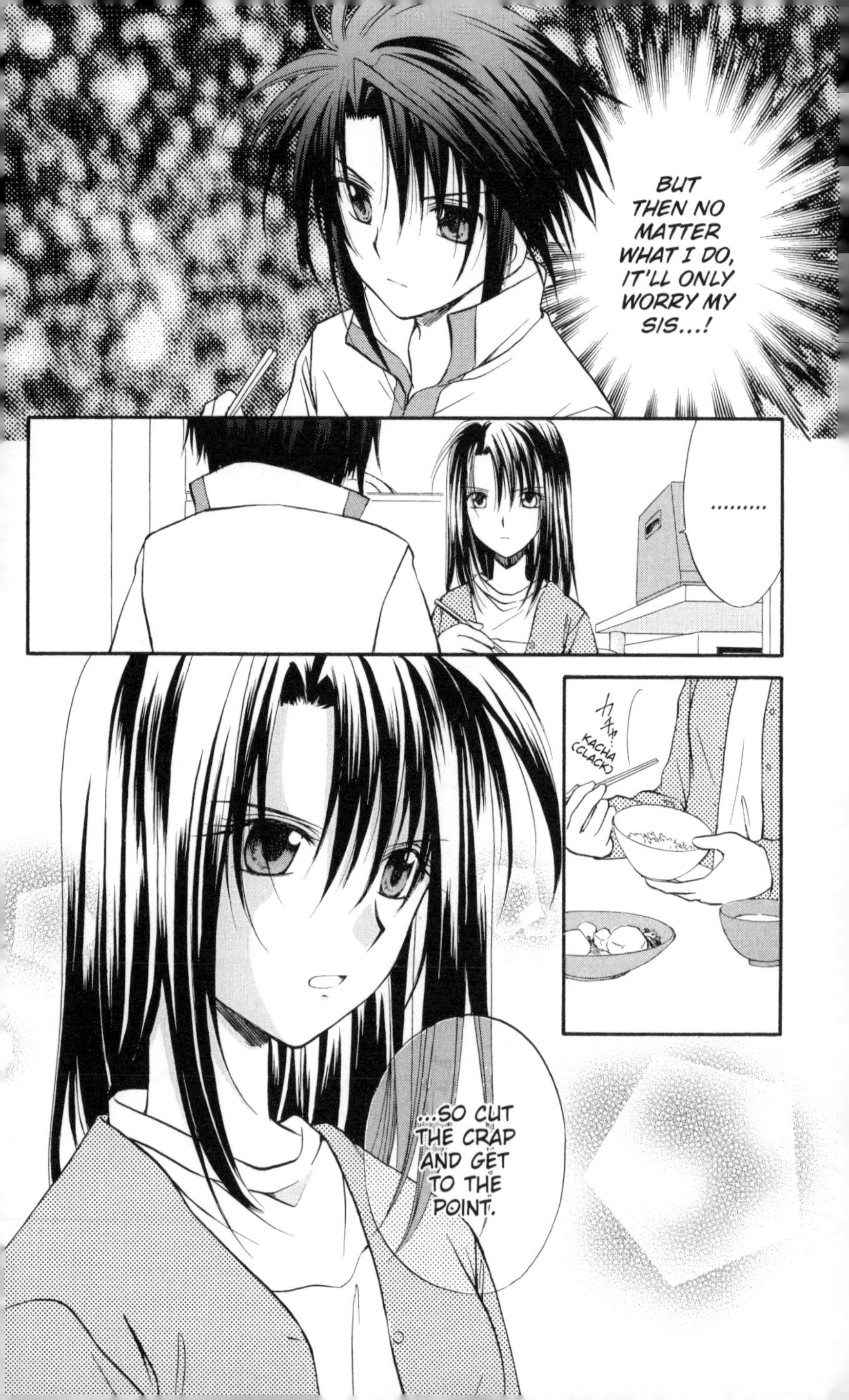
BUT THEN NO MATTER WHAT I DO, IT'LL ONLY WORRY MY SIS...!
....
カチャ...
KACHA (CLACK)
...SO CUT THE CRAP AND GET TO THE POINT.

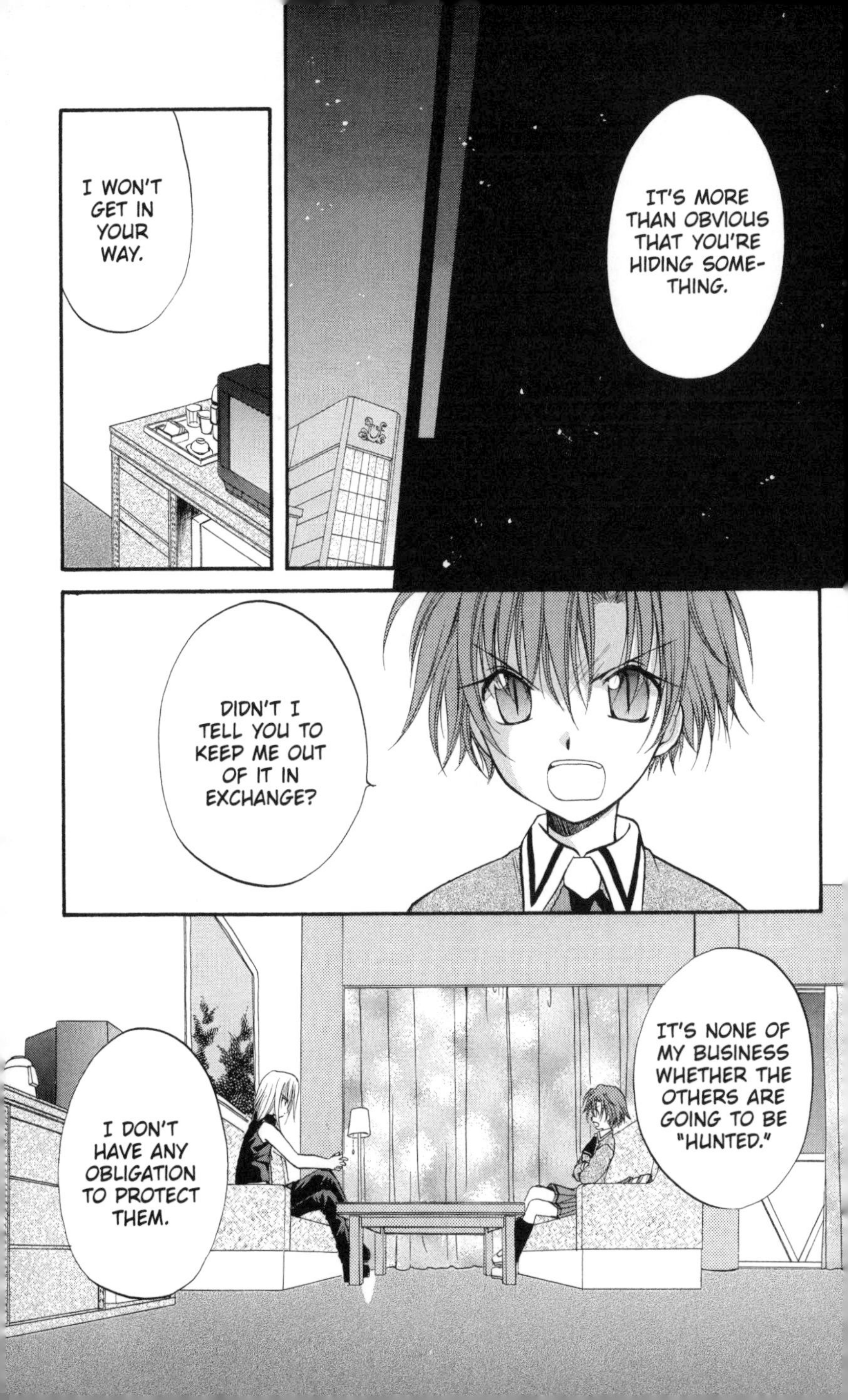
IT'S MORE THAN OBVIOUS THAT YOU'RE HIDING SOME-THING.
I WON'T GET IN YOUR WAY.
DIDN'T I TELL YOU TO KEEP ME OUT OF IT IN EXCHANGE?
IT'S NONE OF MY BUSINESS WHETHER THE OTHERS ARE GOING TO BE "HUNTED."
I DON'T HAVE ANY OBLIGATION TO PROTECT THEM.

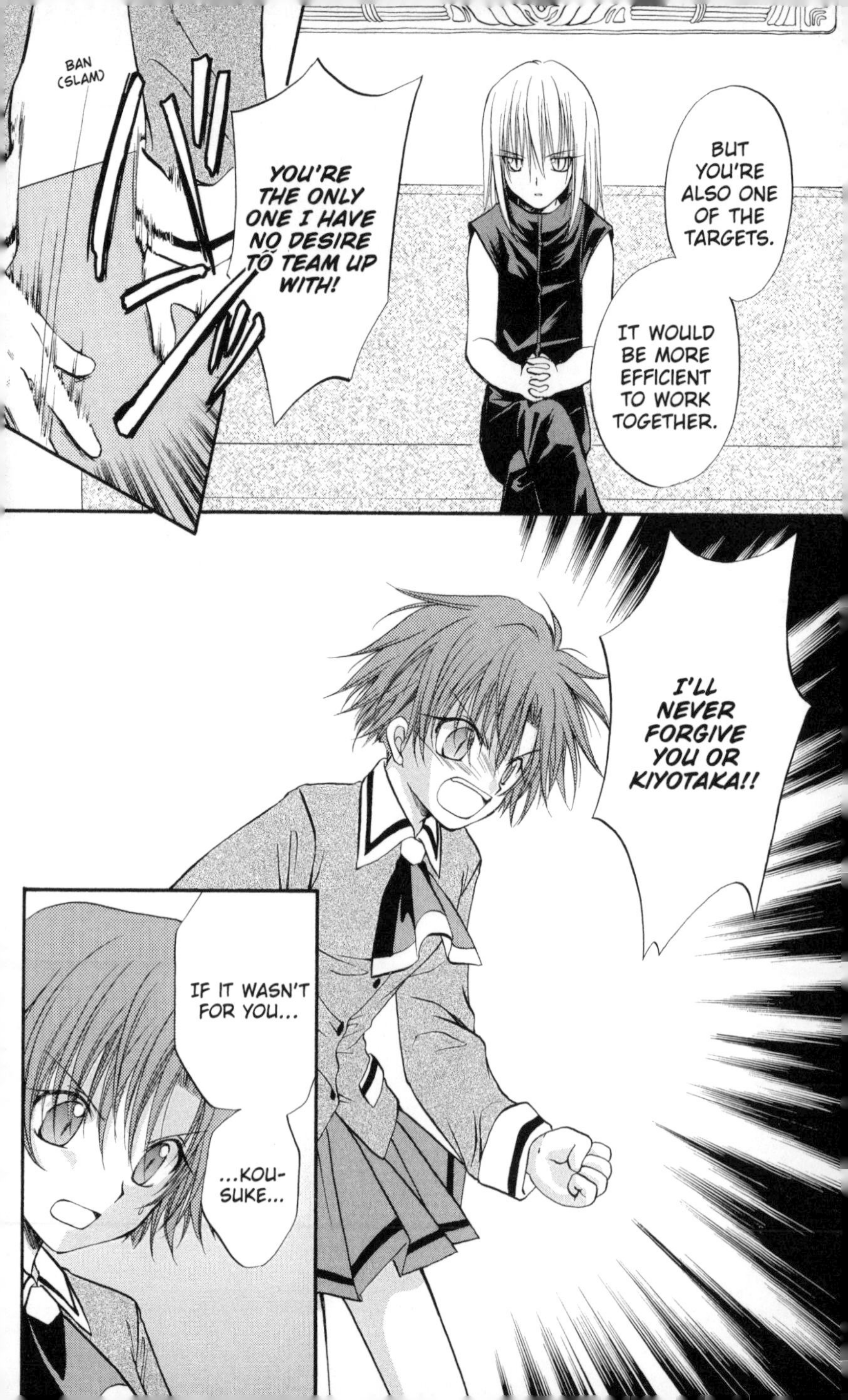
BUT YOU'RE ALSO ONE OF THE TARGETS.
IT WOULD BE MORE EFFICIENT TO WORK TOGETHER.
YOU'RE THE ONLY ONE I HAVE NO DESIRE TO TEAM UP WITH!
BAN (SLAM)
I'LL NEVER FORGIVE YOU OR KIYOTAKA!!
IF IT WASN'T FOR YOU...
...KOU-SUKE...

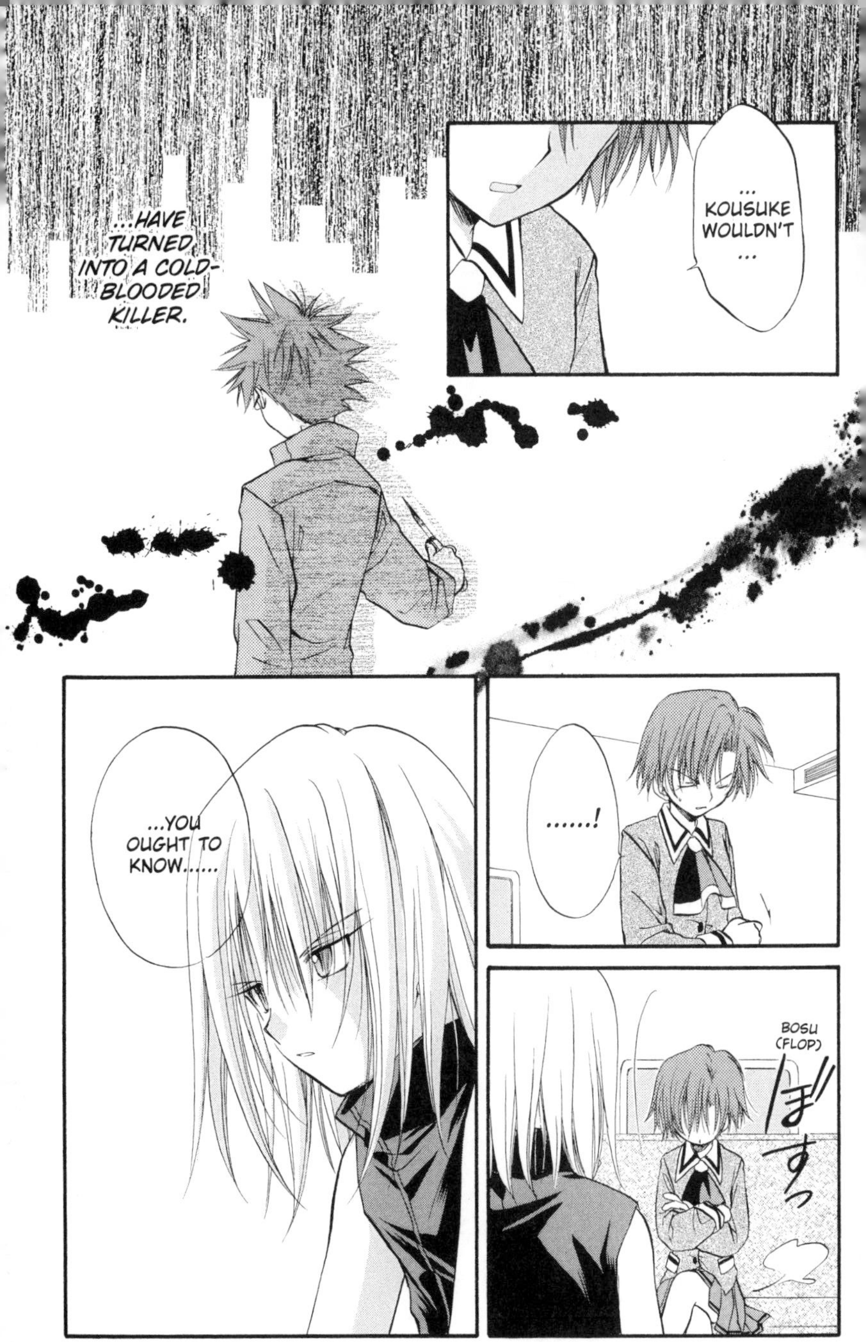
... KOUSUKE WOULDN'T ...
...HAVE TURNED INTO A COLD-BLOODED KILLER.
......!
BOSU (FLOP)
...YOU OUGHT TO KNOW......

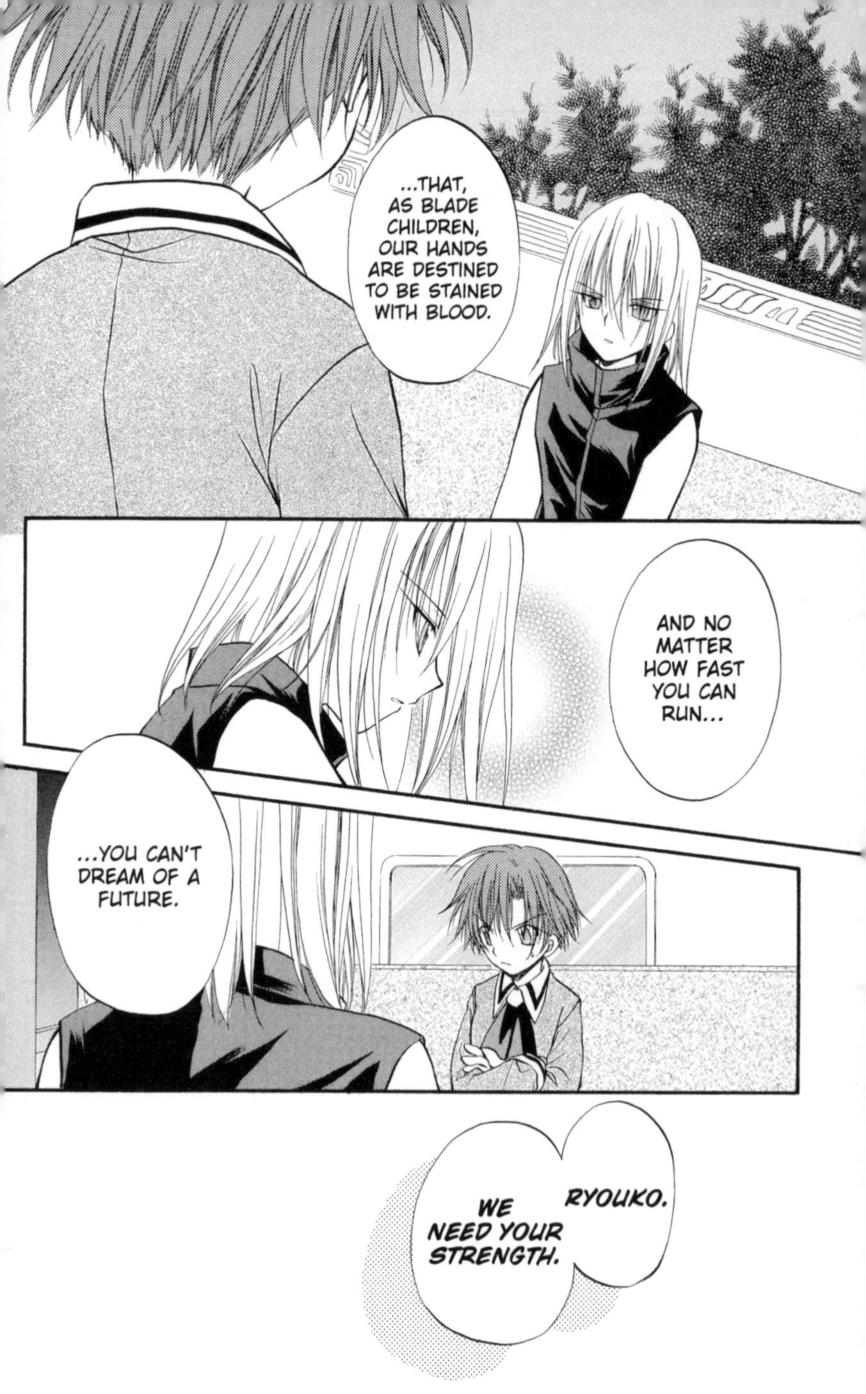
...THAT, AS BLADE CHILDREN, OUR HANDS ARE DESTINED TO BE STAINED WITH BLOOD.
AND NO MATTER HOW FAST YOU CAN RUN...
...YOU CAN'T DREAM OF A FUTURE.
RYOUKO.
WE NEED YOUR STRENGTH.

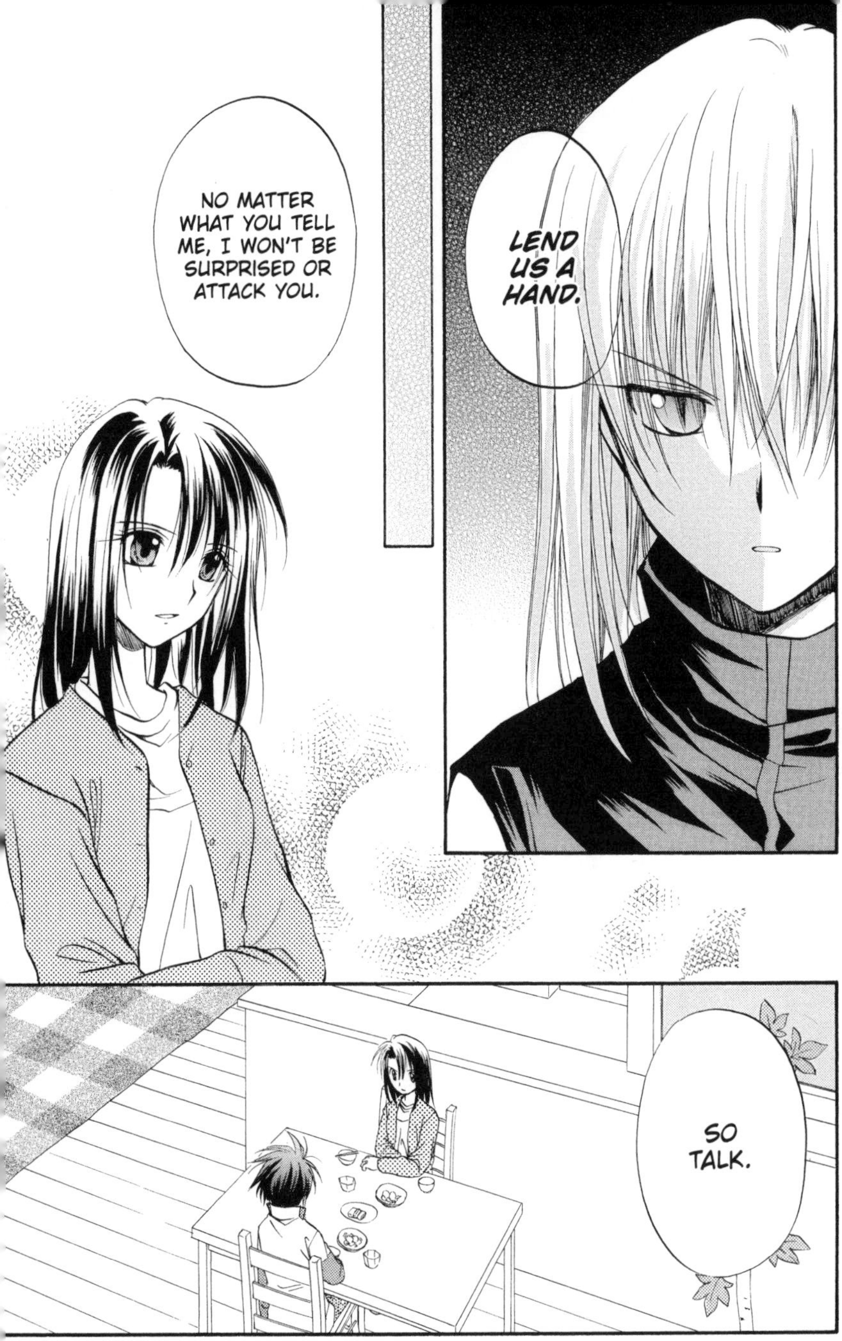
LEND US A HAND.
NO MATTER WHAT YOU TELL ME, I WON'T BE SURPRISED OR ATTACK YOU.
SO TALK.

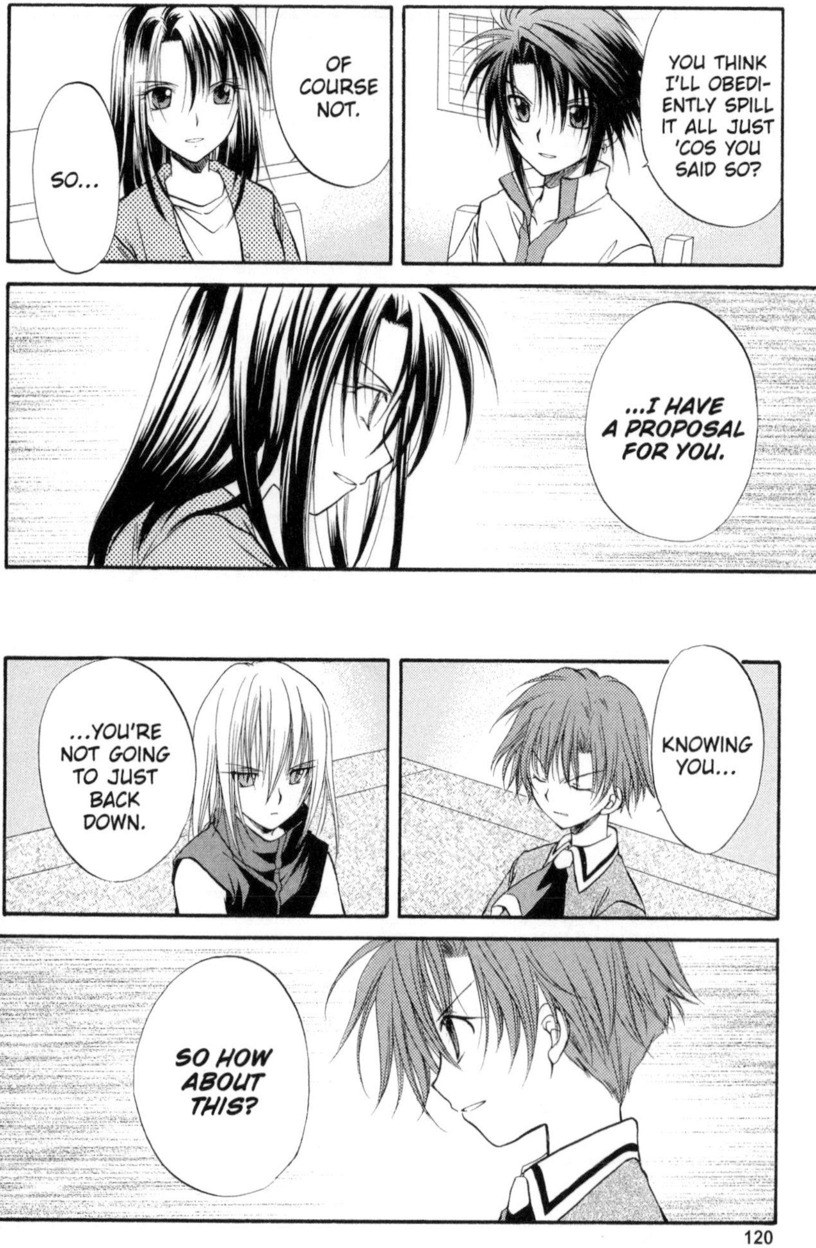
YOU THINK I'LL OBEDIENTLY SPILL IT ALL JUST 'COS YOU SAID SO?
OF COURSE NOT.
SO...
...I HAVE A PROPOSAL FOR YOU.
KNOWING YOU...
...YOU'RE NOT GOING TO JUST BACK DOWN.
SO HOW ABOUT THIS?

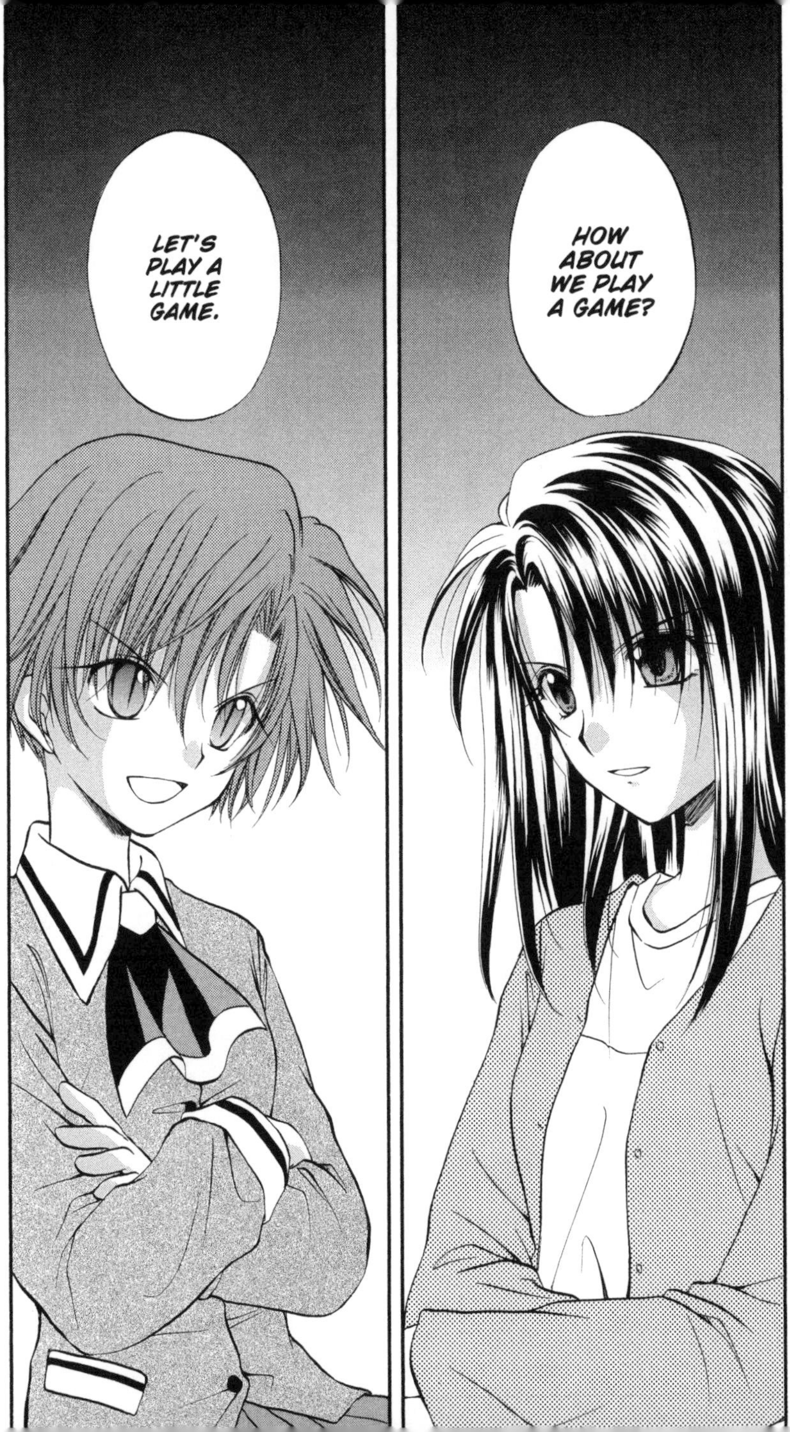
HOW ABOUT WE PLAY A GAME?
LET'S PLAY A LITTLE GAME.

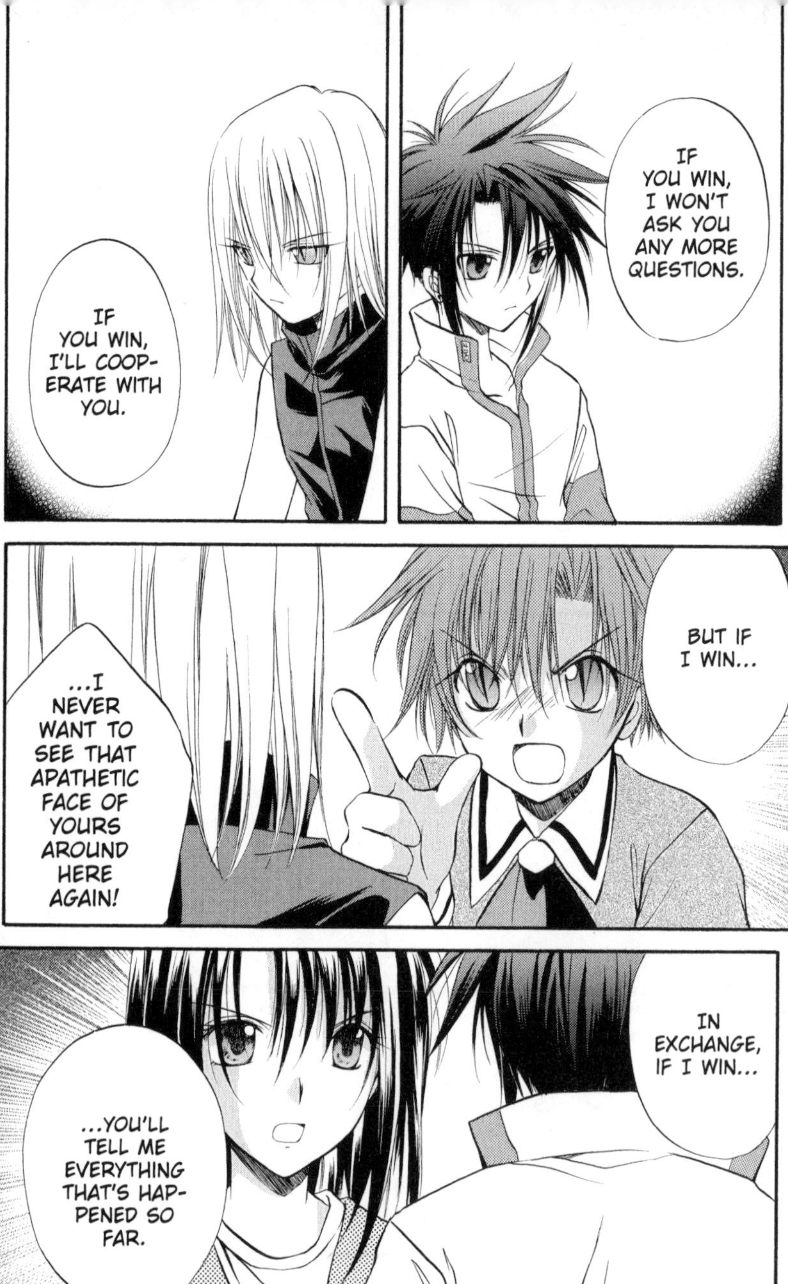
IF YOU WIN, I WON'T ASK YOU ANY MORE QUESTIONS.
IF YOU WIN, I'LL COOPERATE WITH YOU.
BUT IF I WIN...
...I NEVER WANT TO SEE THAT APATHETIC FACE OF YOURS AROUND HERE AGAIN!
IN EXCHANGE, IF I WIN...
...YOU'LL TELL ME EVERYTHING THAT'S HAPPENED SO FAR.

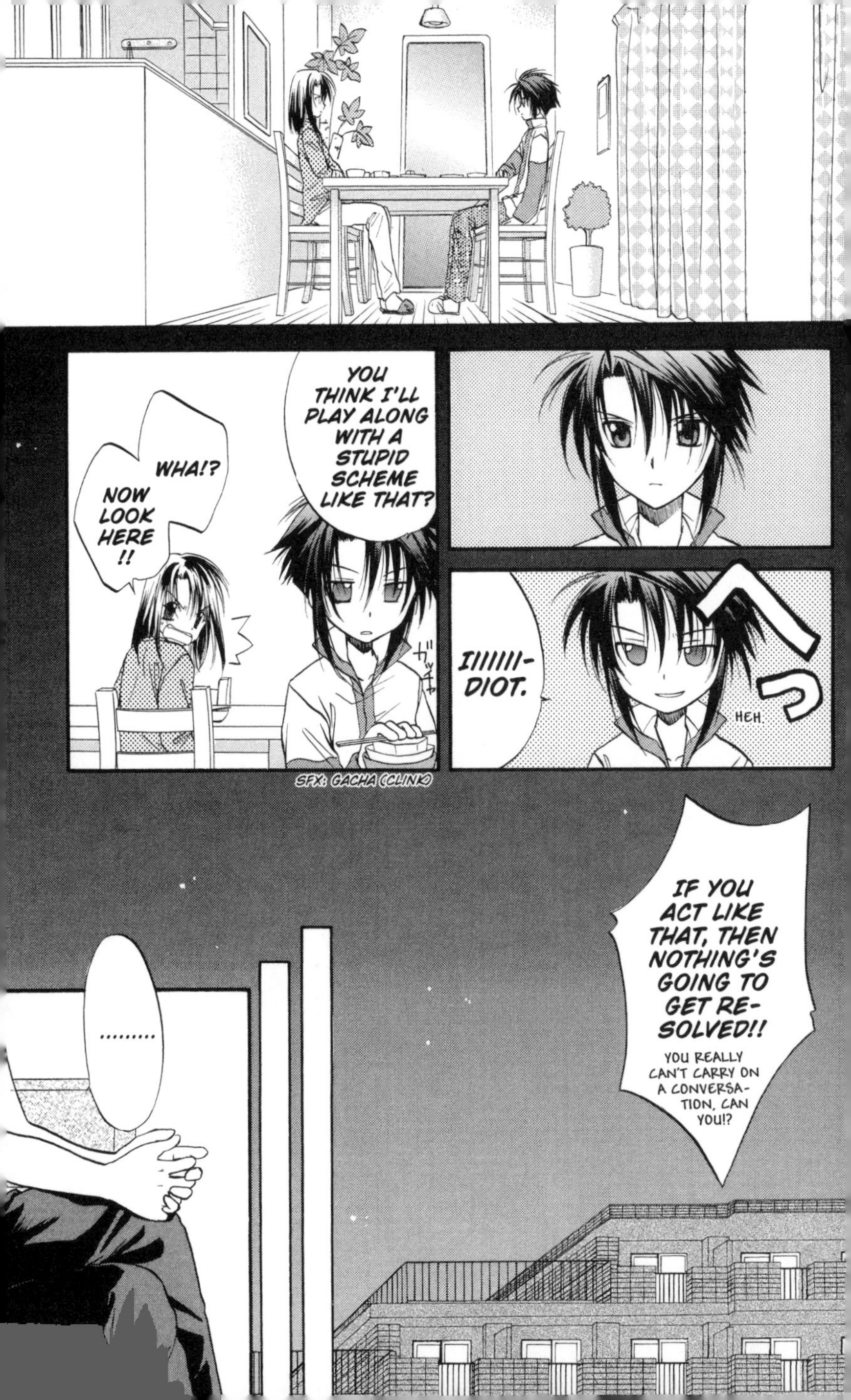
IIIIII-DIOT.
HEH.
YOU THINK I'LL PLAY ALONG WITH A STUPID SCHEME LIKE THAT?
WHA!? NOW LOOK HERE!!
SFX: GACHA (CLINK)
IF YOU ACT LIKE THAT, THEN NOTHING'S GOING TO GET RE-SOLVED!!
YOU REALLY CAN'T CARRY ON A CONVERSA-TION, CAN YOU!?
....

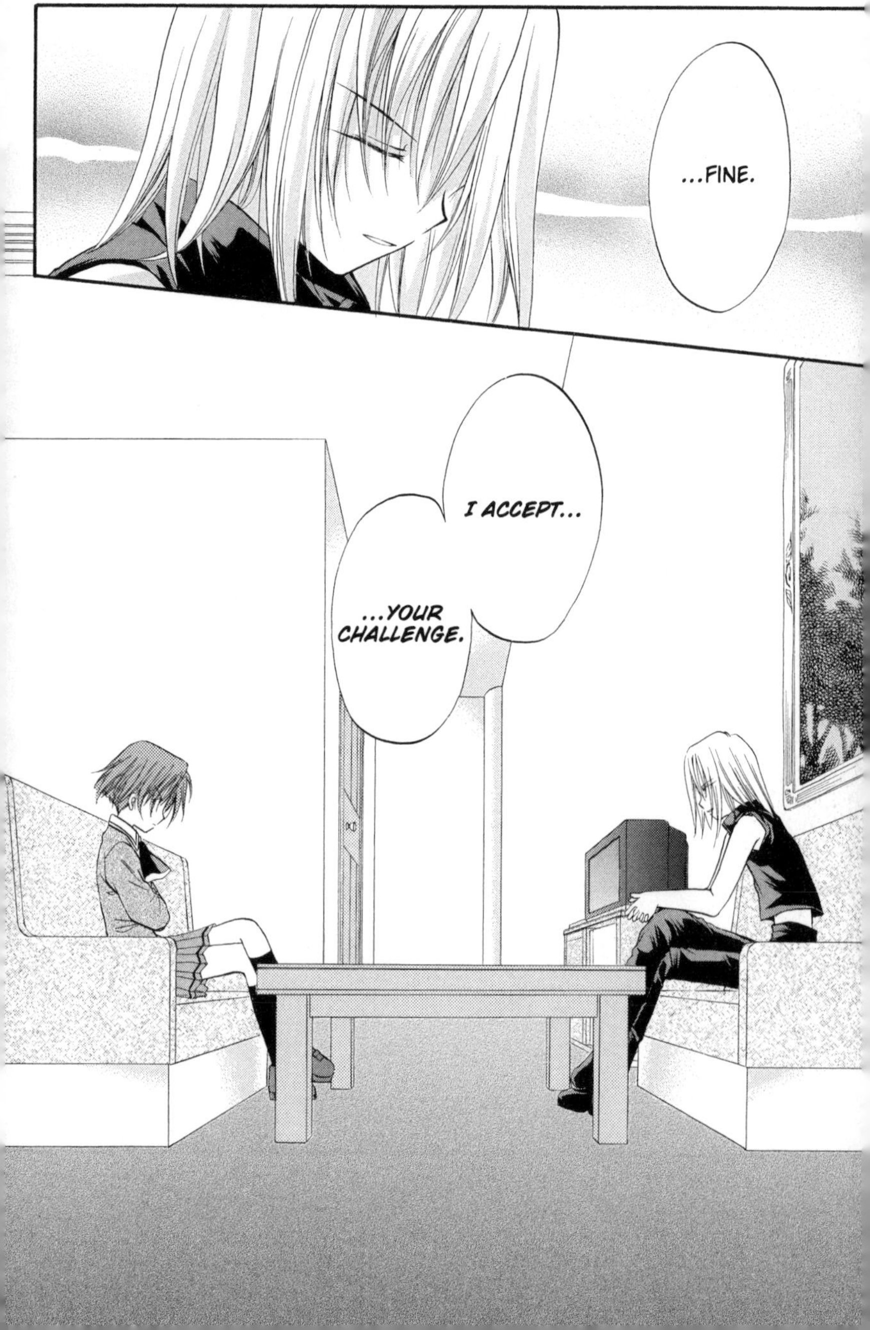
...FINE.
I ACCEPT...
...YOUR CHALLENGE.

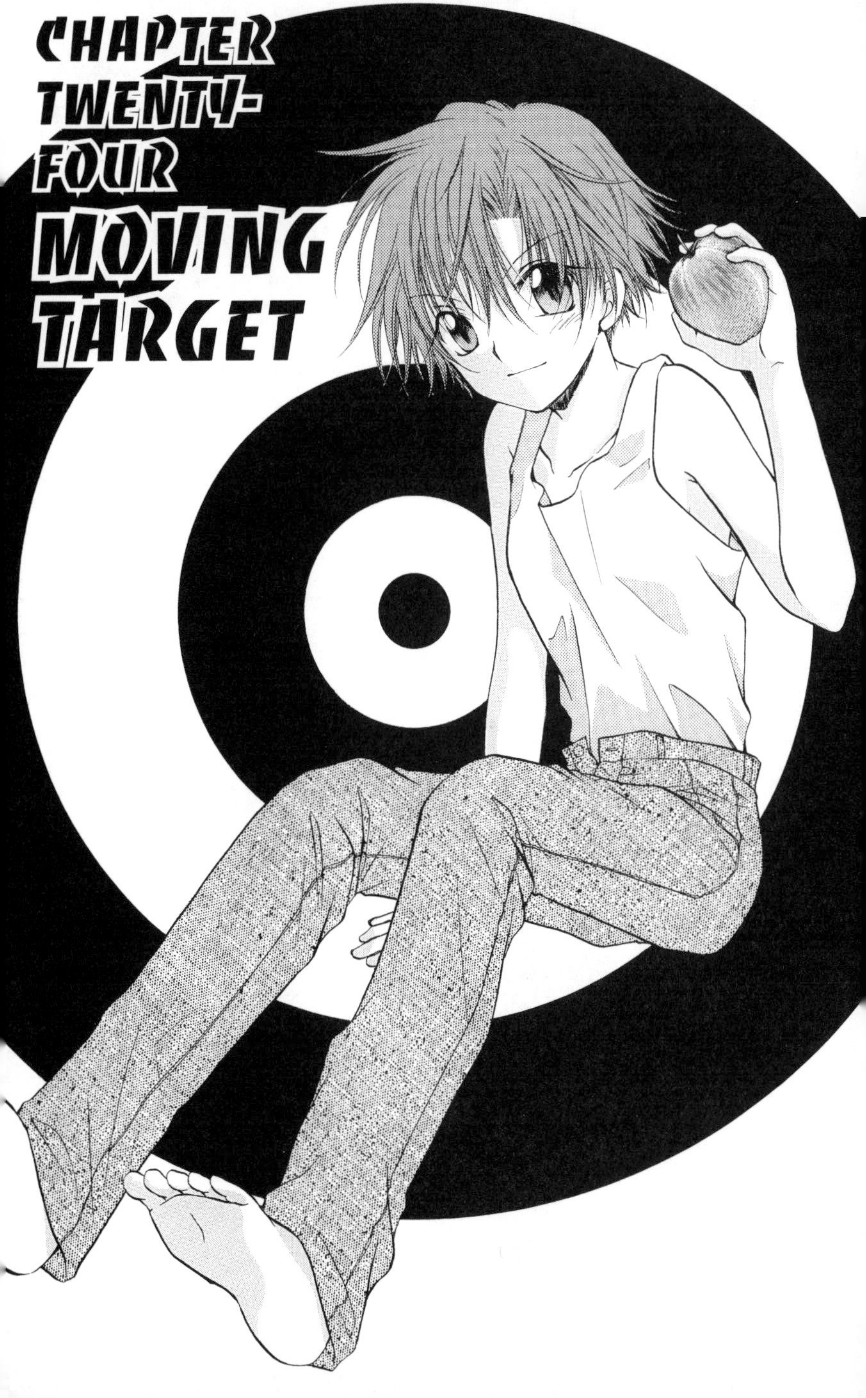
CHAPTER TWENTY-FOUR
MOVING TARGET

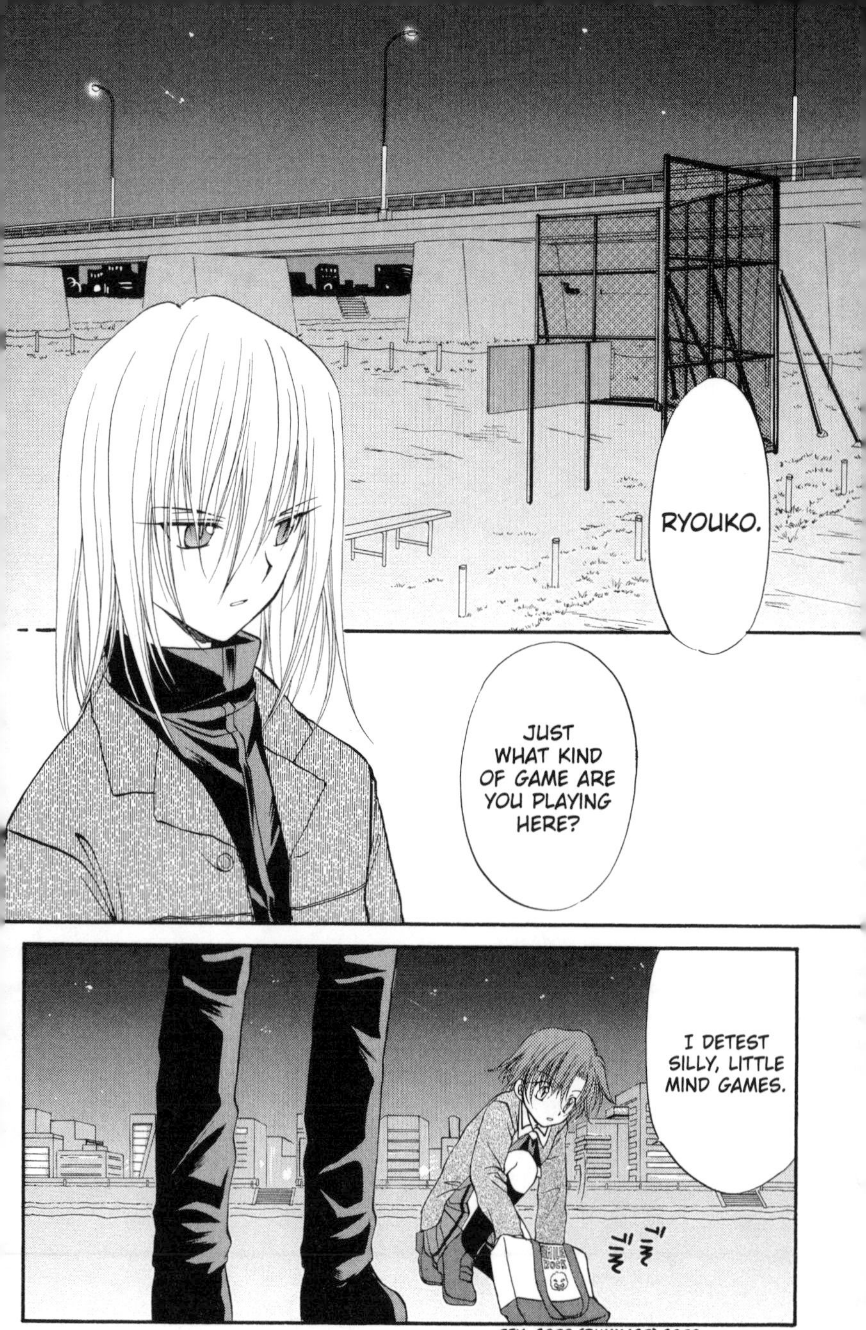
RYOUKO.
JUST WHAT KIND OF GAME ARE YOU PLAYING HERE?
I DETEST SILLY, LITTLE MIND GAMES.

SFX: GOSO (RUMMAGE) GOSO

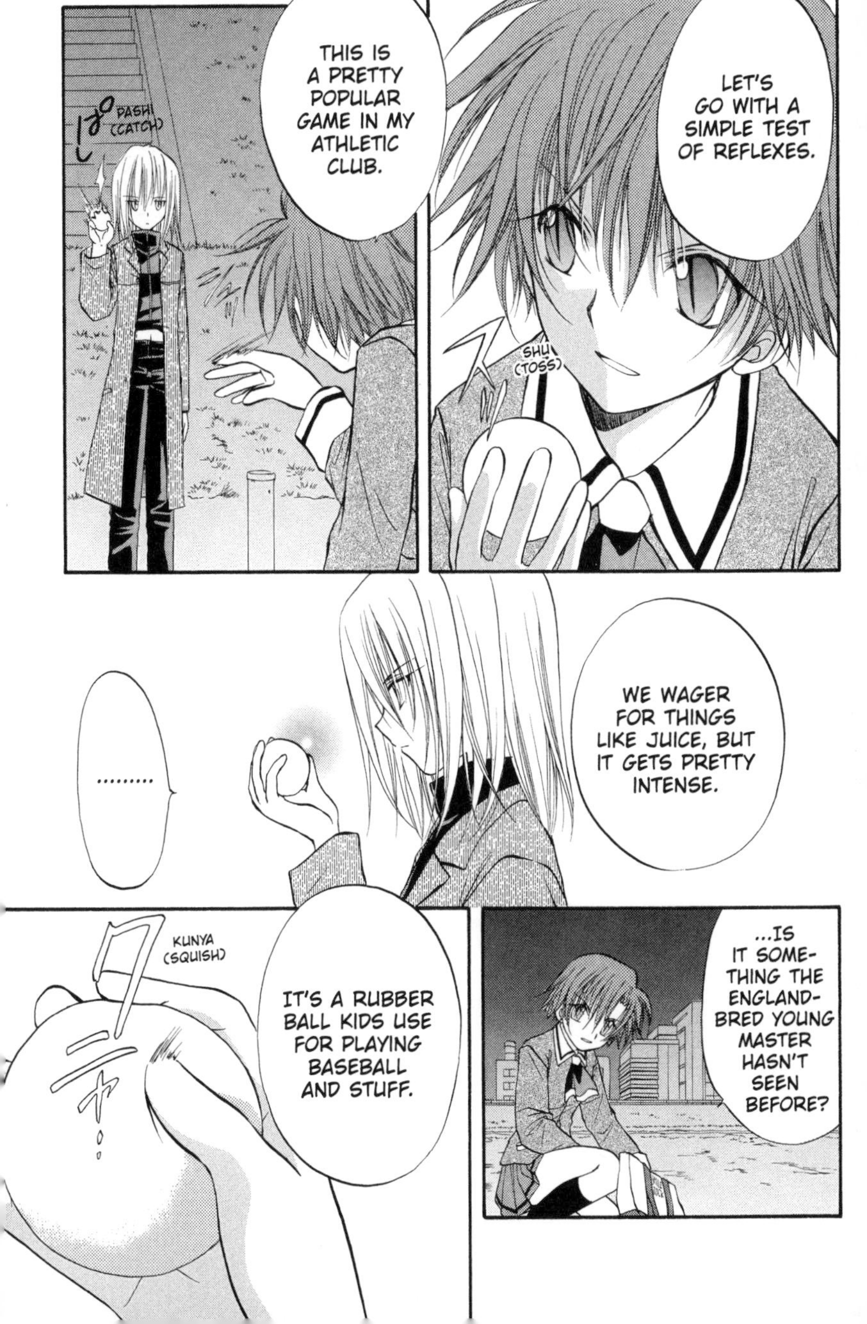
LET'S GO WITH A SIMPLE TEST OF REFLEXES.
SHU (TOSS)
THIS IS A PRETTY POPULAR GAME IN MY ATHLETIC CLUB.
PASHI (CATCH)
WE WAGER FOR THINGS LIKE JUICE, BUT IT GETS PRETTY INTENSE.
....
...IS IT SOMETHING THE ENGLAND-BRED YOUNG MASTER HASN'T SEEN BEFORE?
IT'S A RUBBER BALL KIDS USE FOR PLAYING BASEBALL AND STUFF.
KUNYA (SQUISH)

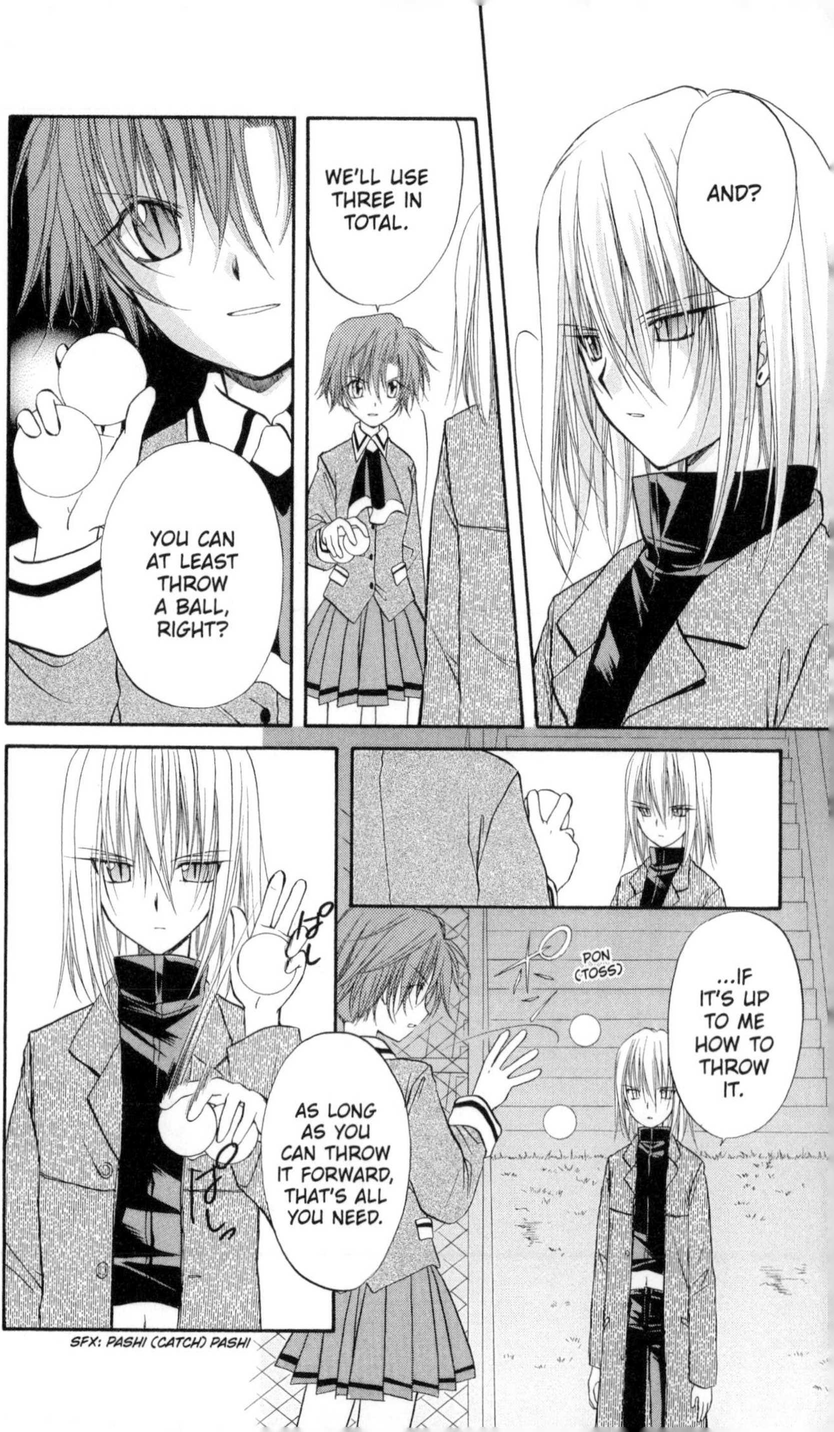
AND?
WE'LL USE THREE IN TOTAL.
YOU CAN AT LEAST THROW A BALL, RIGHT?
...IF IT'S UP TO ME HOW TO THROW IT.
PON (TOSS)
AS LONG AS YOU CAN THROW IT FORWARD, THAT'S ALL YOU NEED.
SFX: PASHI (CATCH) PASHI

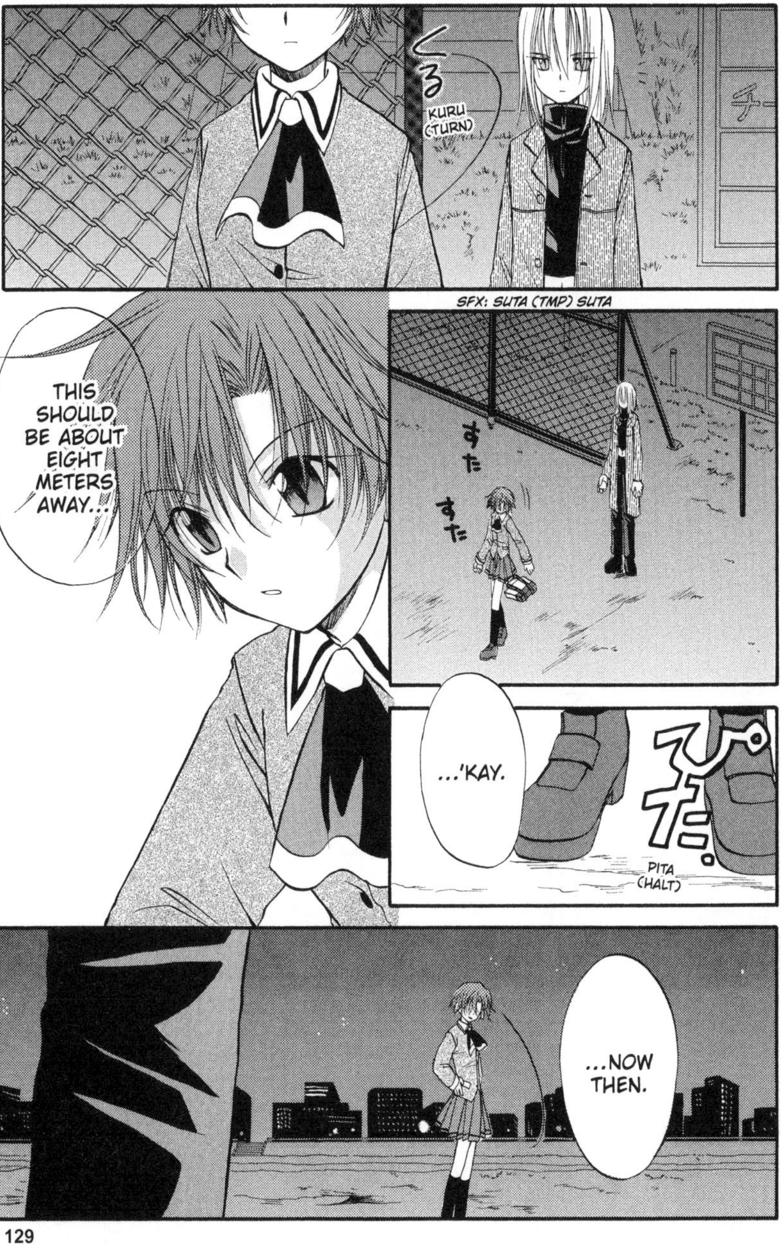
くる
KURU (TURN)
SFX: SUTA (TMP) SUTA
すた すた
...'KAY.
ぴた。
PITA (HALT)
THIS SHOULD BE ABOUT EIGHT METERS AWAY...
...NOW THEN.

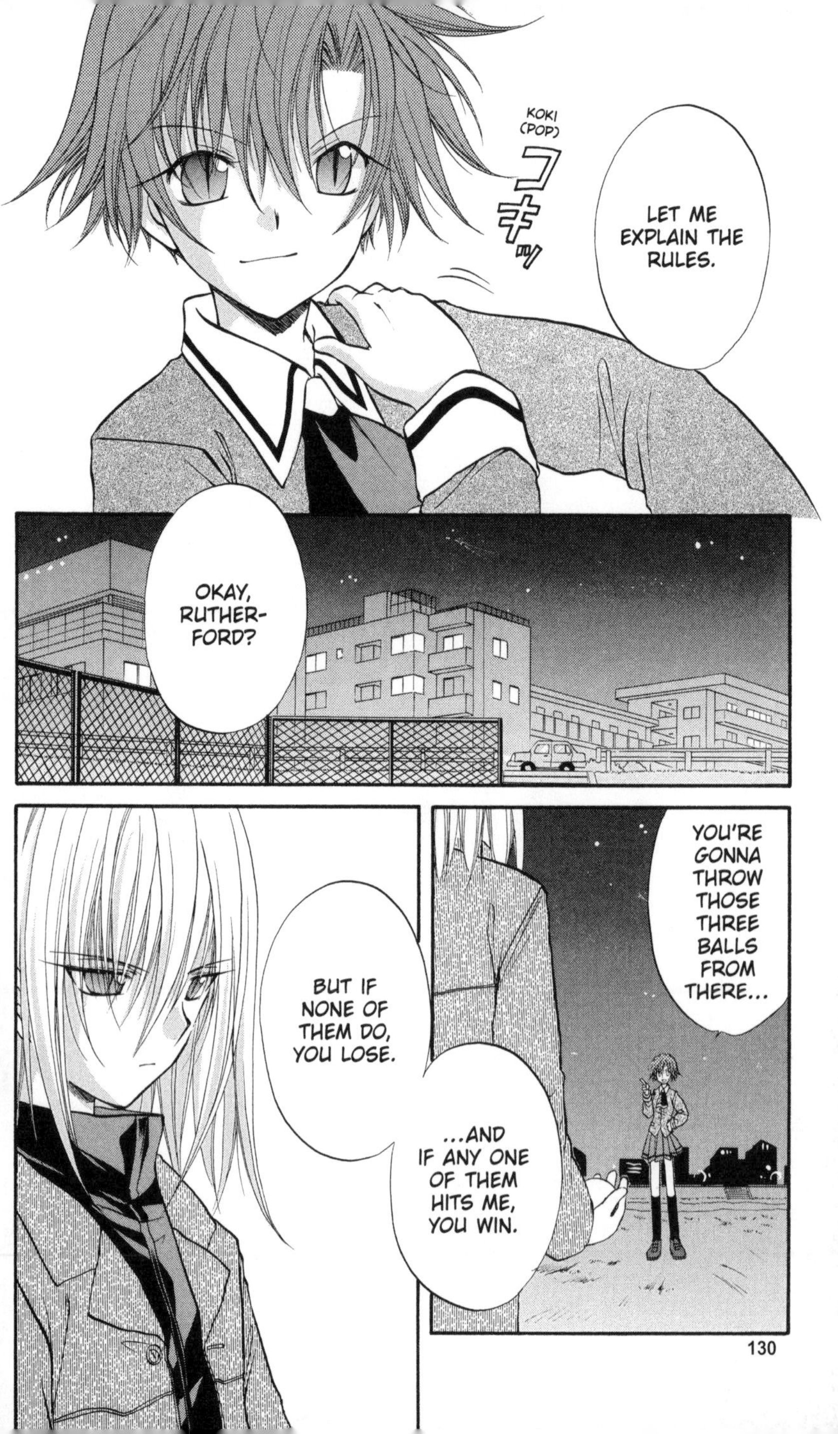
KOKI (POP)
コキッ
LET ME EXPLAIN THE RULES.
OKAY, RUTHER-FORD?
YOU'RE GONNA THROW THOSE THREE BALLS FROM THERE...
...AND IF ANY ONE OF THEM HITS ME, YOU WIN.
BUT IF NONE OF THEM DO, YOU LOSE.

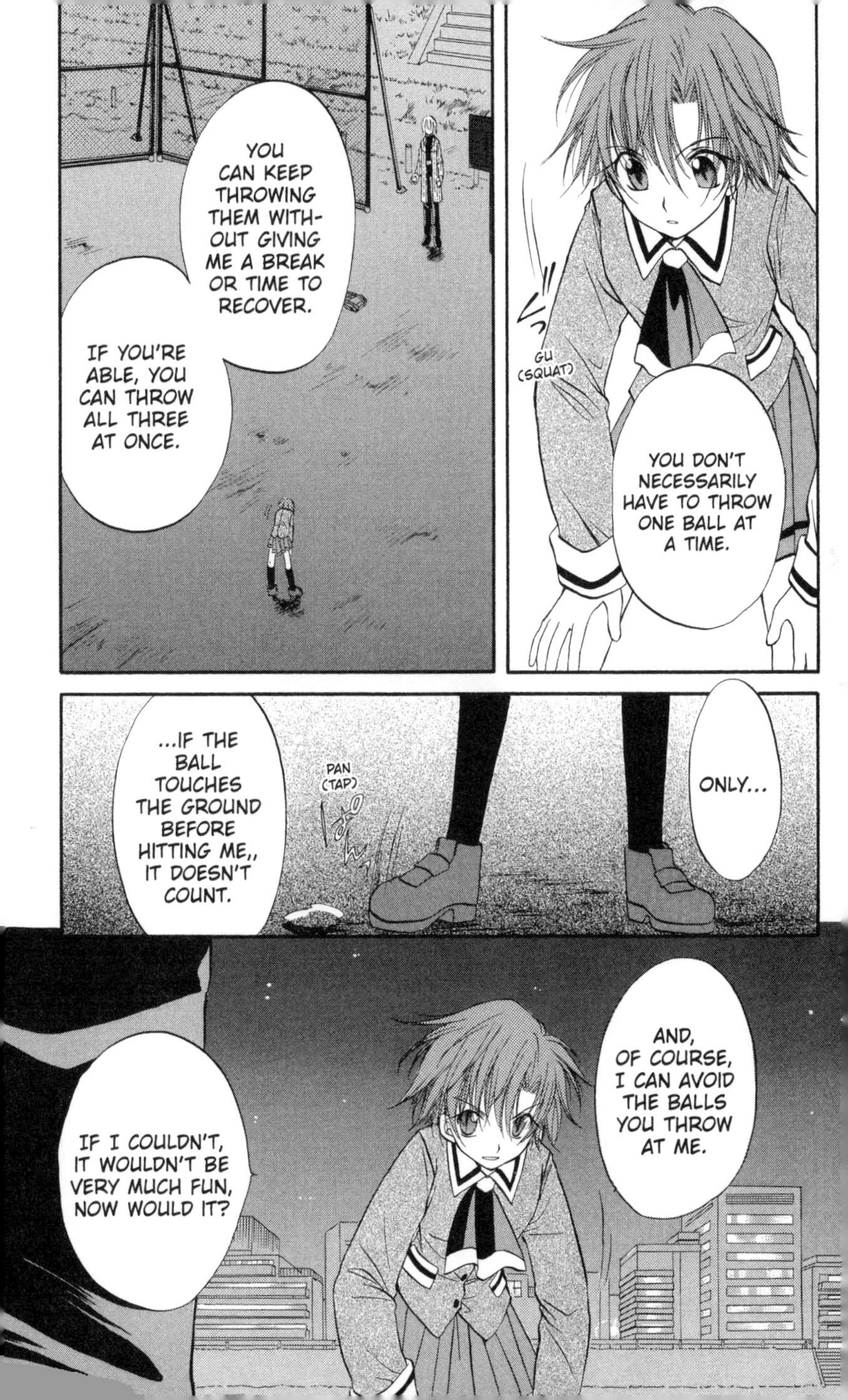
GU (SQUAT)
YOU DON'T NECESSARILY HAVE TO THROW ONE BALL AT A TIME.
YOU CAN KEEP THROWING THEM WITH-OUT GIVING ME A BREAK OR TIME TO RECOVER.
IF YOU'RE ABLE, YOU CAN THROW ALL THREE AT ONCE.
ONLY...
PAN (TAP)
...IF THE BALL TOUCHES THE GROUND BEFORE HITTING ME,, IT DOESN'T COUNT.
AND, OF COURSE, I CAN AVOID THE BALLS YOU THROW AT ME.
IF I COULDN'T, IT WOULDN'T BE VERY MUCH FUN, NOW WOULD IT?

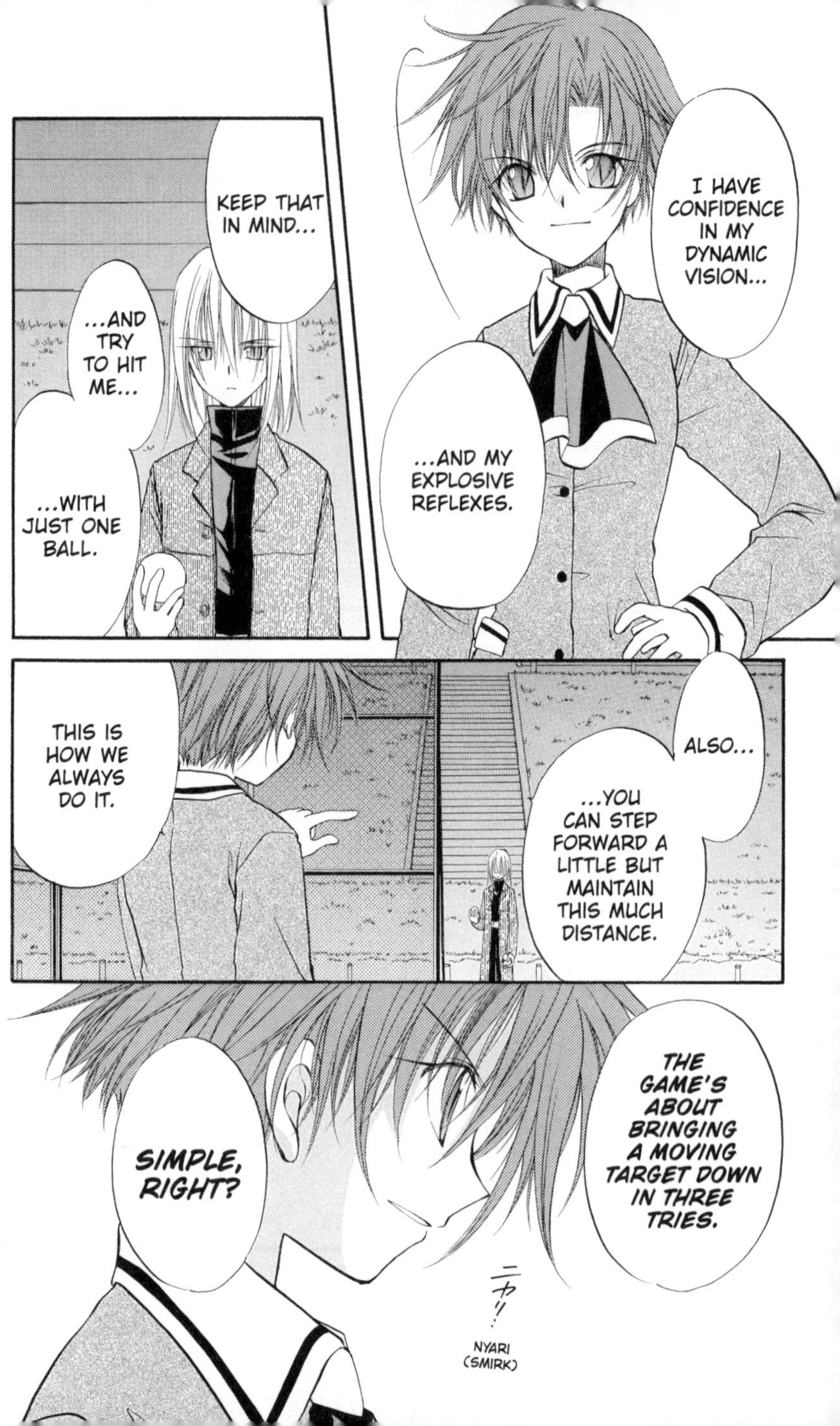
I HAVE CONFIDENCE IN MY DYNAMIC VISION...
...AND MY EXPLOSIVE REFLEXES.
KEEP THAT IN MIND...
...AND TRY TO HIT ME...
...WITH JUST ONE BALL.
ALSO...
...YOU CAN STEP FORWARD A LITTLE BUT MAINTAIN THIS MUCH DISTANCE.
THIS IS HOW WE ALWAYS DO IT.
THE GAME'S ABOUT BRINGING A MOVING TARGET DOWN IN THREE TRIES.
SIMPLE, RIGHT?
ニヤ!!
NYARI (SMIRK)

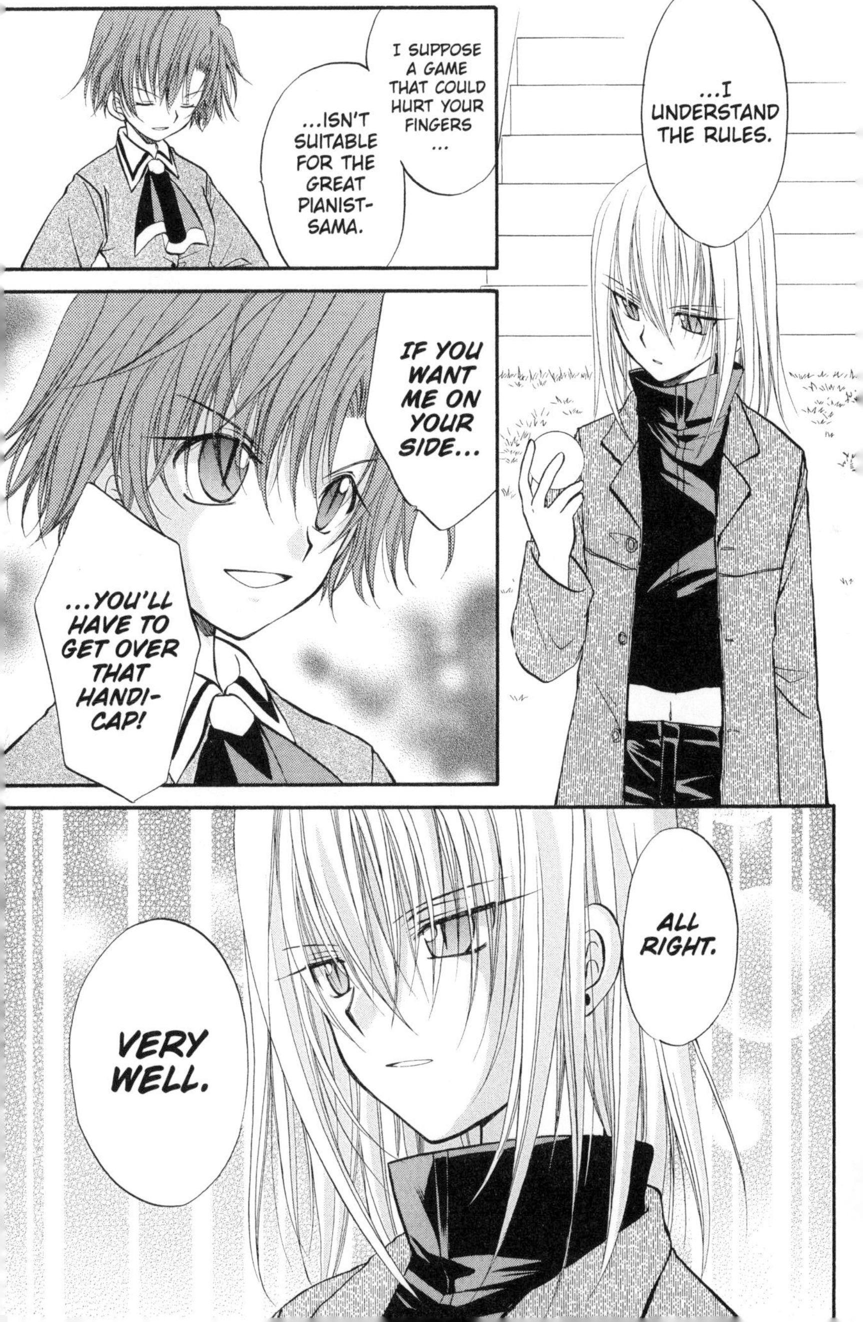
...I UNDERSTAND THE RULES.
I SUPPOSE A GAME THAT COULD HURT YOUR FINGERS...
...ISN'T SUITABLE FOR THE GREAT PIANIST-SAMA.
IF YOU WANT ME ON YOUR SIDE...
...YOU'LL HAVE TO GET OVER THAT HANDICAP!
ALL RIGHT.
VERY WELL.

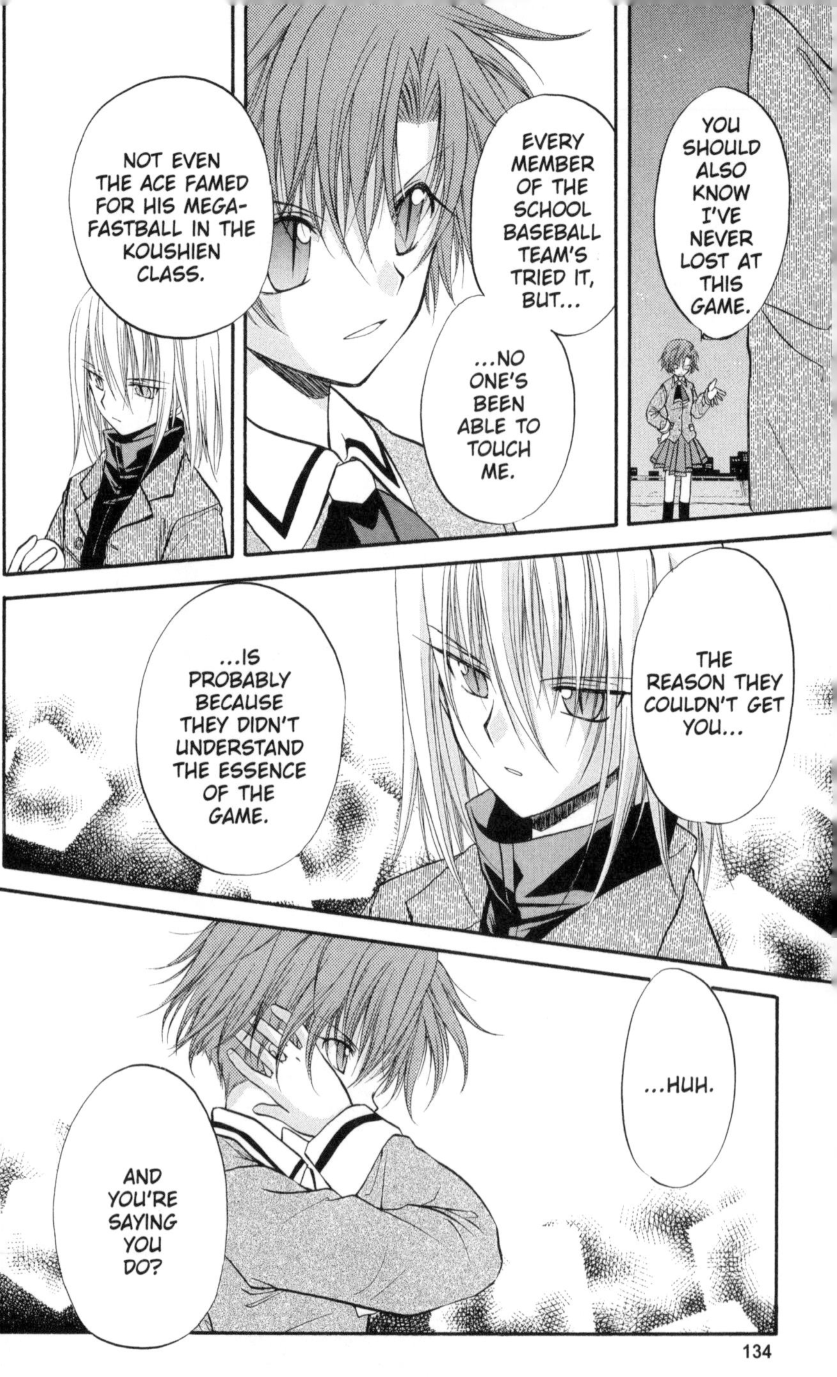
YOU SHOULD ALSO KNOW I'VE NEVER LOST AT THIS GAME.
EVERY MEMBER OF THE SCHOOL BASEBALL TEAM'S TRIED IT, BUT...
...NO ONE'S BEEN ABLE TO TOUCH ME.
NOT EVEN THE ACE FAMED FOR HIS MEGA-FASTBALL IN THE KOUSHIEN CLASS.
THE REASON THEY COULDN'T GET YOU...
...IS PROBABLY BECAUSE THEY DIDN'T UNDERSTAND THE ESSENCE OF THE GAME.
...HUH.
AND YOU'RE SAYING YOU DO?

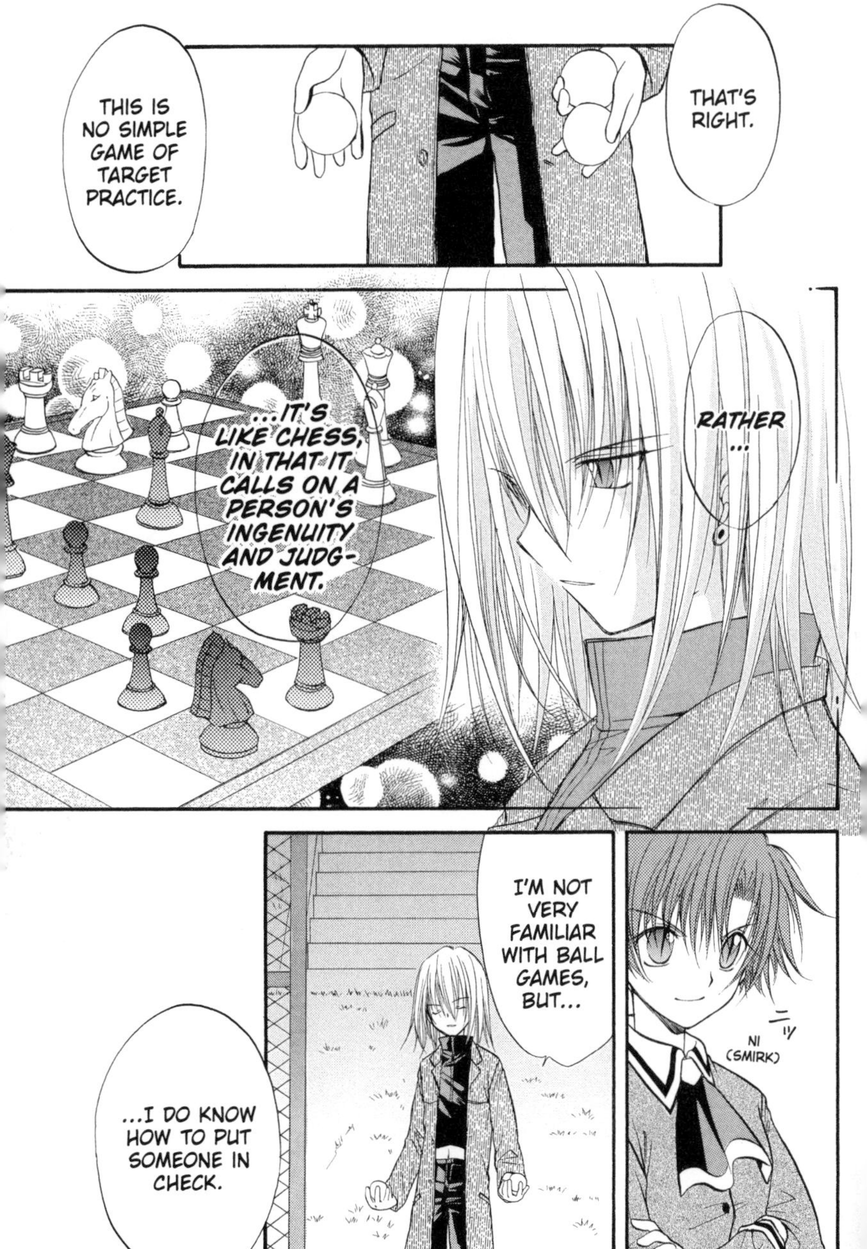
THAT'S RIGHT.
THIS IS NO SIMPLE GAME OF TARGET PRACTICE.
RATHER...
...IT'S LIKE CHESS, IN THAT IT CALLS ON A PERSON'S INGENUITY AND JUDG-MENT.
NI (SMIRK)
I'M NOT VERY FAMILIAR WITH BALL GAMES, BUT...
...I DO KNOW HOW TO PUT SOMEONE IN CHECK.

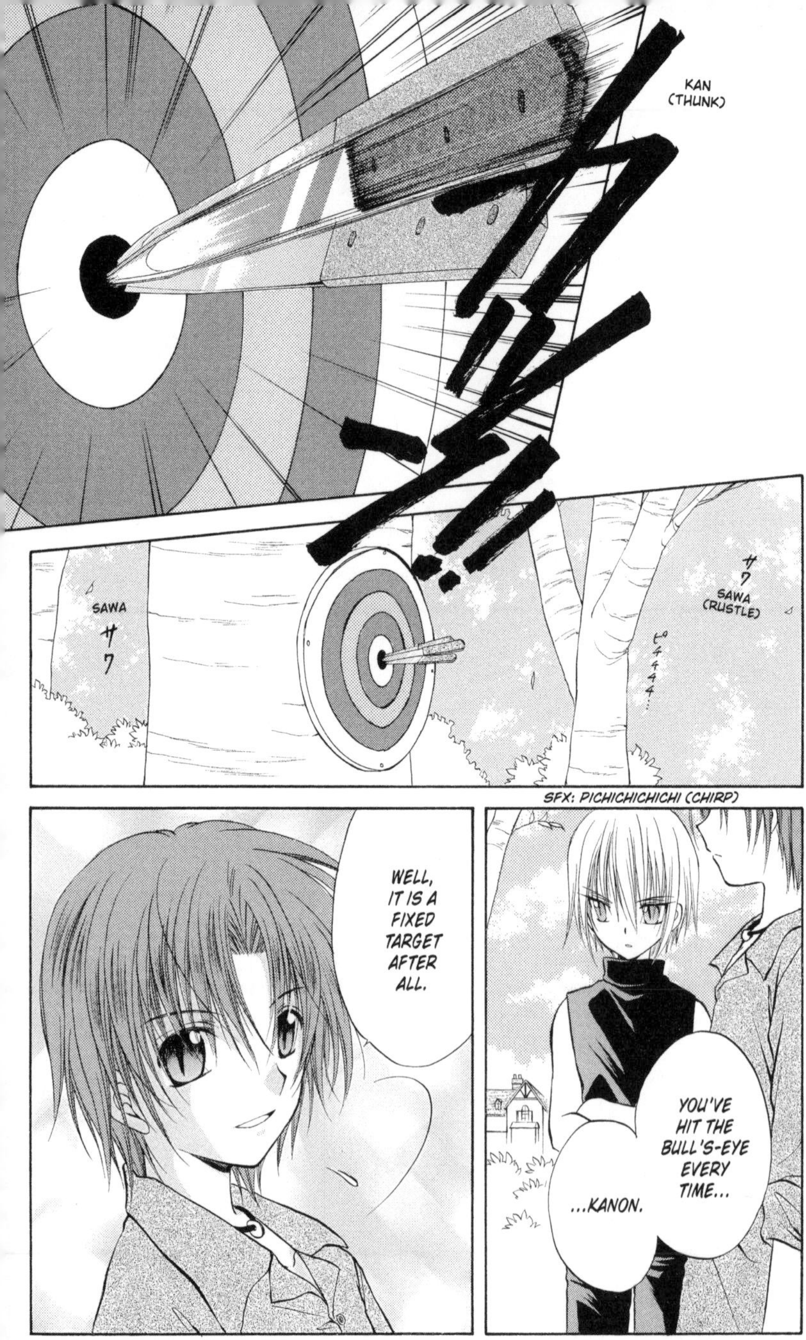
KAN (THUNK)
サワ
SAWA (RUSTLE)
ピチチチチ…
SAWA
サワ
SFX: PICHICHICHICHI (CHIRP)
YOU'VE HIT THE BULL'S-EYE EVERY TIME…
…KANON.
WELL, IT IS A FIXED TARGET AFTER ALL.

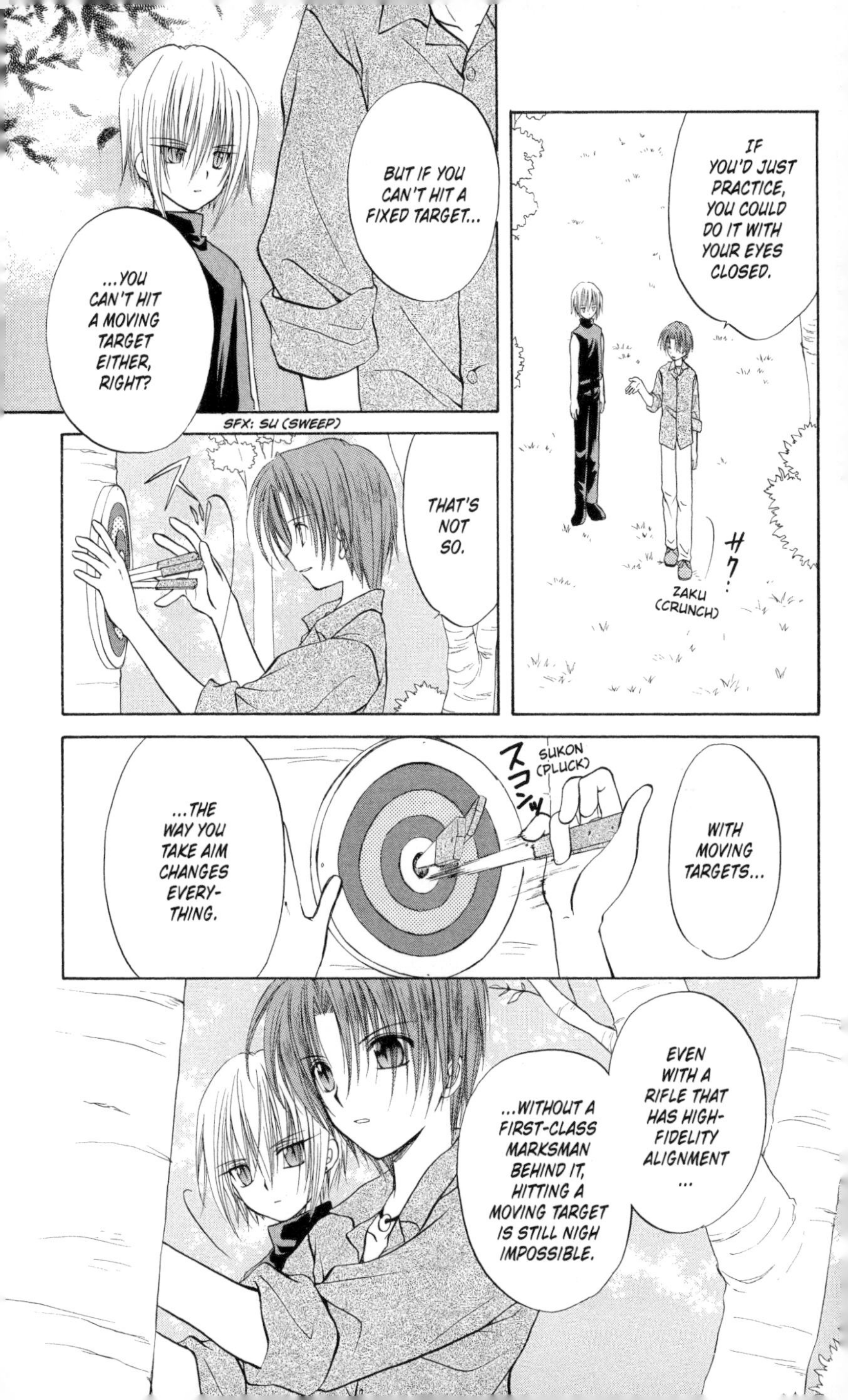
IF YOU'D JUST PRACTICE, YOU COULD DO IT WITH YOUR EYES CLOSED.
ZAKU (CRUNCH)
BUT IF YOU CAN'T HIT A FIXED TARGET...
...YOU CAN'T HIT A MOVING TARGET EITHER, RIGHT?
SFX: SU (SWEEP)
THAT'S NOT SO.
WITH MOVING TARGETS...
SUKON (PLUCK)
...THE WAY YOU TAKE AIM CHANGES EVERYTHING.
EVEN WITH A RIFLE THAT HAS HIGH-FIDELITY ALIGNMENT...
...WITHOUT A FIRST-CLASS MARKSMAN BEHIND IT, HITTING A MOVING TARGET IS STILL NIGH IMPOSSIBLE.

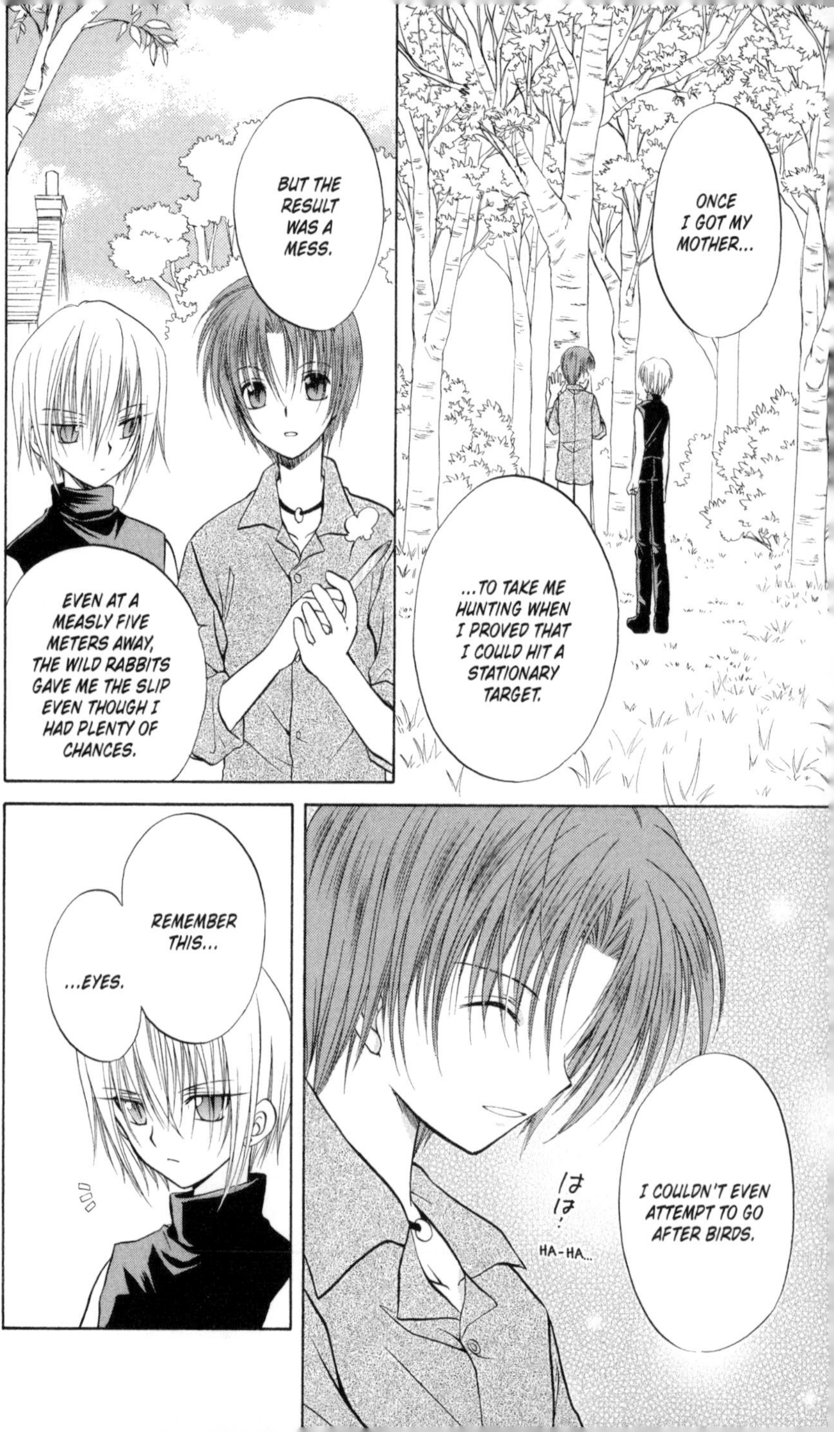
ONCE I GOT MY MOTHER...
...TO TAKE ME HUNTING WHEN I PROVED THAT I COULD HIT A STATIONARY TARGET.
BUT THE RESULT WAS A MESS.
EVEN AT A MEASLY FIVE METERS AWAY, THE WILD RABBITS GAVE ME THE SLIP EVEN THOUGH I HAD PLENTY OF CHANCES.
I COULDN'T EVEN ATTEMPT TO GO AFTER BIRDS.
はは
HA-HA...
REMEMBER THIS...
...EYES.

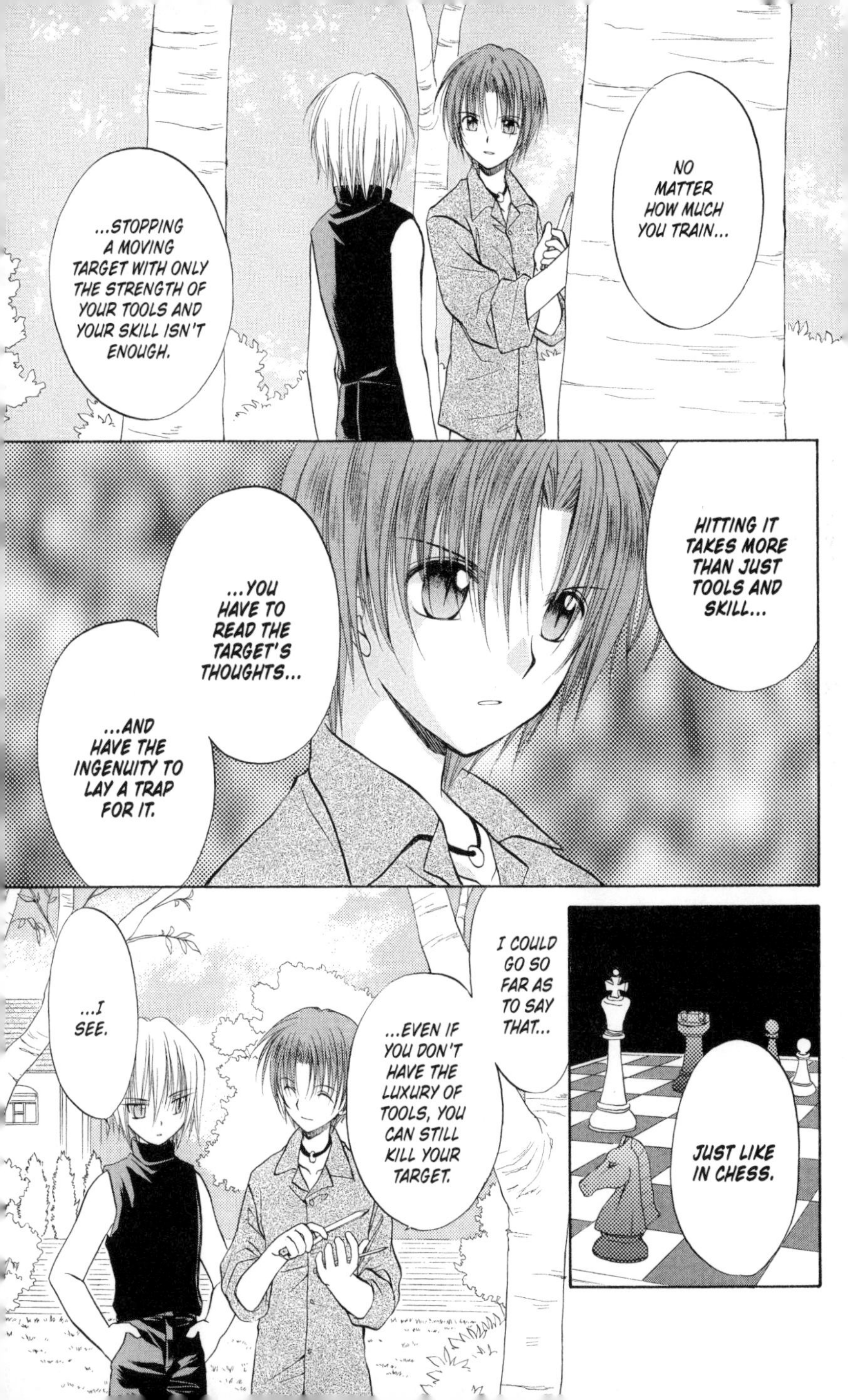
NO MATTER HOW MUCH YOU TRAIN...
...STOPPING A MOVING TARGET WITH ONLY THE STRENGTH OF YOUR TOOLS AND YOUR SKILL ISN'T ENOUGH.
HITTING IT TAKES MORE THAN JUST TOOLS AND SKILL...
...YOU HAVE TO READ THE TARGET'S THOUGHTS...
...AND HAVE THE INGENUITY TO LAY A TRAP FOR IT.
JUST LIKE IN CHESS.
I COULD GO SO FAR AS TO SAY THAT...
...EVEN IF YOU DON'T HAVE THE LUXURY OF TOOLS, YOU CAN STILL KILL YOUR TARGET.
...I SEE.

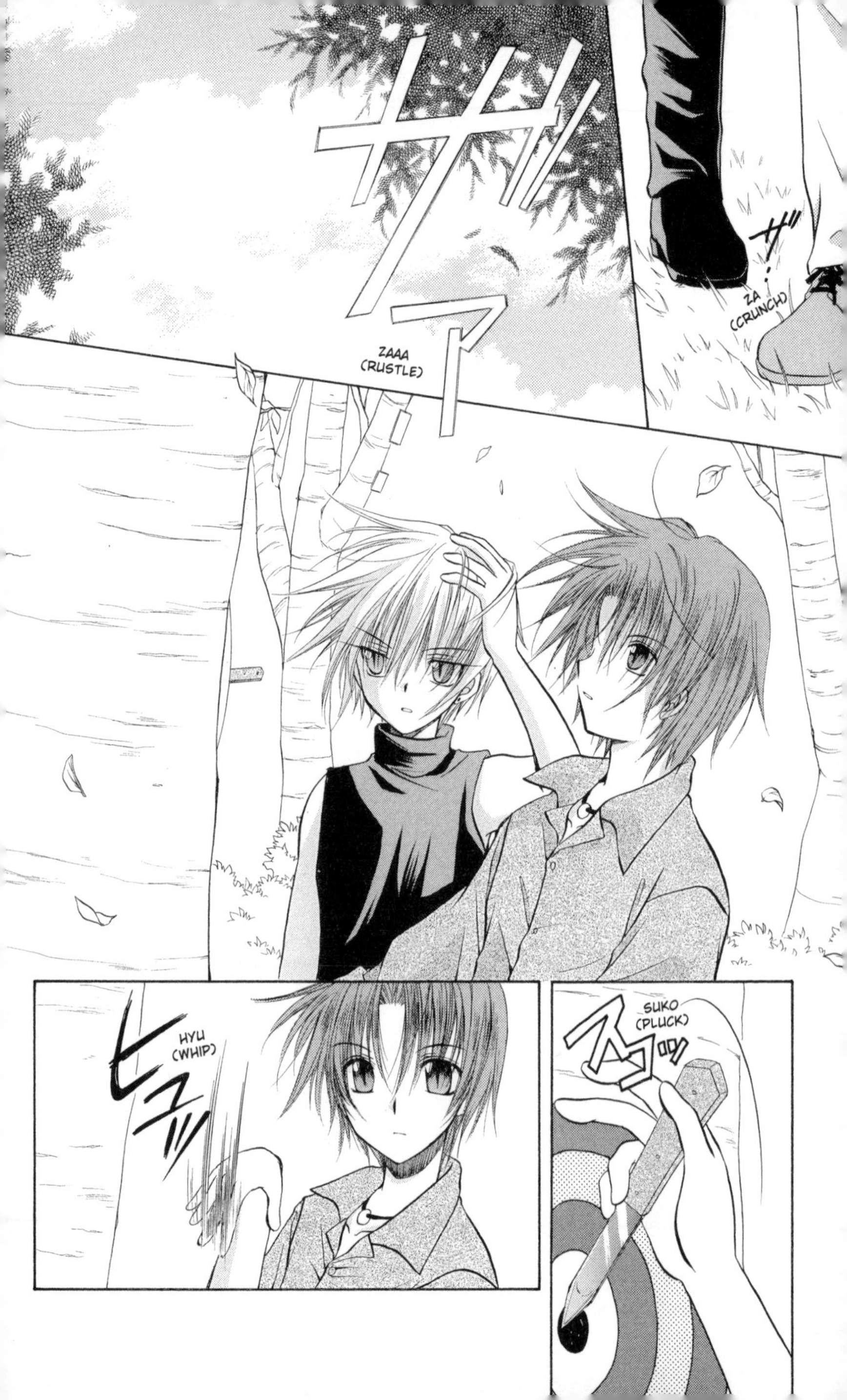
ZA
(CRUNCH)
ZAAA
(RUSTLE)
SUKO
(PLUCK)
HYU
(WHIP)

WELL...

...NOTHING BEATS PRACTICE.

KAN! (THUNK)

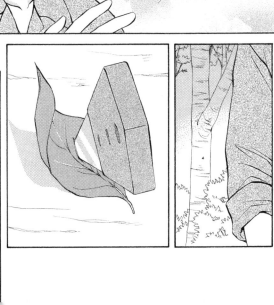

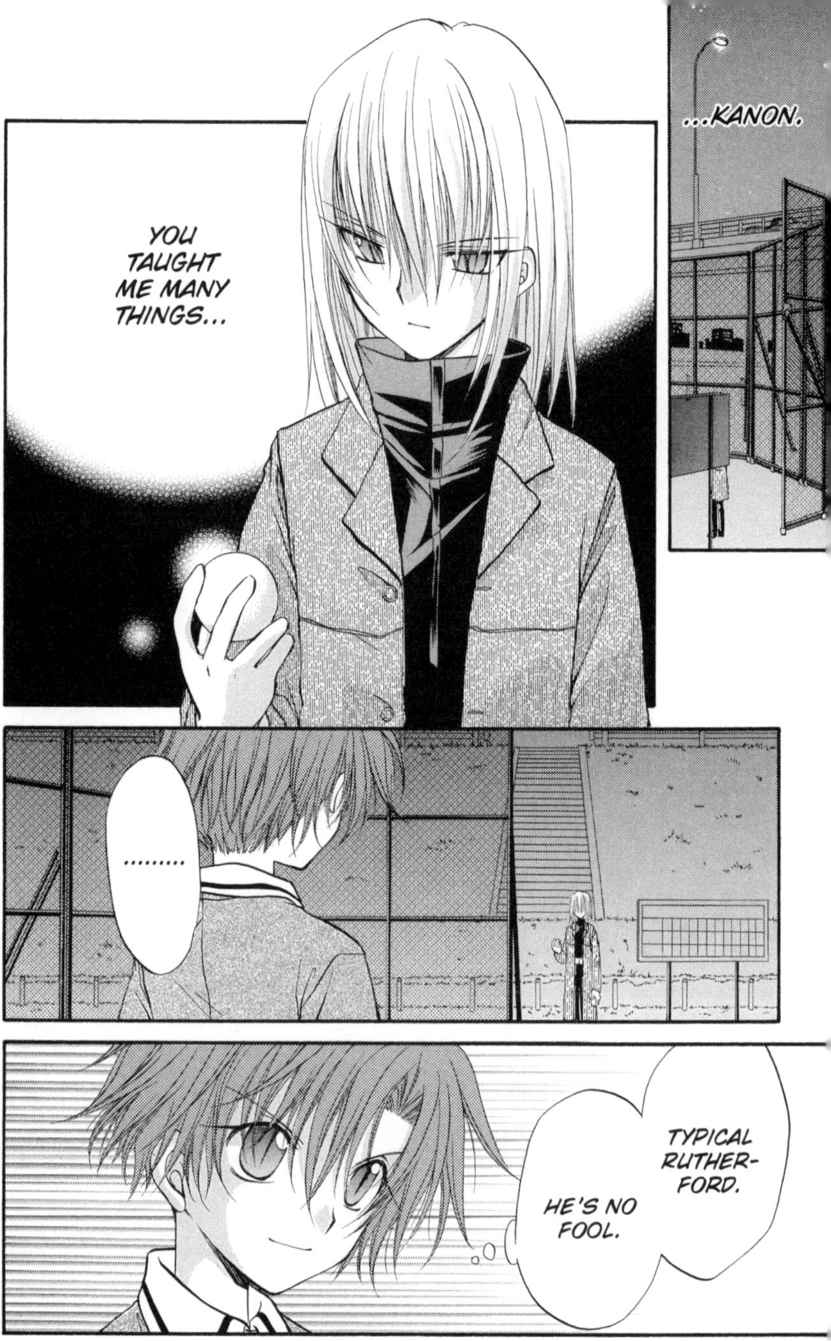
...KANON.
YOU TAUGHT ME MANY THINGS...
....
TYPICAL RUTHERFORD.
HE'S NO FOOL.

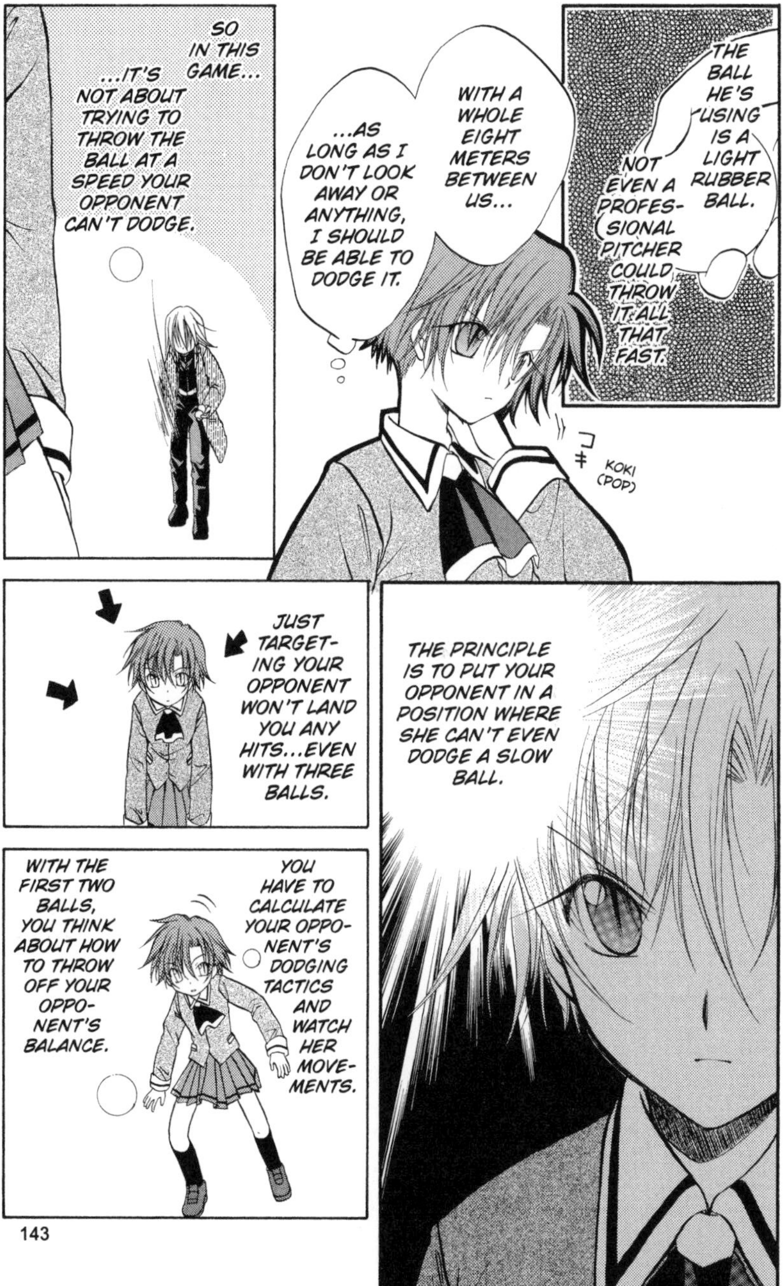
THE BALL HE'S USING IS A LIGHT RUBBER BALL.
NOT EVEN A PROFESSIONAL PITCHER COULD THROW IT ALL THAT FAST.
WITH A WHOLE EIGHT METERS BETWEEN US...
...AS LONG AS I DON'T LOOK AWAY OR ANYTHING, I SHOULD BE ABLE TO DODGE IT.
コキ
KOKI (POP)
SO IN THIS GAME...
...IT'S NOT ABOUT TRYING TO THROW THE BALL AT A SPEED YOUR OPPONENT CAN'T DODGE.
THE PRINCIPLE IS TO PUT YOUR OPPONENT IN A POSITION WHERE SHE CAN'T EVEN DODGE A SLOW BALL.
JUST TARGETING YOUR OPPONENT WON'T LAND YOU ANY HITS...EVEN WITH THREE BALLS.
YOU HAVE TO CALCULATE YOUR OPPONENT'S DODGING TACTICS AND WATCH HER MOVEMENTS.
WITH THE FIRST TWO BALLS, YOU THINK ABOUT HOW TO THROW OFF YOUR OPPONENT'S BALANCE.

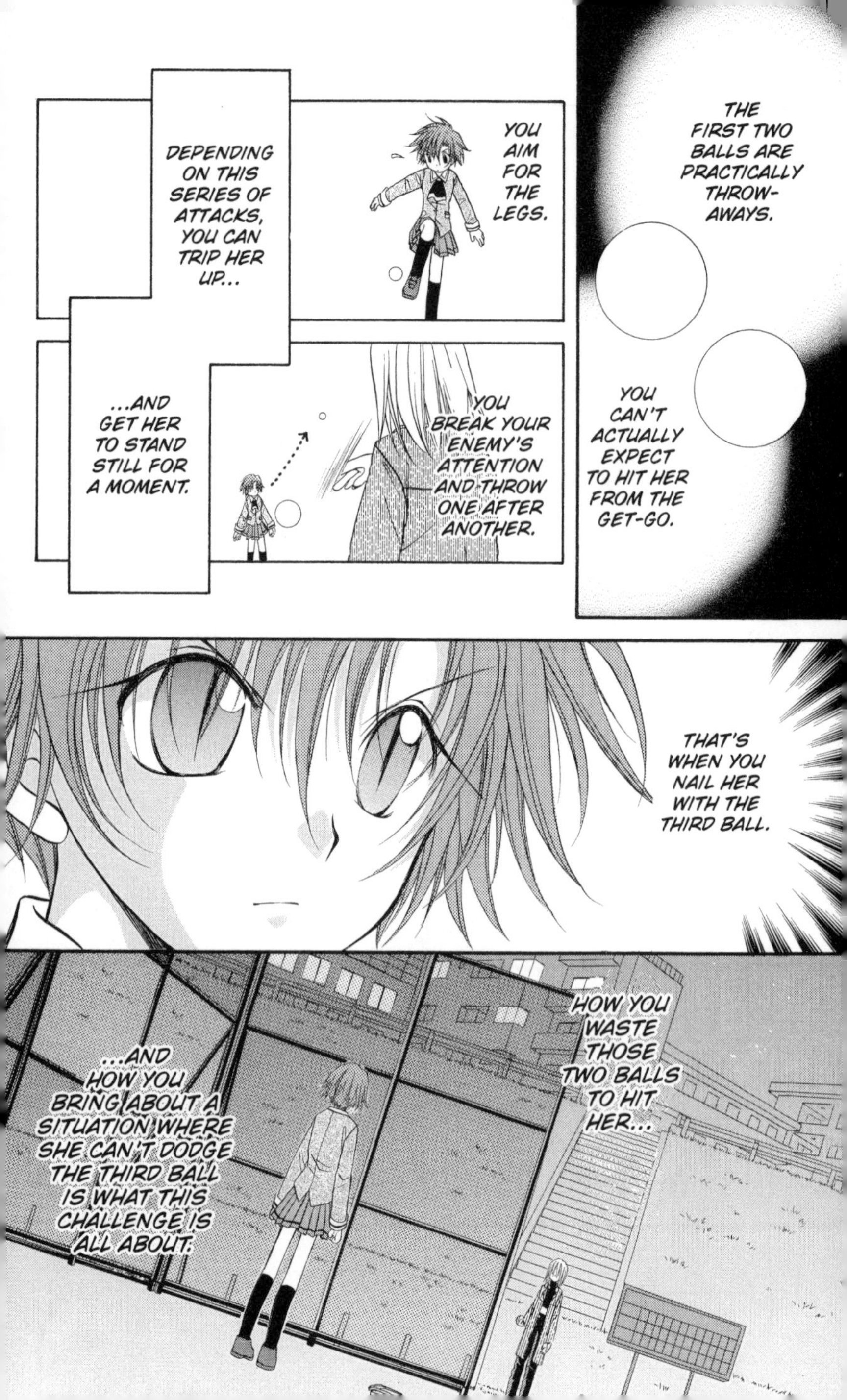
THE FIRST TWO BALLS ARE PRACTICALLY THROW-AWAYS.
YOU CAN'T ACTUALLY EXPECT TO HIT HER FROM THE GET-GO.
YOU AIM FOR THE LEGS.
DEPENDING ON THIS SERIES OF ATTACKS, YOU CAN TRIP HER UP...
YOU BREAK YOUR ENEMY'S ATTENTION AND THROW ONE AFTER ANOTHER.
...AND GET HER TO STAND STILL FOR A MOMENT.
THAT'S WHEN YOU NAIL HER WITH THE THIRD BALL.
HOW YOU WASTE THOSE TWO BALLS TO HIT HER...
...AND HOW YOU BRING ABOUT A SITUATION WHERE SHE CAN'T DODGE THE THIRD BALL IS WHAT THIS CHALLENGE IS ALL ABOUT.

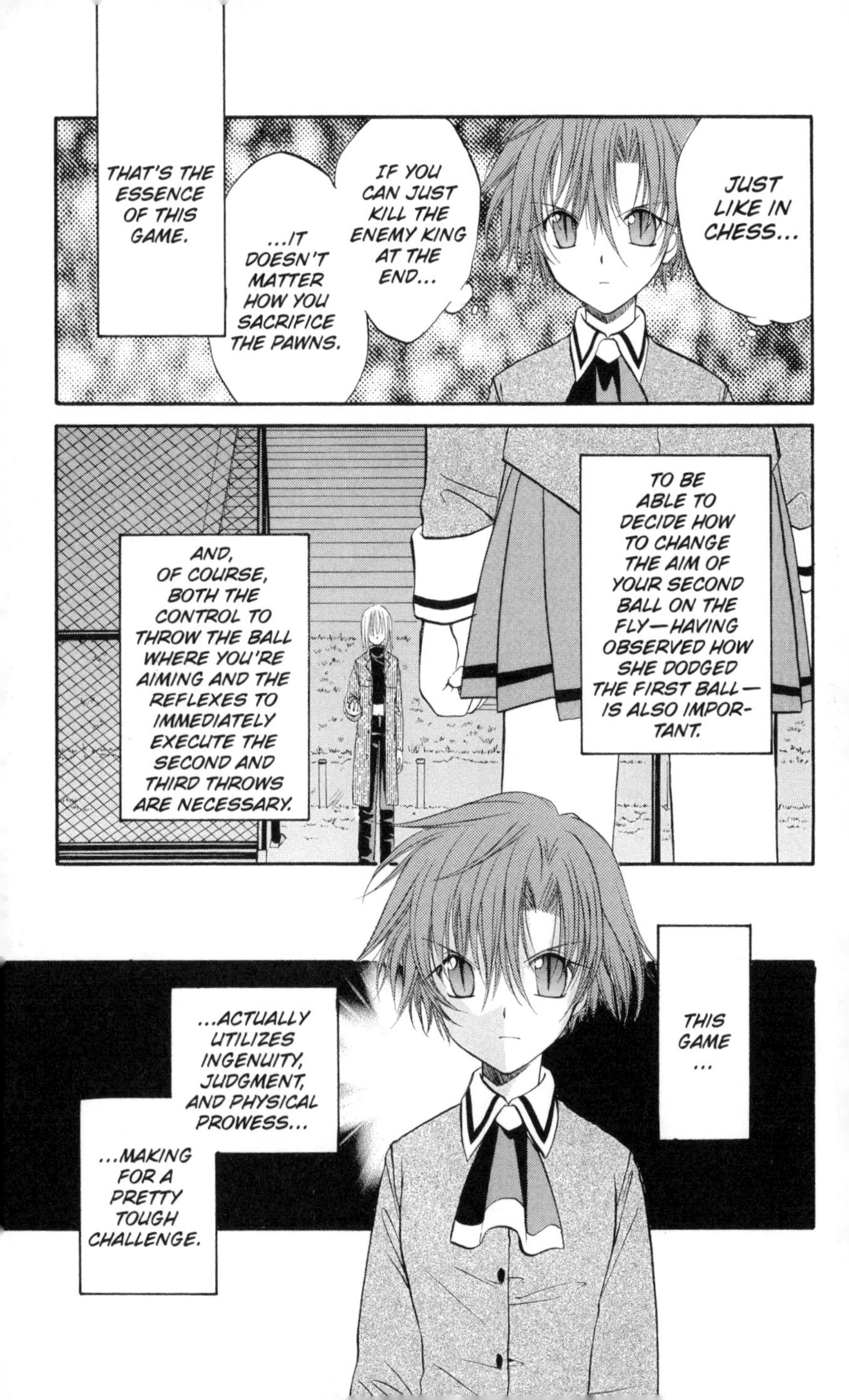
JUST LIKE IN CHESS...
IF YOU CAN JUST KILL THE ENEMY KING AT THE END...
...IT DOESN'T MATTER HOW YOU SACRIFICE THE PAWNS.
THAT'S THE ESSENCE OF THIS GAME.
TO BE ABLE TO DECIDE HOW TO CHANGE THE AIM OF YOUR SECOND BALL ON THE FLY—HAVING OBSERVED HOW SHE DODGED THE FIRST BALL—IS ALSO IMPORTANT.
AND, OF COURSE, BOTH THE CONTROL TO THROW THE BALL WHERE YOU'RE AIMING AND THE REFLEXES TO IMMEDIATELY EXECUTE THE SECOND AND THIRD THROWS ARE NECESSARY.
THIS GAME...
...ACTUALLY UTILIZES INGENUITY, JUDGMENT, AND PHYSICAL PROWESS...
...MAKING FOR A PRETTY TOUGH CHALLENGE.

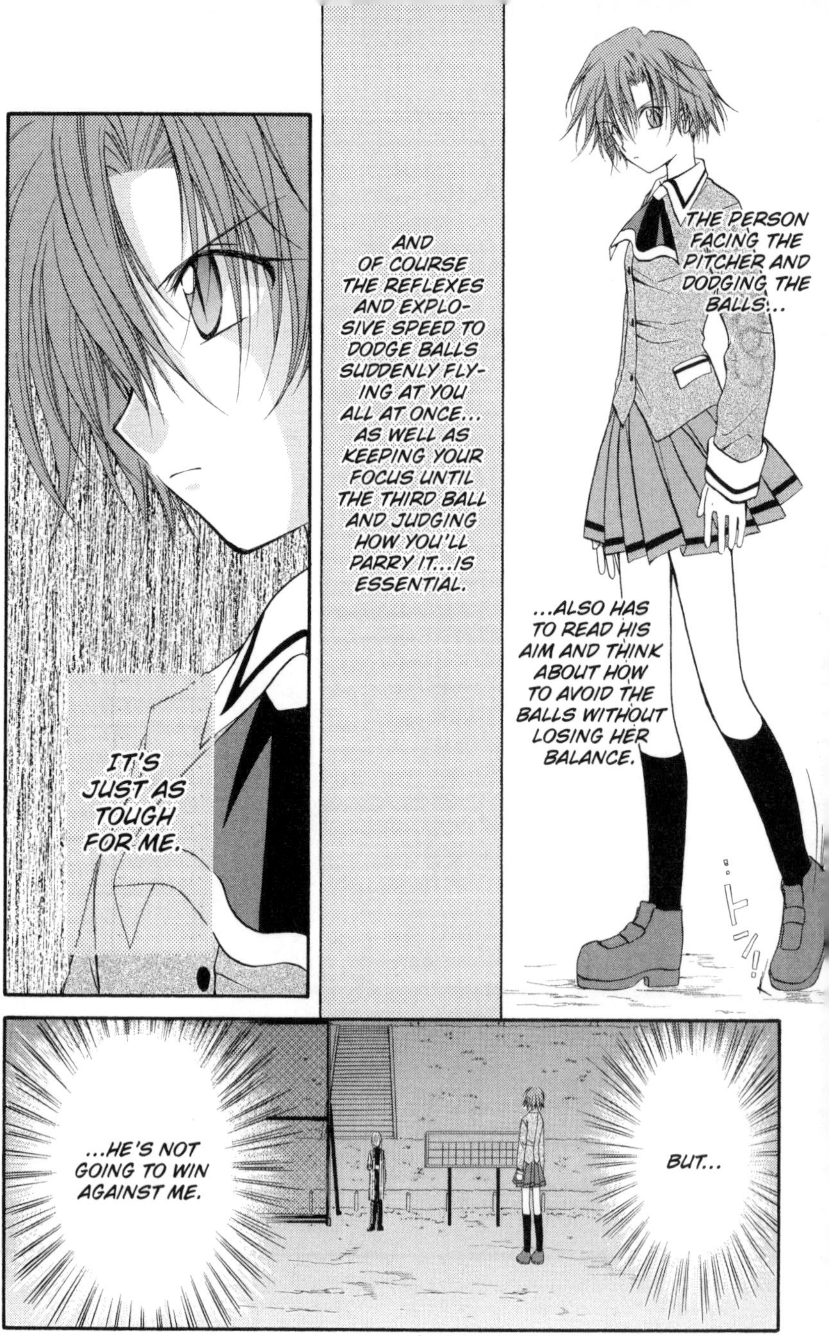
THE PERSON FACING THE PITCHER AND DODGING THE BALLS...
...ALSO HAS TO READ HIS AIM AND THINK ABOUT HOW TO AVOID THE BALLS WITHOUT LOSING HER BALANCE.
AND OF COURSE THE REFLEXES AND EXPLOSIVE SPEED TO DODGE BALLS SUDDENLY FLYING AT YOU ALL AT ONCE... AS WELL AS KEEPING YOUR FOCUS UNTIL THE THIRD BALL AND JUDGING HOW YOU'LL PARRY IT...IS ESSENTIAL.
IT'S JUST AS TOUGH FOR ME.
BUT...
...HE'S NOT GOING TO WIN AGAINST ME.

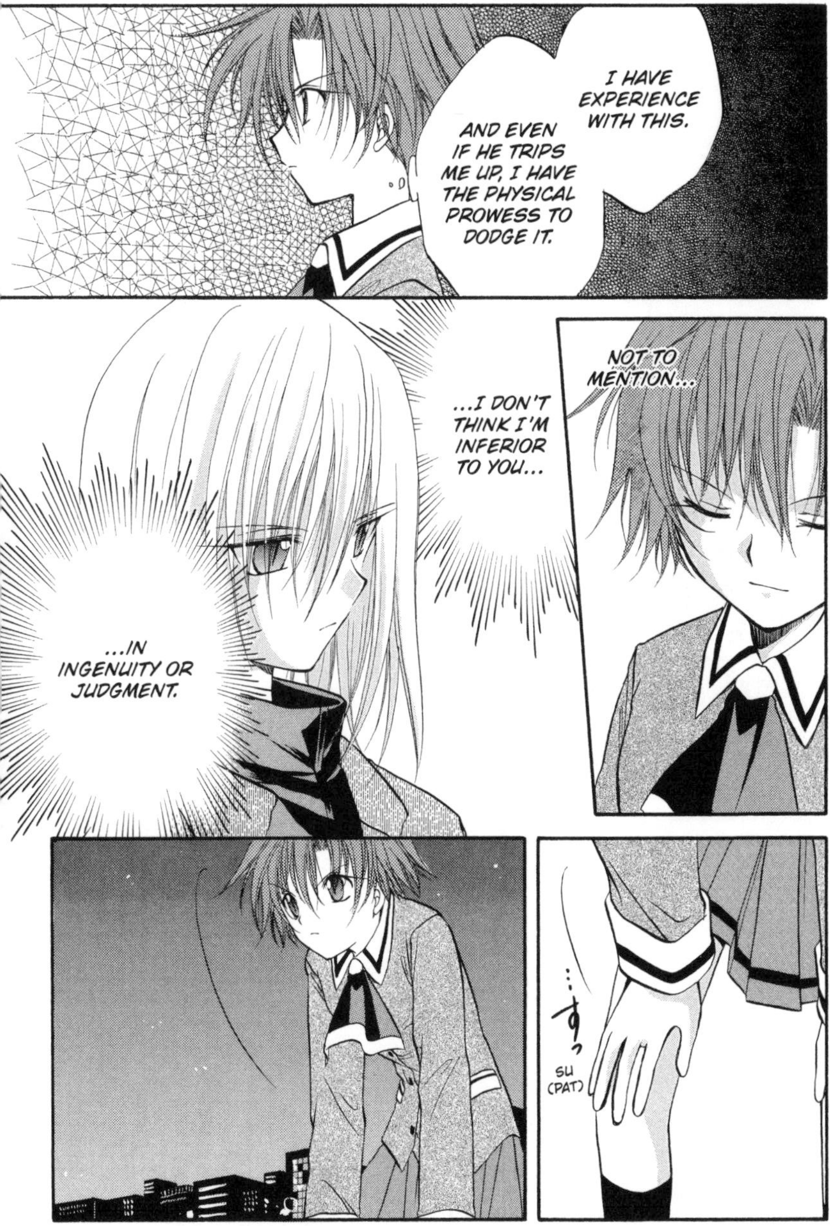
I HAVE EXPERIENCE WITH THIS.
AND EVEN IF HE TRIPS ME UP, I HAVE THE PHYSICAL PROWESS TO DODGE IT.
NOT TO MENTION...
...I DON'T THINK I'M INFERIOR TO YOU...
...IN INGENUITY OR JUDGMENT.
...すっ
SU (PAT)

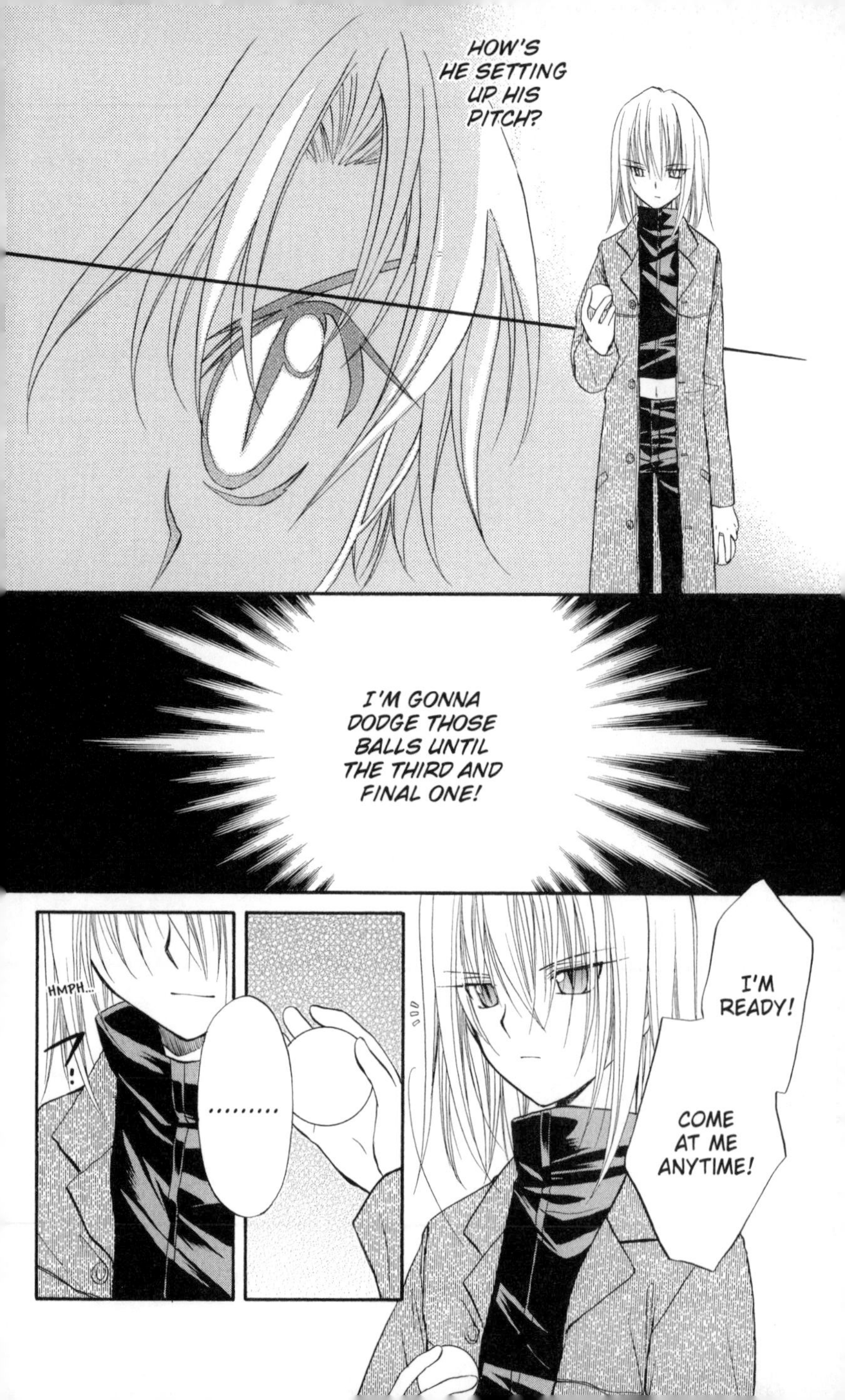
HOW'S HE SETTING UP HIS PITCH?
I'M GONNA DODGE THOSE BALLS UNTIL THE THIRD AND FINAL ONE!
I'M READY!
COME AT ME ANYTIME!
....
HMPH...

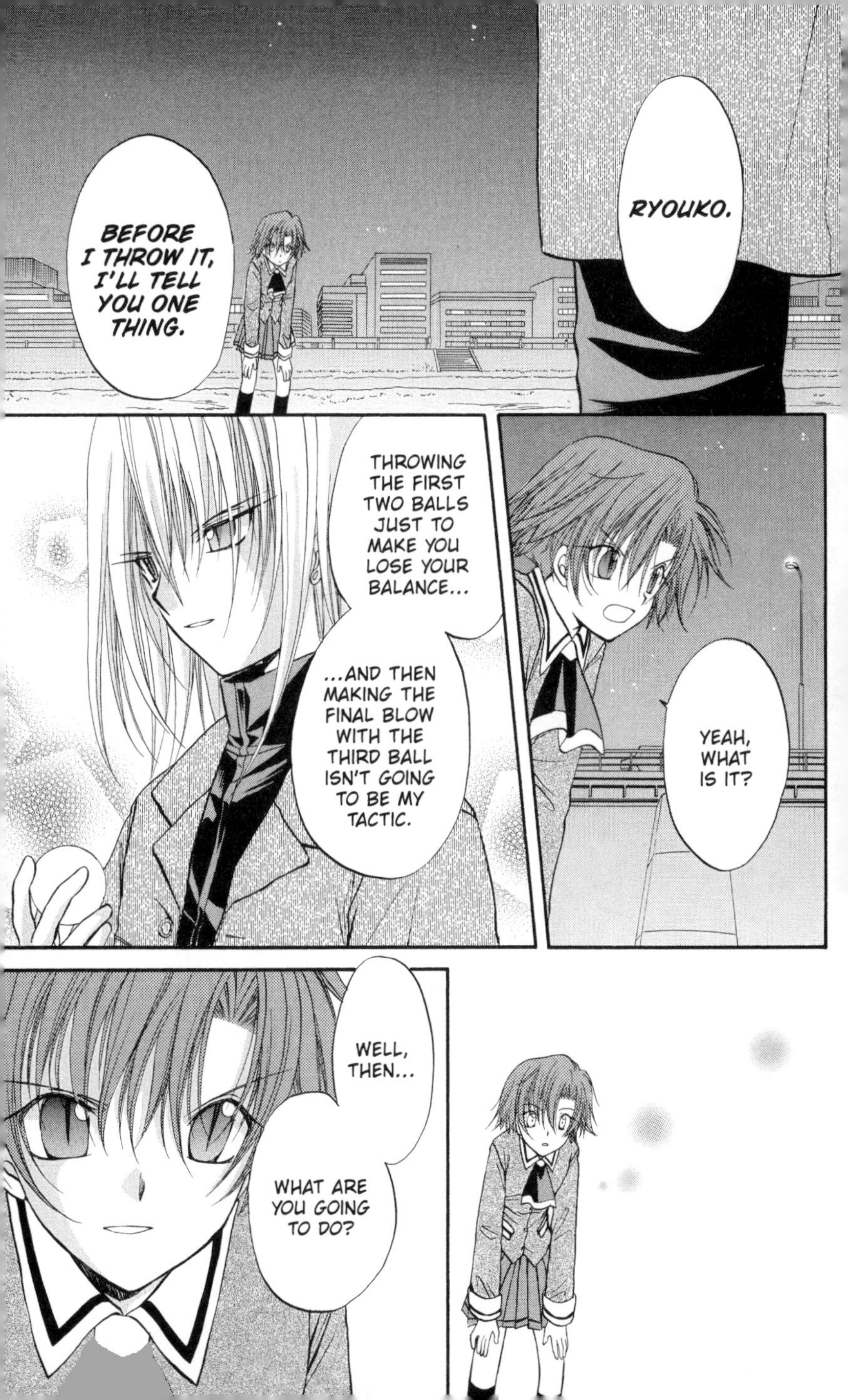
RYOUKO.
BEFORE I THROW IT, I'LL TELL YOU ONE THING.
YEAH, WHAT IS IT?
THROWING THE FIRST TWO BALLS JUST TO MAKE YOU LOSE YOUR BALANCE...
...AND THEN MAKING THE FINAL BLOW WITH THE THIRD BALL ISN'T GOING TO BE MY TACTIC.
WELL, THEN...
WHAT ARE YOU GOING TO DO?

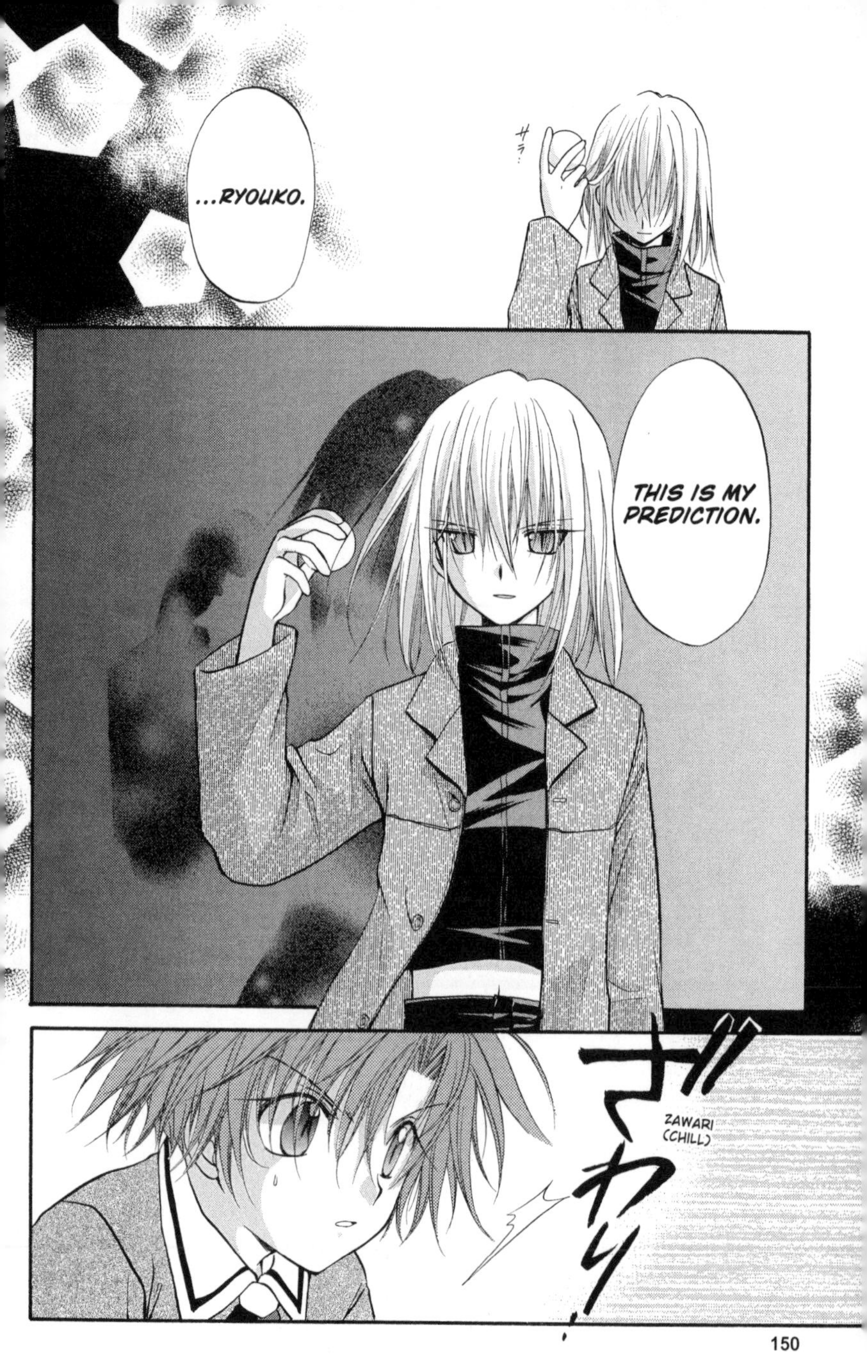
...RYOUKO.
THIS IS MY PREDICTION.
ざわり
ZAWARI (CHILL)

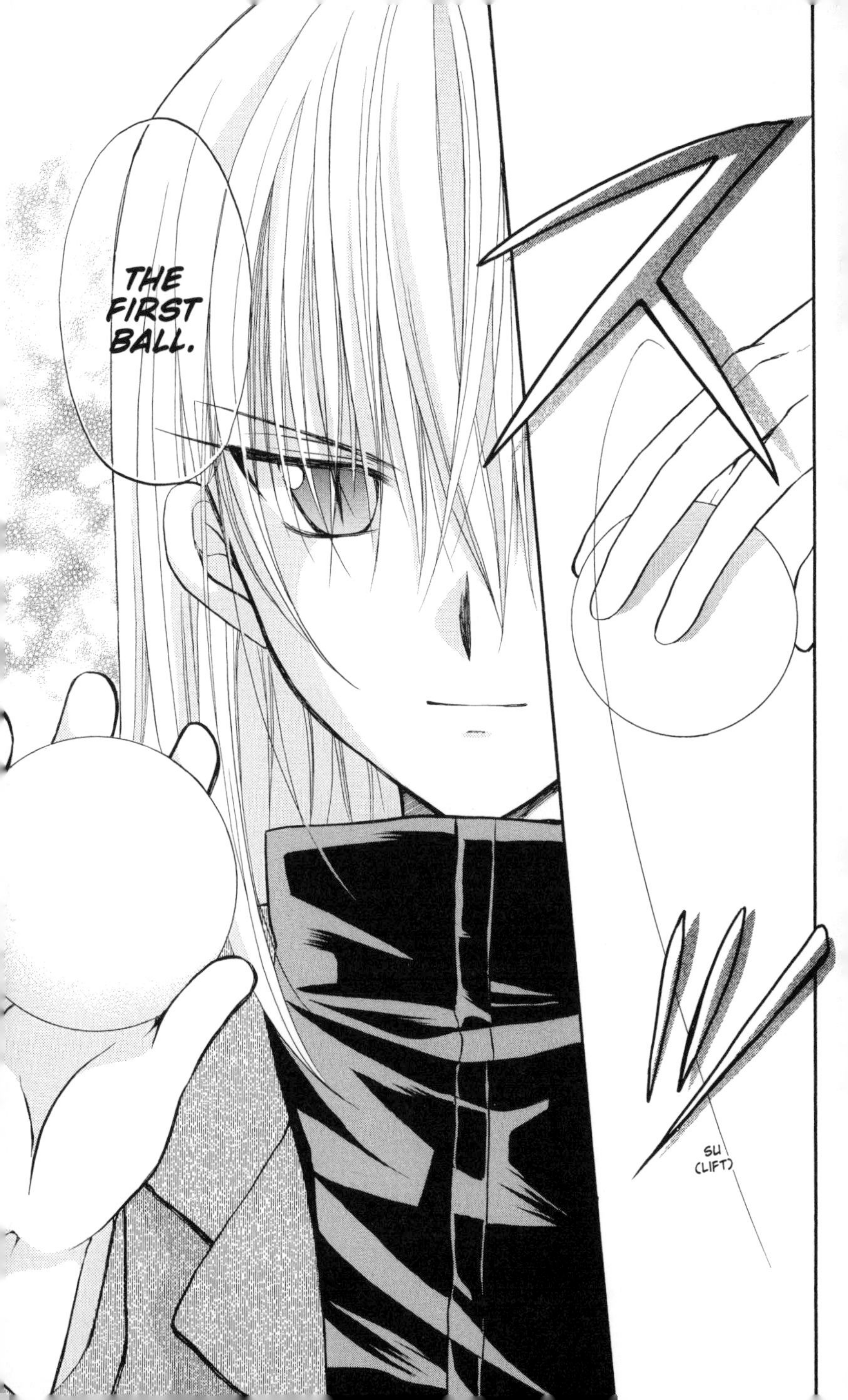
THE FIRST BALL.
SU (LIFT)

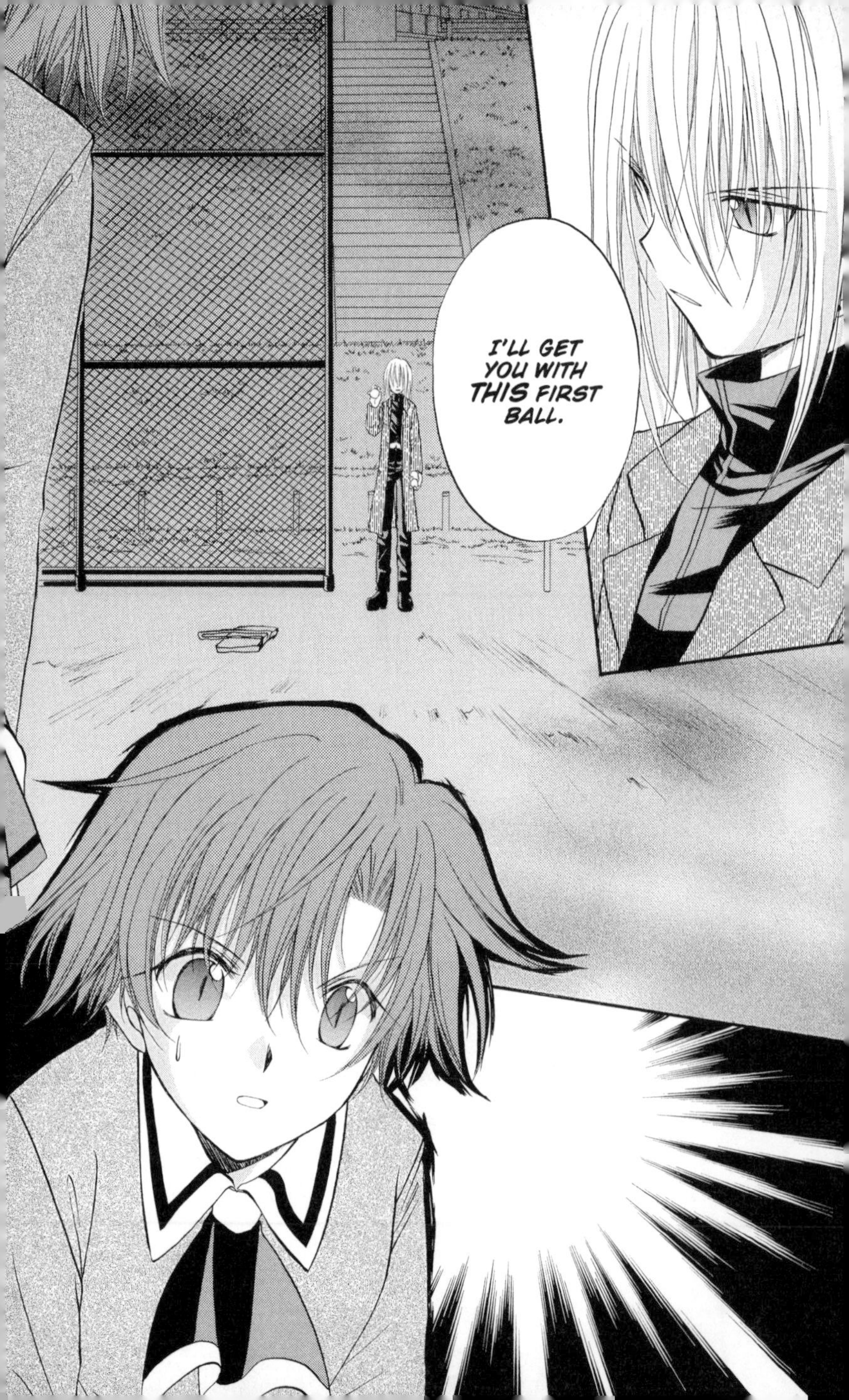
I'LL GET YOU WITH THIS FIRST BALL.

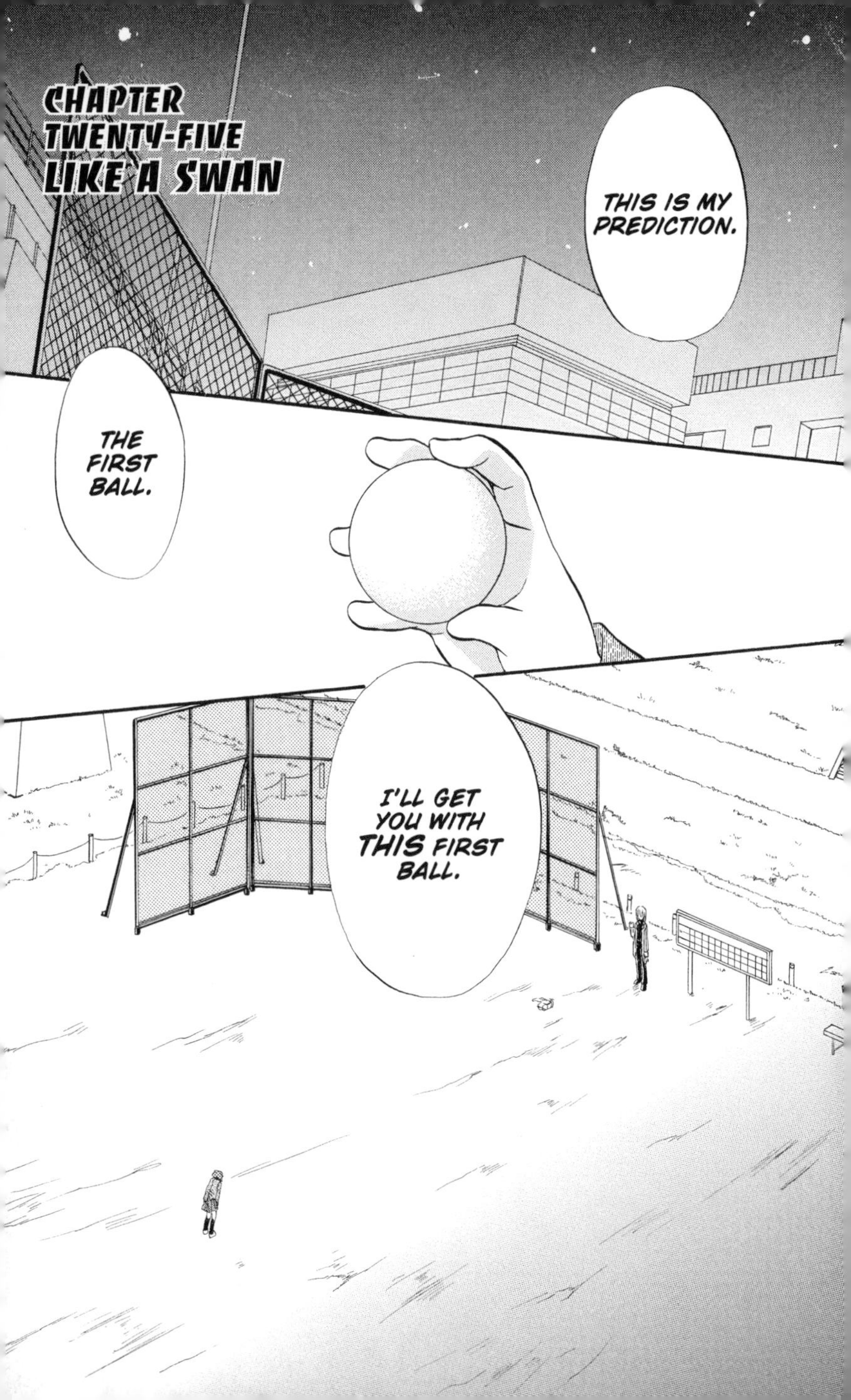
THIS IS MY PREDICTION.
CHAPTER TWENTY-FIVE LIKE A SWAN
THE FIRST BALL.
I'LL GET YOU WITH THIS FIRST BALL.

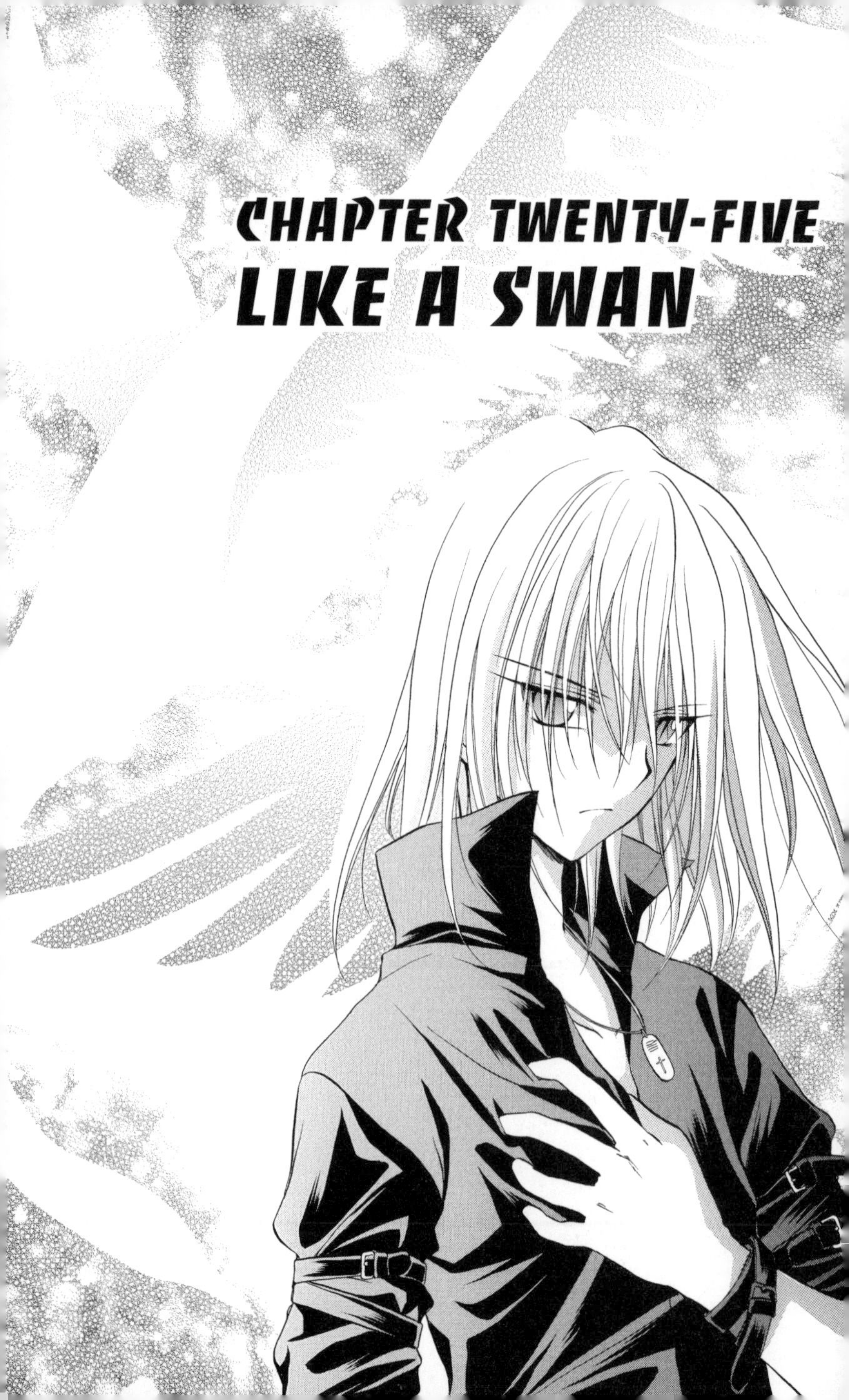
CHAPTER TWENTY-FIVE
LIKE A SWAN

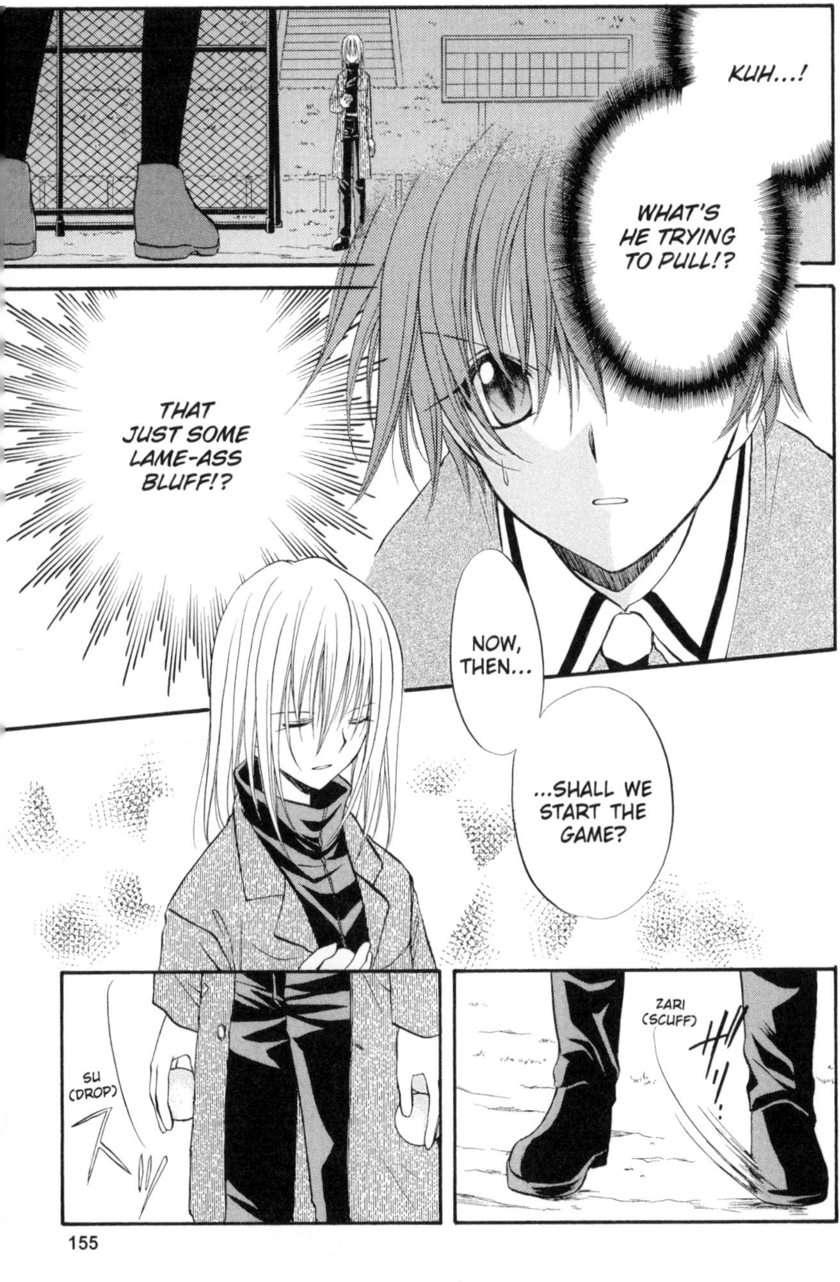
KUH...!
WHAT'S HE TRYING TO PULL!?
THAT JUST SOME LAME-ASS BLUFF!?
NOW, THEN...
...SHALL WE START THE GAME?
ZARI (SCUFF)
SU (DROP)

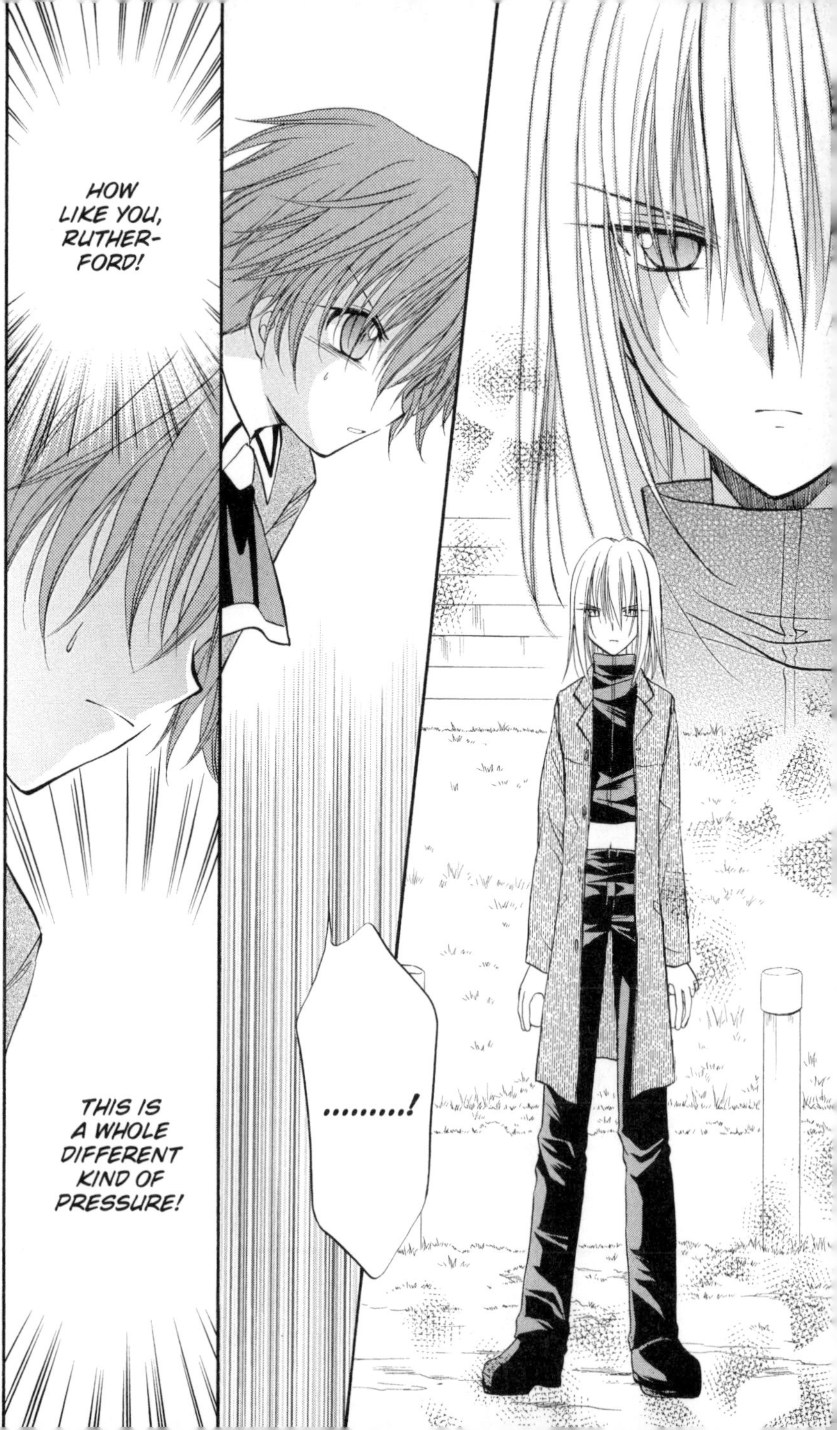
........!
HOW LIKE YOU, RUTHER-FORD!
THIS IS A WHOLE DIFFERENT KIND OF PRESSURE!

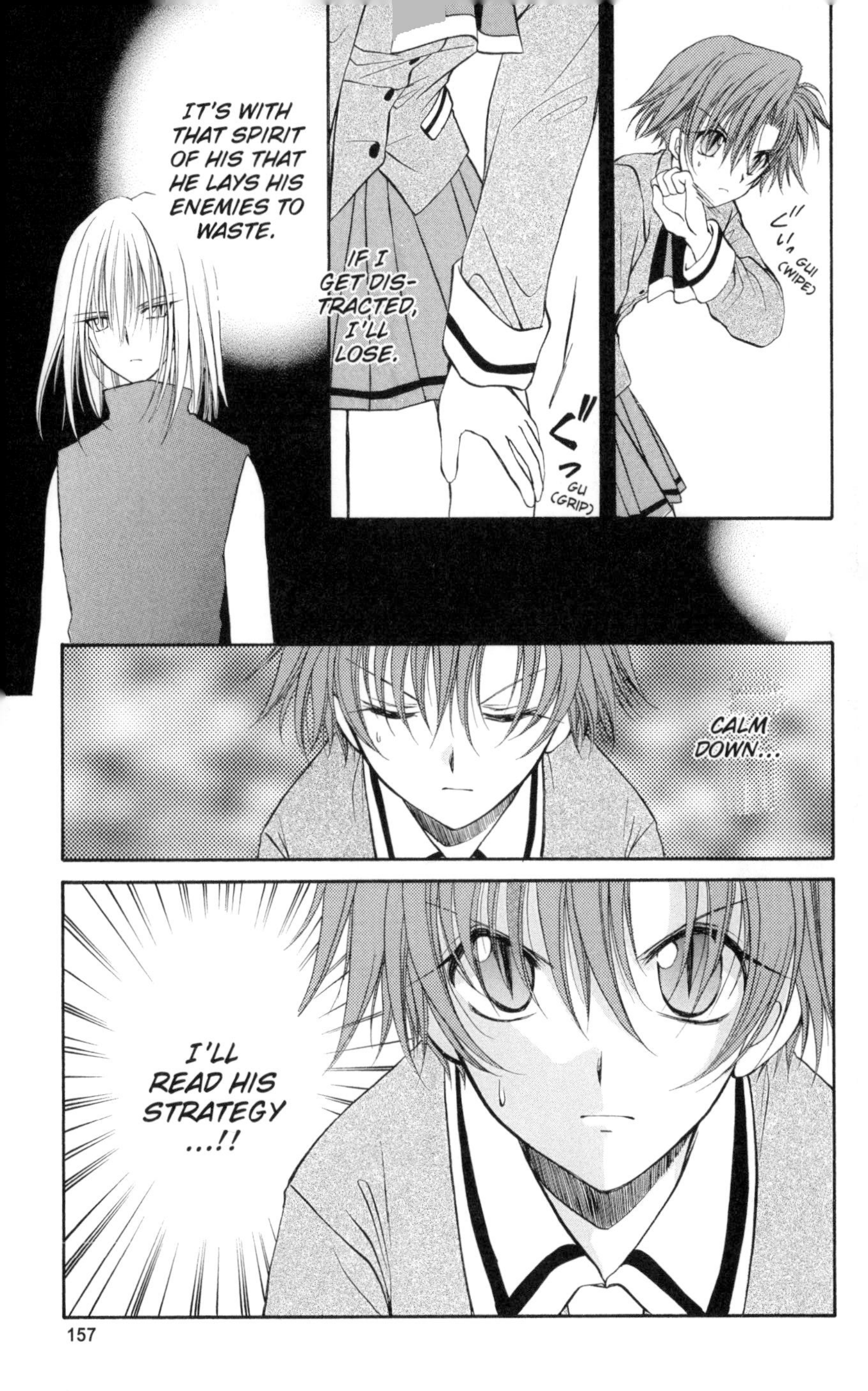
GUI (WIPE)
IF I GET DIS-TRACTED, I'LL LOSE.
GU (GRIP)
IT'S WITH THAT SPIRIT OF HIS THAT HE LAYS HIS ENEMIES TO WASTE.
CALM DOWN...
I'LL READ HIS STRATEGY ...!!

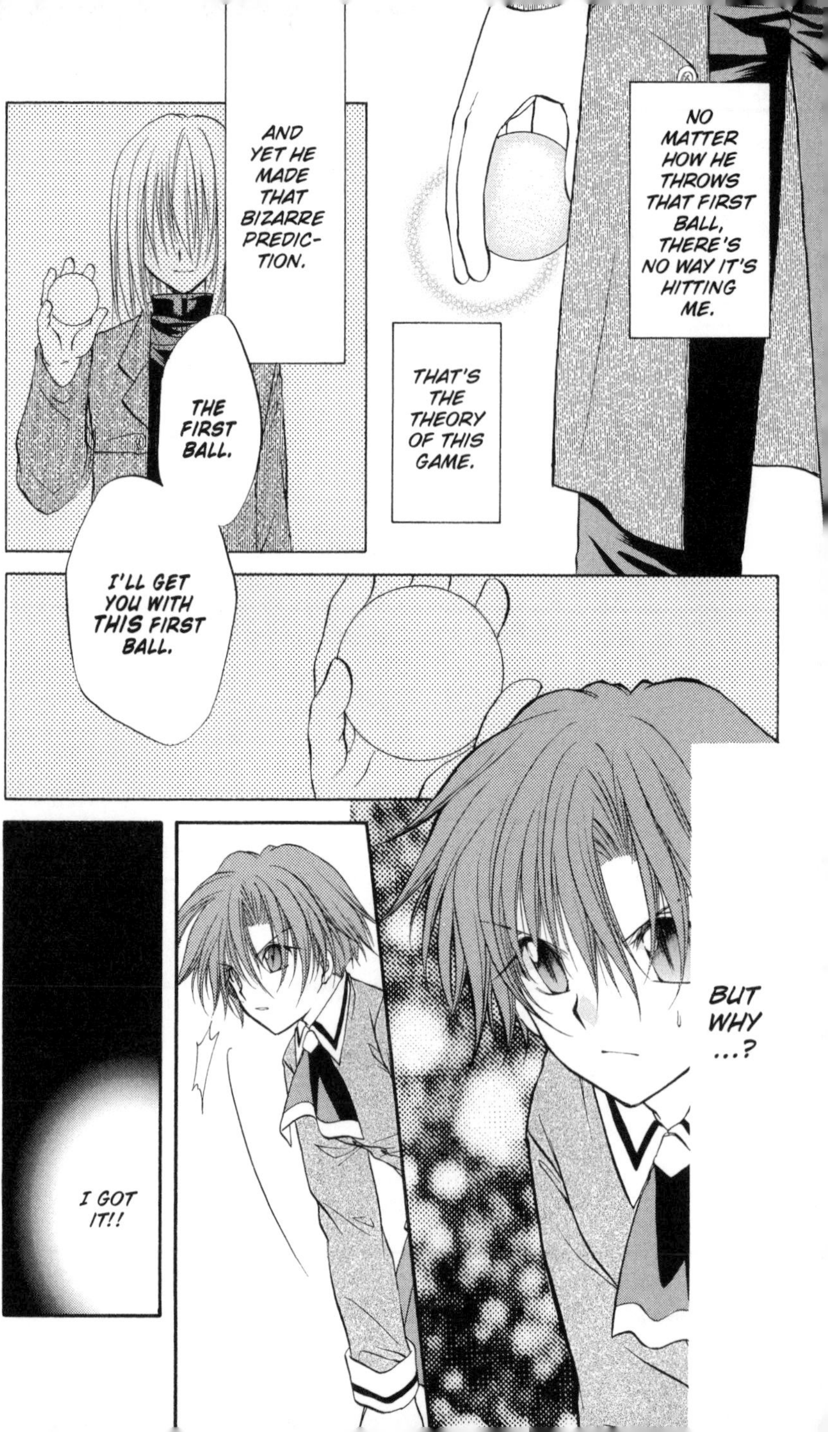
NO MATTER HOW HE THROWS THAT FIRST BALL, THERE'S NO WAY IT'S HITTING ME.
THAT'S THE THEORY OF THIS GAME.
AND YET HE MADE THAT BIZARRE PREDICTION.
THE FIRST BALL.
I'LL GET YOU WITH THIS FIRST BALL.
BUT WHY ...?
I GOT IT!!

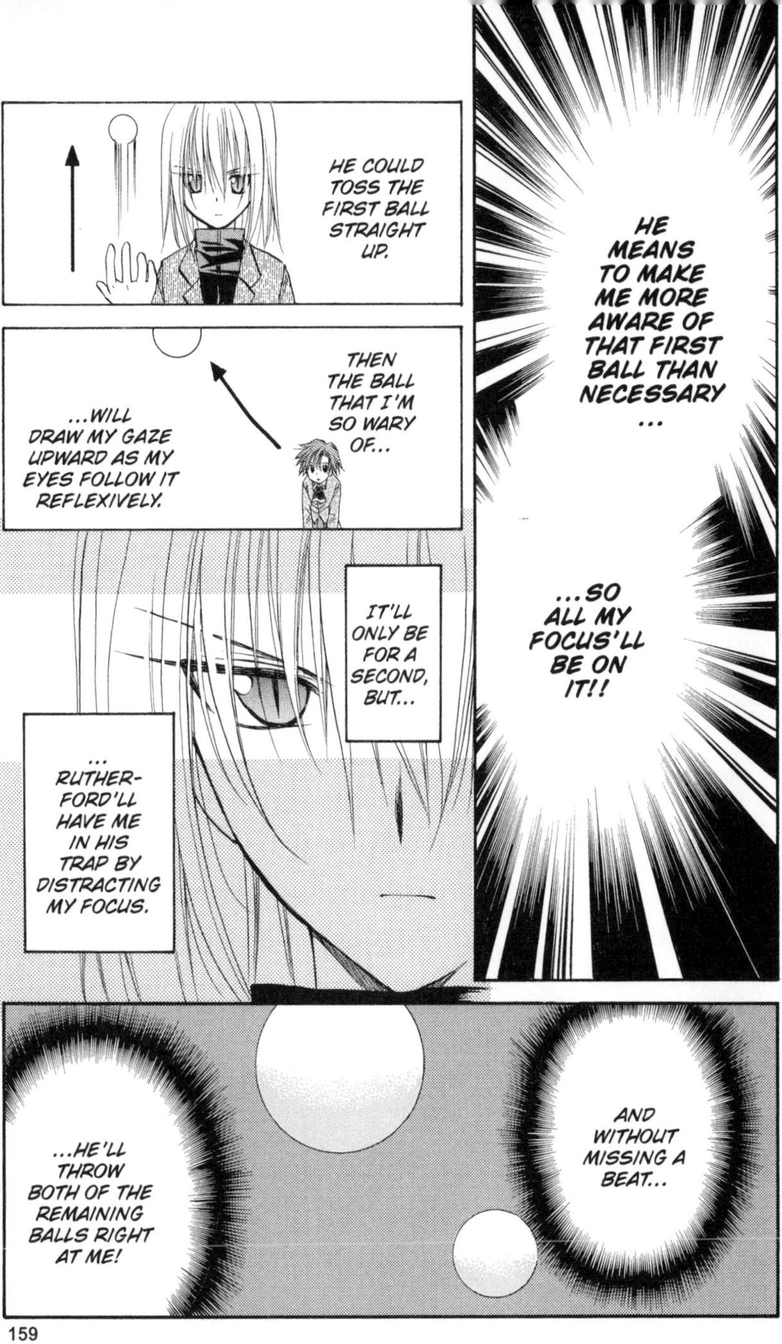
HE MEANS TO MAKE ME MORE AWARE OF THAT FIRST BALL THAN NECESSARY...
...SO ALL MY FOCUS'LL BE ON IT!!
HE COULD TOSS THE FIRST BALL STRAIGHT UP.
THEN THE BALL THAT I'M SO WARY OF...
...WILL DRAW MY GAZE UPWARD AS MY EYES FOLLOW IT REFLEXIVELY.
IT'LL ONLY BE FOR A SECOND, BUT...
...RUTHERFORD'LL HAVE ME IN HIS TRAP BY DISTRACTING MY FOCUS.
AND WITHOUT MISSING A BEAT...
...HE'LL THROW BOTH OF THE REMAINING BALLS RIGHT AT ME!

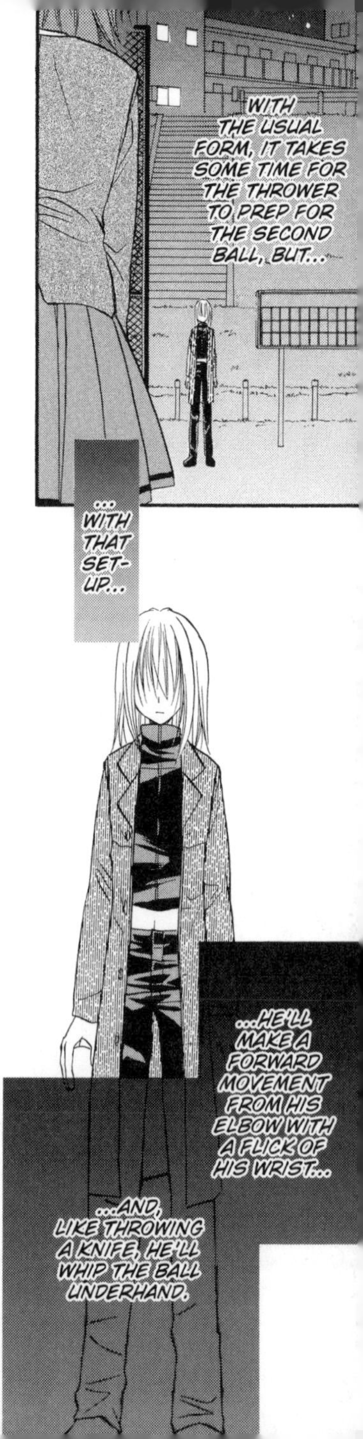
WITH THE USUAL FORM, IT TAKES SOME TIME FOR THE THROWER TO PREP FOR THE SECOND BALL, BUT...
...WITH THAT SET-UP...
...HE'LL MAKE A FORWARD MOVEMENT FROM HIS ELBOW WITH A FLICK OF HIS WRIST...
...AND, LIKE THROWING A KNIFE, HE'LL WHIP THE BALL UNDERHAND.

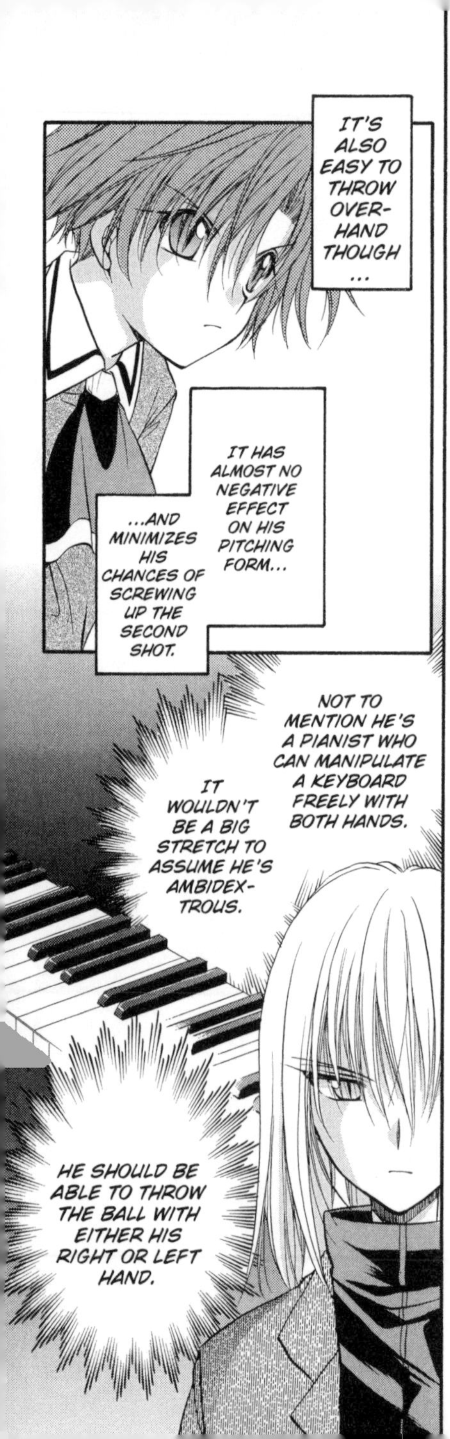
IT'S ALSO EASY TO THROW OVER-HAND THOUGH...
IT HAS ALMOST NO NEGATIVE EFFECT ON HIS PITCHING FORM...
...AND MINIMIZES HIS CHANCES OF SCREWING UP THE SECOND SHOT.
NOT TO MENTION HE'S A PIANIST WHO CAN MANIPULATE A KEYBOARD FREELY WITH BOTH HANDS.
IT WOULDN'T BE A BIG STRETCH TO ASSUME HE'S AMBIDEX-TROUS.
HE SHOULD BE ABLE TO THROW THE BALL WITH EITHER HIS RIGHT OR LEFT HAND.

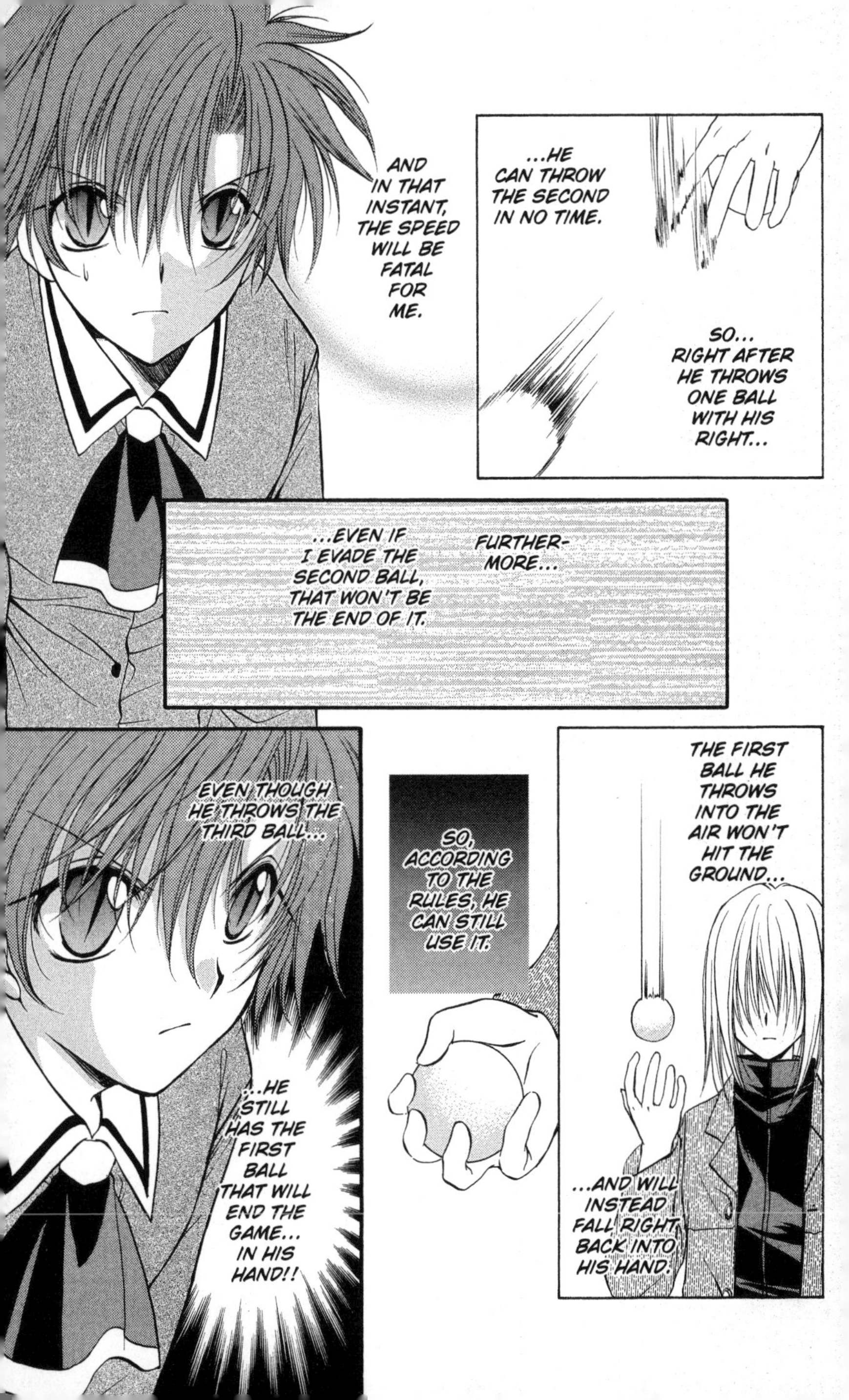
SO... RIGHT AFTER HE THROWS ONE BALL WITH HIS RIGHT...
...HE CAN THROW THE SECOND IN NO TIME.
AND IN THAT INSTANT, THE SPEED WILL BE FATAL FOR ME.
FURTHER-MORE...
...EVEN IF I EVADE THE SECOND BALL, THAT WON'T BE THE END OF IT.
THE FIRST BALL HE THROWS INTO THE AIR WON'T HIT THE GROUND...
...AND WILL INSTEAD FALL RIGHT BACK INTO HIS HAND.
SO, ACCORDING TO THE RULES, HE CAN STILL USE IT.
EVEN THOUGH HE THROWS THE THIRD BALL...
...HE STILL HAS THE FIRST BALL THAT WILL END THE GAME... IN HIS HAND!!

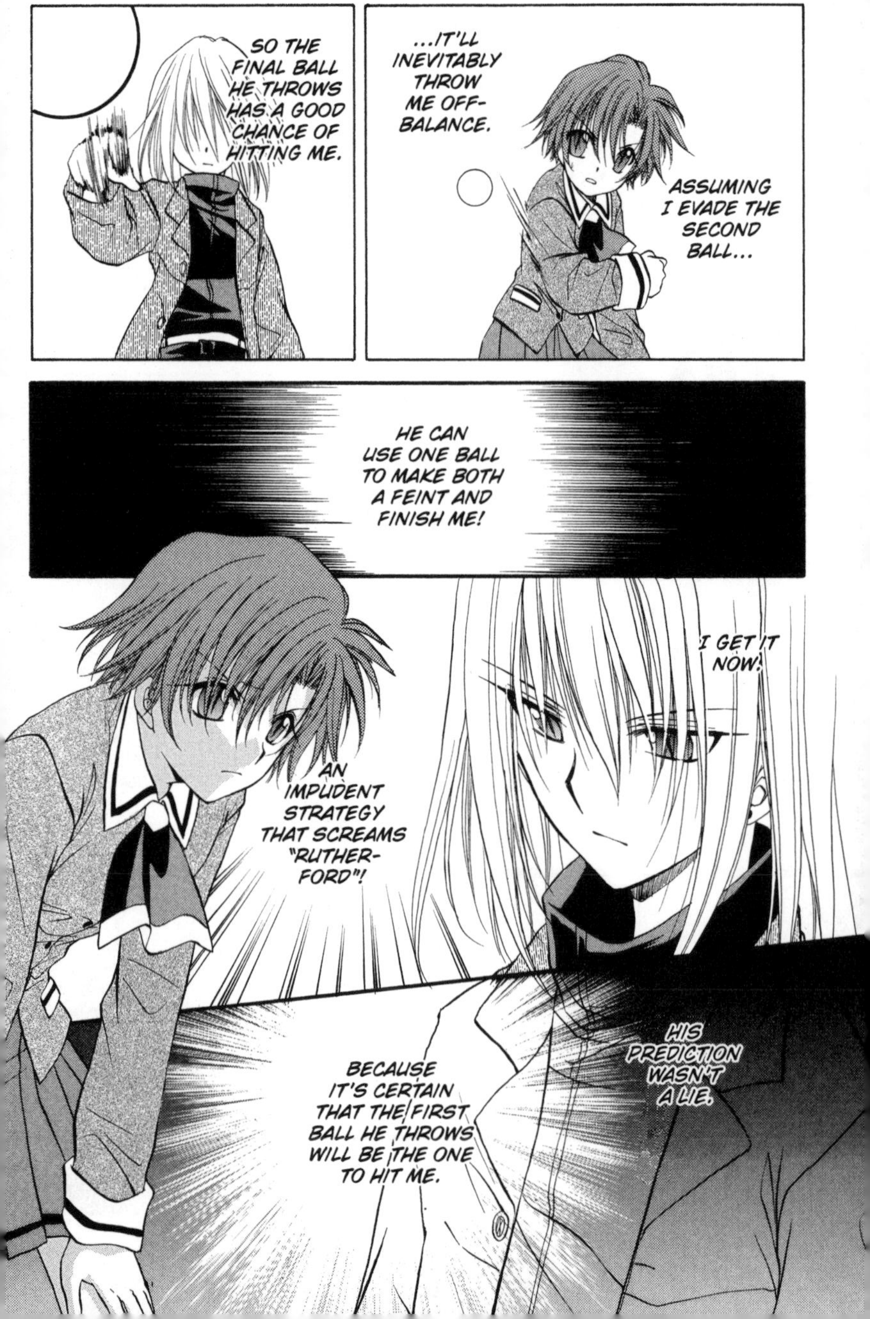
ASSUMING I EVADE THE SECOND BALL...
...IT'LL INEVITABLY THROW ME OFF-BALANCE.
SO THE FINAL BALL HE THROWS HAS A GOOD CHANCE OF HITTING ME.
HE CAN USE ONE BALL TO MAKE BOTH A FEINT AND FINISH ME!
I GET IT NOW!
AN IMPUDENT STRATEGY THAT SCREAMS "RUTHER-FORD"!
HIS PREDICTION WASN'T A LIE.
BECAUSE IT'S CERTAIN THAT THE FIRST BALL HE THROWS WILL BE THE ONE TO HIT ME.

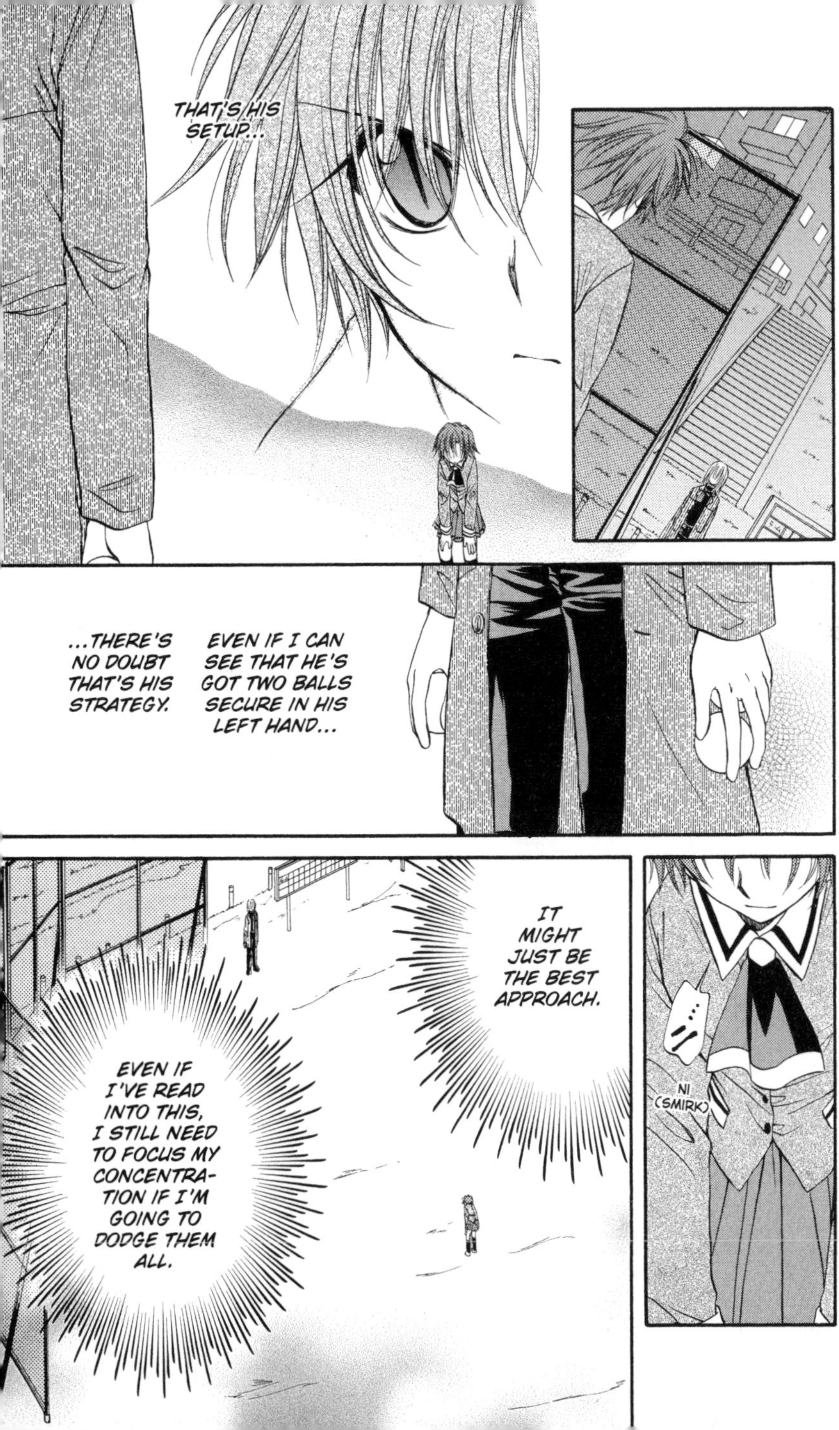
THAT'S HIS SETUP...
EVEN IF I CAN SEE THAT HE'S GOT TWO BALLS SECURE IN HIS LEFT HAND...
...THERE'S NO DOUBT THAT'S HIS STRATEGY.
...!
NI (SMIRK)
IT MIGHT JUST BE THE BEST APPROACH.
EVEN IF I'VE READ INTO THIS, I STILL NEED TO FOCUS MY CONCENTRATION IF I'M GOING TO DODGE THEM ALL.

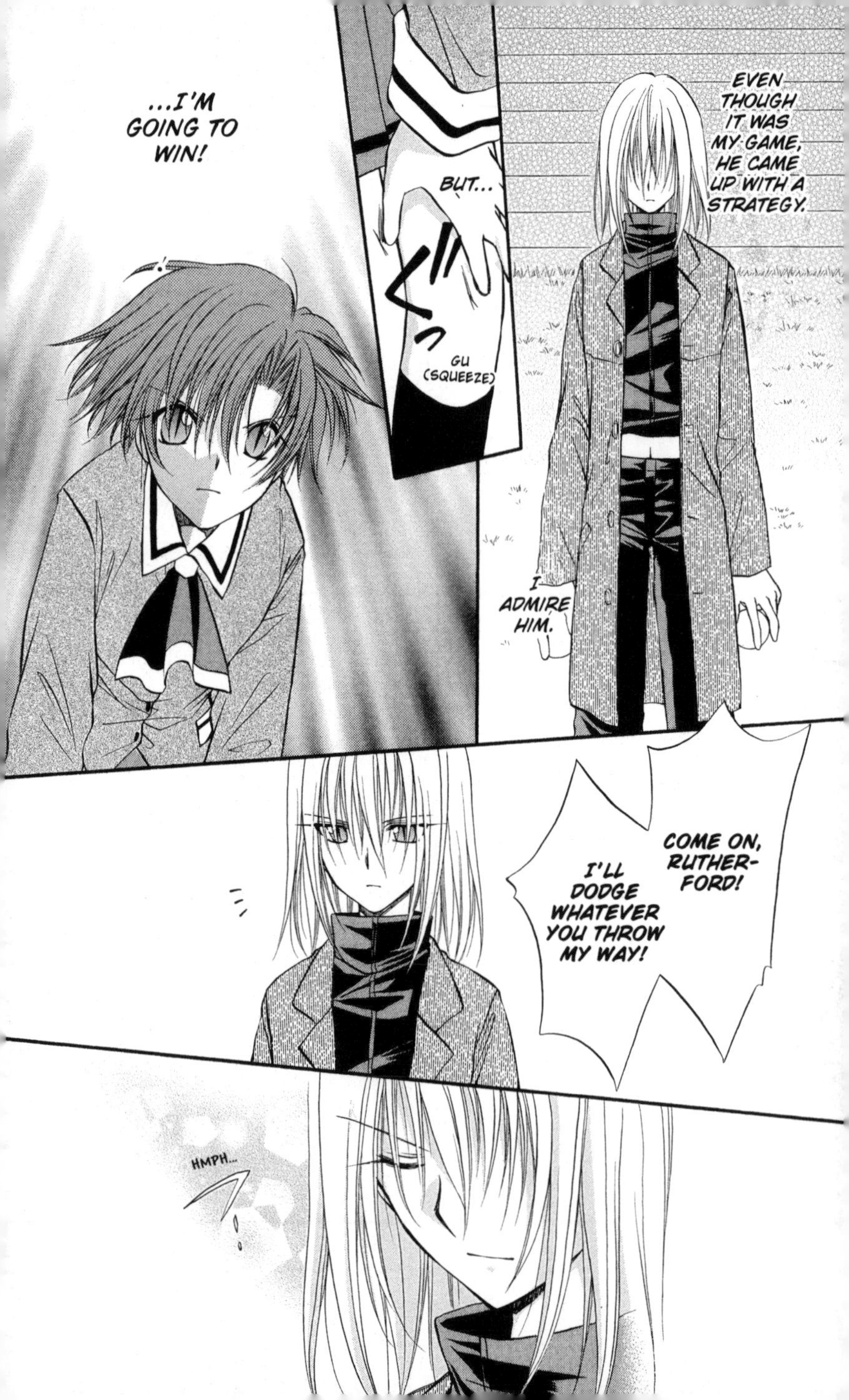
EVEN THOUGH IT WAS MY GAME, HE CAME UP WITH A STRATEGY.
I ADMIRE HIM.
BUT...
GU (SQUEEZE)
...I'M GOING TO WIN!
COME ON, RUTHER-FORD!
I'LL DODGE WHATEVER YOU THROW MY WAY!
HMPH...

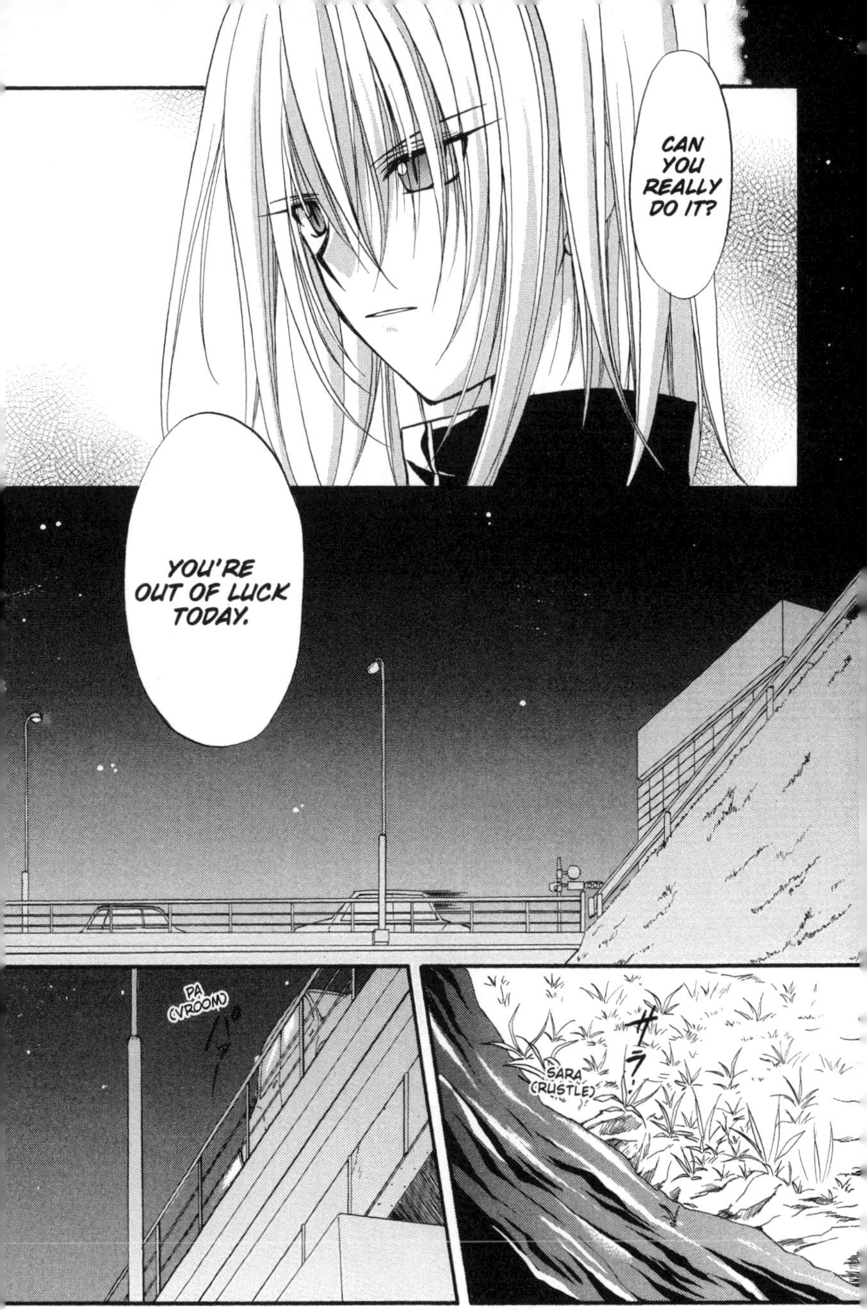
CAN YOU REALLY DO IT?
YOU'RE OUT OF LUCK TODAY.
SARA (RUSTLE)
PA (VROOM)

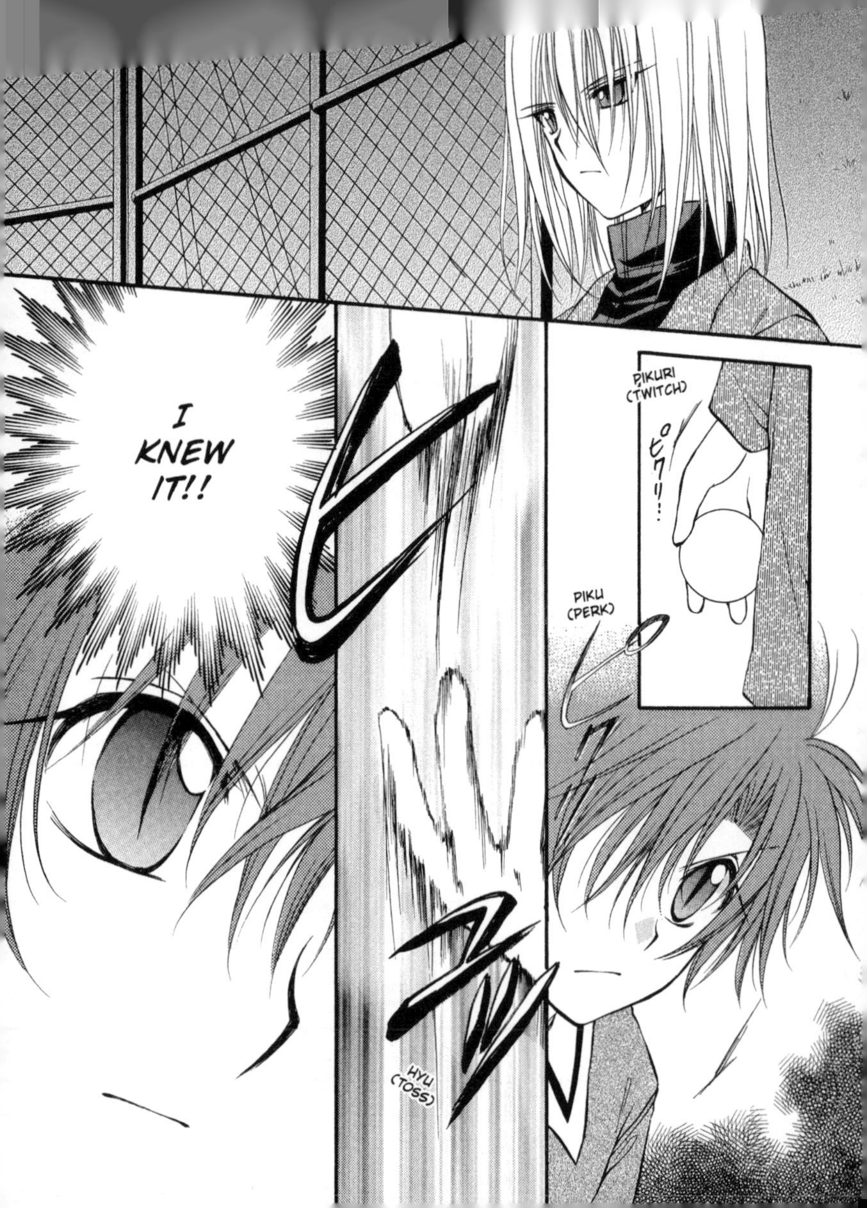

PIKURI (TWITCH)
ピクリ
PIKU (PERK)
HYU (TOSS)
I KNEW IT!!

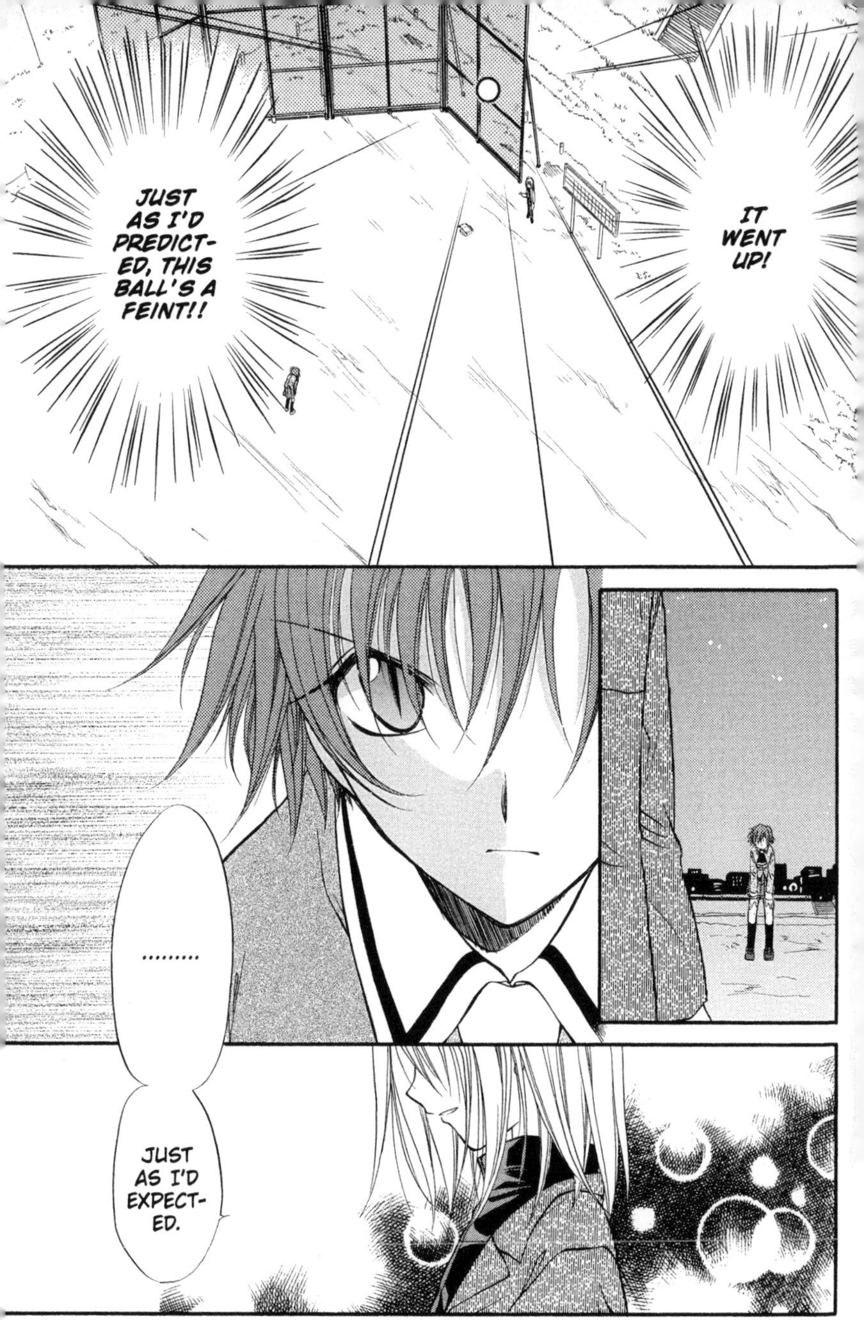
IT WENT UP!
JUST AS I'D PREDICT-ED, THIS BALL'S A FEINT!!
....
JUST AS I'D EXPECT-ED.

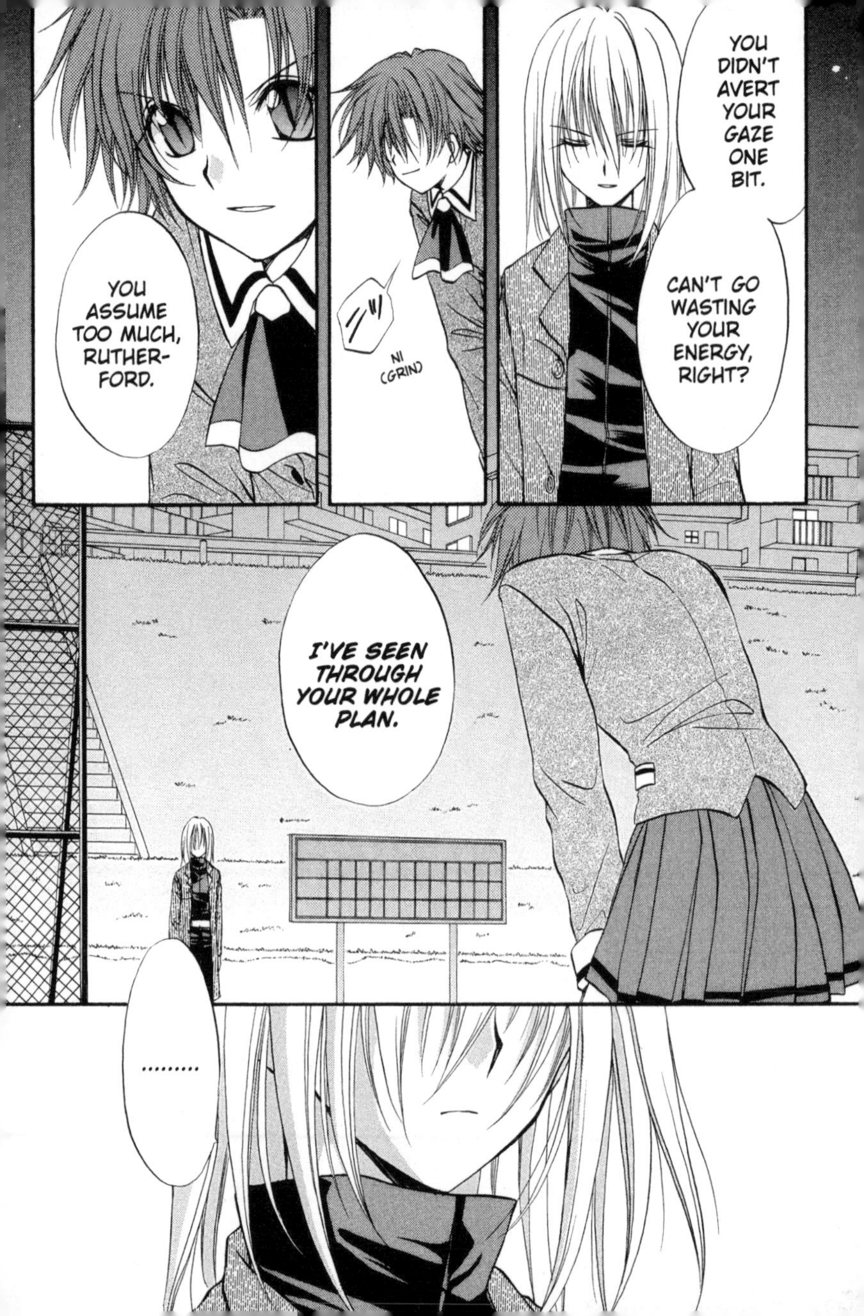
YOU DIDN'T AVERT YOUR GAZE ONE BIT.
CAN'T GO WASTING YOUR ENERGY, RIGHT?
NI (GRIN)
YOU ASSUME TOO MUCH, RUTHER-FORD.
I'VE SEEN THROUGH YOUR WHOLE PLAN.
....

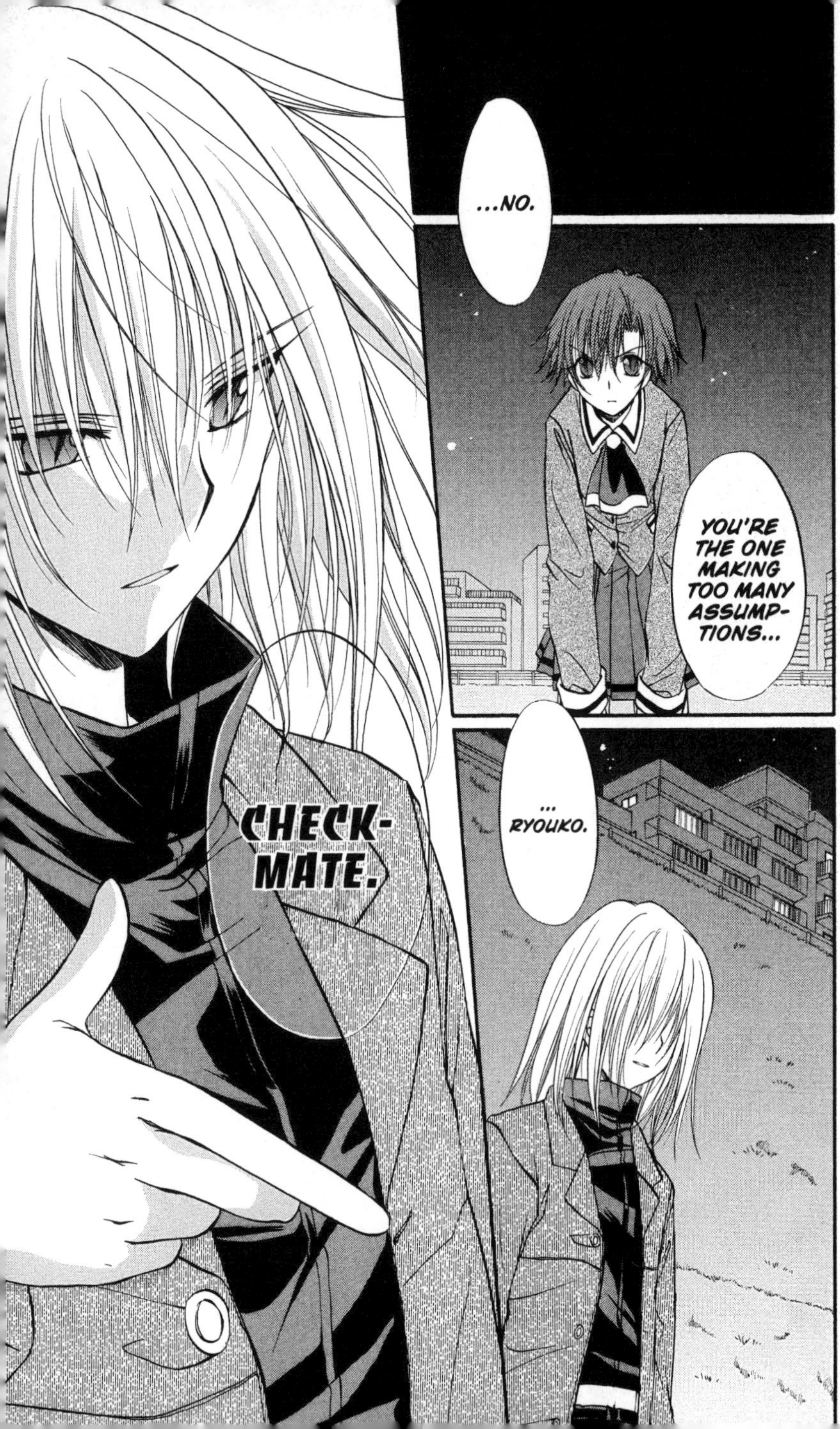
...NO.
YOU'RE THE ONE MAKING TOO MANY ASSUMPTIONS...
... RYOUKO.
CHECK-MATE.

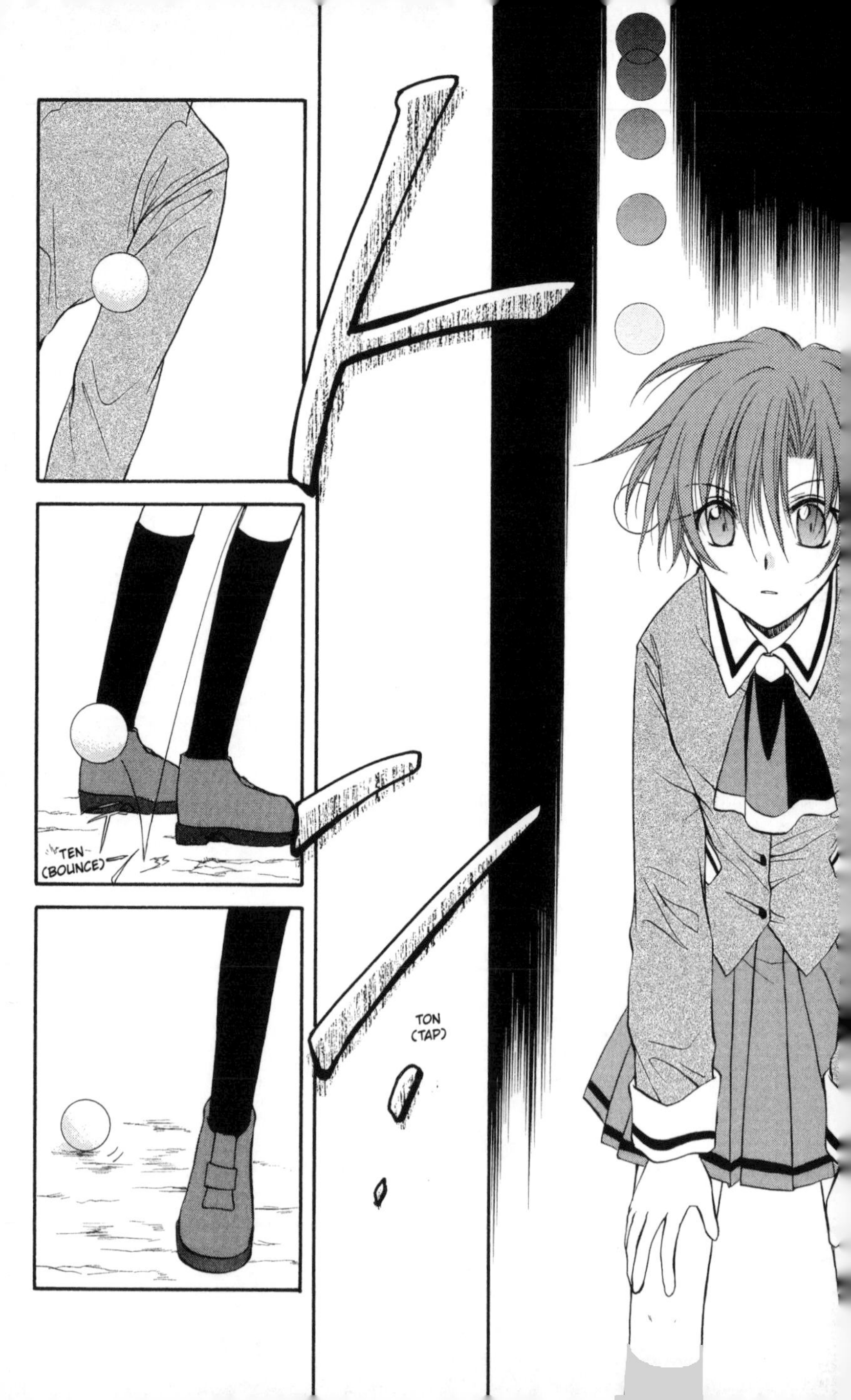
TON
(TAP)
TEN
(BOUNCE)

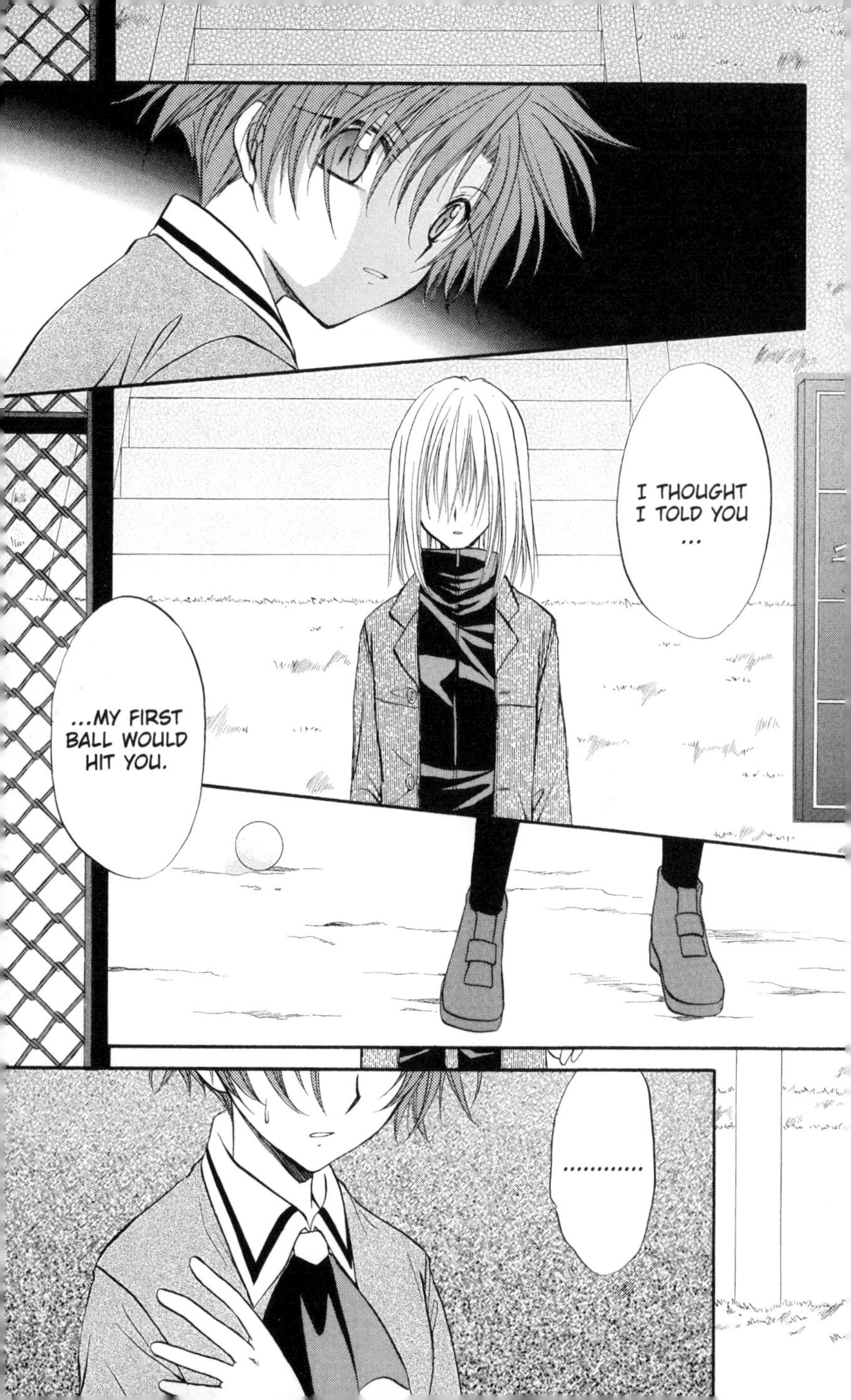
I THOUGHT I TOLD YOU ...
...MY FIRST BALL WOULD HIT YOU.
....

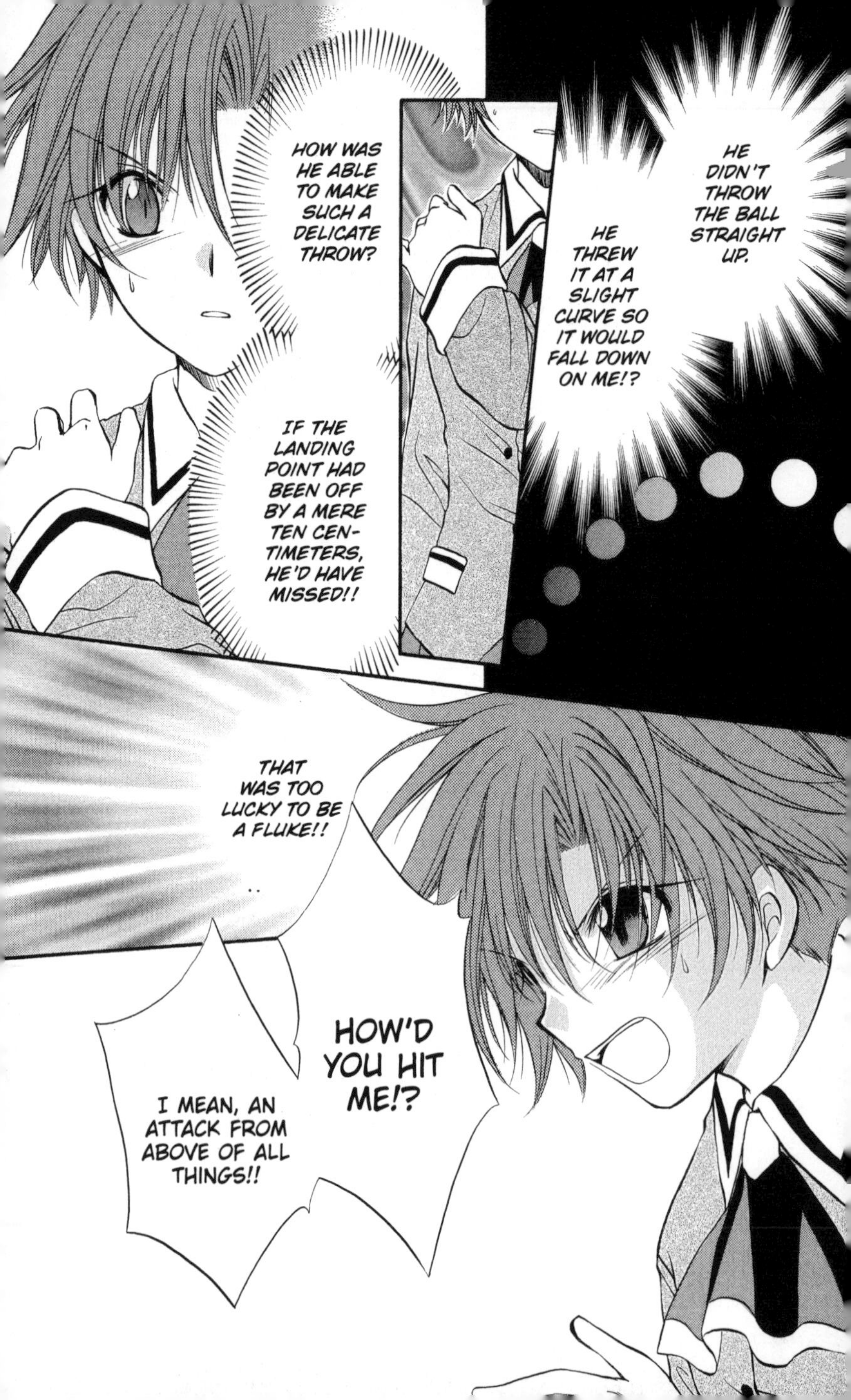

HE DIDN'T THROW THE BALL STRAIGHT UP.
HE THREW IT AT A SLIGHT CURVE SO IT WOULD FALL DOWN ON ME!?
HOW WAS HE ABLE TO MAKE SUCH A DELICATE THROW?
IF THE LANDING POINT HAD BEEN OFF BY A MERE TEN CEN-TIMETERS, HE'D HAVE MISSED!!
THAT WAS TOO LUCKY TO BE A FLUKE!!
HOW'D YOU HIT ME!?
I MEAN, AN ATTACK FROM ABOVE OF ALL THINGS!!

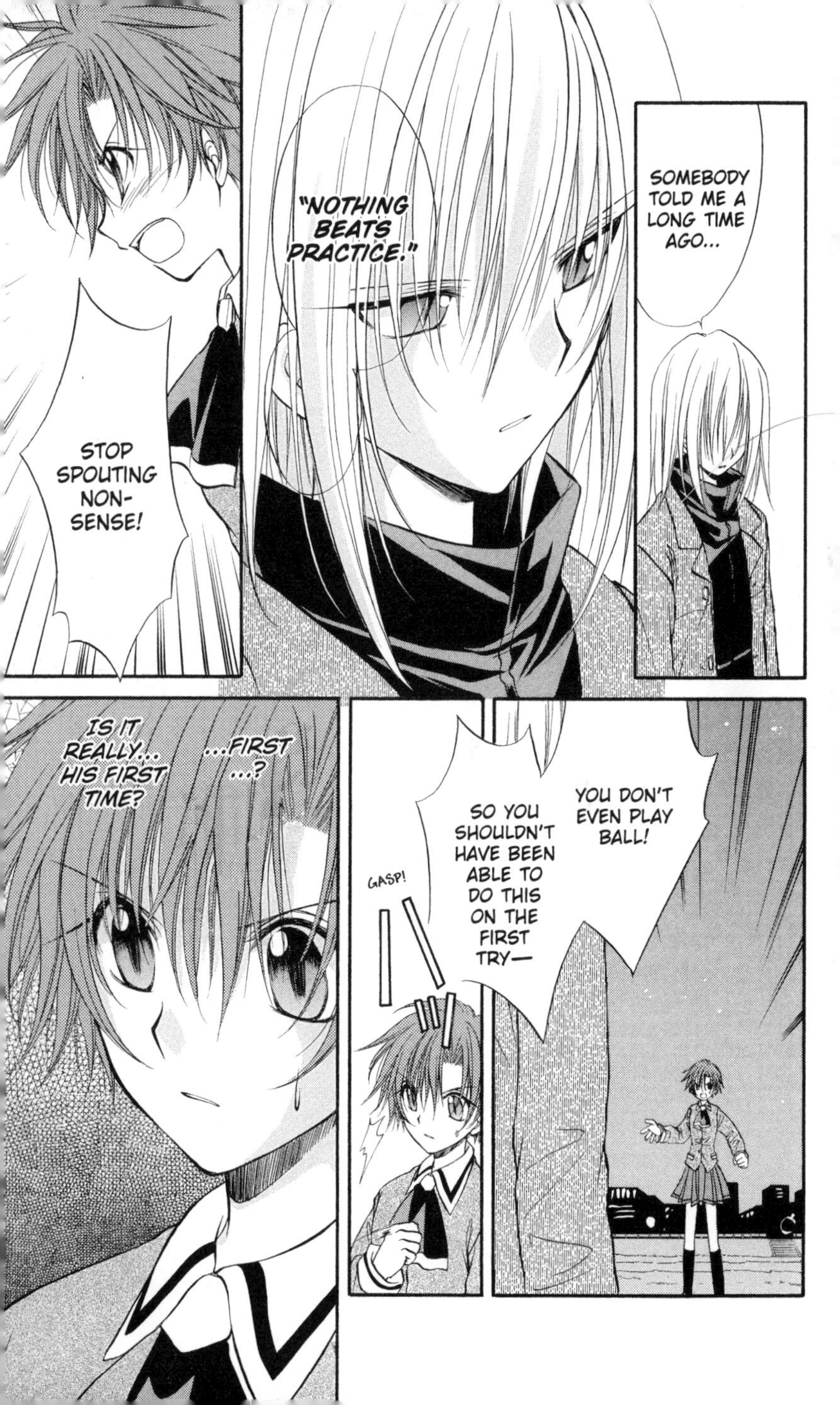
SOMEBODY TOLD ME A LONG TIME AGO...
"NOTHING BEATS PRACTICE."
STOP SPOUTING NON-SENSE!
YOU DON'T EVEN PLAY BALL!
SO YOU SHOULDN'T HAVE BEEN ABLE TO DO THIS ON THE FIRST TRY—
GASP!
...FIRST ...?
IS IT REALLY... HIS FIRST TIME?

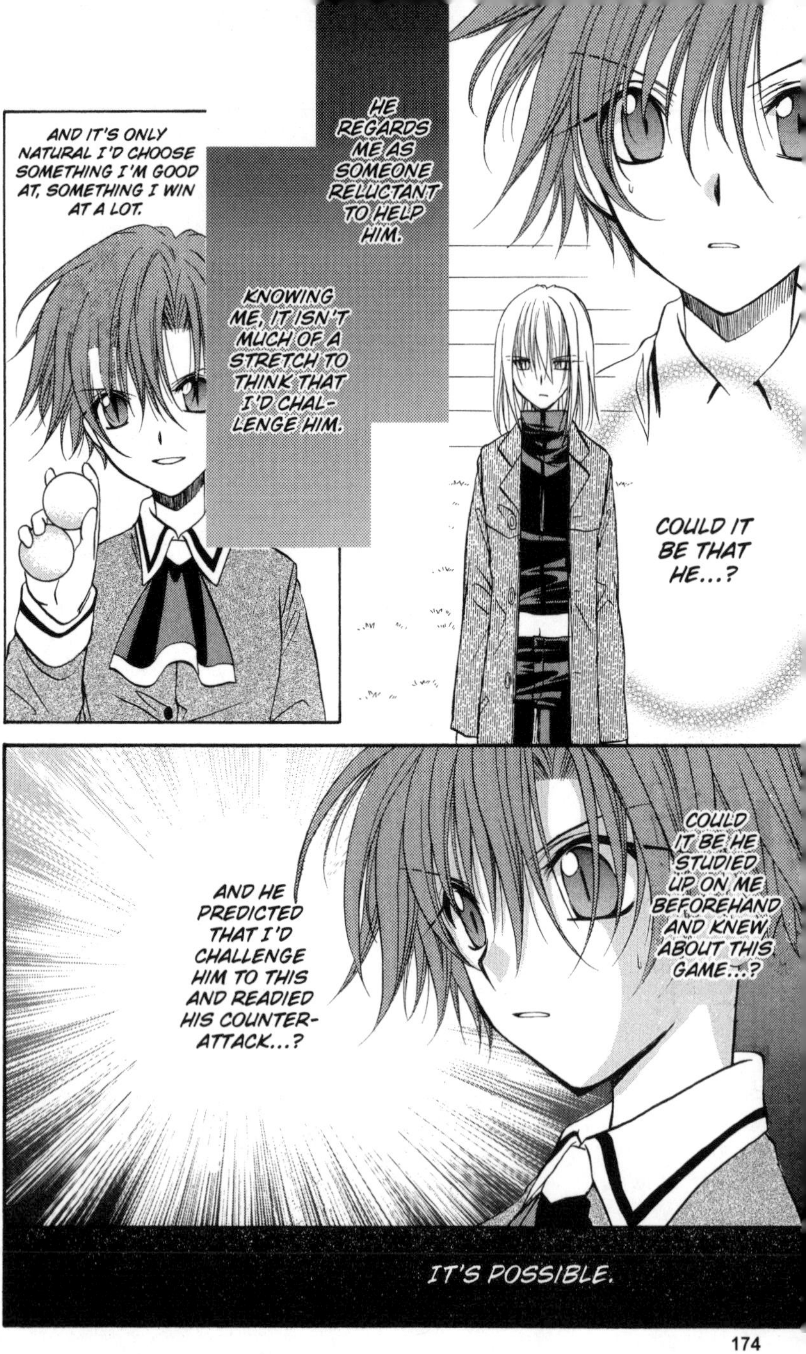
HE REGARDS ME AS SOMEONE RELUCTANT TO HELP HIM.
AND IT'S ONLY NATURAL I'D CHOOSE SOMETHING I'M GOOD AT, SOMETHING I WIN AT A LOT.
KNOWING ME, IT ISN'T MUCH OF A STRETCH TO THINK THAT I'D CHAL-LENGE HIM.
COULD IT BE THAT HE...?
COULD IT BE HE STUDIED UP ON ME BEFOREHAND AND KNEW ABOUT THIS GAME...?
AND HE PREDICTED THAT I'D CHALLENGE HIM TO THIS AND READIED HIS COUNTER-ATTACK...?
IT'S POSSIBLE.

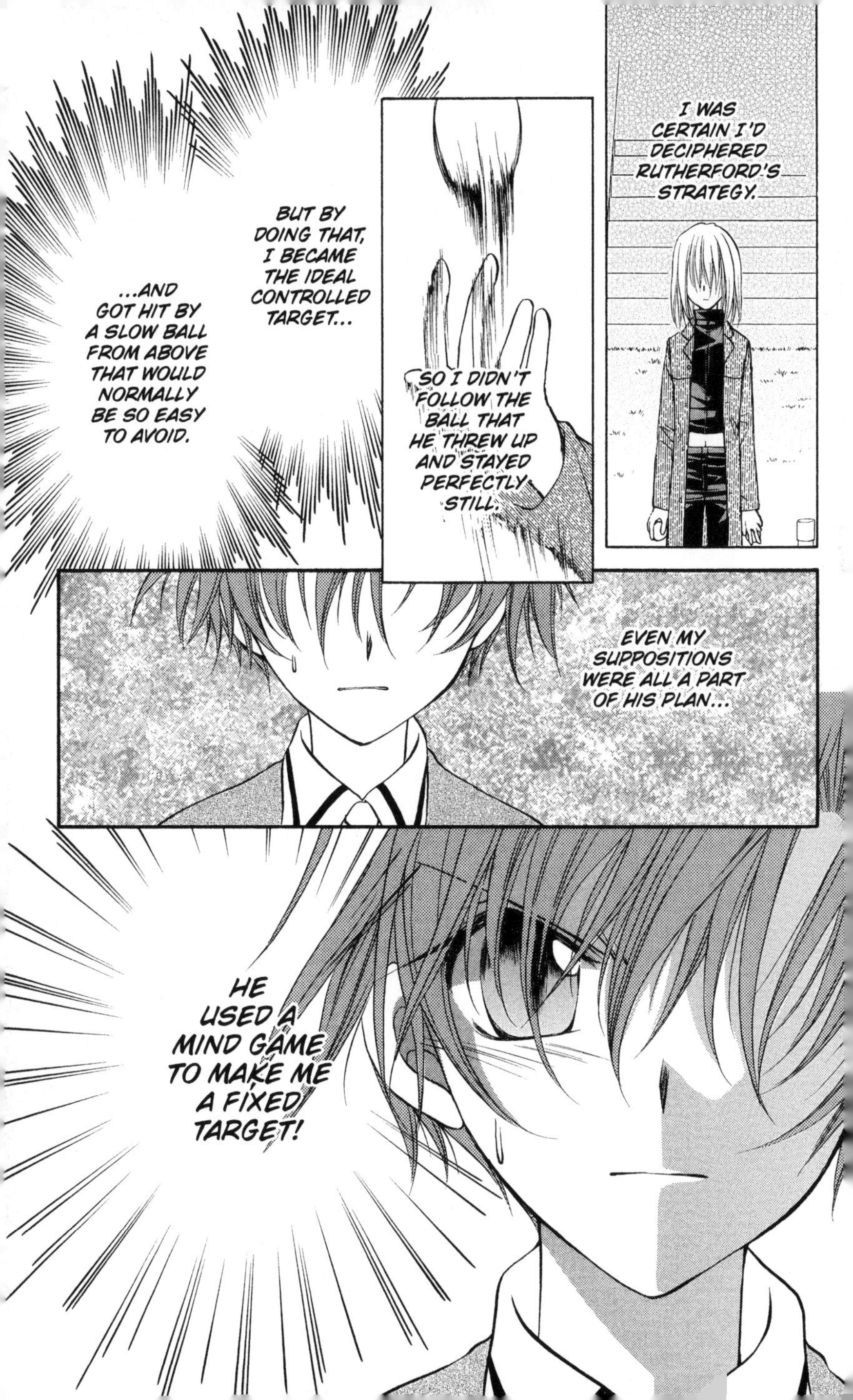
I WAS CERTAIN I'D DECIPHERED RUTHERFORD'S STRATEGY.
SO I DIDN'T FOLLOW THE BALL THAT HE THREW UP AND STAYED PERFECTLY STILL.
BUT BY DOING THAT, I BECAME THE IDEAL CONTROLLED TARGET...
...AND GOT HIT BY A SLOW BALL FROM ABOVE THAT WOULD NORMALLY BE SO EASY TO AVOID.
EVEN MY SUPPOSITIONS WERE ALL A PART OF HIS PLAN...
HE USED A MIND GAME TO MAKE ME A FIXED TARGET!

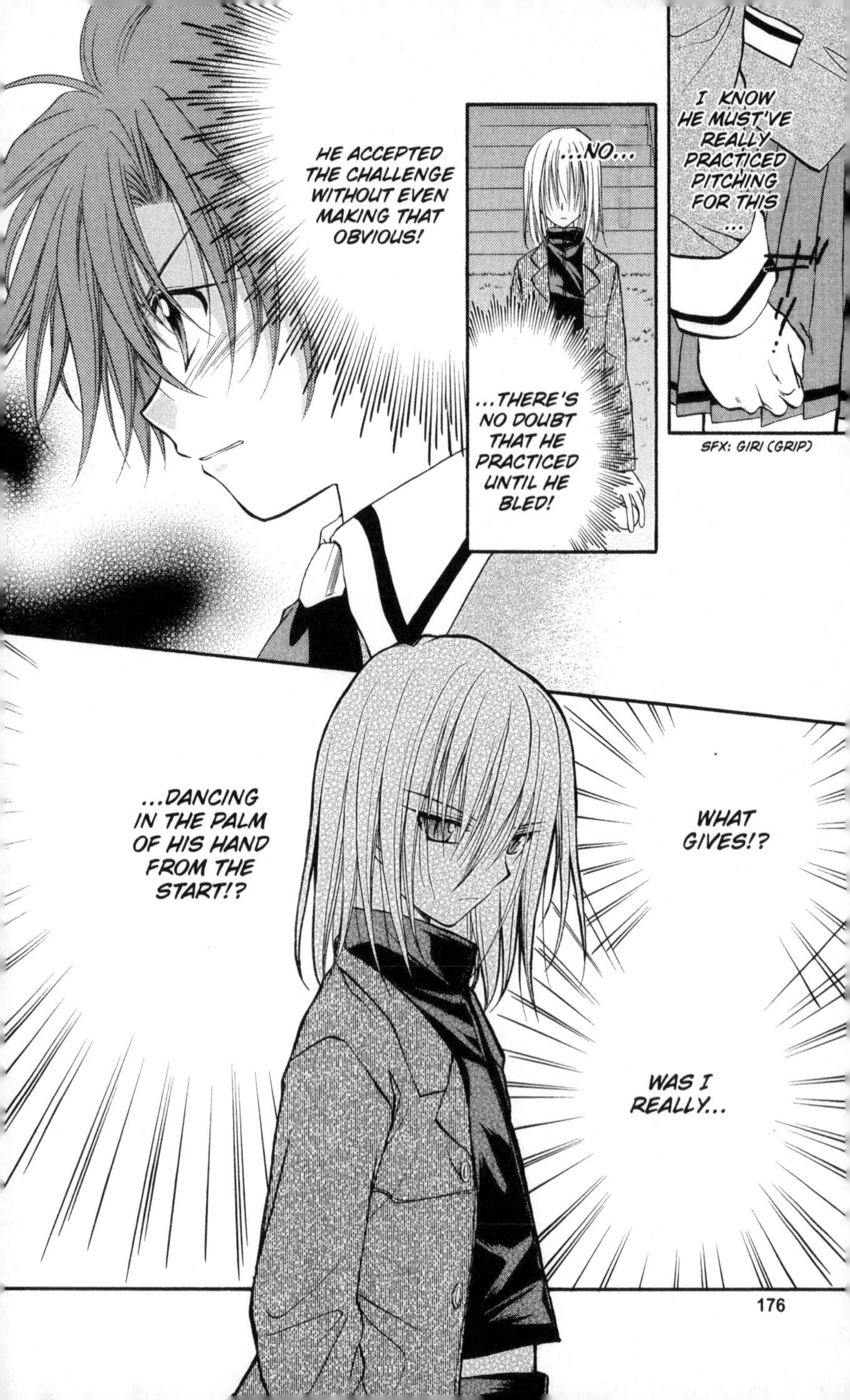
I KNOW HE MUST'VE REALLY PRACTICED PITCHING FOR THIS ...
SFX: GIRI (GRIP)
...NO...
...THERE'S NO DOUBT THAT HE PRACTICED UNTIL HE BLED!
HE ACCEPTED THE CHALLENGE WITHOUT EVEN MAKING THAT OBVIOUS!
WHAT GIVES!?
WAS I REALLY...
...DANCING IN THE PALM OF HIS HAND FROM THE START!?

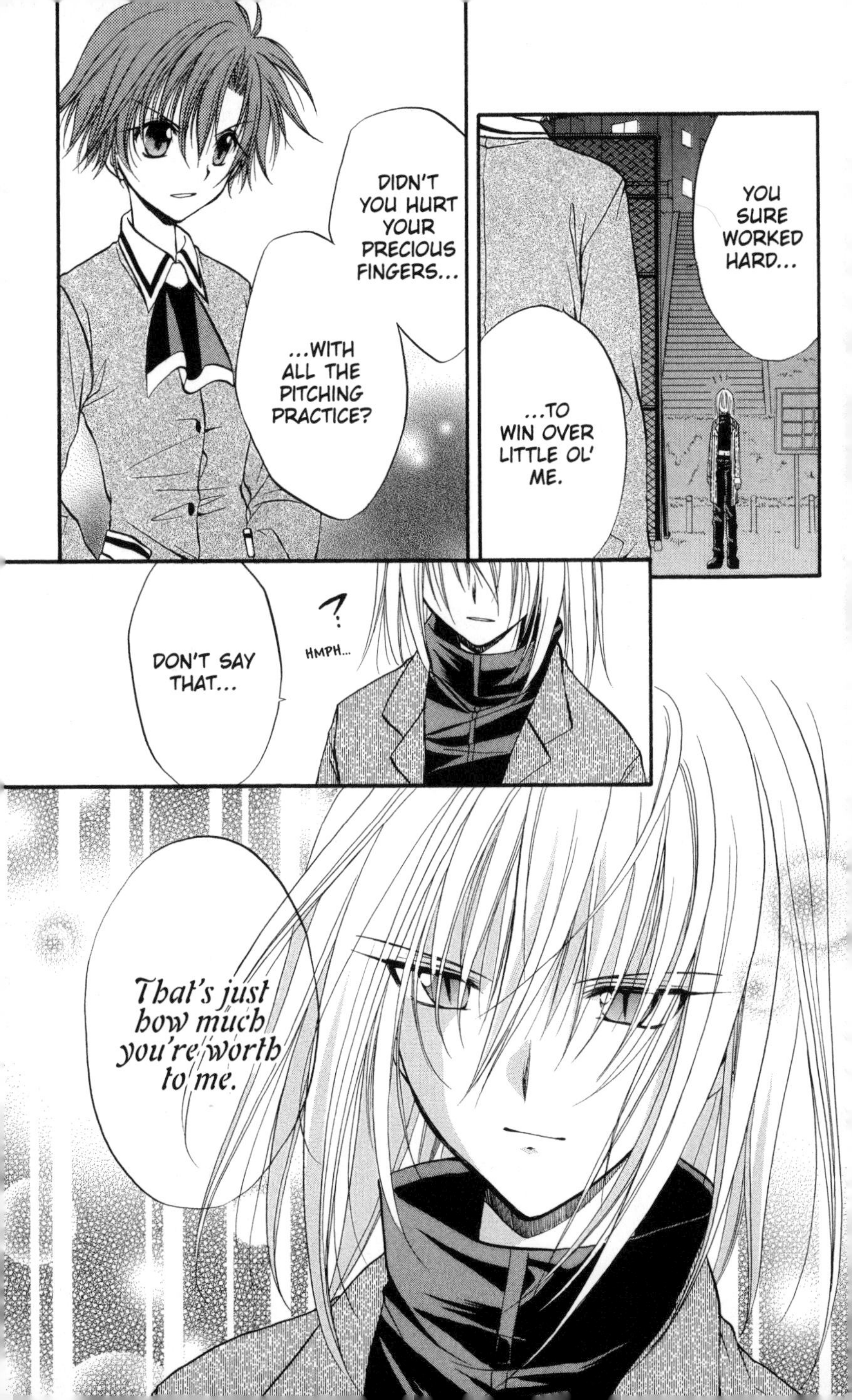
YOU SURE WORKED HARD...
...TO WIN OVER LITTLE OL' ME.
DIDN'T YOU HURT YOUR PRECIOUS FINGERS...
...WITH ALL THE PITCHING PRACTICE?
HMPH...
DON'T SAY THAT...
That's just how much you're worth to me.

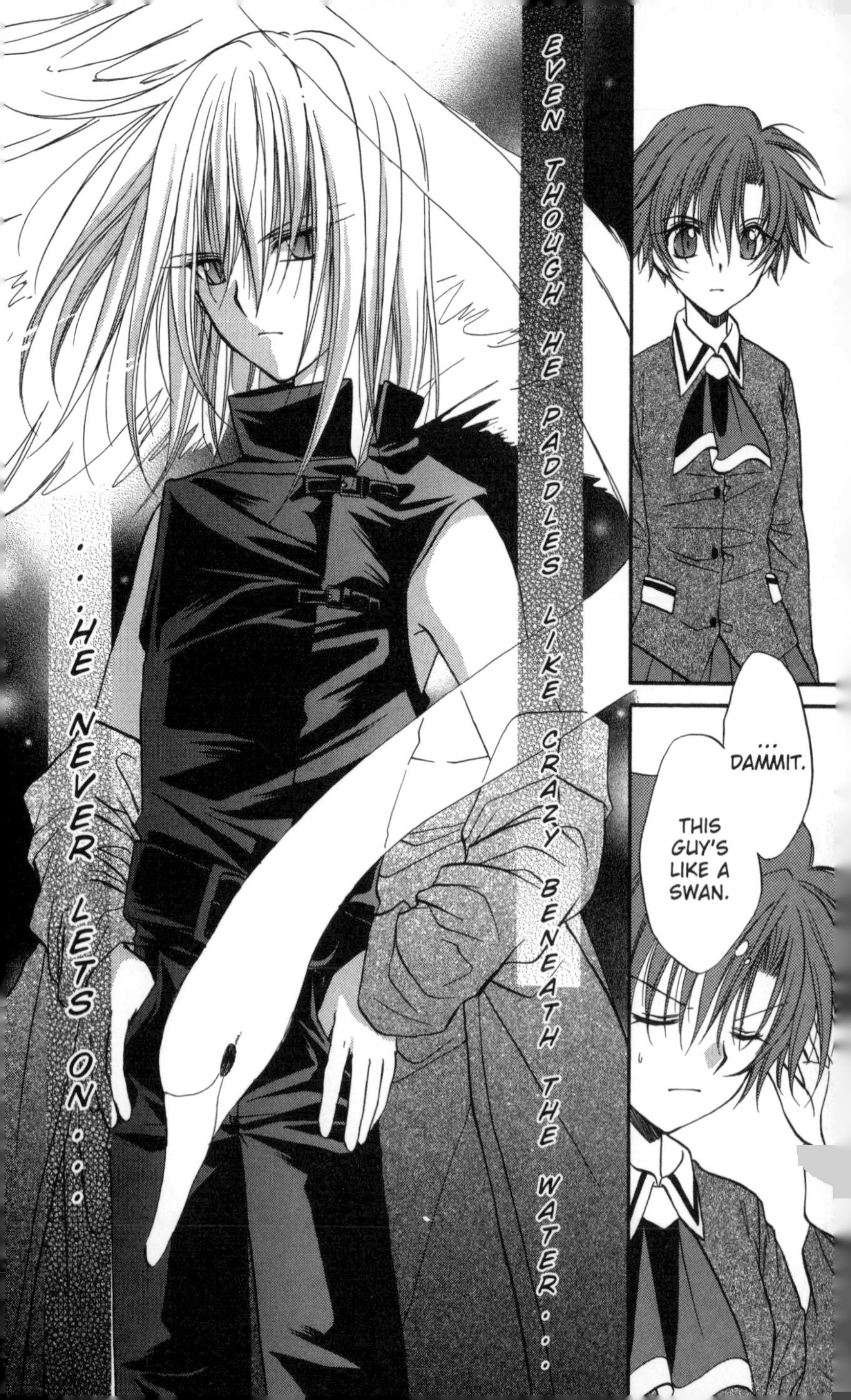
...DAMMIT.
THIS GUY'S LIKE A SWAN.
EVEN THOUGH HE PADDLES LIKE CRAZY BENEATH THE WATER...
...HE NEVER LETS ON...

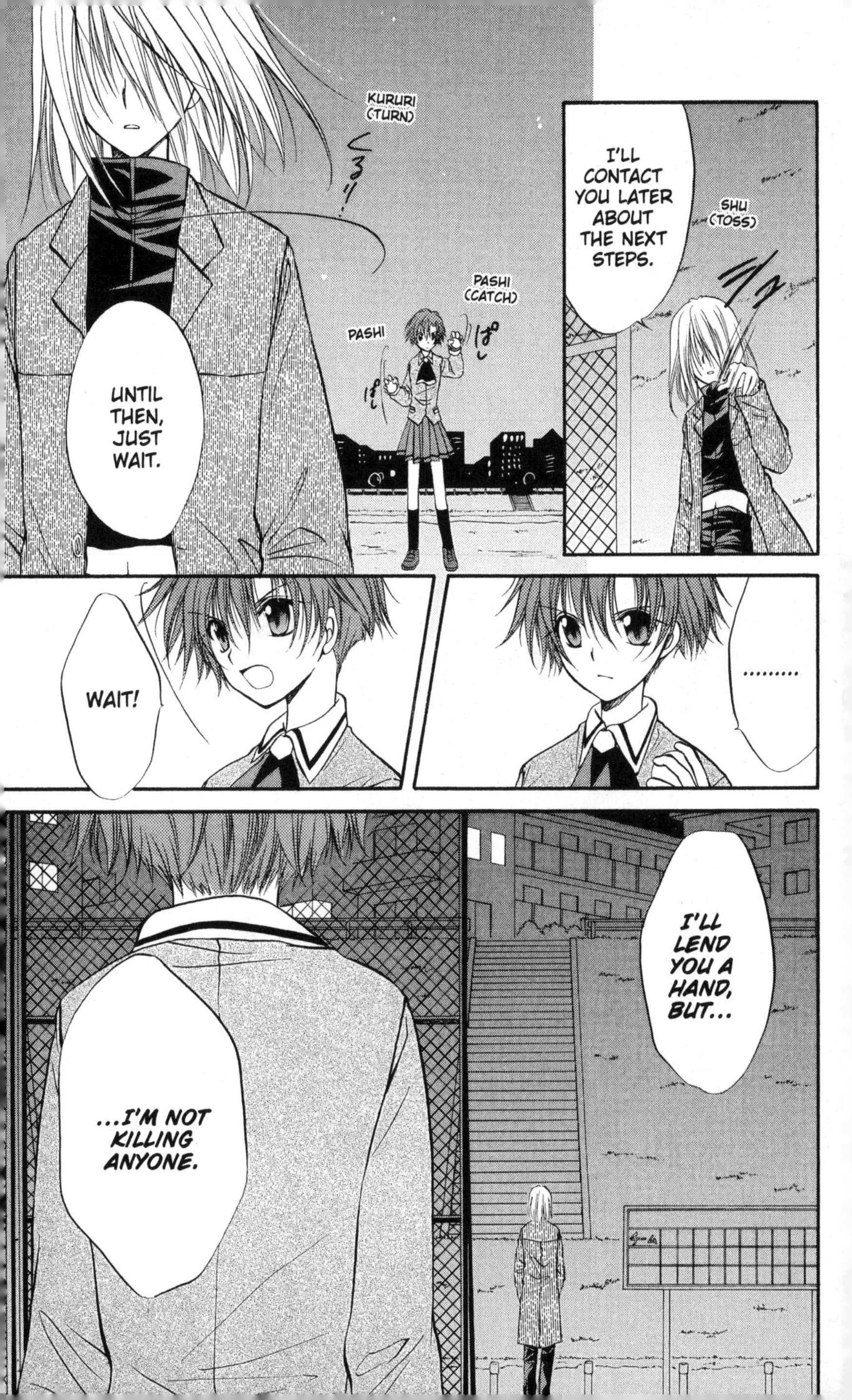
I'LL CONTACT YOU LATER ABOUT THE NEXT STEPS.
SHU (TOSS)
KURURI (TURN)
PASHI (CATCH)
PASHI
UNTIL THEN, JUST WAIT.
....
WAIT!
I'LL LEND YOU A HAND, BUT...
...I'M NOT KILLING ANYONE.

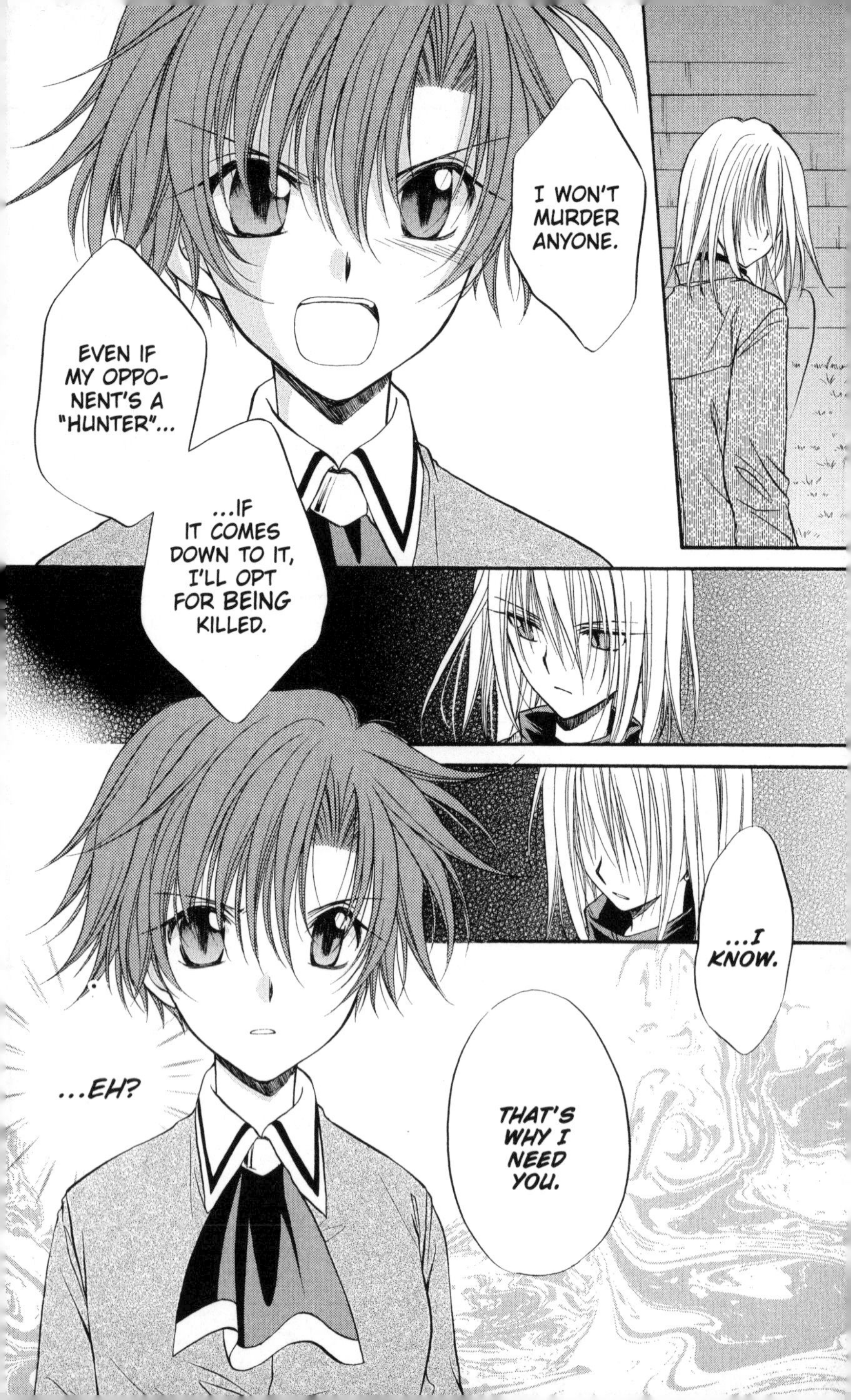
I WON'T MURDER ANYONE.
EVEN IF MY OPPO-NENT'S A "HUNTER"...
...IF IT COMES DOWN TO IT, I'LL OPT FOR BEING KILLED.
...I KNOW.
THAT'S WHY I NEED YOU.
...EH?

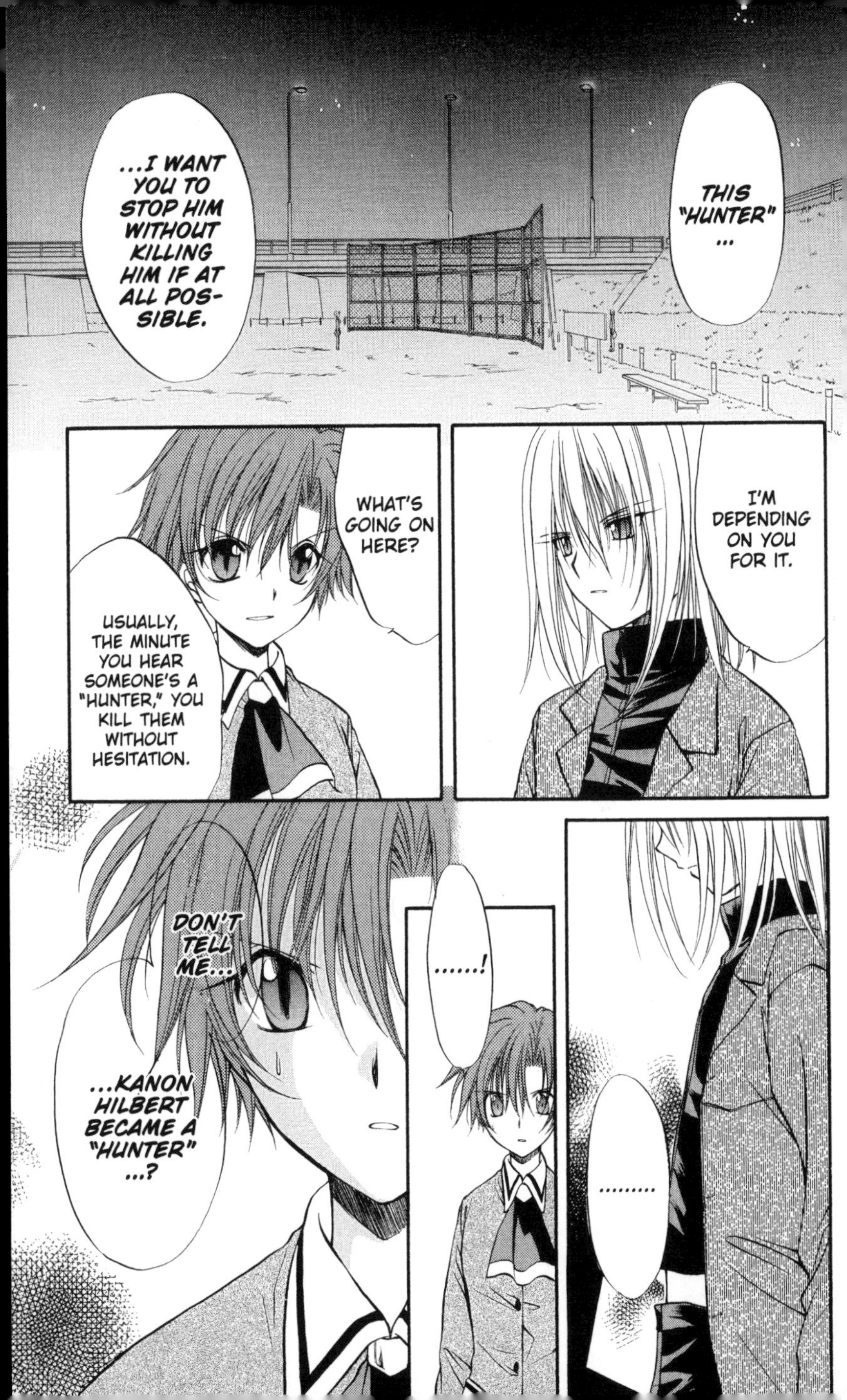
THIS "HUNTER" ...
...I WANT YOU TO STOP HIM WITHOUT KILLING HIM IF AT ALL POS-SIBLE.
I'M DEPENDING ON YOU FOR IT.
WHAT'S GOING ON HERE?
USUALLY, THE MINUTE YOU HEAR SOMEONE'S A "HUNTER," YOU KILL THEM WITHOUT HESITATION.
....
......!
DON'T TELL ME...
...KANON HILBERT BECAME A "HUNTER" ...?

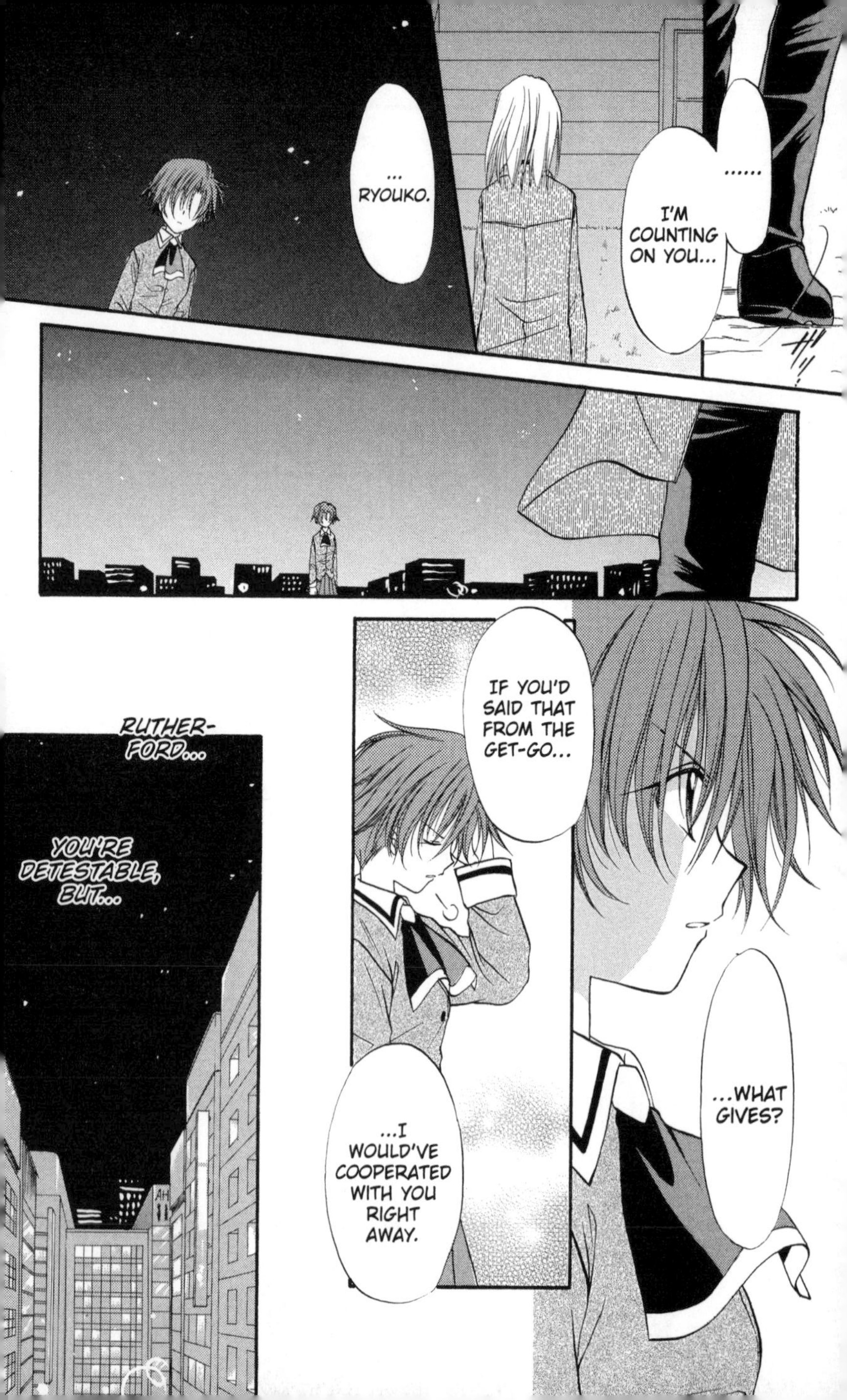

......
I'M COUNTING ON YOU...
...RYOUKO.
...WHAT GIVES?
IF YOU'D SAID THAT FROM THE GET-GO...
...I WOULD'VE COOPERATED WITH YOU RIGHT AWAY.
RUTHERFORD...
YOU'RE DETESTABLE, BUT...

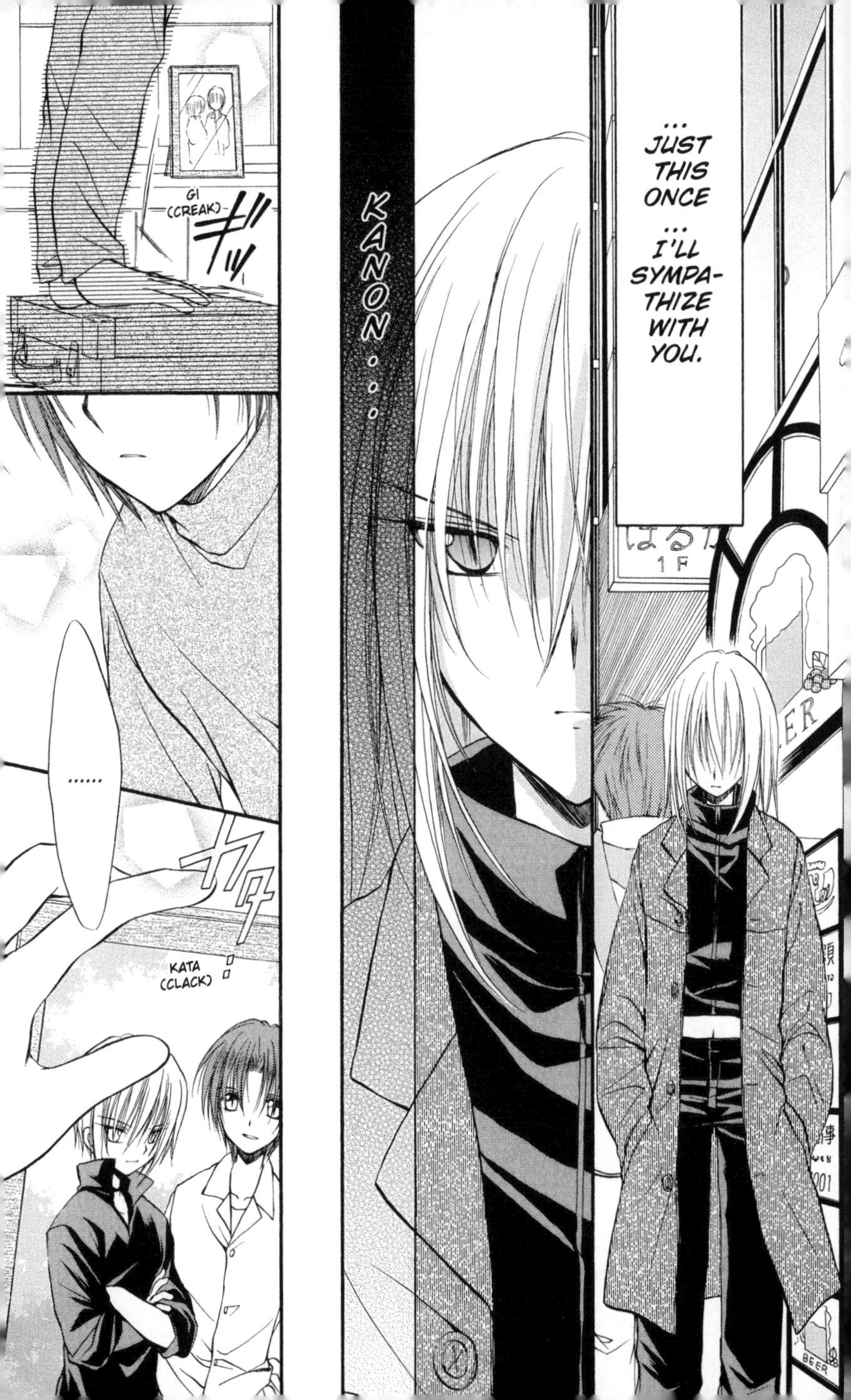
... JUST THIS ONCE ... I'LL SYMPA-THIZE WITH YOU.
KANON...
GI (CREAK)
ギッ
......
カタ
KATA (CLACK)

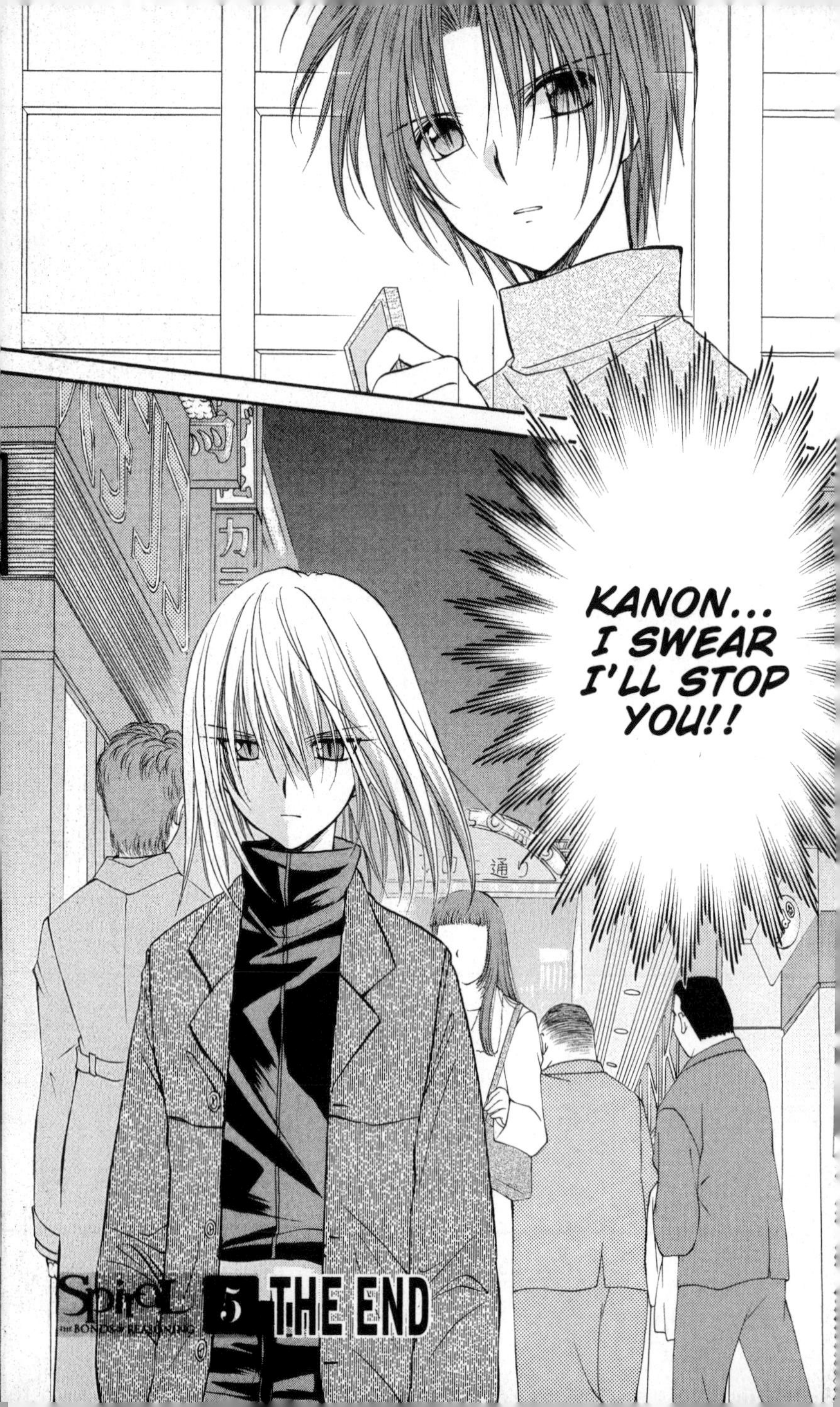
KANON... I SWEAR I'LL STOP YOU!!
Spiral THE BONDS of REASONING
5
THE END

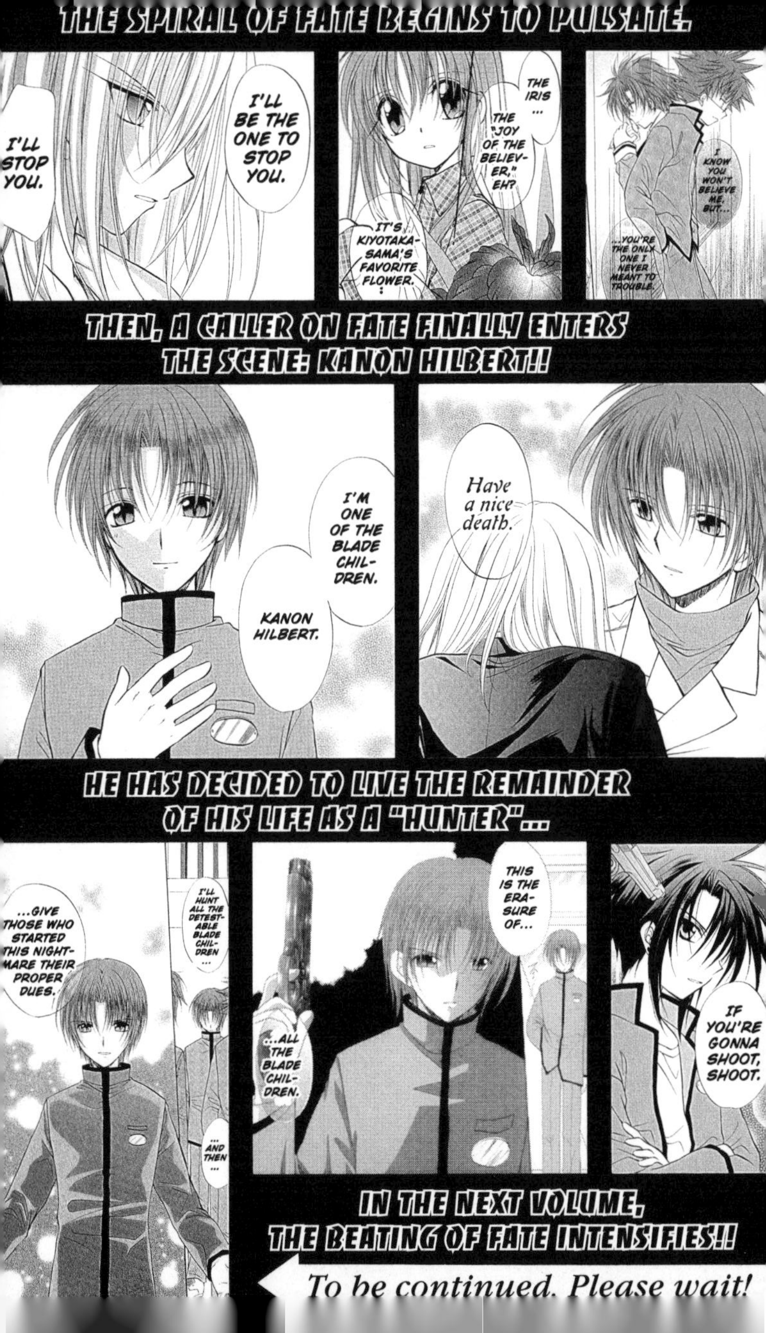
THE SPIRAL OF FATE BEGINS TO PULSATE.
I KNOW YOU WON'T BELIEVE ME, BUT...
...YOU'RE THE ONLY ONE I NEVER MEANT TO TROUBLE.
THE IRIS...
THE "JOY OF THE BELIEVER," EH?
IT'S KIYOTAKA-SAMA'S FAVORITE FLOWER.
I'LL BE THE ONE TO STOP YOU.
I'LL STOP YOU.
THEN, A CALLER ON FATE FINALLY ENTERS THE SCENE: KANON HILBERT!!
Have a nice death.
I'M ONE OF THE BLADE CHIL-DREN.
KANON HILBERT.
HE HAS DECIDED TO LIVE THE REMAINDER OF HIS LIFE AS A "HUNTER"...
IF YOU'RE GONNA SHOOT, SHOOT.
THIS IS THE ERA-SURE OF...
...ALL THE BLADE CHIL-DREN.
I'LL HUNT ALL THE DETEST-ABLE BLADE CHIL-DREN...
...GIVE THOSE WHO STARTED THIS NIGHT-MARE THEIR PROPER DUES.
...AND THEN...
IN THE NEXT VOLUME, THE BEATING OF FATE INTENSIFIES!!
To be continued. Please wait!

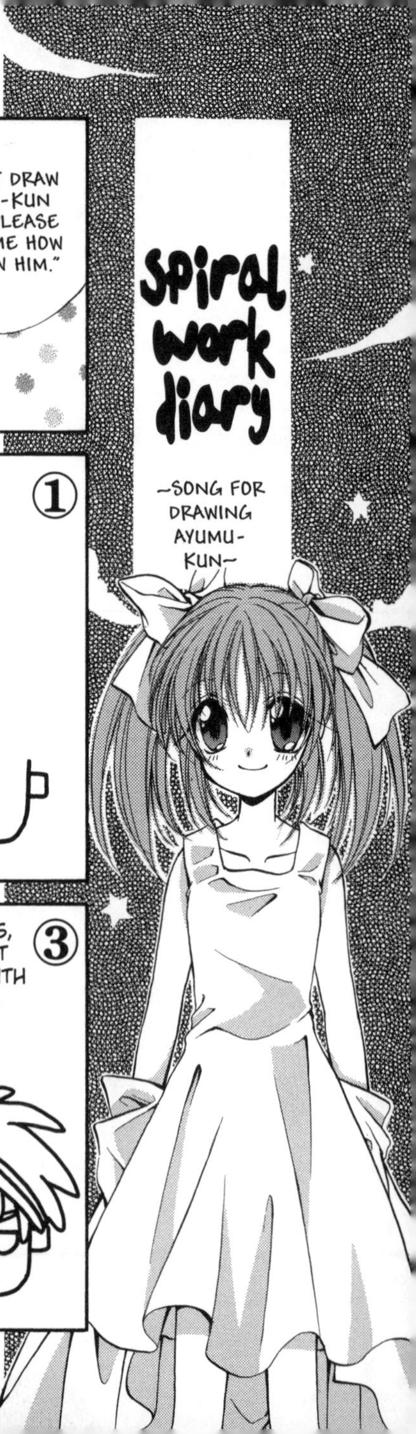
Spiral work diary
~SONG FOR DRAWING AYUMU-KUN~

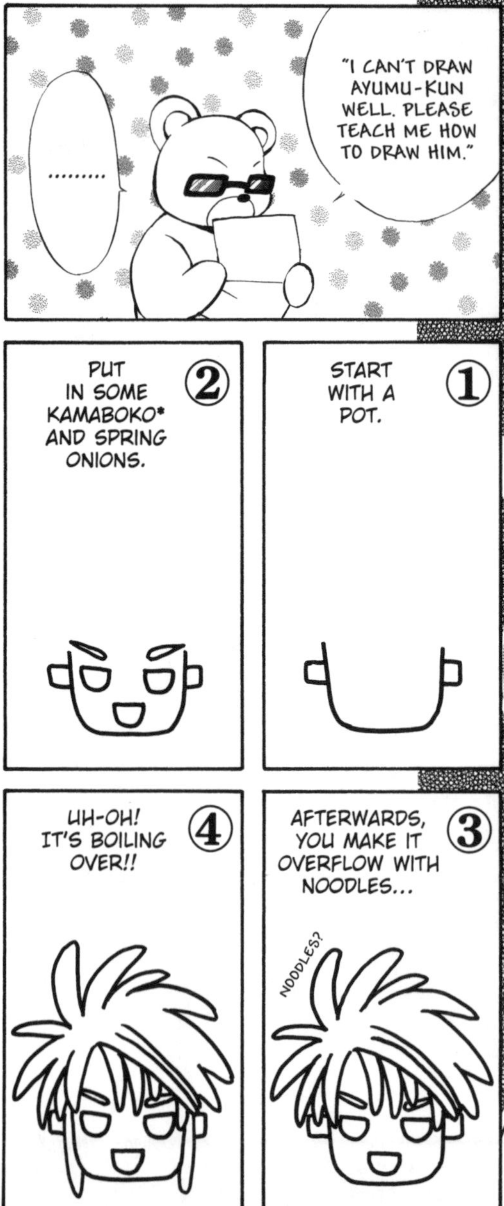
"I CAN'T DRAW AYUMU-KUN WELL. PLEASE TEACH ME HOW TO DRAW HIM."
....
①
START WITH A POT.
②
PUT IN SOME KAMABOKO* AND SPRING ONIONS.
③
AFTERWARDS, YOU MAKE IT OVERFLOW WITH NOODLES...
NOODLES?
④
UH-OH! IT'S BOILING OVER!!

*A PROCESSED SEAFOOD PRODUCT FROM JAPAN WHICH IS SHAPED INTO LOAVES AND STEAMED UNTIL FIRM. WHEN THE LOAF IS SLICED, IT APPEARS SEMICIRCLE-SHAPED, LIKE AYUMU'S EYES AND MOUTH.

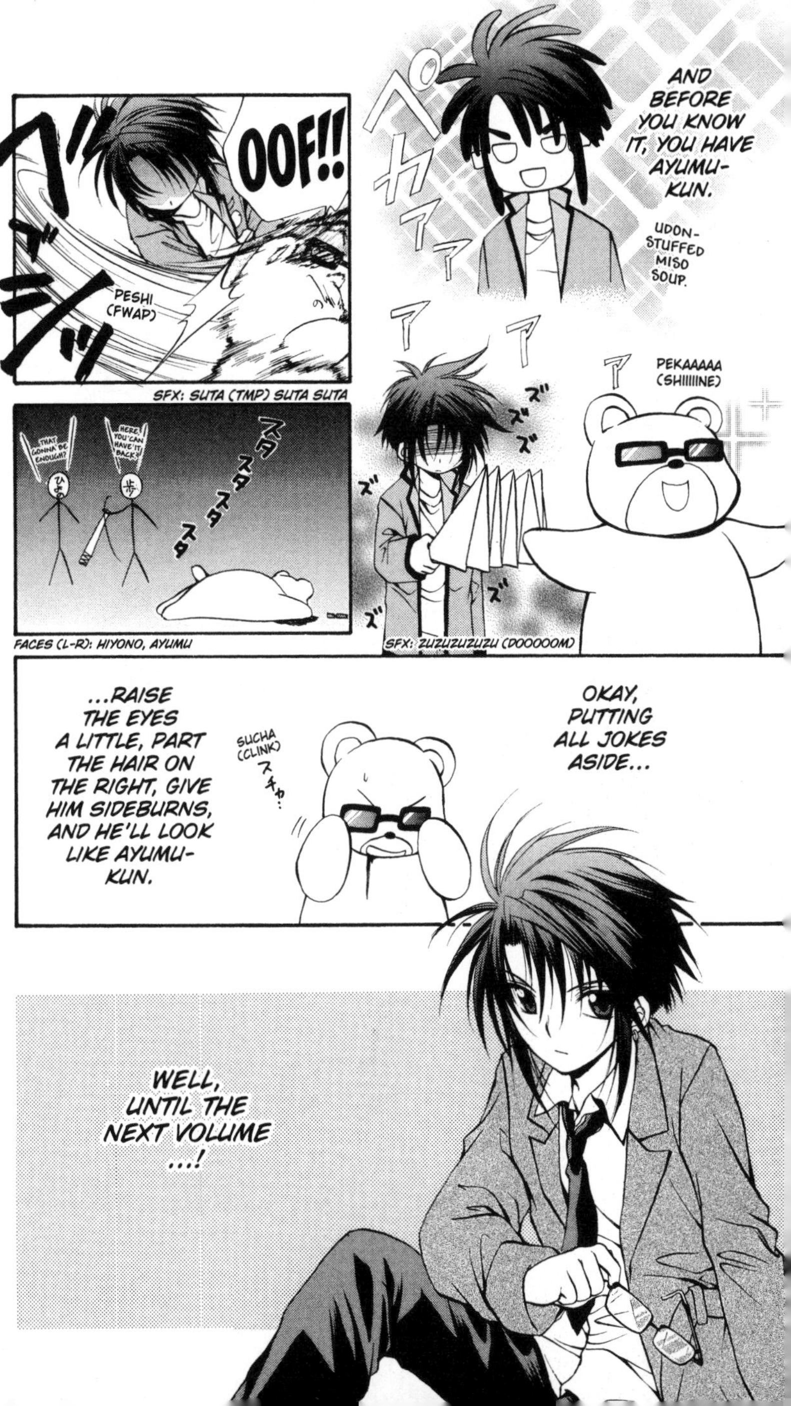
AND BEFORE YOU KNOW IT, YOU HAVE AYUMU-KUN.
UDON-STUFFED MISO SOUP.
ペカァァァァ
PEKAAAAA (SHIIIIINE)
ズズズズズ
SFX: ZUZUZUZUZU (DOOOOOM)
OOF!!
PESHI (FWAP)
SFX: SUTA (TMP) SUTA SUTA
スタスタスタスタ
HERE, YOU CAN HAVE IT BACK.
THAT GONNA BE ENOUGH?
FACES (L-R): HIYONO, AYUMU
OKAY, PUTTING ALL JOKES ASIDE...
SUCHA (CLINK)
スチャ…
...RAISE THE EYES A LITTLE, PART THE HAIR ON THE RIGHT, GIVE HIM SIDEBURNS, AND HE'LL LOOK LIKE AYUMU-KUN.
WELL, UNTIL THE NEXT VOLUME ...!

WRITER'S AFTERWORD

Due to how the page count worked out in Volume Four, I wasn't able to say, "Hi," but this is Kyo Shirodaira. With the comic at a whole five volumes, it would make me so glad to know that all of you who are still following the story have been enjoying the plot so far.

As usual, having passed twenty chapters, the story's begun to take a huge turn, and both our appearing characters and atypical cohorts have increased. I plan for the two new characters introduced in this volume to be key players in the story from here on out. Especially Kanon Hilbert—he will be responsible for a lot that happens. Since there's no doubt that he will do his own crazy thing, ignoring the voice of the fans, I'm keeping my eye on him. But really, it's all very exciting to look forward to. Seems there'll be a lot of bloodshed coming up.

Charged with new and exciting characters, *Spiral* travels further and further away from being a strictly "mystery" manga, and I think I'd like it to continue in a more serious vein as "the heart is a mystery."

Also, I'm still doing the *Spiral* side story—*Spiral Alive*—that's serialized in *GANGAN WING* every other month.

If you're wondering how "side" the story is, almost none of the characters from *Spiral* appear (at most, only their names are mentioned). That's how much of a side story it is. For those of you who are perplexed and wonder just what's going on with it, please take a look at it.

By the way, it seems there have been a lot of fans asking us for profiles of the characters. We touched upon the subject back in the "Spiral Work Diary" from Volume Three.

As the creator, it's my responsibility to answer these requests but, for the sake of the story, there is some information I just cannot share and make public just yet. (I swear I'm not thinking it's too bothersome to think up that stuff, or that none of that information is necessary, or anything. I swear.) So. . .I'm sorry, but you'll have to wait for all of their profiles.

Some things about Ayumu and Madoka are divulged in the drama CD. (Before we knew it, we had one of those released.) So for now, please forgive us and enjoy that.

Lastly—this is something I always announce—but on GAN-GAN NET (http://gangan.square-enix.co.jp/spiral/), the supplementary novelization about Kiyotaka Narumi, the detective, is up (in Japanese!). Since a new chapter goes up on every comic release date, there's also a quiz with prizes. So for those of you who have access, please give it a try.

If you don't have access but still want to read it, Chapters One and Two of this supplementary story are included as back-of-book bonus material in SQUARE ENIX's published novels, *Spiral: The Bonds of Reasoning—The Crime of the Sword Master*, so please look for them there.

Well, I'll be praying that we see each other again in Volume Six!

KYO SHIRODAIRA

Spiral 5
THE BONDS OF REASONING
Omake!

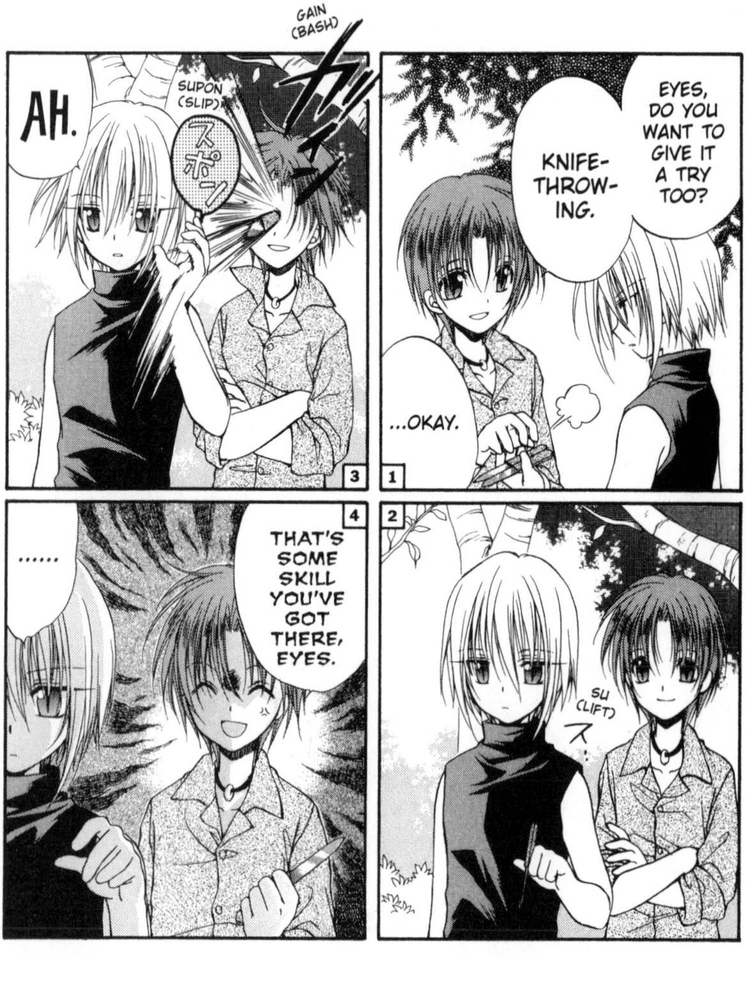
EYES, DO YOU WANT TO GIVE IT A TRY TOO?
KNIFE-THROWING.
...OKAY.
SU (LIFT)
ス
GAIN (BASH)
SUPON (SLIP)
スポーン
AH.
THAT'S SOME SKILL YOU'VE GOT THERE, EYES.
......

SPIRAL
The Bonds of Reasoning
5

by Kyo Shirodaira and Eita Mizuno

Translation: Christine Schilling
Lettering: Marshall Dillon and Terri Delgado
Logo: Kirk Benshoff

Yen Press
Hachette Book Group
237 Park Avenue, New York, NY 10017

Visit our Web sites at www.HachetteBookGroup.com and www.YenPress.com.

Yen Press is an imprint of Hachette Book Group, Inc. The Yen Press name and logo are trademarks of Hachette Book Group, Inc.

First Yen Press Edition: October 2008

ISBN-10: 0-7595-2835-7
ISBN-13: 978-0-7595-2835-2

10 9 8 7 6 5 4 3 2 1

BVG

Printed in the United States of America